Dear Edie - Happy 70th!
Well, here it is at last! Enjoy it,
'tis a great tale. Love to you -
Hank & Jan xxx

World Wheel

One Woman's Quest for Peace

To my mother
Lillian Melba Hamilton

and my father
Paul Hamilton

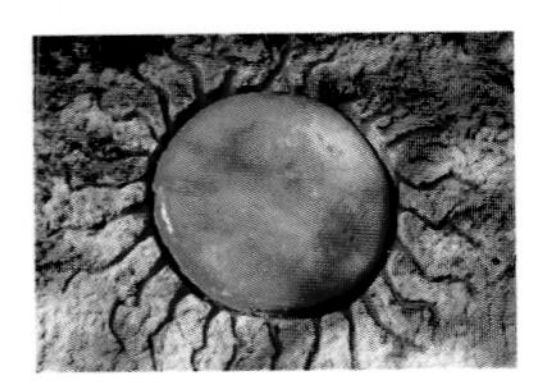

and to you

World Wheel

One Woman's Quest for Peace

VIJALI HAMILTON

with artwork by the author

Introduction by Gloria Feman Orenstein

WORLD WHEEL PRESS
Castle Valley, Utah

www.worldwheelpress.org

ISBN: 978-0-9789055-1-4

Library of Congress Control Number: 2007924530
Printed in the United States of America
10 9 8 7 6 5 4 3 2 1
This book is printed on 80% Silk, acid-free, archival quality, 10% recycled paper.

Cover art by Vijali Hamilton
Cover design by Sara Glaser
Book design by Sara Glaser, Shelley Firth, and Vijali Hamilton
Design consulting and image editing by Henry Swan III

Introduction by Gloria Feman Orenstein

WORLD WHEEL PRESS
HC64 Box 2703
Castle Valley, Utah 84532

Orders copies from:
www.worldwheelpress.org

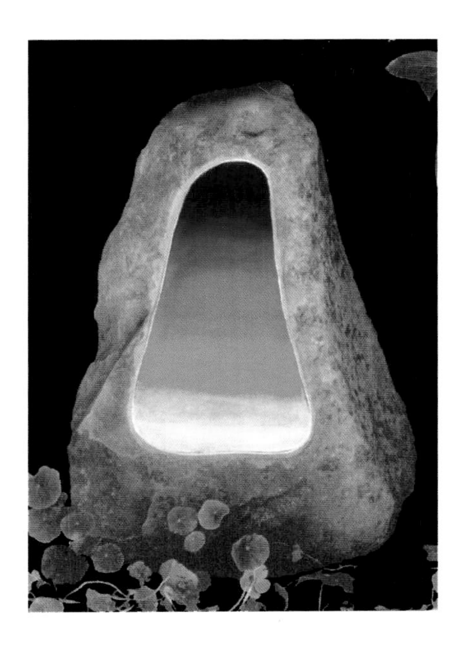

What is our essence?

What is our imbalance—personally, communally, globally?

What can bring us, our community, our planet back into balance?

TABLE OF CONTENTS

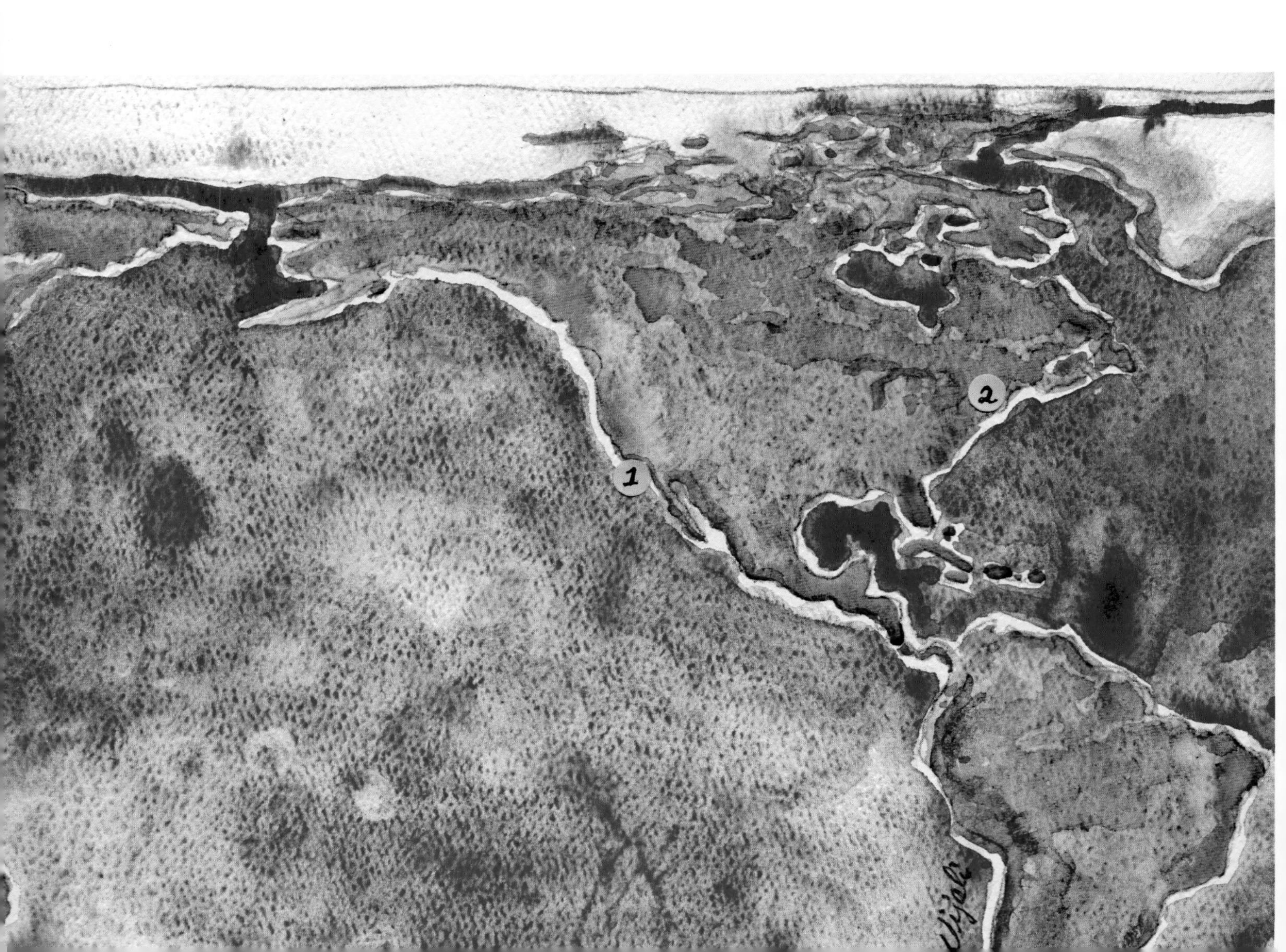

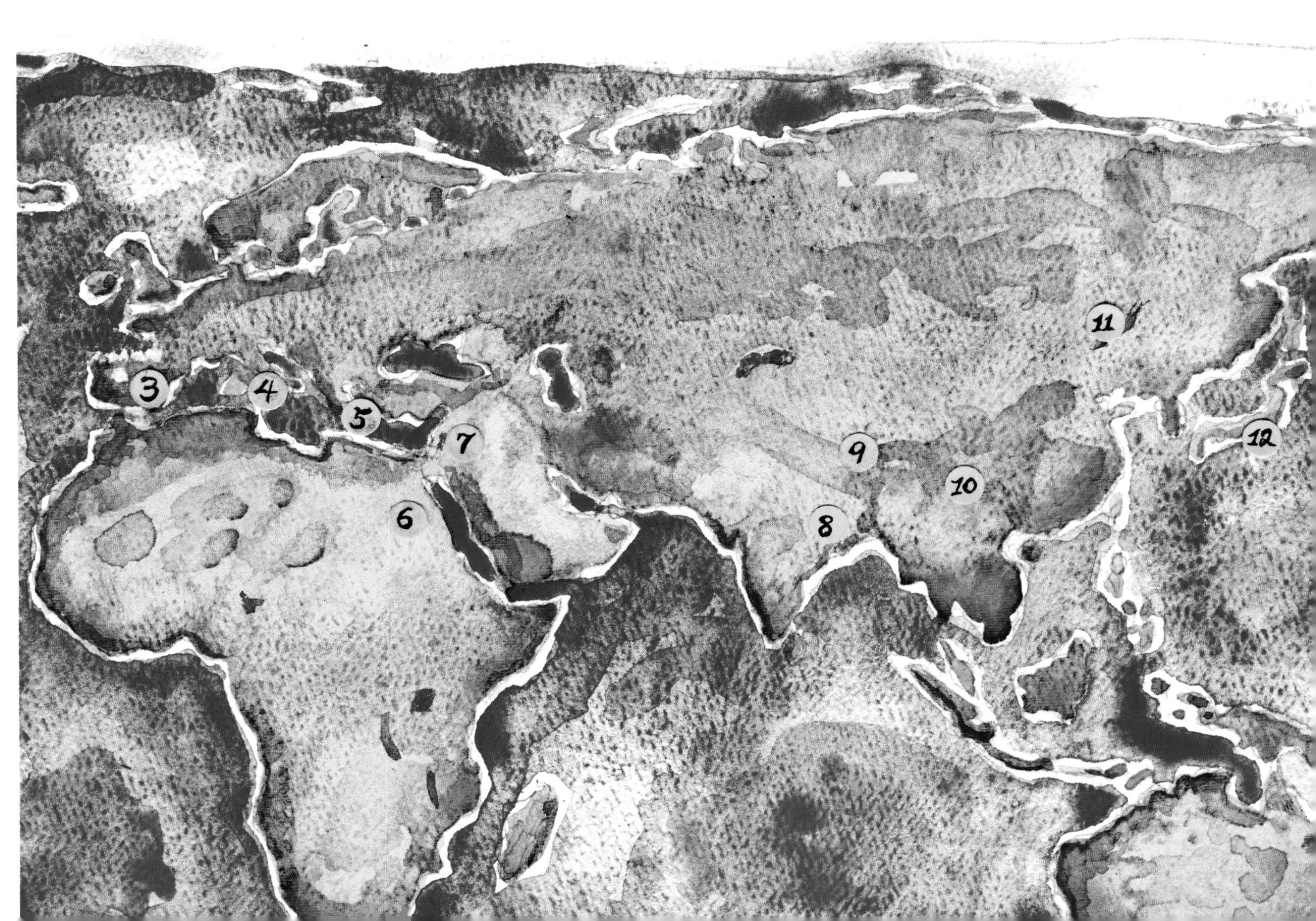
3
4
5
6
7
8
9
10
11
12

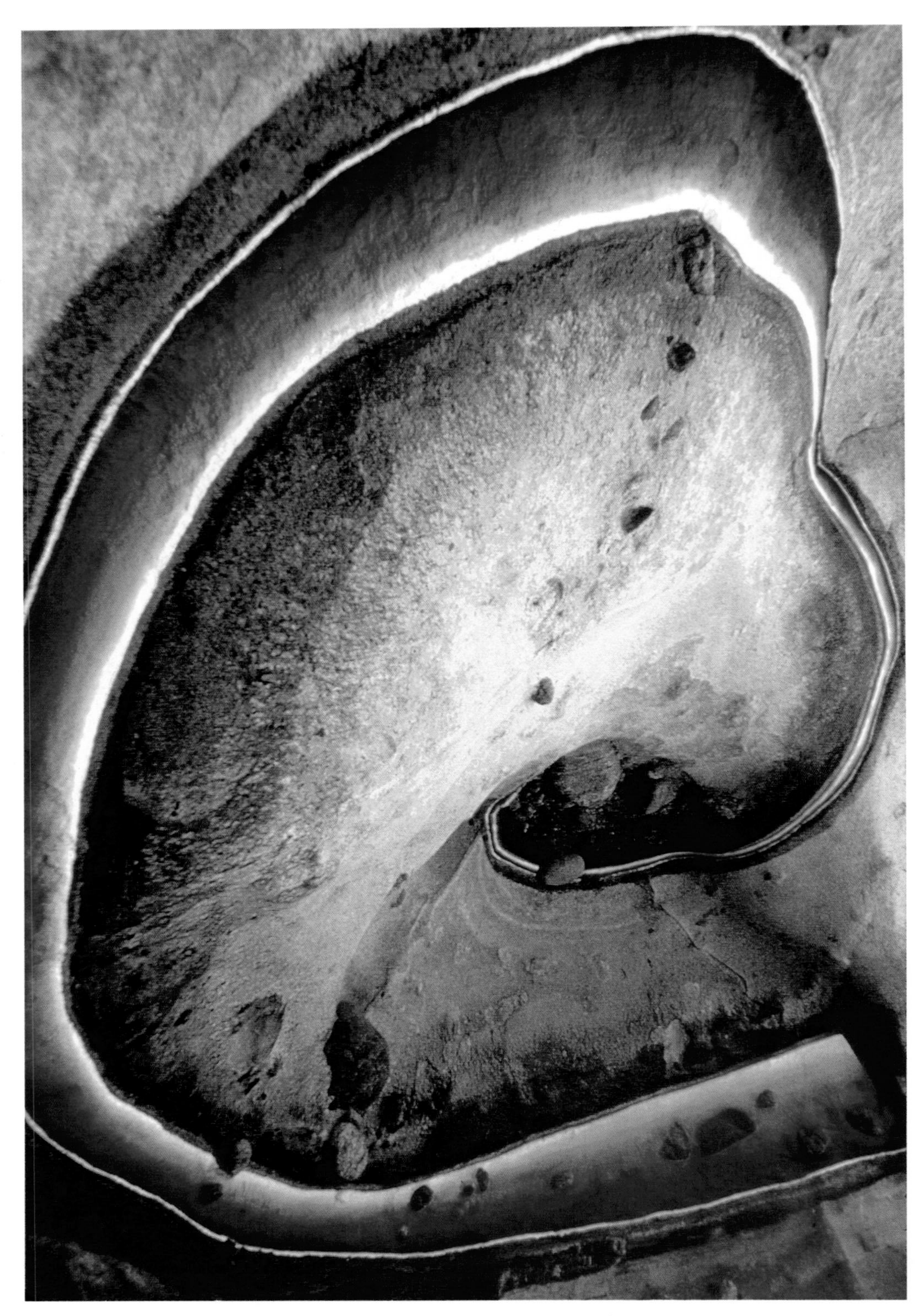

Sculptural Amphitheater (detail), Pepperdine University, Malibu, California

Introduction

VIJALI HAMILTON'S *World Wheel: One Woman's Quest for Peace* is a unique narrative of artistic and pacifist pioneering. Her life-journey has been fueled by intense spiritual inspiration, introspection, meditation, and practice.

When I first met Vijali in the mid-eighties, we made what I then considered a pilgrimage to visit her sculpture, *Winged Woman,* in the Santa Monica Mountains in California. Along the way, I learned about Vijali's early life when she had lived as a nun in a Vedanta convent. This in itself, it seemed to me, was a most apropos beginning for an artist who sculpted rocks while living alone in a trailer in the mountains, and who journeyed around the world, carving faces into huge boulders at old and new sacred sites throughout the planet. We see in Vijali's accomplishments that she not only "talks the talk," she "walks the talk" of a global peacemaker and artist, weaver of the dream of a borderless world.

The Other Self (detail)

The Surrealist poet, Andre Breton, has suggested that we should conceive of our waking lives as merely the punctuation points in the primary continuum—that of our dream lives, rather than the reverse, which is the way we ordinarily conceive of this relationship. Vijali has intuitively lived her life according to that reversal of priorities, always giving the prophetic sense of the dream priority over the solutions offered by ordinary reason and reality, always seeing the positive in place of the negative, always giving heed to the dream's guidance over society's worldly teachings.

She begins her book with the dream that changed her life and galvanized her artistic activity—the dream of a borderless world. In this dream, she saw herself in the future as a sculptor carving huge works out of boulders and creating new sacred sites in countries not yet revealed to her. This dream led to her creation of a performance art/life event of global proportions which she calls the World Wheel—and which continues to this day. The story of her selection of the initial twelve sites along the 34th north latitudinal parallel of the earth—from the Santa Monica Mountains to the ancient Shinto Shrine of Tenkawa, Japan—is interspersed with vignettes from her personal life as a nun, as a wife in two different marriages, and as a renunciate at various critical moments in her transformational journey.

Throughout this immense spiritual pilgrimage/travelogue of changing cultures, languages, climates, foods, cosmologies, ritual practices, friendships, guides, healing ways, theatrical and artistic traditions, there is a constant *basso continuo* in the background, her dream of a borderless world. This guides her emergence from seclusion into the global network of interlaced communities that she connects as she lives out her dream. The monumental carvings that result include *Homage to Andean Woman, Kuan Yin of the People, Winged Woman, Rainbow Bodhisattva,* and *Trinity,* among others.

After reading this book, I wondered from where Vijali's direction and courage came to undertake this life journey. I am struck by the fact that someone who

She Who Opens the Doors of the Earth, Yelapa, Mexico

has resided in caves, meditated in forests, and built altars of stone was born on May 1st -- May Day! -- that archetypical day in which many cultures celebrate springtime rebirth and the renewal of the earth. I feel that Vijali has equally gained strength from her spiritual practices of fifty years: living in many ashrams, as a wandering holy persona, a renunciate, and at one time chanting 700,000 repetitions of the mantra "Om Ah Hung" for the freedom and welfare of Tibet.

The seriousness and integrity of Vijali's vision of a borderless world is felt whenever she chooses not to remain with any particular person or system, husband or healer, but to follow her non-dualistic vision. She decides to leave the world of the amazing curandero Don Hildé in the Peruvian Amazon because he sees things in terms of opposites such as good and evil, while she seeks a place beyond polarities which would not exclude others by positing them as negative. Even though Don Hildé warns that she needs protection from Jesus, Ramakrishna, and other powers in the worlds that she enters so innocently, Vijali chooses to follow her own inner guidance. As she ventures off into forests, caves, mountains, and jungles alone, I can only admire the reality of the protection one earns from many years of chanting, meditation, and prayer. I have observed and marveled from a distance at how Vijali leaves on her World Wheel travels with very few possessions, accomplishes her dream, and always emerges completely unscathed.

Vijali intuitively models a new psychological paradigm, one articulated by writers like Catherine Keller, who maintains in *From a Broken Web*[1] that the true road to individuation is not through the construction of borders between the self and the other, but through expanding the self via the interconnections one makes with the other. Psychological self-realization then becomes an expression of a continual opening. Each life is rendered more complex, more compassionate, more humane through this extension of the boundaries of the self, to the point at which it is seamless with the entire universe.

The more Vijali works to release the face of the feminine hidden in each rock and boulder, the more she joins her voice to the voices of the feminine in oppressed cultures, the more her art becomes a living prayer. The prayer, carefully crafted to answer the question, "What can I do to help the suffering in the world?" is the expression of her life's purpose. Vijali envisioned her network of sculptures like acupuncture needles on the Earth, each one unblocking the energy at a certain point on the meridians of the body of the Great Mother. Through Vijali's work with communities from different cultures, she comes to understand that one person *can* make a difference, *can* make big changes. In order to do this, she realizes that she has made a shift of identity from the small self to the large Self, from the limited to the infinite and unbounded Self. She tells us that:

> *The world became my studio. I was a pilgrim who made offerings and gave voice and form to the spirit of the earth and the people I met along the way. I kept expanding the borders of what*

sculpture was, what art was, integrating it more and more into life itself—the people around me, their problems, their hopes, their dreams of the future. I saw that at the root of these problems is the misunderstanding of ourselves as separate, isolated beings needing to exploit the earth and each other for our personal gain. This dualistic way of thinking is the direct cause of our ecological and social problems, which are rapidly leading us toward global disaster.

The role that Vijali plays for us in this artistic journey is one I would like to call the role of the Peregrine. Whereas a pilgrimage is a journey to a sacred site made by a person in search of a vision or a healing, a peregrinage is a journey to a sacred site made on behalf of the person in need of a healing, by a Peregrine, a person who stands in for those too delicate or too frail to risk the dangers of a long perilous journey. Thus, Vijali's art has become a peregrinage on behalf of all humankind to make offerings at ancient sacred sites, to create new sacred sites, to weave communities together—a rebalancing of the energies of the earth and of all the earth's peoples.

In the latter part of the twentieth century, several other women artists have felt the call to circle the globe several times and interact with women of indigenous communities in ways that remind me of Vijali's peregrinages. Both Betty LaDuke and Suzanne Benton have created paintings, masks, and sculptures with women in diverse cultures, and have been impelled to create their own artistic peregrinages as they, too, circled the globe creating art works and events with people in different cultures, sharing mythologies and sacred stories. Perhaps a new prototype or archetypal pattern is emerging through these journeys.

Within this movement among artists, however, Vijali's work is unique, for she is a spiritual practitioner and a visionary as well as an artist. Vijali's peregrinage has been guided by dreams, visions, and rituals, by her life as a Vedanta nun, by wisdom figures like Anandamayi Ma and Mother Theresa, by her friendship with Anaïs Nin, and by a number of spiritual leaders and shamans from the cultures she has visited. Hers were not visits about artistic interchange alone. They were about spiritual communion, healing, compassion, harmony, and an interconnected global family. Sharing with us the innermost dimensions of her experience during the final ritual in a Shinto temple in Japan, she writes:

I lost my sense of individual identity and opened to universal energy. As the music pulled me to the south, the wail of earth's sadness and the sorrow of her children rose from my belly and poured through my lips. In the west, I felt the darkness of hibernation and dream, and our awakening visions on this earth. In the north, I sang an ancient Sanskrit hymn honoring the Divine Mother of the Universe. My movement stopped in the east, and as emptiness, I stood at the point of new beginnings, the rise of a new sun.

When the ceremony was completed, the Shinto priest turned to her and said: "The Earth and Cosmos have heard your sincere prayer dance, and it will be answered."

Whenever Vijali arrived in a new country, she would ask the people she encountered three questions:

1. What is our essence?
2. What is our sickness, our imbalance—personally, communally, and globally?
3. What can heal this sickness, what can bring us into balance?

The answers she received formed the basis of the themes she worked into her earth sculptures and performance pieces, and always she left these art works as a gift to the communities with which she collaborated.

This book brings her three questions to us in the form of a living example, and it offers us one woman's response to the question she asked of herself, "What can I do to heal the imbalance in the world?" Knowing that a single person with a dream can indeed make a difference is a great source of inspiration and validation. We are encouraged to actualize our own dreams, and to dream her dream further. By following her lead, we may eventually understand that, as the Surrealists once taught us: "The imaginary is that which tends to become real."

Ultimately, Vijali's life story enjoins us all to become peregrines, to make the sacred journeys on behalf of those in need of healing, to make the offerings that will bring about the visions and guidance necessary to lead us on the path to peace and unity. Vijali has re-ignited the cosmic web of the Great Mother. It is now with urgency that we must nurture our planet and keep the spirit of the Mother, our earth, alive.

—Gloria Feman Orenstein
March 2006

Gloria Feman Orenstein is Professor of Comparative Literature and Gender Studies, University of Southern California in Los Angeles, and the author of The Theatre of the Marvelous, The Reflowering of the Goddess, *and* Multicultural Celebrations: The Paintings of Betty LaDuke. *She is co-editor of* Reweaving the World: The Emergence of Ecofeminism.

Dark Roots Luminous, Canyonlands of Utah

CHAPTER ONE

World Wheel-Spoke One

Malibu, California, USA
1984–1987

Western Gateway performance
Malibu, California

I AWOKE IN THE middle of the night on Boney Mountain, the highest peak of California's Santa Monica Mountains that run through Los Angeles and up the coast toward Ventura. From my bed I gazed out of my trailer window into the star-filled sky, my dream still vivid before me:

I am carving a giant face out of living rock—warm, dark granite, rough under my palms in some places, smooth in others. As I chip away at the bottom lip, I have the sense that I am working on a sacred site in a country that I had never before visited. A young woman with a golden complexion and dark, almond-shaped eyes peers up at me and speaks in a language I can't understand. She adjusts the baby on her hip and pulls her woolen shawl over his head as a biting wind cuts across the high, barren plateau. In the distance I see snow-covered mountains disappearing into a topknot of swirling clouds. I stop work, and the young woman joins me as we gather small stones and herbs and place them carefully in my knapsack for a pending ceremony.

The dream shifts and I am in a place that seems close to the Mediterranean Sea. Wearing my backpack, I hike up into an area near crashing waterfalls covered in green grass and wildflowers. I lay my hammer and chisel at the base of a large outcropping of limestone. Three people have followed the same trail and shout to me in another language I only half understand, "Vijali, show us how to carve." I hand them each a hammer and chisel, and we work together as we sing, stop to share the lunch from my pack, and then continue until sunset creating a figure in the stone. Villagers arrive with baskets of food and light candles around the sculpture. We start dancing in a circle—the women's red and blue skirts flaring in the glow of the sinking sun.

Within the context of this dream, I somehow knew that I went on to many countries where I carved giant sculptures of stone to establish new sacred sites. In every community the inhabitants spoke languages I had never heard. And yet, at the end of my stay in each country, we created a ceremony of transformation with music, dance, and ritual—for our lives, for their community, and for the world. In the dream I went from country to country around the globe, creating a giant circle of peace, a World Wheel.

I sat up in bed with a start. The dream gave me an answer to the question that had burned in my soul for ten years—how do I live my vision of a borderless world that came to me unexpected one solitary night?

I had no idea how I would enact what I had seen or where the circle of my dream lay. Where were all these countries? How would I finance my travel to them? How would I connect with these people? I lived with these questions for two years.

Then one evening in 1986, I was sitting on the steps of my trailer and gazing at the full moon. Suddenly it gave me an idea, and I jumped up and went to a world globe that I kept in a back room. I put my

Vijali sitting outside of her trailer at Boney Mountain,
Santa Monica Mountains, California

finger on the 34th north parallel where I lived, and spun the world. Twelve sites leapt out at me: the Santa Monica Mountains where I lived, the Seneca Cattaraugus Reservation in upstate New York (home to a Seneca elder with whom I had spent much time), Spain, Italy, Greece, Egypt, Israel and Palestine, India, Tibet, China, Siberia, and Japan. I realized that this circle of countries formed the giant wheel of my dream, and that the circle represented the interconnection with all life, the tangible experience of my vision. I would begin in my own environment where I could address local problems and learn from resources at hand. Only later I would earn the right to enter other countries.

This thought released a current of new energy, as if the wild, dark roots of my psyche which had lain dormant for so long had come to life and were about to put forth new branches and leaves.

I finished my supper of rice and vegetables and opened the door of my trailer. The hot summer wind tore it from my hand and banged it against the metal side. I stepped outside, braced my body against the step, and managed to get the door closed behind me. I ran up the dirt road that wound through my beloved boulders. The wind tore at my clothes and hair, and I let out a wolf howl. *Ahwooooo!* The wilderness of the void seemed to contain all possibilities, and I wanted to jump in and discover who I really was.

The red sky faded into night, and the boulders retreated into darkness. I took off my clothes and weighted them down with a stone. Removing my hair-clip, my hair fell to my thighs. I ran in total blackness, with only my internal radar to guide my feet.

As I ran, the force of the gale caused me to lift slightly with each stride so that I felt almost airborne. I threw myself into the arms of wind, penetrated by this unknown lover's hot breath. I felt as if I had already jumped into the void, and I trusted that everything would be all right, whatever form that *all right* might take.

Through Anaïs Nin I had become friends with Mary Wright. A few days after I had turned the world globe and had seen the countries of my dream, I ran into Mary at the market. She invited me to visit her at her home in the Santa Monica Mountains, a few ranges from my trailer. I already knew Anaïs's husband, Rupert, and now I would meet Mary's husband, Eric. Both Rupert and Eric Wright were grandsons of Frank Lloyd Wright.

When I drove up to the Wright's house, Mary stood in the doorway waving for me to come in. I sat in her painting studio where she poured me tea, and through the window I saw Eric engrossed in his architectural design in an adjacent studio.

After she heard my artistic vision, Mary's eyes were bright with generosity as she made me an offer. "If you find a location on our land that feels right for your sculpture and performance event, we would be thrilled if you started the World Wheel here."

When we finished tea, Mary introduced me to Eric and went back to her painting. I left the studio and walked down the wooden steps to a path that led into the chaparral. The view was breathtaking, and my excitement rose as I hiked through naturally sculpted stone outcroppings filled with caves. I found myself irresistibly drawn to a precipice of earth jutting over the Pacific. I stood on the edge, breathing in the humid, salty air. To the north I saw the Santa Barbara Channel Islands rising out of the Pacific; to the south, the Santa Monica coastline. I turned and looked behind me. Range after range of the Santa Monica Mountains spread as far as I could see, with their twisting, jutting stone peaks and chaparral-covered slopes.

I sat down on the warm earth and watched a red-tailed hawk circle over my head—and I knew that this was the place for the first World Wheel sculpture and event. I jumped up and walked in a circle. As I did, I visualized a wheel on the ground created by stones. In the center of the wheel, a large upright stone would honor my Celtic background and the megalithic period of standing stones in Europe. On my way up the hill I had grabbed a makeshift walking stick from the underbrush, and now I jammed the point of it into the center of the circle until it held firm. I found a string in my knapsack, tied it to the upright end of the stick, and pulled the string taut as I walked the circumference, dropping flour I had brought for this purpose. As I walked I felt the closure of a circle of my own life: the struggle I had had as an abandoned child and the darkness that had hovered over me from having a schizophrenic mother; the introspection of my ten years in the Vedanta Society convent as a nun; two marriages; and now I was ending a five-year period of retreat in these mountains. When I had completed the circle of flour I stood and gazed out over the ocean. I felt this moment was the beginning of another spiral moving outward into the world, into connection and into community.

On a beach north of Malibu, I parked my Subaru and hiked down the bank through enormous boulders until I spotted an upright granite rock about eight feet high that felt right for the center of my circle. I planned to dig a circular fire pit around the standing stone in the center to represent the union of the male and female qualities.

I called a friend, and an hour later he arrived with his truck. We secured ropes around the boulder and tried to move it, but his wheels only spun in the moist sand. After hours of struggle, the rope snapped, the slab crashed down the embankment into the surf, and the truck almost lunged over the cliff. Sweat poured down my friend's face, and my shirt was wet from exertion and the surf spray.

The next day we returned with chains. Once again, I looped them around the boulder while the truck groaned and spun its tires. After hours of work, we had the stone part way up the bank, but we could budge it no further. Finally, admitting defeat as the sun dropped into the ocean, we removed the chains and allowed the rock to drop to its original home, where it burrowed even deeper into the sand. A wave crashed over it, reclaiming the boulder as its own.

Now I researched the effect of fire on stone. Granite was the wrong material anyway—it would crack and fall apart with continual heat. Yet I needed both the standing stone and fire, as I had visions of men and women sitting in ceremony around its warmth on cold nights. I would have to find a stone that could withstand heat. Lava was the obvious choice since heat would vent through pores caused by escaping gases during its formation.

When I could find no lava rock in the Santa Monica Mountains around our site, I searched for an appropriate boulder in nearby commerical stone yards. The first yard had sandstone, but no lava boulders. The next had lava rock, but nothing large enough to stand upright in the center of my circle.

Santa Monica Mountains, California

Setting the center stone for ***Earth Wheel*** with help from the Wright family

Finally, in a Santa Monica stone yard, I found all the presence and strength I needed in a boulder brought from a lava field in Mexico.

On the following Thursday, the day of the stone's delivery to the Wright's land, in a gesture of purification and sacred rite similar to that used by Native Americans of the area, five of us laid bundles of sage in the pit we had dug. In the afternoon, a truck arrived with the great lava stone. Eric and Mary and their two lanky sons hurried out of their studios, eager to help. Each of us donned whatever protective gear we had—leather gloves, boots—and with wooden planks for levers, six of us pushed and pulled the stone from the truck until eventually it dropped with a thud into the pit. We carefully wedged smaller stones and earth into the hole. Then we stomped around the boulder to pack it tightly.

Once the stone was upright and supported, we stood back, wiped the sweat from our faces, and gazed with awe at this great red monolith. It was *alive*; the hot bubbling, twisting lava of its origin was with us.

Eric broke our moment of silence with a burst of laughter exclaiming, "Wow, what a phallus!" Linda, Mary's cousin, had brought her eight-month-old girl wrapped in a yellow shawl and nursed her as we walked around the stone. She whispered, "To me, she looks like a calm, silent Madonna." And viewing her from another angle, Mary said, "Now she looks like an old woman bent with life experience."

With our center boulder now in place, we needed stones to shape the wheel around it. I called my friend Elizabeth at her home in Malibu. Tall and slender with bobbed brown hair and dark eyes, Elizabeth was called Boo by her friends because she was spunky and straightforward. When the tides were low, we donned sun hats and took our gunnysacks to the beach. We laughed like children as the ocean spray soaked our clothes, and we gathered small multi-colored stones the tide had belched out onto the sand. We tossed the red, gold, black and white stones into four burlap bags until they became almost too heavy to carry. Once a week we met like this, to gather these small stones, load them in the back of Boo's truck, and carry them up to the site.

In a few weeks, friends started arriving at the sculpture site and joined me, helping to dig trenches into the ground along the lines I had marked to form an Earth Wheel. Four spokes ran from the center of the circle toward the four cardinal directions, a fifteen-foot radius. We worked in silence, giving thought to each act as we patted, stomped, and pounded the ditches, making the walls even and firm, breathing in the fragrance of the moist earth.

In the Medicine Wheel—as taught to me by Yehwehnode, a Seneca elder I had been close to for many years—the South represents faith, trust, and innocence. The animal of the South is the mouse or the porcupine which only sees what is under its nose. The lessons learned from this direction arise from the close experiences of home, family, relationship, and the immediate environment. As I worked with my hands to scoop out earth that had fallen back into the trench, I became another earth-bound creature sniffing the soil, forming new relationships with a family of co-creators. Just as the sun set over the Pacific, Mary grabbed one end of a gunnysack and I the other. We walked South, pouring the red sea-washed pebbles Boo and I had gathered earlier into the trench.

During the next week we completed the trench running west, the place of introspection, and from a second sack we dumped black stones. The animal representing the West is the black bear, and with the strength of the bear the goals of our dreams are accomplished. In this direction, we let go of the past in order to enter a brighter future.

As I worked, I re-experienced my own dark path of introspection and reached into myself, into the unconscious, which this direction represents. For a long period of my life I had dwelled in these dark corridors as I attempted to understand the roots of my own despair and isolation.

Patting the earth firm on the Earth Wheel, I pulled myself out of my reverie. How much time has passed, I wondered, as I saw the sun begin to set. I thought of the bear as he wakes from his hibernation and reenters life. I had to give myself permission to live out my dream in the world—to let my art bring understanding within ourselves, and within and between communities.

During the next week I worked in the northerly position, that of the wounded healer. The animal of the North is the buffalo or the moose, which is strong and paces itself. In order to survive some crisis or near-death experience, we must find the road out of our difficulties. The wisdom gained as we journey from confusion to understanding becomes our gift to others.

Shirley Graham and Peter Levitt, two writer friends, joined me. They picked up shovels and helped to deepen the trench. Shirley's long blond hair blew in the breeze as she shoveled the earth out of a trench; Peter put his shovel aside to squat and scoop the soil away with his hands. As his amber eyes danced with playfulness, I realized how all the sorrows and fears and longings of my childhood had brought me right here, digging trenches to create my dearest wish—the family I lacked in childhood, a world family drawn together without boundaries.

After Shirley left for work and Peter to teach his writing class, I poured out the first bag of white stones, which symbolized wisdom and the purity of regeneration. As I worked, I saw how the pain of isolation in my childhood had pushed me to find a way out of my own despair, and how my artwork had allowed me to transform my own life. As I poured in the last heavy sack of white stones, still marked with the salty stains of seawater, I wondered if I could ever have dreamed of the World Wheel if I had not been wounded. Would I ever have connected to this web of life?

Soon other friends arrived, and we completed the trench running East and filled it with gold stones, representing illumination and farsightedness. More friends arrived, and everyone joined in the work, moving the four large boulders to the outer ends of the four trenches now filled with colored stones accenting the cardinal directions. When we had completed the work, we sat and gazed at the wheel. As the eagle of the East flies high and sees the larger picture, I looked up at the expanse of sparkling blue ocean and considered the journey ahead of me.

Peter Levitt, Mary Wright, and Vijali working together to create *Earth Wheel*

Later, after everyone had gone, I sat alone in the circle of stone and surveyed what we had accomplished. The setting sun streaked orange across the circle and seemed to set the monolith on fire. The smell of baked earth and the warm breeze on my bare arms evoked a childhood memory:

I am seven years old. I run out of the house and through a tunnel of dry grass taller than my head. The heavy fragrance of earth reaches me. I find my secret place, a little spot of ground hidden from view of the house by the high grass. In this private place, I have arranged stones in a circle and an upright stone at the center. When I reach my sacred hideout, I lay dandelions around the stone. I am crying when I go there, but as I sit in the circle, everything feels all right again, and my heart fills with peace.

Earth Wheel at the first World Wheel site, Malibu, California

The pulse of the crickets' song pulled me out of my reverie. It was late as I stuffed the remainder of a sandwich and my notebook into my backpack and returned to my car. From the Wright's land I drove north, away from Malibu and the Los Angeles area, along a winding road through the Santa Monica Mountains until Boney Mountain loomed before me. My heart pounded as it had the first day I laid eyes on those jutting stone deities rising against the sky. I drove the last mile on the eroded earth road and parked my station wagon in front of the broken-down trailer that had been my home in this wilderness for the past five years. My life had become very simple. How would it feel to be "in the world" again?

The next morning I arose before sunrise, greeted the rising sun and returned to the site to meet with the others for the Monday practice of our small group, *Theater of the Earth*, which I had formed to develop a performance for the closing event of the first World Wheel site. I had met Georgianne Cowan in a performance class. With two or three other friends, we had been meeting twice a week at her home in Santa Monica to create the performance. But now we decided to meet at the site on the Wright's land, at the Earth Wheel sculpture itself.

I drove to the practice laden with concern. Would we be prepared for the ceremony in time? What roles would we play, and how would our costumes reflect the content? Arriving before the other performers, I left my station wagon, climbed the hill to the *Earth Wheel* and sat for a moment before the presence of the upright stone. Then I went to where my friend Boo and I had piled some grey stones. One by one I carried them to the upright boulder and arranged them around the base to form a circular fire pit. The shape reminded me of the *yoni*,[2] which in Hinduism is used to designate the sacred feminine. As I worked in the shadow of the *lingam,* I felt the presence of ancient people and tried to sense their thoughts. It seemed to me that they felt more than fertility in those phallic stones. They felt a force, a vibration that entered the body and mind and brought change and clarity.[3]

I finished arranging the stones and sat in silence until I heard the wheels of a car crunch on the dirt road coming up the hill. Georgianne had arrived, accompanied by Anne Mavor, a performance artist and writer. The two of them joined me at the *Earth Wheel,* and we each found our own place to sit on the ground within the circle.

A tangible silence drew us inward for a time. Then I led a few theater exercises centered around the three questions I had contemplated since childhood: *Where do we come from? What is our problem? What is the solution?*

Georgianne reached into her backpack and drew out a costume she had been working on. She slipped on the transparent, membrane-like body suit, tugged and pulled until it covered her whole body and face. Then she danced—her body tall and slim, undulating like water in answer to the first question, *Where do we come from?* She sat down and said, "I want to use my fleeting birth memories to understand myself and the conflicts I am having in my life. I feel we evolved as a species from water."

Anne asked, *What is our problem, what is our sickness?* She brought out her costume, and when she slipped it on, she looked like a football cheerleader. She bounced around our circle with exaggerated gestures as her short red skirt flared out with each step.

"How is your problem or sickness effecting our community, our planet?" I questioned her.

"I've asked Ron from our performance workshop to rant and rage about the 'true' path, as I cheer him on. Then I plan to have us all end up in a fight about who has the *right* way."

Anne had a severe stutter, and, while many of our sessions were an emotional struggle for her, through her performance she found her voice and a passion for working with words. After the World Wheel event, she had the confidence to perform solo for the first time.

"I feel connected to the third question," I said. *What is the solution—what can heal us and bring us into balance?* I took out my skimpy deerskin skirt, slipped off my jeans, and tied it loosely around my hips. I would play the role of Gaia, the ancient Greek word for Earth. Through the image of Gaia, I would convey that harmony might be restored if we could find again, not only our real relationship with the earth, but also that we *are* Earth. I walked to the edge of our stone circle, picked up a dried tumbleweed, and clipped it on my head. As I wove my long hair through its web, I imagined how our bodies formed out of earth's evolution and are made of the same elements—how the trees, stones, and animals are our brothers and sisters.

One warm day in June, I left my work with the performance to meet a friend, Richard Feynman, the physicist and Nobel Prize winner who developed the landmark theory of quantum electrodynamics and the "Feynman Diagrams." We met at the entrance to Winter Canyon behind the Pepperdine University campus, where a few years earlier I had been given permission by the university to create two environmental sculptures.

I pulled up in my station wagon and spotted Richard's car already parked along the curb. I gave him a hug and hid my surprise at how frail his body had become, eaten away by cancer. He had only a few more months to live, and his last request of me was that I personally show him one of my sculptures.

His tall frame was now gaunt and his sandy brown hair now gray, but his eyes still lit up mischievously whenever I looked back at him. We hiked along the steep bank to the right of the waterfall. I heard him slip once and displace a few stones which tumbled down the embankment. I slowed my pace and paused, ready to help him over the next boulder, but he stiffened as a child might at the sight of my hand, and I could see he wanted to manage the trek himself.

When we reached the summit of the bank at the top of a waterfall, we stopped to catch our breath. After a moment Richard said, "If a cataclysm occurred, so that all scientific knowledge was destroyed, and you were allowed only a one-sentence hypothesis to pass on to the next generations, what would you say?" He turned to me, but he answered himself. "I'd

Vijali working on the *Shelter Sculpture* in Winter Canyon,
Pepperdine University, Malibu, California

Vijali carving in cave for *Sculptural Amphitheater* in Winter Canyon, Pepperdine University, Malibu, California

say that all things are made of atoms—particles that move around in perpetual motion, attracting each other when they are a little distance apart, but repellent when they are squeezed together."

"Like humans," I said, acknowledging his irony.

We walked down to the stream and he crouched by the bank to put his hand in the water. He let the drops fall from his fingertips. "Imagine this great drop of water, with all these jiggling particles stuck together. The water keeps its volume; it doesn't fall apart because of the attraction of the molecules for each other. If the drop is on a slope, as this stream is, where it can move from one place to another, the water will flow, but it doesn't just fly apart—because of molecular attraction."

Richard stood up and wiped his hand on his shirt, and then we crawled on our bellies through the dried grass tunnel I had crept through for two years while I worked back in the canyon. I could hear his labored breathing behind me, and when I emerged on the other side, I had to wait several seconds for him to catch up. I extended my hand to help him to his feet, and this time he grasped it. I expected warmth, and instead I felt bones, hard and cool. Though there had always been an attraction between us, a respect for the other's creativity, we were never sexually or romantically intimate. Rather, we brought out in each other a childlike playfulness. Now I looked at him with concern, as we each brushed the other free of the dried leaves and grass that had stuck to our clothes.

But Richard's eyes twinkled as he brushed bits off my chest saying, "I like this." And then, seriously, "You know I'm going to die very soon."

"What do you think happens after death?" I ask.

"Nothing. Death is the end of our existence, and I'm ready." He gave me a little push when he saw my sad face. Then he spotted the sculpture: a cave with a giant blue spiral carved and painted into the recess. It appeared to be a twisting slice of sky that opened the stone to its intrinsic space—the space that Richard knew so well in physics. He stood with his hands on his hips. "Now, that's something!"

I leapt up into the natural amphitheater with its five levels and the caves that I had carved and painted. The stream flowed over the central portion of the stone outcropping, forming tadpole-filled puddles on each level that poured over their rims onto the next.

"Here, give me your hand." I leaned down and stretched to pull him up to the first level. We climbed to the upper cave by using natural toe-holes in the sandstone, and when we reached it, he turned around as if delivering one of his dramatic lectures at Caltech, and bowed.

"It's marvelous." He placed his hands on the center of the spiral in the cave and then with his fingertips followed the radiant blue in its outward curve.

We sat down in the partial shadow in the cave and I pulled our lunch from my backpack. "A sandwich for you, a sandwich for me." In my elation over Richard's enthusiasm for *Sculptural Amphitheater,* I almost sang the words.

The grass tunnel in Winter Canyon

Sculptural Amphitheater (detail) with Vijali

We looked across to the other cave, where I had carved and painted a giant blue wave. I felt Richard taking in the image, and could see by his pallor what the trip had cost him. Silently I gave thanks for this time with someone who immediately understood what I had attempted to convey, and for these precious moments so close to the end of a dear friend's life.

After lunch, I suggested that he rest.

"No," he said. "Let's explore the other cave." As he stood up, he teetered at the edge of the outcropping.

I gasped and grabbed his shirt to pull him back, and then we climbed over to the other cave. We sat in silence and ran our hands over the tumbled river stones, caught like jewels in the layers of sand that eventually, through pressure and eons of time, had become sandstone—the Sespe Strata.

I waited until he was ready, and then we silently worked our way to the base of the amphitheater, led by the stream, and trekked back without mishap through the canyon. At the car in a long hug goodbye, I recognized fatigue in his eyes. A part of me had worried he would collapse on the trek, but I saw now that he had finished the trip as much for me as for himself.

Back at the sculpture site, Eric Wright and his son deepened and readied a natural basin in the ground with a small bulldozer and filled the dry earth with water, lilies, fish, and all the elements that comprise a natural lake.

Over the months of the project, each of us worked with our own question and on our own section of the performance, to heal our audience and ourselves. We chose our own music, decided with whom we would collaborate, and made our own costumes. Though I coordinated and directed the overall performance, I wanted my colleagues to feel that the ceremony was their creation as well. Throughout the process, we danced, sang, acted out, and responded to the three questions, still keeping with our theme of transformation. Everything changed daily. As the performance day approached, we settled on the choreography, but even then we made alterations on the final day.

The day of the performance coincided with the Harmonic Convergence, August 16, 1987, a time when planets aligned in harmony and groups around the world gathered in ceremony and good will. Was the timing a coincidence? Perhaps. Or did the forces of the universe bring many projects to their completion

Sculptural Amphitheater (detail)

Spectators gathering for the *Western Gateway* perfomance

on this date? The Church of England ordained the first female Anglican deacon. Gorbachev met for three days in Washington and signed a treaty to ban all short- and medium-range nuclear weapons from Europe. The Soviet cosmonaut, Yuri Romanenko, returned to earth from the Mir space station after a record 326 days in space.[4]

Early that morning on Boney Mountain, I left the trailer and hiked the dirt road that wound its way up to the plateau where I greeted the sun. A deer darted across the path and stood frozen when she saw me. Our eyes locked in a moment of recognition and acknowledgment, and then she bounded into the chaparral, leaving my heart leaping. When I reached the top of the plateau, the stone circle I had formed when I first moved to the area drew me. I walked its circumference until I arrived in the east and stopped to admire the sun's golden rays as they shot over the rim of the mountain. Simultaneously, a prayer surfaced in my heart: *I have been here five years, and you, Boney Mountain, are my Gaia. Please remove my ego, and anything that stands in the way of your presence, so that the people who come today can experience the silence that you have given to me.*

Two hours before the ceremony, I rubbed rich brown earth and colors onto my skin, making my limbs as dark as charcoal. My hands and face were earth brown, turning red, to signify the heat of bubbling lava. On my head, I tied the tumbleweed I had found at the sculpture site, and wove my long brown hair into its dried branches. The effect was that my hair seemed to stand on end, with flames lapping over my face. Through this ritual preparation, I transformed not only my physical body, but my consciousness as well. By the time I had finished, I truly felt I was no longer Vijali. Made of the elements of earth, I *was* Gaia, the earth herself.

Through the invitation of friends and by word of mouth, almost seven hundred people had arrived by five-thirty in the evening. They seated themselves on the sloping ground, with the lake in front of them and rocky cliffs beyond. Caves dotted the sandstone outcroppings, setting the stage for the Guardian Spirits of Earth, performers dressed with indigenous animal masks. The hawk, a snake, coyotes, and deer showed as silhouettes against the sky. Colorful flags flapped and twisted in the breeze. The performers moved slowly, as animals, periodically punctuating the silence with primitive instruments.

At six-thirty, the performance began. Georgianne and a male African-American dancer friend had dressed as androgynous beings in tight translucent fabric that resembled white membrane with veins showing through. They emerged from two cocoon-like forms, which lay in the sand. In a process of birthing, they slithered into the water, and then, like amphibian creatures, they climbed under waterfalls

Georgianne and partner in the *Western Gateway* performance

Georgianne Cowan as androgynous being in the *Western Gateway* performance

and onto rocks where they stretched in the sun. At the water's edge, they writhed out of their skins to reveal the veined flesh of a black man and a white woman.

A hush fell over the people. Three children walked close to the lake to watch the dancers. Then a loud drum roll sounded and a procession of six people marched out dressed in modern day costume. They set down a "soap box" platform on the slope of the hill, and each one began to rant about how *his* or *her* way was the right way. This was Anne's response to the second question, *What is our sickness?*

The audience roared with laughter. This was the Heyeohkah part of the performance, which means *contrary* in the Lakota tradition. The Heyeohkah is a powerful shaman, often the clown, mimicking people's characteristics so that they can see themselves.

From the hill above, an Australian didgeridoo sounded. I stepped to the crest of the hill, earthen skinned, silhouetted against the sky as primordial Gaia. In one raised hand, I held a dried tree branch. In the other, I held an eagle's wing. My hair, wildly entangled in the dried tumbleweed, writhed upward, snakelike, against the blue sky. I felt the audience holding its breath. Some stood up and took a few steps toward me. I felt lava bubbling through my veins and the surface of the earth through my skin, crusting and twisting as it cooled with the touch of air. As I stood on the precipice, I was not Vijali, but the voice of stone, the movement of air and water, and the sprouting of trees.

Georgianne Cowan birthing as Woman in the *Western Gateway* performance

I could feel the presence of my beloved mountain moving through me, drawing people up the hill and around the Earth Wheel. My body very slowly began to move as if it were the turning of earth around the Earth Wheel, pulling the audience with me into their own center. Energy moved up my spine, continuing through my arms, legs, and out my eyes into the eyes of the participants, pulling them into one center of silence. I felt that some force came through me, connecting each person in that circle to earth, to the spirit within matter.

Next, a friend of ours appeared as "Woman" with water and herbs. She entered the wheel from the southeast, traveling counterclockwise. A beautiful woman, she stood within the circle and loosened her dress until it fell to the ground. From a large conch shell, she bathed in water. Then she put on a fresh cloth and wrapped it around her as the wind caught the material, flag-like, and picked up the flaming color of the setting sun.

Another friend appeared as "Man" carrying long bamboo poles with leaves at the tops and furled flags. His skin glistened under the last rays of sun as they penetrated the earth. He entered the wheel from the northwest and unfurled the flag. With poles and flag he erected the Western Gateway, which had become the name of the performance.

I, as Gaia, rose from where I had been sitting by the monolith and drew Woman and Man to me. With the slowness of the seasons, Gaia poured water over them from a vessel painted with a skyscape. Next Gaia gave fire by igniting sage sticks in the roaring fire at the base of the megalith, and giving one to Woman and one to Man. They circled the audience in a dance, smudging the environment with sage smoke.

Gaia moved ever so slowly out of the wheel and arrived at the very precipice of the hill. Woman and Man offered ladles of water to each other to pour over the center stone. Steam shot off the hot monolith

Vijali as Gaia in the *Western Gateway* performance, Malibu, California

with a spitting sound that united with one gesture the elements of water, earth, air, and fire.

Other performers, as animals and birds, came out of the mountains and caves and entered the circle of alchemy. They picked the couple up in their arms and lifted them high into the air as their fingers touched, and then carried them through the Western Gateway. The audience, now becoming participants, entered the Earth Wheel and poured water on the *lingam*. They, too, left the circle through the Western Gateway and danced with the performers and with each other down the hill to a clearing where fifteen drummers played on into the night.

As the drumming and dancing built to a crescendo at the bottom of the hill, I sat on the precipice. I felt I had been sitting there for four billion years, and would be there another four billion years in utter stillness as Earth herself. I thought I would never move again. I thought that I would be like the dead coyote I had once found and for seven days had watched disintegrate. First it swelled, bloated with maggots until the whole body moved and undulated with the activity of this new birth—until it burst. The odor still comes to me in dreams. On the seventh day there was complete stillness again; the flesh was gone, leaving only holes for eyes. This night, as I sat on the precipice, I believed that this would be my own process, that I would watch my body disintegrate on this spot.

Peter Levitt, my poet friend, recognized the state I was in. He looked into my eyes, and then others came, one by one, to sit in front of me in a similar manner. He told a friend of his, who felt uncomfortable with this scene, that I was a Boddhichita, an enlightened presence. His friend then came and sat in front of

Vijali as Gaia, sitting on precipice after the *Western Gateway* performance

me and later told him, "As I looked into Gaia's eyes, I experienced extraordinary comfort, as if my deepest self was being looked into without any judgment. My own mind stopped its judging and became quiet."

Some cried. Some friends became upset, thinking I was on an extended ego trip. Eventually the wind blew in off the sea to twist my hair and branches and tug at my mud-smeared deerskin clothes. From stone I became space, and the wind blew straight through me without hindrance. After some time, the movement of wind entered my limbs and I was able to walk down the hill.

Over the next few days, I distributed the money remaining from the contributions made to the performance to homeless people in Los Angeles. I released the trailer on Boney Mountain back to its owner. I sold my car, gave away my possessions, and with a tiny bit of money from artwork I had recently sold, I purchased a ticket that would take me to the Seneca Cattaraugus Reservation in upstate New York, the next site of the World Wheel. I packed my hammer and chisels, a camera, one change of clothes, and my journal. Then I, too, became a person without a home.

CHAPTER TWO

Invisible Sources

Los Angeles
1941–1948

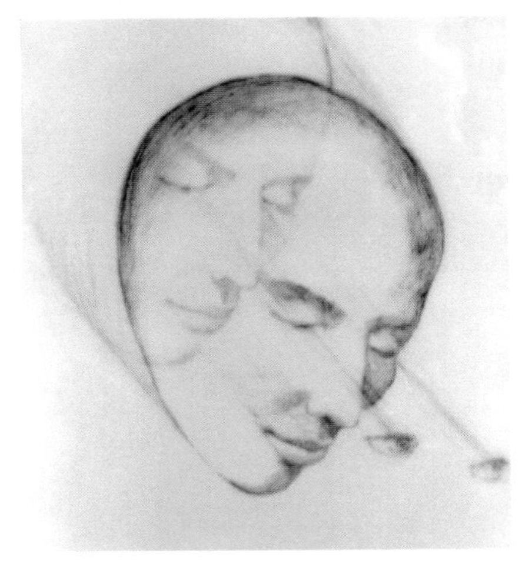

Invisible Sources

When I was two years old, my father drove to my mother's apartment in Los Angeles while she was away at work. He opened the front door and a foul odor confronted him. He walked down the hall and into the bedroom where I sat crying, locked in a dog kennel. Excrement had dried in smears over my body. He could smell me from yards away. Tears streaked my cheeks and my eyes had glazed over. I had been alone all day, without food, without water.

Whether I retain actual memories of this time or have formed them from accounts others have told me, some details remain vivid. I remember recognizing my father's voice, and as his soft face became clear through my tears, I cried out. "Daddy!"

He bent down toward me and I smelled the ink and paper of his office. He put his hand on the kennel, and I waited for him to unlock the wire door and pick me up, to cradle me against him. But instead, his lips pressed tightly together, he adjusted the collar of his blue suit and turned away. I heard his leather shoes scuffing against the wooden floor as he retreated. When the front door closed with a bang, I screamed until my throat was raw.

Late at night, my mother came home from work. The telephone rang as she walked down the hall. I cried so hard she said she couldn't understand my father on the other end of the line. "Quiet," she said. As she listened, her face drew taut and lines formed between her eyebrows.

When she hung up the phone, she dropped her blue coat on the arm of a chair and went to the bathroom to draw a bath. Then she came to the kennel and lifted the wire door that kept me in my prison. My crying stopped when she picked me up and took me into the bathtub—but I shook all over. Her body was warm, the water was warm, but she didn't look at me. She seemed preoccupied, in a world other than my own.

The next day my father picked me up before he went to work and took me to a foster home. A woman answered the door and invited us in. I didn't know her or the two children I saw playing in the living room. I hung onto my father's pant leg and hid my face in his trousers when the woman tried to talk to me. My father moved to leave and tried to loosen my grip. When he closed the door, I howled.

For a week, I cried every day and wouldn't play with the other two children in the house or eat my food. The woman hit me when I wouldn't eat, and her husband hit me when I cried.

The next time my father came to visit, he held my face and peered at it, turning it one way and then another. I heard angry voices. He ripped drawers and closet doors open and threw my things in my suitcase and a box. Then he took my hand and we left.

After two more attempts to find foster homes, my father sent me to live with his parents in Dallas. There, through the front door of my grandmother's house, I often watched children walk down our tree-lined street holding the hands of their parents. One day I stood with my forehead pressed against the screen. I turned to Grandma, "Why am I the only child without a mommy and daddy?" She didn't say a word.

Grandma permed her thinning gray hair into curls. Her breasts hung like deflated balloons at night, but during the day, a laced corset held them up; worn for her fallen womb, she said. When I suffered from asthma attacks in the middle of the night, she massaged my aching back, her hands gnarled with arthritis.

Grandpa was bald with bushy eyebrows. He seemed to think that a daily switching was the way to raise a child. He never talked to me, and I kept as much distance as I could between us. I don't remember what he switched me for, only that he used the willow branches growing by our side porch—perhaps because I had peed in bed or had knocked over a glass of water. Grandma always rubbed an unpleasant smelling yellow ointment on my bleeding legs after the switching. Around this time I began to see a light hovering around me when I was alone, as if a presence existed there, holding me, letting me know that it protected me, that it loved me.

When we ate together, Grandpa slurped his vegetables from a big bowl set at his place at the end of the table. He rarely spoke. Sometimes, when I found him looking at me from under his shaggy eyebrows, I lowered my eyes and retreated into my own silent world. I squirmed in my seat and waited until I could leave the table.

Grandpa allowed no mirrors or lipstick in the house, and he didn't drink or smoke. We read the Bible every day and tuned to classical music on the radio. As we listened, I stood on a box and conducted the music with waving arms. Sometimes I sang along with the melody.

Each week Grandma dressed me in a blue taffeta dress she had made herself, with a bonnet, and we took the bus to Sunday school. I couldn't understand why the teacher said a child in Africa would go to hell if they didn't accept Jesus, because I knew that many children had never heard of him. Yet, I listened carefully to the stories of the life of Jesus, who was kind and loved everyone. I knew he could love me, too, so I asked him to come into my heart. I wanted to be just like Jesus when I grew up.

My mother came to visit in 1944, when I was five. I saw her walk up the front path. "My mommy, my very own mommy!"

I leapt and danced until she leaned down at the doorway to pick me up, wrapped her slim fingers around my waist, and lifted me off the ground. Those long days and even nights alone in the dog kennel vanished in one glorious moment.

That night we bathed together in Grandma's bathtub. I crawled close to her and played I was a baby in her arms. I tugged at her soft breasts with my lips until she told me to stop. She didn't put the quinine and Band-Aid on my thumb as Grandma did to stop my sucking, and she let me curl up against her warm back before we both fell asleep.

In the early morning, my mother shook me awake and whispered in my ear, "You can live with me if you don't tell Grandma and Grandpa."

I tumbled out of bed and dressed in my plaid pinafore as fast as I could. I giggled, and my two braids flopped in the air until she shushed me.

She grabbed an armful of my clothes. "Shhh," she said, and we slipped out the back door.

"Do you mean it? Do you really mean it?" The black Packard with its deep seats felt like a new home, the home I wanted, and we drove away as the first glimmer of light appeared on the horizon.

"Climb in the back seat, honey. Pull your blanket around you and try to sleep," she whispered.

But I couldn't stay still. I kept looking out the windows into the world of passing oak trees, their phantom shapes taking form in the dawn. When we entered the Great Plains with its open skies, seemingly ready to lift me right up into the clouds, I finally nodded off to sleep.

After what seemed like an entire day, with dreams of running horses and birds flying toward the sun, I woke when the car stopped suddenly.

My mother's face appeared over the back seat. "Wake up sleepy-head. We're here."

Through heavy eyelids, I saw that we had arrived at a farm with big fields and orchards.

"I promised you we could live together." She loosened my hands from the blue blanket. "This is the Picketts' farm. We're near Little Rock, Arkansas."

Mr. and Mrs. Pickett came out of the old farmhouse and approached the car. They seemed about Grandma's age and looked very serious, but I had neither seen them nor heard of them before. My mother shook hands and introduced herself. The extra polite way my mother talked with Ma Pickett told me that she had never met them before either. After only a few moments in the farmhouse, Mr. Pickett took my hand and walked me to the cherry orchard. A slim man with a weatherworn face, he wore cowboy boots and a cowboy hat.

This must be heaven, I thought: to be with Mommy and to have a cherry orchard and a cowboy, too! Mr. Pickett lifted me onto a branch of a cherry tree, and I munched all the cherries I could eat, their red juice staining my fingers and lips. When we returned to the farmhouse a half hour later, Mommy had gone.

I wouldn't talk to anyone.

"She'll be all right," I heard Ma and Pa Pickett reassure each other in the next room.

That night, I lay in bed in the dark with a photograph of my mother in my arms. I cried. I remembered our bath and how she let me sleep close to her. I thought of her soft brown hair and warm breasts. Finally, I fell into sleep—but in the middle of the night, I woke to loud snoring in the next room. From beneath the patchwork quilt, I crawled into the chilly air, squatted over the metal pee pot Ma Pickett had left on the floor, and felt my release. Then I crept back into the warm sheets with my mommy's picture.

The next morning Pa Picket put me on top of the big dark horse he used to plow the fields. The moist

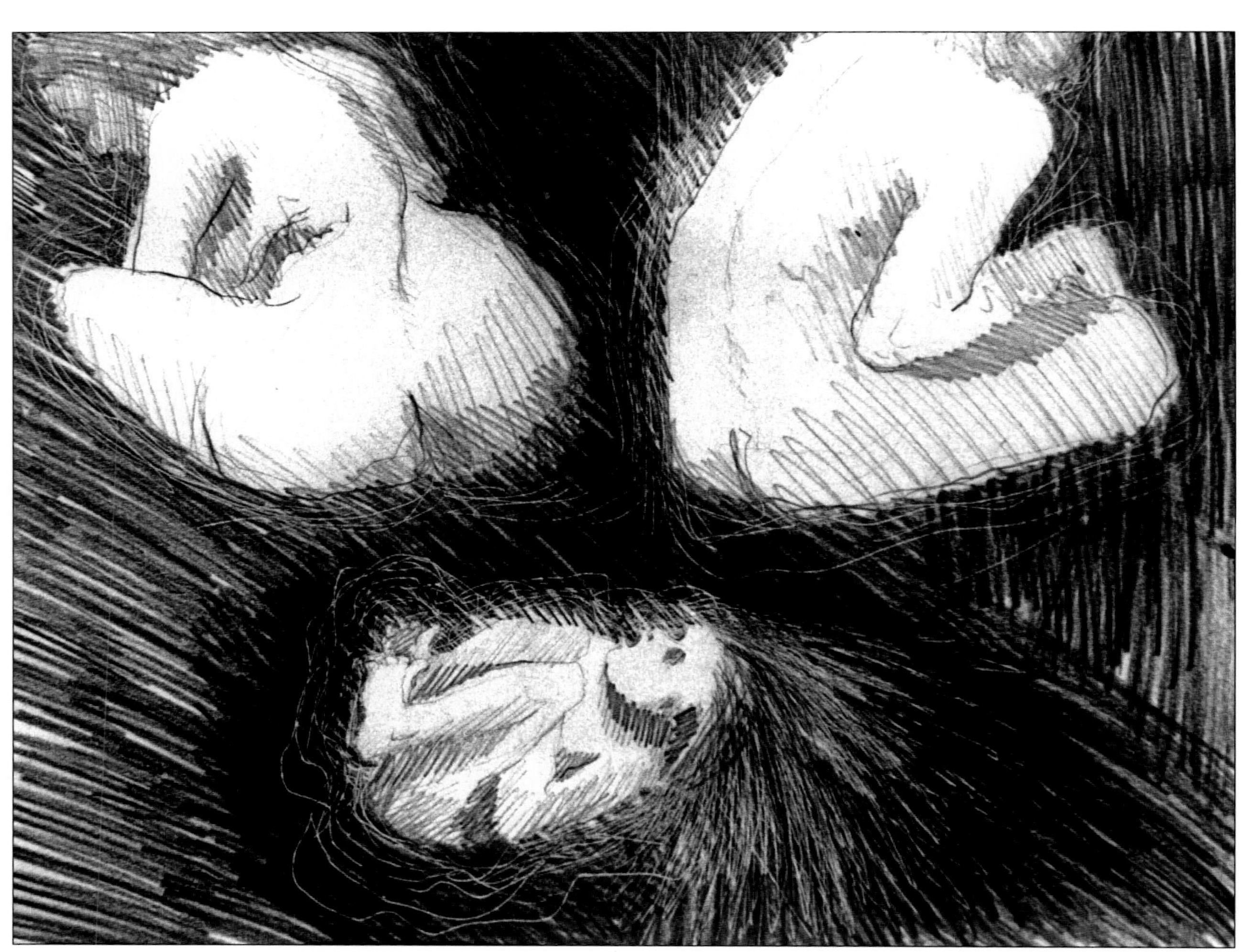

Alone

smell of uncovered earth rose around us, and when we stopped work, the sun shone directly overhead. We washed up at the well and went into the house for lunch, but the house seemed strange and empty. There were no figurines to play with, as in Grandma's house, and no books. I looked around for paper to draw on, but found none. Someone came to the door with a package, and Pa Pickett signed an X on a long piece of paper. Then we sat down to a big hot meal I couldn't eat. Pa Pickett frowned, but Ma Pickett put her hand on his arm.

Ma Pickett, plump in a flower-print dress she had made from feed sacks, sat by the fire in the evening after supper knitting with red yarn. Her needles clicked as she rocked in her chair. She turned to Pa Pickett and said, "I'll show you later."

"Show me, too. Show me, too," I said, not knowing what she referred to. She wouldn't answer, but let me crawl onto her lap and pull on the brown warts that stuck out on her face like baby cow tits. But when I tried to touch the little box I felt between her big breasts, she made me leave the room. I peeked through the cracks of the door and saw Ma Pickett take the green tin box from between her breasts and open it. As she took out the money, she and Pa Pickett talked in hushed tones.

The next morning Pa lost his patience and I got a switching when I failed to eat my biscuits. "You won't be going outside for a week," he said.

Ma Pickett let me watch as she made a dress for me out of the feed sack Pa Pickett brought in from the barn. "You'll always be skinny," she said, "if you don't eat your biscuits."

Days passed. Finally the Picketts allowed me to go outside as long as I didn't play with the children down the road at the next farm. I sank my bare feet into the earth and its fragrance rose up to greet me. A few mud puddles remained after the spring rain, so I splashed and made designs with my feet, and then, singing, I ran into the tall green grass at the edge of the vegetable garden. Within this forest of grass, I found an open space of earth that felt silky to my toes, and I knew right away that this would be my special secret garden. I ringed my hideaway with pebbles I found in the grass, and stuck wildflowers from the edge of the garden in between the stones.

Inside the circle of grass and stone and flowers, I grew quiet as a presence hovered over me. I saw a light by my hand and felt comforted. Grandma always talked about Jesus. Maybe the light was Jesus. Or maybe the light was his mother Mary who knew that my own mother had left me all alone.

One Saturday evening, Pa Pickett grabbed my arm and we walked down to the barn, up the ramp, and through the barn doors, where we stepped into a world of light and color and sound: red and yellow ribbons tied to the rafters, people playing fiddles, others singing and dancing, the women's skirts flying in streaks of blue and orange. I wanted to dance so badly my feet itched. I jumped up and down until a little man with a big hat and heavy boots took my arms and swung me around the floor. I laughed and laughed and wanted to dance forever. I felt as if the big sky I had seen over the plains had taken me up through the barn roof. But then the man with the big hat brought me back to my standing place.

Snow came and we made popcorn balls for the Christmas tree. Santa Claus brought me crayons and paper, so I drew and drew—people and trees and mountains and sky.

Sometimes I saw the face of Jesus in the clouds and I knew that at any moment he could come down to my hideaway and sit by my side. Some point of light, some humming presence, remained always with me, pressing behind the movements of my hand, appearing to me in clouds, calling me to remember. I knew I was part of a vast playground that extended into the earth, into the life of insects and weeds, with their delicate flowers and pungent smells, and into the evening twilight with its summer fireflies.

At night, when I looked into the black sky at the stars overhead, I imagined they said, "We are here with you." As I lay awake in bed, lights glowed in the dark, sometimes at the window, sometimes hovering around me. This presence remained always close at hand, ready to pop out and greet me at any moment. I had only to look, turn around, bump into it, or reach out to touch it, and it would be there. But the stones in my secret hideaway were the strongest reminder. They gave me the feeling, "Hey, you belong to us."

My father hired a detective. He found me and put me on a train with a big tag that sent me back to my grandparents' home. I was not sure that Grandma and Grandpa wanted to have me back, and no one ever told me why my mother left me on the farm. I carried a dark cloud in my heart, and only years later, when I was old enough to ask the questions, did I receive answers.

The Second World War ended. We were listening to the radio program *One Man's Family* when a special announcement came on saying that Germany had surrendered. My grandparents raised their voices in prayer, "Thank you, Lord, for bringing an end to this fighting." Then Grandpa brought the Bible to the table and showed me the signs of the end of the world in Revelations. He had drawn red lines under the printed words. He said, "When tensions arise in the Middle East, the third and last world war will begin. Evil will be consumed by fire and Jesus will come again."

I wanted Jesus to come. Yes, I needed Jesus to come, badly!

My father visited me in Dallas once a year. I got flutters in my stomach when I knew he would be coming, and I concentrated on nothing else. I lined my dollies up on the front porch in their best dresses and then sat with them, waiting and waiting, scrutinizing every car that drove down the road. Often he called and canceled the visit, but when he did arrive, I ran and leapt into his arms, and he swung me around until the world became a kaleidoscope of greens and blues.

"Stay with me," I begged. "I like it when you talk to me and take me places."

"Shhh," he said.

He gave me a book, *A Museum of Art for Children*. He painted pictures of my cat, Skipper, and made tiny elephants of blue clay that I preserved in the refrigerator long after he left.

When I was seven, I visited him in California. Grandma and I traveled on a train and stayed with Grandpa's sister. One day my mother came to see me. She took me for a drive and I gave her a blue handkerchief. On it I had embroidered, "I love you Mommy," in red. She did not return me to my great-aunt's house. Instead, she drove me to her rented cottage, where she kept me for two months.

She put me in a day care home while she worked, and I cried and hid my face and wouldn't play. After that first day, I refused to go back to day care. I stayed alone in the house and hid under the covers, afraid of the factory whistle that shrieked close by. When she returned, she seldom held me, and she often went out at night. I knew when she would go because she dipped her little finger in a tube of red lipstick and smeared it on her lips. I wanted her to paint my lips, too, and sometimes she did. Then she finally told my father where we lived, and he sent me back to Dallas to live with his parents again.

At this point, my grandma said she had something she needed to tell me. She acted extra cheerful and hummed a little tune under her breath, the way she did when she was worried. She took me on her lap, and I said, "Tell me a story, tell me a story of the olden days," which she often did.

"No, I have something else to tell you. Your mother's been committed to a state mental hospital. She thinks she's the Virgin Mary and has been diagnosed as paranoid schizophrenic."

The words were too big for me and I couldn't understand what was so bad about being the Virgin Mary. I played at being Peter Pan every chance I got. But I did understand that she was ill.

That night I prayed before going to sleep: "Dear Jesus, please take my hands in exchange for my Mommy getting well." My hands were my most precious possessions because they could draw and paint. After my prayers, I curled up with my mother's photograph, the cold frame against my cheek.

The next morning, I ran out of the house through a tunnel of dry grass. In a spot hidden from the house, I created a secret shrine like the one at the Picketts'. I laid dandelions around the large stone in the middle of a circle of stones. I sat in the circle for a long time and cried. The soft light hovered around me, touching me gently, as if the fingers of the unknown wanted to let me know I was all right, that life was bigger than my grandmother's world.

I played hide-and-seek into the twilight with our neighbors, Nancy and Gordon, who were close to my age. Often we would run through mud, climb trees, and hide in the tall grass until the fireflies came out and Grandma called me home. I considered the ants and the doodlebugs my friends. I watched their movements for hours as they maneuvered through the soft earth beneath our porch. Sometimes a beautiful cloud distracted me—perhaps one that took the shape of an eagle moving fast across the sky, so that in my mind I would fly with her, on her wings, looking out over great distances to the horizon, down onto the tops of mountains and forests and valleys.

One day I peeked through the fence and saw our neighbor, Ethel, bent over weeping in her garden. I crawled under the fence and ran to her, my pigtails flapping as my bare feet sank into the freshly watered lawn. I put my hand in hers. With my other hand, I held out one of my paintings. It was an ordinary painting of green trees with gnarly roots descending into the earth, but above the trees, clouds that resembled eagles sailed across a blue sky. She took the painting and her face changed and her tears stopped. She looked into my eager face and said, "Yes, yes, yes!"

Introvert

Grandma later told me, "Ethel said that you changed her life at a time when she wanted to give up. Her husband had just left her and she was thinking of suicide. You connected her with hope, with the beauty in the simple things around her, with God."

When I was nine years old, my father moved my aging grandparents and me to California where we would be closer to him. He enrolled me in a girls' boarding school in Temescal Canyon, and then the next year at Parnell Preparatory School for Girls in Whittier.

I was the only ten-year-old girl I knew with budding breasts. They caused my puritanical grandmother much worry and many uncomfortable moments.

"Now that you're getting bosoms and hair," she told me when I returned home for Christmas, "there will be a time when you will have blood and you will have to wear pads."

I shared this information with the girl next door, fascinating her with the news that we would soon have blood coming out of our breasts and would wear pads in our bras so we could have babies.

My father took me once a year to see my mother, who remained in various hospitals until her death twenty years later. I always saw my mother through the eyes of my childhood, with nothing other than love and admiration. To me she was not crazy. She was as beautiful as I had remembered her, with long brown hair and a heart-shaped face, singing hymns with her rich contralto voice—but she would disappear from my life without warning or without a reason that I could understand. She always fell through my fingers like water. In later years, I had dreams in which she looked straight through me as if I didn't exist.

Later, when I had grown up, I asked my father about these years, and he said, "Your mother was jealous that I had custody of you, so she'd steal you away to get back at me."

"But why didn't *you* take me?"

"Honey, it didn't occur to me that I could take you. I had to work." He wiped his eyes as he continued, "I was immature and really didn't know what to do. I connected you with your mother and the trauma I went through with her. My heart closed to both of you for a while. When I saw that your mother couldn't take care of you, I got custody and made other arrangements. I always paid for the foster homes and your boarding school, and I didn't abandon you. But all that has changed. I'm so proud of you, and of the way you turned out."

"But when you're a child," I said, "you don't understand or care that someone is paying the bills. You weren't there! That was all I knew. I adored you. I longed day and night for you. In my emotions, you abandoned me."

I carried no conscious anger toward either my mother or my father, but my repressed anger turned inward. It took many years to unwind the pain and find a way to love and accept myself.

I remember sitting in the guest room of the state mental hospital with my father, waiting for my mother to come. For two years the doctors forbade me to see her because she had slipped into a catatonic state, but new drugs had pulled her out. The room had that unpleasant hospital odor. There were no pictures on the walls, and the furniture was made of gray plastic. Through a little window in the door, I saw my mother walking down the hall. A warden opened the door and she came into the waiting room, quietly saying hello to my father. She looked nothing like I had remembered her, with her beautiful face and graceful body. She had grown heavy, with a puffy red look and a scar on her right cheek. Her teeth were gone, her eyes glazed. She moved stiffly, not looking to the right or left. We walked to the lawn outside and sat on a bench.

My mother turned to me, and for the first time that I can remember, she looked into my eyes. She said, "Please forgive me for what I have done to you." She never looked directly at me again.

CHAPTER THREE

World Wheel-Spoke Two

Seneca Cattaraugus Reservation, New York, USA
1988

Unity (detail), Seneca Cattaraugus Reservation, New York

I STOMPED OUT INTO THE forest on the Seneca Cattaraugus Reservation in upstate New York where I had been living for the past month in a trailer beside Yehwehnode's ancestral home, preparing for the second World Wheel event. When I arrived on the reservation, I thought it would be easier. "I hate being restricted to houses, cooking, and the role of 'woman,'" I fumed as I burst into the cool darkness of the forest. "I want the freedom the Seneca men have here." That morning when I went to sharpen my chisels, I found a new sign on the tool shed, "Off limits." The women seemed secondary here, supporting the men as they did their "important work" as Yehwehnode, the Seneca elder I had known for a decade, called it. When I asked if the men ever cooked or did a dish, her reply was, "We can't build the office building."

I simmered down as I walked on the trail through a grove of oaks with ferns and white and purple trillium hiding the ground on that June day. The path led to the blue dome tent that I had put up despite Yehwehnode's concern for my safety. As I neared the stream running by the tent, I increased my pace, anticipating its clear running water to cool my hands, my face, my spirit. I leaned against the moist slope and scanned the weavings I was creating for the performance. Memories flooded in, of myself as a teenage nun living in the Vedanta Society convent. I wanted to be a man so I wouldn't need permission to do the things I really loved. Now, I thought, I just give *myself* permission and never wait for it to come from outside. I take the freedom along with all the risks rather than live half a life, timid and frightened.

I took some California white sage from my backpack and lit the dry leaves. With a vulture feather I fanned the smoke over my body, around and inside my blue dome. Then it felt like home. The light faded quickly and I zipped myself in the tent just as darkness swallowed me and the forest. I stretched out on the mat, pulled the sleeping bag around me in contentment as I mused, "Only now with this attitude of freedom am I happy to be a woman. I feel blessed to have been born with the innate intuitive wisdom of woman. Perhaps the woman's part to play at this time in history is the deciding factor in restoring our society to harmony in a true spirit of partnership with man." I fell asleep dreaming of flying horses as I often had in my childhood.

In the middle of the night, I woke to a loud voice, *Why are you here?* My answer came, "Because I love you and want to find a way of sharing without taking away from you." I believed the voice was the voice of the woods.

In the morning I woke up happy, full of joy and thankfulness for each moment I could be in the forest. During the day, I continued to gather the giant forest vines, twisting them into medicine wheel weavings that I hung between the trees for the upcoming performance.

I stood for a moment in the light that filtered through the trees. I remembered when I first came to this spot. I knew immediately that it was the perfect place for the second World Wheel event. I can always feel it in my body. My breath deepens. My mind becomes very still and clear.

At noon I walked back to the house to fix lunch for Yehwehnode and her extended family. Her home was built by her grandfather's father-in-law in 1858 when he was forced by the government to move from the Buffalo Creek Reservation and live on this new reservation. Expansive green lawns surrounded the two-story wooden cottage painted white, shaded by enormous oaks and weeping willows.

After lunch I fixed tea, and Yehwehnode and I went to the living room and made ourselves comfortable on her couch. Yehwehnode's long gray hair was braided and pinned in a bun at the back of her head, her eyes sparkling above her firm jaw. In her late seventies, she was still a beautiful woman. I had first met Yehwehnode through a Chumesh Medicine Man, Kote, who said, "You must call Yehwehnode, she is also a Stone Woman." When I called her, she said, "I had a dream of the canyon you are working in. I want to come to California and see you, see the canyon." She did come and stayed with me and we spent time where I was carving in the canyon.

Yehwehnode was a dedicated teacher. She had incited bitter opposition from many on the reservation for offering her medicine wheel teachings to all she judged sincere in their search for truth, regardless of race or nation. As a result, when outsiders came to the reservation for her teachings, her opponents dubbed them "boat people"—a reference to the Mayflower landing and invasion by the Europeans.

Four years earlier, I had formed a circle of twelve women and another circle of twelve men based on Yehwehnode's teachings, which she called the "Wheels of Truth." She came out to my Boney Mountain retreat for their initiation into the World Clan Lodge. The Senecas are born into a clan through their mother, Yehwehnode told me. Extended family members are said to hold the characteristics of the totem animal of that clan. The wolf is the teacher and the pathfinder. Since we non-natives were not born into the clan, our initiation was into a sub-group inspired by Yehwehnode, who, acting as a bridge between cultures, lived the brave spirit of her name which means Whose Voice Rides the Winds.

Our women's circle met once a month, but I was uncomfortable with the group which I had started at

Seneca lodge at Yehwehnode's home

Yehwehnode's prompting because I felt that my work could not be bound to any one culture. Yehwehnode had initiated me into the Wolf Clan Lodge and wanted me to be a teacher of the Seneca wisdom, even giving me a certificate that allowed me to teach. She had honored me by the invitation to bring the World Wheel to her home, but I needed to share my mind and let Yehwehnode know what was really going on.

We sat sipping our tea and I decided this was the moment to tell Yehwehnode that teaching in the Seneca tradition was not my way. I fumbled with my cup, then put my hand in hers. "One evening in the mid-seventies, my perception changed. The borders between me and the environment seemed to dissolve. I saw a lattice of light radiating from all objects and myself, connecting all life. My life changed at that moment. I feel my work since that time reflects that borderless world. That is what this new project, the World Wheel, is about—a way to communicate the essence of who we are, that common denominator running through all cultures, all religions, and all life."

Yehwehnode finished her tea and I noticed a pendant hanging from her neck and resting on her full breasts—a colorful, beaded wolf-head. She looked into my eyes, "Your vision is true and you have a real calling to bring this understanding." She got up and motioned for me to follow her to her room. We sat on her bed and she took her grandfather's hat from the side table and handed it to me. "Take this to your trailer and dream with it. Grandfather Shongo will help you through your dreams." Then she added, "I remember when my grandmother found her 'helper plant.' Grandfather had asked her to sit and wait until one of the plants spoke to her. One of the violet flowers seemed to become brighter than all the rest, so he told her to eat it. It would become part of her, as her helper. Grandfather would say, 'If everyone could see the world as it really is, they would see all as moving light-sound.' Trees, grass, everything shimmers with sound, movement, and color. Light and sound link things into one. They travel together. We have to identify with that sound, with that One. His understanding was similar to your vision, although he experienced sound with the light. You have a connection with Grandfather, he will help you."

I gave Gram, as we called Yehwehnode, a hug, happy for her support for my new vision of direction, and walked past the medicine lodge cabin to my trailer carrying Grandfather Shongo's hat. The trailer was similar to the one I lived in on Boney Mountain. It had old wood paneling, no bathroom, and no water or electricity. What could make me feel more at home?

The following day I hiked deep into the forest with Jim, Yehwehnode's son, and his friend, Rick. Rick, who was one-half Native American, lived with his wife and children in a cabin on Yehwehnode's land. Walking back through the forest to the house, I said, "I wish I'd been born Native American. Your outlook on life is closer to my own."

"No, you don't," Jim said. "When I was a kid in school, the boys used to tie me to a tree and torture me for being 'Indian.' They used to burn my skin with matches and make my blood run by sticking their penknives in my flesh. They'd laugh at me when I had to answer questions in school. I didn't have any friends."

His story reminded me of what Yehwehnode had said about her childhood. "When I was seven, the government took me away from my family and put me in a 'white' boarding school along with all the other Native children. They gave us Christian names and would not allow us to speak our Native language. When I grew older and had my first job, the boss thought he could approach me sexually, and would slap my behind because I was an 'Indian' girl. I wouldn't put up with it."

Yehwehnode wanted me to carve a stone and create a site close to her house. I would go each morning and sit by the boulder that had been moved to the front entrance to the lodge, enjoying its power. But I always received a feeling of "no" from the stone when I proposed the question of carving it. The stone was complete as it was. But Yehwehnode insisted and I gave in and started the work.

The chipping away on the stone was very slow. There was a natural spiral on the top of the granite, which I developed with my hammer and chisel. On the four sides of the stone I carved faces for the four directions representing the four root races. One face looked American Indian, one Chinese, one African, and one European. These faces were already in the stone and had been peering out at me. The name of the piece emerged as I worked: *Unity.* The granite had crystal areas in it and was the hardest stone I had ever worked. It ate away at my tools, and the crystal sections resisted being carved at all. I sharpened my carbide-tipped chisels twice a day. My body felt strained with the hardness of the stone and the joints in my fingers, wrists, and elbows ached. I felt the stone saying as I worked, "I told you so. I told you so. I told you so." At the end of the day I would come in for dinner blanched and exhausted. But Yehwehnode loved the sound of the hammer and chisel. She wanted to record it. She said there was a message coming through the taptaptap—tap—taptaptap—tap; a code from beings in another dimension.

During my time at the reservation, life continued as usual. The annual five-day Women's Council was held, and I helped prepare the house and the lodge. My favorite time was the dancing and singing at night—150 women dancing in concentric circles on the earthen floor of the lodge.

During the Council, I entered a circle of pine trees just as Yehwehnode walked by. "I love this circle of trees," I said.

"They're sacred trees. You have a gift for spotting natural medicine wheels. The grass grows taller in a circle and sometimes in another direction. The circle is the shape of harmony. On this land many of these natural medicine wheels have been developed further by placing stones in the circle of energy or by planting trees, as in this circle."

That evening we had a ceremony in the pine tree circle for Judith, one of our extended family. Earlier, she had lived for a year in Yehwehnode's home. She had just been released from the hospital. She had an abortion with complications and wanted to stay with us for a week. We gathered inside the circle surrounding Judith and Yehwehnode spoke. "In our tradition, we feel that the child in the mother's womb has part responsibility for the parent's decision to abort. The child-spirit was drawn to the mother and father, but then sees that the circumstances of the birth would not be good for any of them and puts this suggestion in the consciousness of the parents." Yehwehnode turned a loving look on Judith and then continued, "The ways of the Great Mystery are beyond our social conventions."

But the next evening, when I was ready to go to my tent in the forest, Yehwehnode worried. "I don't feel comfortable with you being out in the forest alone. It's a dangerous place."

When I insisted that I needed to absorb the feeling of the forest for the project, she said, "Well, take someone with you." Revital Arieli, a young woman from Israel who had been living with Yehwehnode for a month, volunteered. We gathered her things, then trekked out to the site singing Israeli songs just as the light dropped behind the trees.

As the days passed, I understood Yehwehnode's frustration. Most of the Seneca people on the reservation had no interest in her teachings—many were more interested in television and movies and other trappings of the outside culture. Perhaps that motivated her generosity to me and others like me who became a part of her family. Also, many of the Seneca elders on the reservation criticized her for giving their secrets to us "boat people." This criticism had grown through the years and caused Yehwehnode great stress and hardship. That may have been why her teachings changed and became less centered on the Seneca, and more centered on truths that were channeled to her through her Grandfather and Red Jacket, a Seneca historic figure.

"We're just now ending the 'fourth world,' the period of division and fear," Yehwehnode told me. We sat together in the kitchen with a cup of tea. "It's my mission to preserve the teachings and pass them on to a few people who can carry this wisdom into the 'fifth world,' the era of peace and unity that has just begun."

After a long talk, Yehwehnode went sleepily to her room for the night. I returned to the trailer, pulled my journal from under the bed, and sat for a while, filled with gratitude for my time with Gram. I began to write:

May 22, 1988:

> *My ideas for the performance are coming slowly, growing out of my days here, out of carving on the boulder, cooking together, doing dishes, and dreaming with Grandfather Shongo's hat by my bed.*
>
> *Sometimes I get a wave of fright that I may not have anything completed for July 9th, the date we set for the performance ceremony. The Seneca actress, who was to take the role of young Yehwehnode talking about her grandfather and telling his stories, died last month.*
>
> *After the initial panic, I always stand back with awe and observe how art comes together, especially ritual performance, out of the elements that are actually here this moment and not out of what my head has planned. It is a continual practice of surrender and focus. The surrender allows the void of all possibilities to be present, and the focus draws into that void the appropriate elements.*

That night when I put my pen down, I finished reading the book that Yehwehnode had put in my hand when

Unity, sculpture in granite and crystal with four directional faces

I first arrived, *The White Roots of Peace*, which tells about the Peacemaker. According to Native lore, the Peacemaker was born five hundred years before Christ on the north shore of Lake Ontario. When he grew into manhood, he had a burning passion to bring peace to his world—now the eastern United States—at a time of war and butchery similar to the present time. The Peacemaker built a canoe of stone in which he crossed the lake to begin his mission. There, in the forest on the other side of the lake, he met Hiawatha, who had become a wanderer after losing his wife and children. The Peacemaker convinced him to change his life and help bring the New Mind into the world. Hiawatha became his spokesman because the Peacemaker had a speech impediment.

They left together to find the house of a woman who lived close by the path that the warriors took. When the Peacemaker and Hiawatha arrived, the woman greeted them and placed food before them. After they had eaten, she asked the Peacemaker to speak his message. "I carry the Mind of the Great Mystery," he replied, "and my message will bring an end to the wars between East and West. The Word says that all people shall love one another and live together in peace."

"Your message is good. I embrace it," said the woman, "but words are nothing until they are given form and set to work in the world. What form shall this message take when it comes to dwell among the People?"

The Peacemaker thought for a while, and then he said, "It will take the form of the longhouse in which there are many fires, one for each family, yet all live as one household under one chief mother. Reason shall replace conflict, and there shall be one heart, one mind, and one earth law. You were the first to accept the good news of peace. Henceforth you shall be called Jigonhsasee, meaning 'New Face,' because your countenance conveys the New Mind, and you shall be known as Mother of All Nations."[5]

Peacemaker then went to the Mohawks, Oneidas, Senecas, and Cayugas, and finally the Onondagas.

In each encounter, he met great trials and overcame each one, bringing the five nations together in peace to form a confederacy. This confederacy, the Haudenosaunee (called Iroquois, by the French), lived for hundreds of years in peace—until the white settlers arrived from Europe. Few people are aware of the fact that the Iroquois Confederacy influenced the structure and content of the Constitution of the United States.[6]

When I finished the story, I wept. I felt myself deeply connected with the Peacemaker because the World Wheel carries the same message in a different form. I knew this was the story for the performance and was a confirmation of my own life's work.

For the next few weeks I wrote, culling the essence of the Peacemaker story into a working script for the World Wheel performance ceremony. In my mind, I saw Yehwehnode in the forest, sitting at the base of a guardian tree, weaving a basket and telling the story as the characters silently interacted with each other in the forest depicting the action.

One evening as I sat with Yehwehnode, I said, "I've been living the Peacemaker story day and night. I think my own calling to create the World Wheel, especially in this time of upheaval, is the same mission as the Peacemaker's. The World Wheel is a continuation of what he started."

Yehwehnode lit up, looked in my eyes, and said, "You are Jigonhsasee, who was called the Mother of All Nations."

I nodded and continued, "When the Peacemaker came to Jigonhsasee, she said, 'Your words have no power. You need a form.' She must have been a sculptor like me. I've heard myself say those very words to people who come to me with their personal vision and frustration with their own impotence. 'You need a form that will contain the energy of your vision and communicate it to other people. The form is the conduit between spirit and manifestation,' I tell them."

Yehwehnode said, "I'll help make your ceremonial dress, your Jigonhsasee dress. The story of the Peacemaker needs to be told at this time."

Forest Wheels hanging, Seneca Cattaraugus Reservation, New York

The next morning, I went to Yehwehnode's room and said that I needed to go to the forest alone. I spent the day in its silence working on the vine *Forest Wheels*.

At twilight, I walked through the forest and let its damp, pungent aroma saturate my body. I threw kisses into the running stream, and put a wild strawberry on a large green leaf in front of my dome tent with a wish that an animal would come and take my gift. I sang to the forest, "I love you."

I felt I wanted to create a song for each of the twelve sites of the World Wheel. My voice on the reservation had been tight and closed, but the next morning I stood between two trees, put my arms around them, and asked the hemlock to help me sing. My voice opened up and a clear, melodious, effortless tone poured from me. I felt the trees singing through me.

The rains came in July and forced me to stop work. When the sun came out again, it was too strong for me to sculpt during mid-day, so I used the late morning and early afternoon hours to work on the performance. The cool of the morning drew me out early, and I emerged again in the evenings to sculpt. The work became exhausting. Or maybe it was the heat or the endless cooking and day care and other work that I contributed to help the pressing needs of Yehwehnode's household. Three of us were doing all the cooking and cleaning for about twenty people.

The day I completed the sculpture, I gave money for four trees to be planted in the four directions circling the stone. The flowers of the trees were to be the colors of the directions: red, black, white, and yellow. When they grew tall they would provide shade for people who came to sit and contemplate the stone. Yehwehnode already had ideas for a continuing ceremony after the performance was over. And, in the forest of hemlock, the *Forest Wheels* were completed and hung between trees. Birds were already making their homes in the twisted vines.

Three days later, Morna Watson arrived from London, and I picked her up at the Buffalo airport. Morna and I had been corresponding for the previous six months, but this was the first time we had met. We were proof of the evolution of thought, I felt, because she had formed a theater group in London called "Theater of the Heart" at the same time that I was starting "Theater of the Earth" in California. She called her project in London the World Tree, and her stage manager, who happened to be in California, had seen the advertisement for the first performance of the World Wheel in Malibu and had attended. She called Morna immediately to tell her about my work and relate the similarity of concept. We exchanged letters, and when I understood that she wanted to be involved in the World Wheel, I invited her to come to the reservation and direct the performance.

The first two days after Morna's arrival were tense. Her British reserve seemed out of place on the reservation among these down-to-earth people. I saw a wall come up almost immediately between Morna and Yehwehnode. Gram's face would become fierce and she would cross her arms and knot her fists. All of a sudden, I was not family but "white." I overheard Gram's comment to Morna, "There is too much *white* energy." My heart sank. I realized there was no need for a director when I knew that the message of our Theater of the Earth was simple: the deep and transformative relationship with the earth and others.

My body became so heavy at times that I could not move, and I just sat in my own heaviness and sadness, staring blankly. I felt trapped. I wanted to support Morna, as my guest, but I felt the pain and awkwardness her manner caused my family on the reservation. All I could do was wait.

Yehwehnode's teachings finally penetrated Morna's reserve and with only two days left before the ceremony, Yehwehnode asked Morna if she wanted to be initiated into the Wolf Clan Teaching Lodge. With the preparation for the ceremony and the chance for Morna to step into another place in herself, the atmosphere eased. After the ceremony we were again one family—almost.

I had spent many delightful evenings working on the performance with Jim and his friend, Rick, as they gave their responses to my three questions: *What is our essence? What is our sickness? What is the solution?* But now I sensed that they distrusted Morna and resented her "white energy" on the reservation. They did not want to take direction from a woman and seemed to be looking for an excuse to drop out of the ceremony—which is exactly what they did.

During this time, as I dreamed with Grandfather Songo's hat, a holy man came to me. He stood in front of me in his long tunic, a compassionate expression on his bearded face, and he said, "I wish you peace and wisdom."

It took me aback that he wished me something I thought I had already. I realized that through the stress of developing the World Wheel, I had lost the peace and bliss that I had lived in continually on Boney Mountain.

Late one night, Jim broke into my trailer, very drunk. His whiskey breath permeated the trailer and he flopped down on my bed and tore at my clothes until my blouse was ripped and my breasts exposed. I tried to push him away, but the weight of his body pinned me down. Finally, I inched away. I could not get him to stand up, and finally he totally collapsed on my bed in a drunken stupor. I was determined he would not spend the night there. With all my strength I rolled him onto the floor. Dripping with sweat, I tugged and pushed until at last I got him to the front door and let him tumble down to the ground. He lay there for a long time until the coolness of the night sobered him up and he dragged himself to his cabin. The next morning Jim apologized. I was fond of him as a friend and readily accepted.

Some time later, Jim spotted a fire in the performance area. Rick and Jim immediately jumped into the truck and rushed out to the forest where dense growth forced them to walk the last stretch to the site. Finally, they saw red flames which transformed into billowing black smoke as they doused the fire with water. Yehwehnode's concern about using the forest as the site for performance had become a reality. She interpreted the fire as a warning from neighbors against her interaction with the "boat people." Because of the damage only three days before the performance, we had to develop a new forest site. We brought the vine hangings, a symbolic container of water, and red earth from the original site to the new location.

When I had first arrived on the reservation, I couldn't understand why Gram worried about my working and sleeping in the forest. I kept insisting on sleeping there, believing that she restricted me in a way she wouldn't restrict a man, but the fire showed me that Yehwehnode had been correct. Now I suspected that voice in the forest asking, "Why are you here?" was not the spirit of the forest speaking, but a neighbor.

As the sun came up on the day of the event, we walked to the site. To our dismay, we found that during the night someone had bulldozed a large pile of debris, blocking the entrance to the new site. Two friends, however, worked hard to turn this ugly twisted mess of rubbish into something beautiful. Working with

Vijali in her lace leaf veil and ceremonial dress for *The Peacemaker* performance

Yehwehnode (Twylah Nitsch) telling the Seneca creation story

shovels and rakes, they created a powerful spiral earthwork. The performance started as planned.

Many Senecas from the reservation came in their colorful native clothes and participated. Valerie Rainbow Weaver opened the ceremony. She was a young Mohawk woman in her mid-twenties who had lived with Yehwehnode off and on for ten years. She lit the white sage I had brought from California and left it to burn in an abalone shell. Then she smudged the circle of people who had gathered around her, using her eagle feather to sweep the smoke onto each person. She turned to honor the four cardinal directions, raising the shell with its billowing smoke to the North, the South, the East, and the West.

A change came over Rainbow Weaver's face as the spirit stirred within her. She danced as if moved by some other force, and her heavy form appeared as light as a feather. In the fringed white ceremonial clothes that accentuated her wind-like quality, she became the spirit of the eagle.

Then Yehwehnode walked to the Turtle Mound, a raised part of the ground shaped like a turtle with green lawn growing over it. Dressed in her colorful Seneca clothes, white buckskin with ties and beadwork, she sat down with an eagle feather in her hand. We all gathered around her, some fifty of us. Because Morna had decided that the Peacemaker story was not to be told in words, only gestures, I arranged for Yehwehnote to speak in resonance with my first question, *What is our essence?*

"One afternoon, as I sat down at my grandfather Moses Shongo's feet, just like you children here, he said: 'Long, long ago, before there was time and place or even human beings like you, there was Swenio, the Great Mystery in endless space. Within this space of mystery, a cloud-like substance grew and became known as the Field of Plenty. This is where life began.'" When Yehwehnode finished her grandfather's story of creation she sat looking at the people gathered before her.

Everyone rose, and a Native man, dressed in his traditional Seneca clothes, started drumming and singing. He was one of the people from the reservation who had not spoken to Yehwehnode for many years because of the animosity that had arisen over her sharing the Seneca teachings with non-Natives. We all formed a line behind him, singing and drumming with our own drums or rattles. We followed him into the forest where we had hung the *Forest Wheels* for the second time. As I listened joyfully to his strong, melodious voice and watched his Seneca headdress bob up and down, I felt the spirit of the people. Single file, we walked the path to the forest, past the spiral earth sculpture created out of anonymous debris, and, one by one, we entered the woods to join the forest spirits.

The performance ritual seemed to take on a life of its own, beyond anyone's direction during its creation. It had brought up fears and contention, but in the end it drew many people from the reservation together into one family again. I cannot say that all problems and tensions dissolved on the reservation, but the people who came were drawn into the atmosphere of goodwill and seemed to let go of past grudges.

As everyone settled down beneath the trees in the clearing, I moved very slowly in front of one of the *Forest Wheels.* Earlier I had gathered large leaves eaten by insects to reveal their delicate amber skeletons, and I had woven the leaves together to form a lace mantle that now hung over my face above my golden deerskin ceremonial dress. My personal part of the performance was to show my relationship with the forest. I danced—as the spring that flowed out of the hill by my tent—as the red disintegrating root earth at the base of the tree—as the fire that consumed the first site—as the wind that blew through the trees making them sing. These four elements inspired my solo part which was the introduction to the forest ritual performance. My own will dissolved, and my body moved in response to some other force, just as it had at the ceremony in Malibu.

I became the slowness of earth. I lifted the red sod and let it fall through my fingers onto my clothes and skin, returning me to earth. The wind started blowing, and my leaf veil rose and fell with the movement of my earth body. I became Water, and from a container hidden in the ground, I lifted water in my hands and let the droplets fall, returning them to their source in staccato rhythms accompanied by Jonathan Glasier on his rain stick. Jonathan, now playing the zylophone, slowly changed the sound into that of flames as I lit the dry wood before me. I moved as flames, becoming the essence of Fire, the essence of all life.

As the music died down and became silent, a Native boy emerged from the forest dressed in traditional buckskins. He had only arrived on the reservation that morning, and he had offered to step into Jim's abandoned role of Peacemaker. He met Hiawatha, now played by one of his friends in Rick's place. They mirrored each other as they looked through one of my *Forest Wheel* hangings.

Seneca drummer leading us into *The Peacemaker* ceremony

Morna, believing that no story needed to be told in words, only in movement, stood on the sidelines gesturing with her hand and a nod of head, cueing each person to come into the center opening of the forest. I was not sure if the audience understood what was going on. I knew this was not the right choice. I understood the people on the reservation and their love of storytelling. Many teachings are handed down through the oral tradition. I was left questioning the idea of collaboration. How much control is it wise to give up? I had wanted Yehwehnode to tell the Peacemaker story in her own words as she sat under a tree relating to the audience. But this did not happen.

Silently Yehwehnode walked forth as Jigonhsasee, and Native people representing the Five Nations emerged from the forest. Peacemaker and Hiawatha met each person's eyes and in turn drew us all into a circle, our hands joined.

Now, a theater group from the area interrupted our circle of peace, depicting the arrival of Europeans. This was in response to my second question, *What is our sickness*? In comic form, a man with sunglasses stumbled into our circle carrying a large black sound box with blaring rock and roll. He beckoned to his friends to come, and they broke our circle, setting up little white fences and laying down fake green lawn in their individual sections. They argued over the borders of their sections and eventually fought with each other.

In response to my third question, *What is the solution?,* a gloved hand emerged from behind a tree and drew our attention. Then the ancient Seneca legend depicting the "First Messenger of the Great Mystery" began. The Four Aged People, two men and two women, sat in a circle around a fire as they recited a poem written by Yehwehnode. Then these four elders joined hands with all the people present and led us, singing, out of the forest to the sculpture *Unity* by the side of the lodge. Still holding hands, we made a big spiral that became tighter and more compact. Then

Gathering in forest for *The Peacemaker* performance

we flowed in the opposite direction and opened the spiral out. The elders led us into the lodge where we all sat down in a large circle.

A Lakota man from South Dakota had heard about the World Wheel ceremony and had arrived that morning. Inside the lodge, he led us in a traditional pipe ceremony. As a "pipe holder," he had been entrusted with the pipe on the understanding that someday he would share it with non-Native people. For him, the World Wheel ceremony was that moment. He honored the earth directions, and ceremonially assembled and lit the pipe. Then he passed it around the circle for all to partake in prayer and complete the unity of our day.

I learned much during my time on the reservation that would serve me on my upcoming journey. I understood now that I must always listen to my inner voice and act on that knowing even when it threw me into uncomfortable confrontations and the possible loss of friendships. As Morna and I got to know each other, we realized we shared creative ideas and became close friends. Three women—Yehwenhode, myself and Morna—each with our own resistance and fears, were gradually drawn together by the land and its history. Perhaps in our small way we were being guided to follow one of Yehwenhode's fundamental teachings: "The original people recognized the differences between themselves, and that they could all learn from each other. They realized that the wolf and bear and eagle could also teach them, and so they learned from the animals."

Even so, the experience left me with some pain. Because Morna had flown all the way from London, I felt I couldn't retract my offer for her to direct. I traded my power to a professional theater director at the cost of some precious relationships. And I had carved a stone that did not want to be carved by

The Peacemaker and Hiawatha with the *Forest Wheels*

denying my own inner knowing. I came to realize that I *can* reconsider if I see I have made a mistake.

In a larger sense, I also came to see that there are no real "mistakes." Real growth comes from the unexpected, which is inevitably stressful. I saw that the process of the World Wheel had a life of its own with its own creative solutions, provoking fears and contentions, but in the end being a conduit for healing.

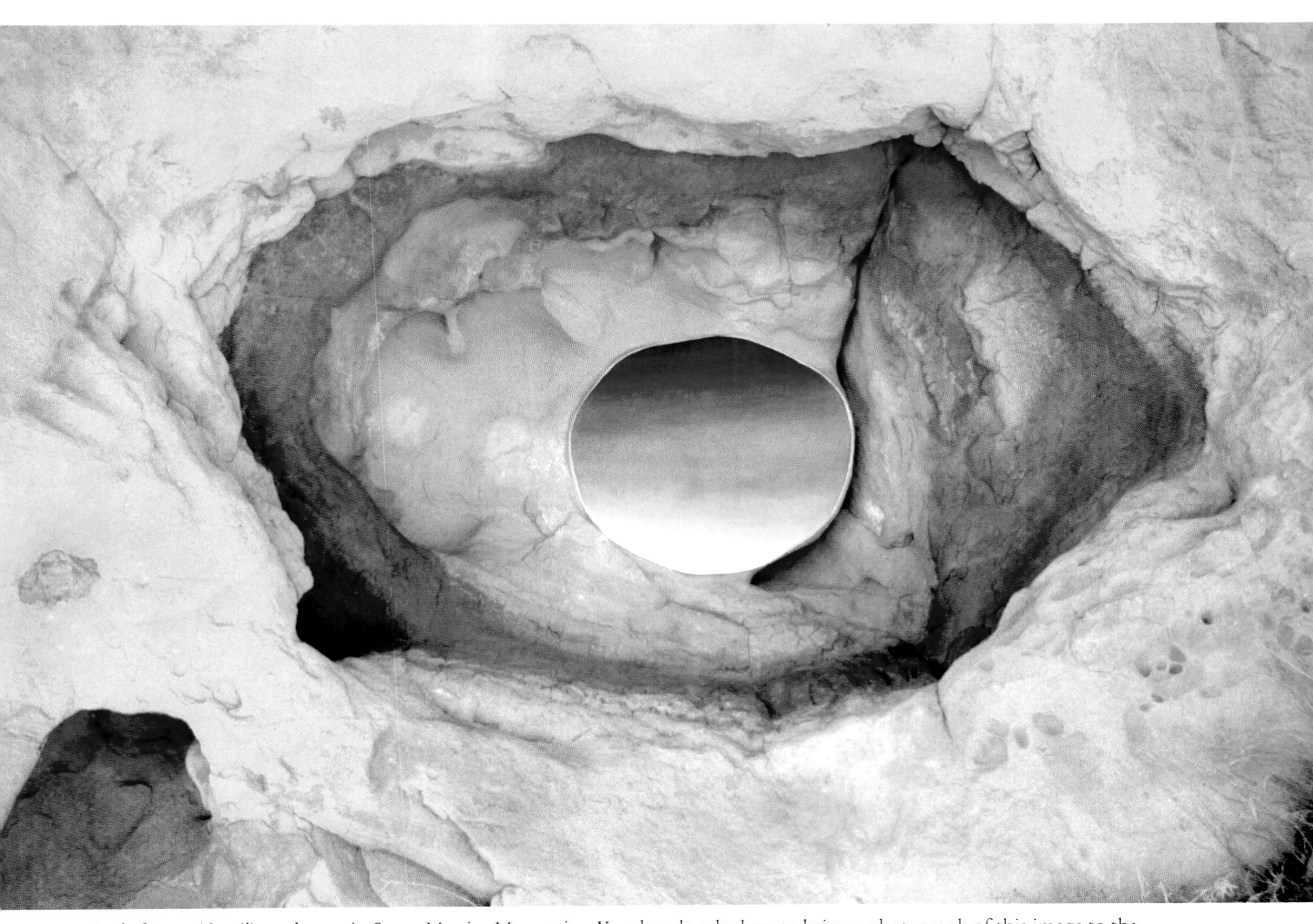

Seed of Space (detail), sculpture in Santa Monica Mountains. Yewehnode asked me to bring a photograph of this image to the reservation. It represented for her the essence of life as described by her grandfather, Shongo, a Seneca medicine man. "There is one thing that holds everything together. We call it The Great Mystery. Everyone is connected. The connection is the earth."

CHAPTER FOUR

The Vedanta Convent

Santa Barbara, California
1948–1963

One, Ramakrishna and Sarada Devi

When I was ten years old, my father placed me in a girls boarding school, the Temescal School for Girls in Pomona County. He came to visit me once a month. One day, he took me to the Vedanta Temple in Hollywood to visit his guru. As we pulled into the parking lot of the Hindu temple, a small version of the Taj Mahal, I mused at how my prayers had been answered: a new friend—a father—had entered my life. Since my mother and father's divorce when I was two years old, I had seen my father only once or twice a year.

My father and I entered the temple where incense and music surrounded us. He had been attending the Vedanta lectures for a year. He had searched the Christian path, but he felt more satisfied with Vedanta's answers to his many questions about life.

Swami Prabhavananda spoke at the pulpit. After his talk my father took me to a private room where Prabhavananda sat in a large cushioned chair. Light streamed in through the window and made his already golden skin glow. He grinned and I shyly smiled back. I told him I wanted to meditate, so he gave me my first mantra, *Jai Sri Ramakrishna*—"Hail to Reverend Ramakrishna." Later, one of the Vedanta Society nuns gave me a rosary to count the repetitions.

As soon as I got back to the boarding school, I made a shrine under a drooping avocado tree in the orchard behind the schoolhouse. I went there regularly to talk with God and say my mantra. My childhood attachment to Jesus gradually expanded to include Ramakrishna, the late nineteenth century Bengali saint that Vedanta practitioners followed. What touched me the most was that the force of Ramakrishna's love had changed everyone who met him.

Ramakrishna was born in a small village in Bengal. He spent most of his life in spiritual contemplation and teaching at Dakshineswar on the banks of the Ganges River outside Calcutta. He accepted all spiritual paths: Hinduism, Christianity, Islam, and others. As he practiced each tradition, he reached the same experience of union with the Godhead.[7] After Ramakrishna's death at the turn of the twentieth century, Vivekananda and several other Ramakrishna disciples carried the impact of his life and the essence of his teachings to the United States and England through a philosophy called Vedanta. Vedanta means "the end," the last portion of the Vedas, the ancient scriptures of Hinduism. The movement accepts all the religions of the world and recognizes the same divine inspiration in all the great prophets and teachers.[8]

As with my father, the Vedanta community gave satisfying answers to many of my deepest questions: *Who was I other than this abandoned child? Could I now go on and find a life that had meaning for me? Could the "heaven" of the Christians be a consciousness that we could obtain right now, in this life?*

I also visited the Vedanta convent in the hills of Santa Barbara, where nuns lived in semi-seclusion, and soon, at the age of ten, took my first retreat there. The convent grounds lay nestled in the chaparral and boulder-studded slopes of the Santa Ynez Mountains overlooking the Pacific Ocean. I loved the nuns, the shrine where we sat for meditation with burning candles and incense, the flowering oleanders that lined the path, and our time eating and working together. A family!

On Ramakrishna's birthday in February, three years later, Swami Prabhavananda initiated me in the temple at the main center in Hollywood and became my guru, my teacher. The ceremony was simple. Swami was sitting in meditation in the shrine when I came in carrying flowers and fruits. I bowed to the shrine and to Swami, and peeked at his face from under my bangs. We meditated for a while, and then he gave me a new mantra—different from my first one—by repeating it aloud in his resonant voice. He said to me, "Repeat the mantra three thousand times a day to start, using this rosary made of rudraksha seeds." He showed me how to use the rosary, going around it with his right hand, counting how many times he went around with his left. Then he handed it to me.

I returned to my girls boarding school, but spent summer vacation at the convent in Santa Barbara. The mantra turned in my heart and carried me through every moment of my day and night as I walked, worked, and fell asleep. One morning as I vacuumed the living room at the convent, I became aware that as Swami Prabhavananda sat in his favorite chair reading the newspaper, he watched me. He was on one of his bi-monthly visits to the convent from the Vedanta Society center in Hollywood. When I turned off the vacuum, he hummed a Bengali tune and repeated it in English: "The vision of the Divine Mother comes like a flash of lightning." Then he said, "Vijali—that is your name, a flash of lightning."

During my stay in the summer of 1952, Aldous Huxley and Christopher Isherwood came for retreats. Both were early followers of Vedanta in this country, and Aldous Huxley sometimes brought his wife, Maria. She was a fine, intelligent woman with an aura of dignity, and was always by his side to support and admire him. Once, as we ate dinner together around the oak dining room table, Maria adjusted her flowered cotton dress and leaned forward, "The fire burned everything, all of Aldous' manuscripts, all the personal details of our lives."

Aldous added with a resigned look in his eyes, "I have spent the last year rewriting, and rewriting, but new ideas and stories have come."

"He is almost blind," Maria told us as we straightened up the kitchen after our dinner.

On Aldous' next visit he came without Maria. The nuns assigned me the job of escorting him to the shrine for meditation, through the winding paths of the convent, to the main house with its kitchen, living room, and dining room, and to his guest room at the entrance of the property. He was tall with a full head of graying, bushy hair, and an inquisitive expression. As we walked the paths, he noticed minute details in spite of his poor eyesight. "That one cluster of oleander blossoms is drooping," and "Don't you think this lily is a brighter pink than the others?" About a sandstone boulder he remarked, "Now that looks like a turtle, wouldn't you say?" Or "Look at that frog sitting under the hibiscus by the side of the path." He noticed many more details than I ever did.

Later, when we waited on the porch of the main house for the supper bell to ring, he was transported by the shapes of the clouds that filled sky, and he named the cumulus overhead and the cirrus closer to the horizon. He always observed the world with wonder and interest. For him, nothing was insignificant.

Aldous told me at the dinner table one evening that he had used my name for one of the main characters in a new book he was writing, *Island.* When the book came out, the Swami forbade us to read it because of its explicit sexuality. I fumed silently and obeyed, until many years later. Sure enough, "Vijali" was one of the characters.

In 1953, at the age of fourteen, I announced my decision to become a Vedanta nun. I saw no other example around me of a life worth living. I imagined that a life of meditation would bring me the peace and understanding I longed for, and I wanted to devote the rest of my life to the pursuit of enlightenment.

My father believed I was too young and that I needed my education. Swami Prabhavananda said it was not the policy of the order to take in people so young. But I was determined, and I devised a way to

The Other Self

continue my education: I would ride my bike the four miles to the school bus stop every day and attend high school in Santa Barbara.

After a year of my constant imploring, my father agreed, and Swami Prabhavananda admitted me to the convent of the Vedanta Society in Santa Barbara. I was the youngest person ever to become a Vedanta nun in the Order. Now they have established a minimum age of eighteen, although they prefer women and men to come after their college education.

I became passionately involved with the *pujas,* or ceremonies, and with the lives of saints. My father, no longer bearing the responsibility of my financial support, followed the conviction of his own beliefs and joined the same order. The Vedanta monastery for men was situated in Trabuco Canyon in Orange County, but because of my father's executive capabilities, Swami Prabhavananda asked him to reside at the main center in Hollywood. I was again destined to see my father only once a year, now at the time of *Durga Puja*, our public celebration at the Santa Barbara convent.

The first four years were blissful. We meditated three times a day. In the evening, we had vespers and sang together and played musical instruments. I continued to pour my inner feelings into drawing and painting, as I had in childhood. I would retreat to my studio, a tiny room tacked onto the back of the garage, and there I might work on an oil painting of Swami, his face deep in meditation, or on a drawing of our shrine in the eucalyptus grove. Swami visited the convent twice a month, and we all sat together with him in the evening and read *The Gospel of Sri Ramakrishna* by Mehindranath Gupta,[9] discussing it afterward until bedtime.

When we were without guests, we enjoyed illicit gin and tonics while we watched the red and purple sunsets spread over the curved coast of Santa Barbara. Swami, on the other hand, loved his port before bed—so much so that on a trip to India the two nuns who accompanied him had to go through wild schemes to get his port to him without detection.

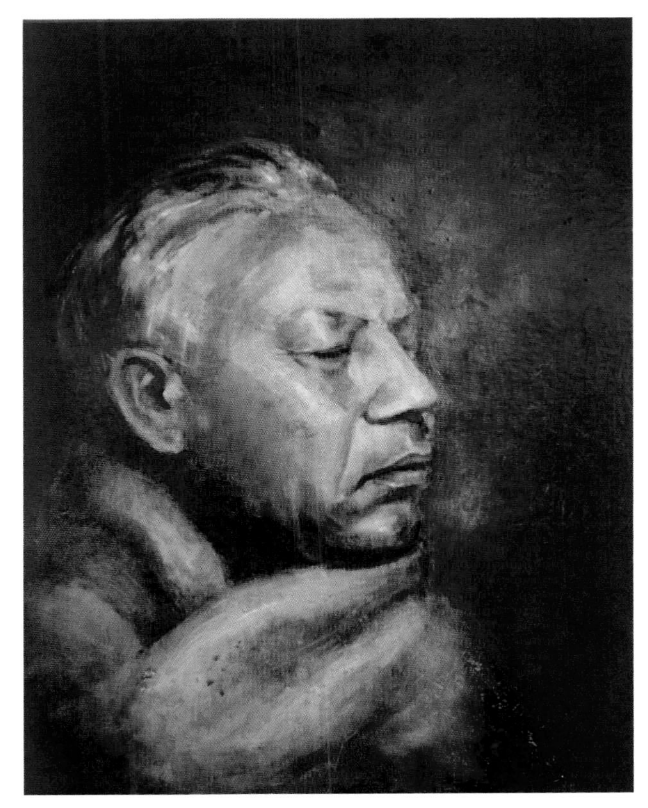

Swami Prabhavananda

On one visit to the convent, Swami sat with his feet tucked under him in his big leather chair in the living room, and said to us, "You have no friend but the Lord. That is a nun's and monk's life. Unless you have the Lord and Mother, life is empty. You have them! They are your very own. You belong to them."

"But why can't we see Him?" asked Sarada, one of the nuns. "If He just gave us even a little vision, wouldn't that help?"

"Never mind. In good time He'll reveal himself to you. Surrender yourselves to the Lord. Feel that He is there. This is my attitude. I don't care for visions and all that. Just let me have love, devotion, and knowledge. Maharaj, my guru, told me that God's love is so great He doesn't let you know how much He loves you."

Swami gestured toward me. "Vijali has many special blessings, but she doesn't realize their extent or she would go crazy, they are so great. She cannot hold the knowledge, so Mother gives her a little ignorance. Right now your body wouldn't hold the vision of God, but in a few years, with practice, it will. Keep constant remembrance of the Lord by making *japa*, by repeating the name of God. That is the best way."

In my fifth year, at the age of nineteen, I took my Brahmacharya vows to live a celibate monastic life. For a whole year after taking my vows, I followed a special practice called *purascharana*. Starting each month on the dark of the moon, I recited my mantra a thousand times, counting on my rosary. Each night I increased the recitations incrementally until, by the full moon, I repeated my mantra fifteen thousand times a day. Doing so many repetitions caused profound joy to rise in my being, which permeated every moment of the day and night. I felt I never wanted to stop *purascharana,* and I believed that complete renunciation of the distractions of the world, including my sexual feelings, was the only way I could find and live in truth. Yet the world leaked in.

Painting, sculpture, and music became more and more a focus for my spiritual and emotional life. I would retreat to my room behind the garage while the nuns were napping in the afternoon and study the voluptuous Indian sculpture which grew close to my heart, alongside the simplicity and majesty of Egyptian sculpture. I modeled the Indian Goddess Kali from clay for our yearly *puja* and painted her black. Kali, with her four arms, grapefruit-shaped breasts, swaying hips, and penetrating black eyes, typically dances on the breast of the inert white Shiva, her husband. He symbolizes the transcendent aspect of God, *purusha*, as Kali symbolizes the dynamic aspect, *prakriti*, or the primal energy taking form. Wearing a girdle of severed arms and a necklace of skulls, Kali holds the bleeding head of a demon in her lower left hand, a sword in the upper left. She

Kali

makes the sign of fearlessness with the upper right hand, and offers boons with the lower right—destroying ignorance, preserving world order, and blessing and liberating those who yearn for God-realization. I longed for her wildness, and threw myself into her creation.

That Christmas, I found an old wooden door. I carved a deep border into the wood and painted an earthy Mary and Jesus of warm bright colors. But this Mediterranean carpenter's wife, with skin tanned from work in the sun, was not to one nun's liking. I saw that she considered lighter skins superior to dark.

Appearances were apparently more important that creative risks. It seemed to me that the removal of dust from our French provincial furniture was more important to the nuns than the expansion of consciousness. The head nun glared at me and withdrew her warmth whenever I did anything she considered improper—the stove's inner ledges were not immaculate, or my hair was not up in a tight bun at all times. "Your long hair showing is sensual," she said, and indicated that my full hips and breasts were enough to contend with.

I sneaked out of my room on full moon nights while the nuns slept and danced in the oleander grove with my mind on Krishna, the legendary God-boy of Brindavan, who steals the hearts of the milkmaids. I put on my white cotton sari without blouse or underwear. In the warm summer evenings, I would dance and sing, sometimes sensually, sometimes madly. The breeze played through my hair. In the secret of the night, I let it down. The warm wind and my own long hair kissed and caressed my skin. The night-blooming jasmine permeated my senses. I sang out, "I want to make love! I want to make love with Krishna!"

As time went on, my curiosity and growing passion fostered a deep depression, until sometimes I felt myself about to explode. I touched myself, thinking of God, and I developed my own sexual tantric practices, never having read the literature that is now freely available. I learned to direct my sexual energy in meditation to bring it up my spine into my third eye and crown chakra. But then I wondered what a man would look like.

The sisters, twice my age, seemed not to have sexual feelings at all—at least they didn't admit to them. Once in a while one would say, "I am glad I don't have to do *that* every night," and I wondered if I was oversexed, maybe even a nymphomaniac. Lying on my bed one night in my late teens, my desire turned into anger and I kicked a hole in the wall.

I had a paralyzing fear of being shamed, of the nuns saying that I was a "bad" person, something that took me back to my childhood. At age seven, I had gone to the corner candy store by myself for the first time. The owner had said, "Come into the back room and I will give you your candy." I went, and he said, "Sit on my lap and I will give you your candy." When I did as he told me, he slipped off my panties and stuck his finger in me.

I knew Grandma always wanted me to keep my legs down and my panties on, so why did this man ask me to hold my legs apart while he looked at what Grandma said was dirty? He told me not to tell anyone, but one day I told my grandmother I had something to tell her, and that she must not tell *anyone*. She promised. Within a few days, my father flew out from Los Angeles, and sometime later we appeared in court. I was so small my father put me up on a chair. When the prosecutor asked me to describe what had happened, my thoughts closed and I turned red and perspired like a grown-up. The man from the candy store sat in the first row. Finally, someone repeated the story, and I only had to say, "Yes."

At the convent, I finally decided that it would be better to take a risk and talk to the nuns about my anxieties rather than to continue to hold everything in. One evening when Padma and Sarada sat in Prabha's room having a drink, I entered and sat on the bed.

I said, "I need to talk about the feelings I carry around inside of me. I think I need a sexual experience to know what it is I must renounce."

Padma reacted immediately and viciously. "You're ungrateful for this opportunity for a spiritual life. You're a slut!"

I jumped off the bed, pulled up my skirt, spread my legs, and said, "See, I'm a slut! I'm a slut!" I threw my shoes—the object in India that represents the lowest, most unclean part of the person—at Prabha's meticulously decorated shrine. They shattered the glass on the photographs of Ramakrishna and his wife, Sarada Devi, and pieces spewed over the carpet. I ran out of Prabha's room, out of the cottage, through the convent grounds, and out onto the road leading into town. I raced down the country road in total darkness, chanting, "I will not go back! I will not go back!"

Mary and Jesus

After a long time, I heard a car approaching. As it neared, I recognized it as our convent car. Sarada slowed by my side and asked to talk with me. She said, "We'll find a counselor for you to talk with, so you can understand yourself better."

Convinced that they would help me, I got into the car and returned to the convent. But as the weeks passed, they avoided the subject, skirted around it, until it became all but nonexistent.

At this time two other young girls entered the monastic life, and Swami had the three of us write essays on Vivekananda's talks on the four yogas:

Mary and Jesus (detail)

Bhakti-Yoga, union with God through love; Karma-Yoga, union with God through selfless work; Jnana-Yoga, union through the intellect; and Raja-Yoga, union through meditation. Swami corrected our essays, marked them with a red pen, underlined passages, and made comments in the margins. He asked me to come to his room to pick up my notebook. When I entered, he turned to me and said, "Vijali, you are the only one here who truly understands the Bhakti-Yoga path."

That night I had a strange dream: A bull came to me, his muscles shining as they rippled under his healthy coat, and mounted me as he would a cow, and vigorously made love to me. I woke up in the midst of climax, though I did not know what an orgasm was then. I had read in the scriptures that Shiva sometimes comes in the form of a bull to initiate a person, so I mused on this throughout the day.

In May of 1961, I had my twenty-second birthday. Swami had arrived for his bi-monthly visit to the convent from the main center in Hollywood. He was alone in the living room reading the newspaper and put the paper down when I asked, "How can I obtain the grace of God?"

Swami said, "But you do have his grace. Do you think it is any little thing that you enjoy doing worship and mental *japa?*" Swami put out his hand and invited me to move closer. I sat on the floor in front of his chair, and dug my fingers into the deep pile of the green carpet.

He looked thoughtful, and then he said, "Cover everything with the Lord. Then you can't go wrong. Do you understand? Yes, struggle, but in the right way. Don't be shy. Come. Sit closer."

"I need to set the table," I said smiling as I got up and went to the dining room. On the smooth waxed finish of the convent table I set the stainless steel knife and fork by the side of the stoneware plate. Clink! The fork accidentally hit the glass at the ninth and last setting for our evening meal. I was alone in the dining room as Swami entered, took my hands, and put his arms around me. His body was soft, pliable, and warm under his blue cashmere sweater. He held me for a long time, his cheek against my face; he was only an inch or two taller than my five-feet-two inches. His breath felt warm on me, and his body and clothes emitted a sweet mellow fragrance. With his arms around me, he said, "I love you. I want you to be happy."

He pressed full, moist lips against mine until I felt his breath deepen. His tongue slipped into my mouth. Then someone was coming along the path and he stepped away, but as we separated, he whispered into my ear, "Come to my room tonight after midnight, after everyone is asleep."

I slid out the kitchen door and walked up the path through the chaparral to the Temple for the evening service, thinking all the while of Swami's lectures on Sundays, and in particular his words, "Shut the doors of the senses, rise above the sensual pleasures of the world to find God." I felt stunned, happily stunned, mysteriously stunned. Imagine, a swami—a monk—kissing me, a nun!

After midnight, when I was certain that the nuns were asleep, I opened the window in my room and stepped out the screened porch door into the bright moonlight. The oleanders were in bloom, and the night-blooming jasmine perfumed the warm night air. I heard an owl as I glided over the flagstone path in my slippers and entered the porch outside Swami's room. I stood on the other side of his door for a moment, my bathrobe covering my nightgown, and then I knocked shyly. Swami opened the door and immediately held me closely in his arms. Then he led me into his room, took off my robe, and held me again for a long time. He kissed me and tenderly stroked my head and face. He said, "You are truly my *Shakti*, my divine feminine, and know this for certain: I am your *Shiva*, the sacred masculine. This relationship is eternal. Never look upon me as an ordinary man. I feel the divine *Shakti* within you—and that is what I worship."

Swami placed his tapered fingers at the opening of my nightgown, unbuttoned the blue button, and let the gown slide over my shoulders onto the floor. He held my breasts in his two hands, and leaned down and kissed my nipples. They stood pink and erect, and lightning shot through my body until my legs quivered and my groin ached. He put his arm around

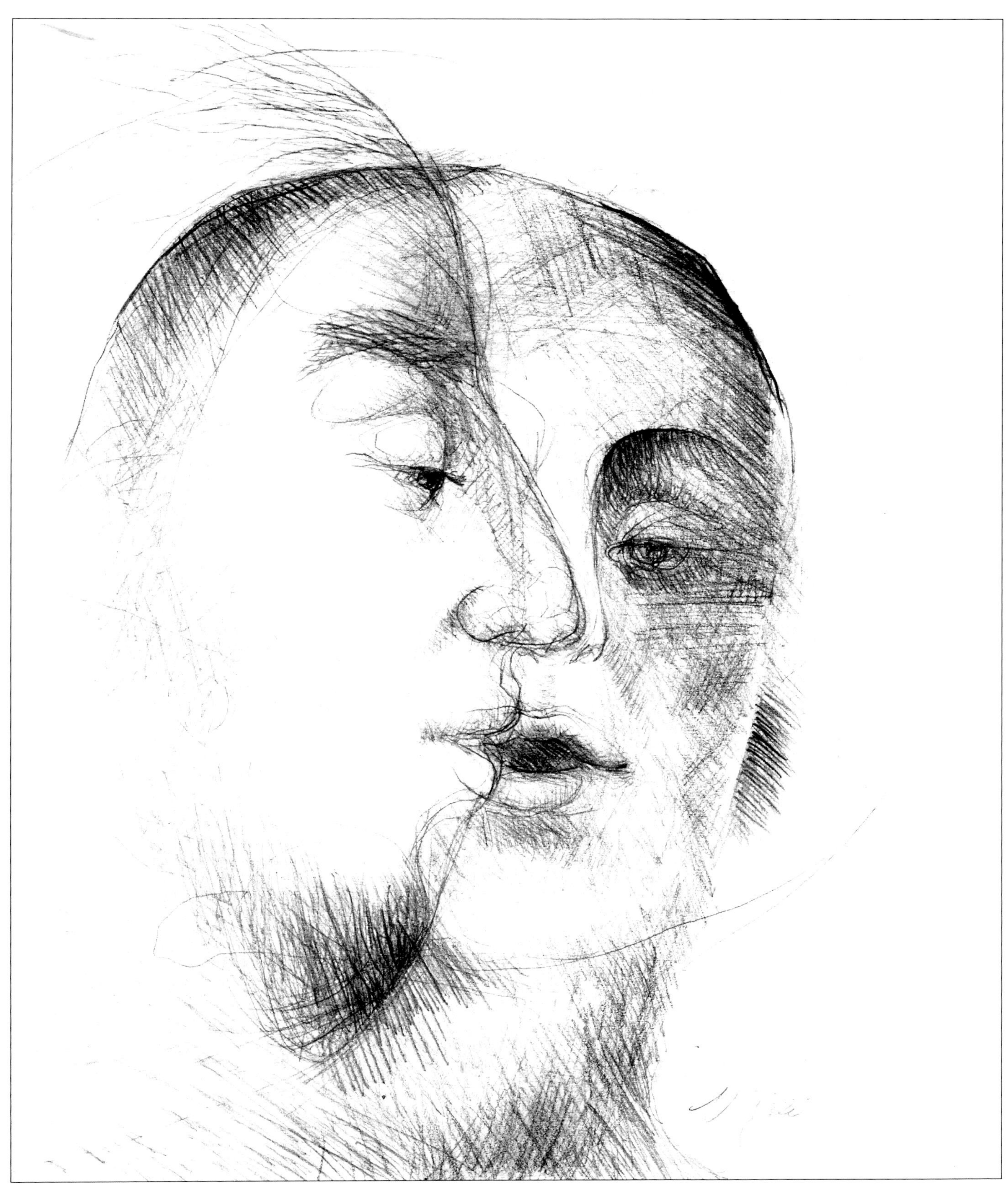

The Kiss

my waist and led me to the bed, where he untied the drawstring of his pajamas and let them cascade off his hips. He stood nude and his broad shoulders and narrow waist reminded me of the dark boy Krishna and his love exploits with the *gopis*, the cowmaids. At first, I couldn't speak. I had never seen a man in the nude. But here stood Swami disrobed from his Sunday tunic with black curly hair cradling his semi-erect penis. He took my hand and drew me onto the bed, lying half on top of me as his lips found my breasts again. He tugged on their tips with his lips and teeth. Then he kissed my neck and let his hands follow the curve of my body, caressing my back, my buttocks, my thighs. He pulled me on top of him as we moved in rhythm, his dark *lingam* pressing to find my humid *yoni*. Heat flared inside of me. He sat up in the meditation position and I sat cross-legged, wrapping my legs around him.

He whispered to me, "Yogis have developed control." We toppled over and lay outstretched on the bed, so that he moved on top of me, and came onto my pubic hair and stomach.

We lay for some time in each other's arms until we heard the mourning doves cooing, and then Swami said, "You must go quickly now, so no one sees you." He whispered after me, "Come to my room tomorrow afternoon when the nuns take their naps."

I moved through the day in a stupor. I had no idea Swami had these feelings after all the effort he made to keep us away from involvement with men, away even from the occasional book or movie with sexual content. I stumbled as I did my morning chores in the convent, dropped objects, and could not unlock my mind from the images and experiences of the previous night. I had known Swami since I was nine—thirteen years! He was sixty-seven and I was twenty-two.

When the nuns were all either napping or reading, I went to Swami's room and stood timidly before his door, knocking gently.

He immediately opened the door and embraced me, saying, "My *Shakti*, my love." He quickly led me into his room, and a little sheepishly he said, "Waiting for you I got so excited, I—I've already come."

There was a semen spill on his shorts, and he chuckled about his comment of the night before, about the Yogi's control. We tumbled onto the bed, and removed each other's clothes, caressing, whispering, kissing, and laughing.

In the afternoon, as Swami held me in his arms, I said, "I love you more than anyone in the world. But I don't understand. I've been reading in the scriptures that it's necessary to keep absolute continence in order to progress spiritually."

"That isn't so. Ancient Indian sages had children. There's nothing detrimental in the sexual act itself."

"Then why," I asked, "do people enter the monastic life and this convent you've established?"

"So as not to get entangled in attachments to family, wife, and children," Swami said. "The *complications* of desire interfere by taking time away from thinking of God and practicing spiritual disciplines."

To myself I wondered, "Then why don't you share and discuss your own evolution of thinking on this subject with the group?"

For the next three years, Swami continued his schedule of bi-monthly visits to the convent. He and I got together at every opportunity, and he was always passionate, taking the lead, the authority, as if he knew what he was doing.

He would lie on top of me and ask me, "Am I on the right place?" However, he never penetrated me the entire time we were together.

Now I know he was referring to the clitoris, but I wasn't sure what he was talking about then. I had no knowledge of my clitoris.

"It is important for my *lingam* to be touching the right place," he would say. "Have you come?"

And I would say, "Oh, yes," not knowing what *come* meant. Later I decided that he hadn't had much experience or he would have known that I never climaxed.

The same desire that took me into the convent at age fourteen—to realize Truth, to live with awareness, to live with consciousness of heaven on earth—led me out ten years later. The convent structure became limiting, and brought nightmares of confusion between the ideals of the convent and my continuing relationship with Swami. I could not come to terms with the conflict. I felt the hypocrisy of continuing to live in the convent, and I began to see Swami as two-faced and dishonest about his own feelings and private life. I would wake in the middle of the night screaming. In darkness, panic grabbed me and I could not breathe.

I craved study and hungered for knowledge of all kinds. I longed to go to a university, and finally asked Swami, "May I go, please. May I go?"

He refused my request, and only once did I discuss with him the confusion I felt. As I laid out his ocher robes for the Sunday lecture, I said, "Swami, I came into the convent young—fourteen—and I think it's necessary for my development to have a variety of experiences,even to make mistakes. That's part of spiritual development." I buffed the shoes I had recently polished and placed them back in his closet. "I don't have the opportunity here. Maybe if I go to the convent at the Hollywood center I will experience more."

Swami said, "I understand, but what can I do? Going to the convent in Hollywood won't do—not with access to the public."

I wanted a broader life. Even the Catholic orders allowed nuns to study and to develop service through their hospital work or schools, but Swami wanted to keep me cloistered.

When I announced my decision to leave, Swami said, "Do what you have to do."

The day before I left, Padma said, "We will find a counselor for you, like we promised many years ago, if you will stay. A nun leaving the convent is caught between two worlds and never finds happiness."

But on the morning of my twenty-fifth birthday, with one hundred dollars borrowed from the father of one of my sister nuns, and the conviction from a small but confident voice inside of me that I knew I must follow at all cost, I left the convent and headed for Canada.

Sri Kali Yantra, ancient East Indian symbol for the divine feminine, womb of the cosmos, carved by Vijali

CHAPTER FIVE

World Wheel–Spoke Three

Alicante, Spain

1988

River of Light

ON AUGUST 6, 1988, I ARRIVED with shaky knees at the airport in Madrid—unable to speak Spanish and feeling that I had just jumped off a cliff, not knowing what was at the bottom, or if there was a bottom at all. I had the address of a youth hostel in my notebook, in case the one person from whom I had received a letter about the project was not in Madrid at the time. She had not answered her phone when I had called continuously from New York. My hands shook on the handle of the airport cart as I wheeled my backpack, heavy with tools, camera, notebook, and one change of clothes, toward a telephone. I fumbled with the foreign coins and waited as I held the receiver to my ear. Ring. Ring. Ring. Ring. My heart pounded.

"Hola." A warm female voice rang out at the other end.

"Hola, is this Geraldyne?"

"Vijali, is that you? We were giving a workshop in southern Spain where there was no phone. We drove all night to be back in Madrid when you arrived. Come right over."

My knees stopped shaking and I loosened my grip on the cart to wipe sweaty hands on my skirt. A friend in the United States had given me Geraldyne's address after she had read a description of her conservation work in a New Age journal.

I spent a few days in beautiful Madrid with its Spanish style tile roofs and courtyards filled with potted flowers. I suffered painful eye irritation from the air polluted by car exhaust, but I saturated myself with the majesty and strength of the Goyas and El Grecos in the Prado Museum. Then, as Geraldyne and her companion, Marysol, suggested, I traveled to the site and community that Geraldyne thought was right for the World Wheel event in the mountains outside of Lorca in southern Spain.

I arrived at an abandoned forester's house isolated on a pine-covered range. Cathedral-like sandstone outcroppings eroded into swirling caves punctured the mountain crest. This would be my home for the next two months, but nothing would come easily.

Two men and one woman had been living there for a month developing a community on land given to them by the government—twenty-five square miles to be restored through the planting of trees. The Spanish earth was drying, and trees and plants were disappearing along with the animals. In the air there was a sense of urgency to turn this around and bring life back to the earth of Spain. Another person joined us, and we became five people plus a guest or two.

We lived and worked together, planting trees and repairing the house. We cleaned out rooms that had formerly housed animals to use as bedrooms. The house had no facilities, so we cooked in the fireplace, relieved ourselves in a hole in the ground, and bathed and washed dishes outside where we drew water with a rope and bucket from a holding tank. I loved it. I had my first taste of Spanish cooking over the fire, paella, and Spanish wine, now my favorite of wines.

Joaquin, a weaver, brought with him a large loom, which filled one of the rooms in the forester's house.

He had building experience, and started taking carving lessons from me as I worked on sculptures in our spare time. At thirty-five, he was six feet tall with a head of curly hair, the long limbed body of an El Greco painting, and the grace of a dancer. His parents had insisted that he go to trade school after high school to learn electrical wiring instead of to art school as he had wanted. Then, after eight years in the military, he decided to change his life. For the next eight years he lived in the mountains and worked the land, and during four of those years he herded fifty goats. He knew the earth, and he knew how to weave. As an added bonus, he was skilled at the art of cooking in the style of southern Spain.

It is hot! I wrote in my journal. *The light is a different light than I have ever experienced. It is white, reflecting from the white limestone of the parched earth and the stone houses painted white. The hot, dry breath of the afternoon makes everything stand still. I now appreciate the Spanish house with its thick walls and tiny windows. You can make it dark inside on these glaring afternoons. This California girl never thought she would like tiny windows. But centuries of life on this tierra has formed the perfect house for this land and climate. It is cool and calming inside—just right for an afternoon siesta.*

In the early mornings I rose ahead of the sun and hiked the mountain before the heat of the day set in. The smell of pine and earth greeted me. On the highest peak I discovered a wall of giant stones. This would be the site of the next World Wheel sculpture and performance. It was so silent, unlike the silence of Boney Mountain which was always punctuated by the sound of airplanes. I heard not one plane in my two-months' stay.

But the sounds in the house! The place was mad with emotions and incompatibilities. The two men had personality conflicts from before I arrived and there had even been one incident of violence. The woman in charge bristled at my presence, and refused to tell the authorities in Lorca that I would be creating a sculpture on the land.

"I will only get permission," she said, "when the community is running smoothly and we have the work on the buildings completed."

So, in an effort to create some sense of harmony and cooperation, I drew us together in council meetings, gave yoga classes, acupressure treatments, taught sculpture, and suggested we meditate together regularly. But my efforts only fed her insecurity and jealousy. She read my astrological chart. She analyzed my every move and word. The negativity and daily fights between the two men continued.

I felt lost without the support of real friends. One night, feeling misunderstood and isolated, I slept beneath the stars with a pine tree by my side. I closed my eyes with a prayer on my lips. How was I to live out my own vision of unity—not on an isolated mountain top as I had done previously, but in the midst of everyday conflicts? I felt the support of the earth against my back and thighs. The fragrance of the pine tree suggested incense in a vast cathedral whose vaulted ceiling was the sky painted with the beginnings of creation. Night sounds murmured—choruses of crickets and distant wolves. Then something very gentle touched my lips. I opened my eyes as a bat darted away into the black night, leaving my parted lips tingling with its kiss.

I left to give a presentation at a New Age conference in Madrid. Such meetings were a rare occurrence in those days. When I returned to the community, I waited outside Lorca on the road going into the mountains with my thumb in the air. No public transportation extended into the mountains. Car after car passed, packed with families, children peering out the windows, but I saw no women driving. Finally a car stopped, driven by a single man. I thought of the great hospitality extended to me from the local farmers and residents and I got in.

We drove for a while, until he leaned over abruptly and grabbed my breast. I yelled at him and pressed against the door to keep my distance. Then he unzipped his pants and pulled out his penis. I screamed for him to stop the car as he grabbed my throat. I pushed him off, opened the front door to throw my backpack out of the moving car, and jumped. When I saw him stop the vehicle, I left my bag and ran. My legs responded like rubber and I stumbled down the embankment as fast as I could go, tripping over logs and my own feet. When I finally turned around, I saw him head for his car and drive off.

I wobbled back to the road and was grateful to see my backpack still there. There were no telephones at our forest retreat and no transportation, so I drew on my courage and put my thumb out again, but only for cars with families. At last one stopped with just enough room for one person to squeeze into the back seat between passengers. The driver tied my backpack to a rack on top and I climbed in and sat in the back with two elderly men.

After forty minutes, they stopped and left me where the quarry trucks could pick me up. I had spoken to the truck drivers before and felt comfortable riding with them to the quarry. From there I could walk the remainder of the way.

The first truck that came along slowed down. "Hey, do you need a ride?" the driver shouted over the noise of the engine. Relief flooded my body when I saw it was one of the drivers from the quarry.

"I sure do!" I almost yelled. I hopped in, and instead of just driving to the quarry, in half an hour we were at the forestry house. I jumped out and shook his hand in gratitude.

I walked in the front door to find the group in the midst of a horrendous fight. Joaquin, always fiery in temperament, had his hands around Juan's throat. My arrival broke up the fight, but they continued to glare at each other. "Vijali," they all spoke simultaneously, "we have decided to disband the community."

"What will you do?" I asked.

"Each person will return to his former life, with the exception of me," the woman said. "I will stay on by myself."

We busied ourselves packing and cleaning up our rooms. I felt very relieved as I stuffed my clothes, journal, books, and tools into my backpack. Juan came to my room and gave me a goodbye hug.

New friends from the conference in Madrid had invited me to another mountain in the Alicante area by the Mediterranean Sea. Now I was free to accept their offer. Joaquin decided to go with me to the next site and continue his apprenticeship as a sculptor. Luckily, a friend of Joaquin's arrived in his car. The crunch of its tires on the gravel was music to my ears. We both stayed at the friend's house while I located a car to buy, an old Citroën for one hundred dollars.

The new site was different altogether. As soon as we arrived, my body relaxed and my breath came easier. Centuries ago, the Moors had inhabited this land, a thriving work community. They had built terraces and vineyards and small stone cottages for shepherds and laborers. Each house had rooms for goats and donkeys, so that families and animals lived together. But blight had spread through the vineyards and, after a failed attempt at fruit orchards, the community had dispersed, leaving the stone houses to crumble into the semi-ruins they are today. The valley descended straight to the Mediterranean, about a twenty minute walk away, and meandering streams culminated in dramatic waterfalls on their way to the sea.

The owner of the land, Jan Semmel, a Madrid artist and writer I had met at the conference, gave Joaquin and me one of the small stone houses in which to live. Moreover, trusting my relationship with the earth and stone, he gave me complete freedom to create as I liked, only viewing the sculptures two months later at the final ceremony.

Joaquin and I cleared the land and dug the dirt away from around a large boulder in front of a stone wall in ruins behind the cottage. I saw the stone as the east point of an Earth Wheel. It looked like an eagle with outstretched wings flying out of the earth. To the west of this circle were two trees with a feeling of a passageway between them. I felt this was

Vijali drawing Christina's shadow for the sculpture image, *Woman of Space Pregnant with Sun*

my own passageway into a new situation of joy and cooperation.

Eventually another person came to help—Christina Serrentino, an herbalist from the United States and an Italian beauty with a Mona Lisa presence. I had met her at the Seneca Reservation during the Women's Council. When she first arrived in Spain, I couldn't sleep for two nights—to have a woman friend to talk with in English!

I wrote in my journal, July 3, 1988:

Today is the day of Las Piedras, *The Stones. The three of us disassembled the crumbling ends of the stone wall leaving the center portion intact where a large boulder was embedded. This stone reigns over the land like a Madonna in a cathedral. As shadows fell across its surface, I saw a woman rising from the stone, her arms upraised into the heavens. The north point of the Earth Wheel pointed toward her. Joaquin, who has disassembled ruins before, warned us that it would be hard work removing the many stones built into the thick wall, and, at the end of this first day, I understand too well what he meant. It will take two more days with three of us working in a line, handing stones from person to person. I have been relocating them in other forms as they come out of the wall, and already we have built a retaining wall to protect against erosion and have made a circle from the large stones completing the Earth Wheel. When the sun went behind the mountain, we finally stopped work. Our muscles and backs ached, and yet, as we walked back to the cottage, we joyfully collected red crystals we found mixed with the earth shining underfoot.*

When we arrived at the cottage, we built a fire immediately because the house is like a big refrigerator, built for summer use only. The wind comes in around the doors and windows, so we eat, study, write, and draw all huddled by the fire. The huddling is the best. On the personal level, this is what the World Wheel is about—developing a world family. Yes, I feel that today.

When the side walls of the ruin were completely disassembled, we dug trenches for the four directions and a moon and sun shape in front of the woman-boulder in the wall. We filled the trenches with the white powdery mortar collected from between stones in the ruin, so that we used every part and discarded nothing as unimportant. I showed Christina how to sculpt,

Woman of Space Pregnant with Sun, Alicante, Spain

and, together, we carved the symbols in the stones for the four directions. The environment itself seemed to tell us what to do. Day by day the project took its unique form.

For days I worked with the large stone in the center of our sacred wall and felt the spirit of the Moors still present in the valley. *Woman of Space Pregnant with Sun* emerged. Her thick thighs rose out of the earth, her belly grew pregnant with the sun, the condensed male energy. Her breasts were full and her arms rose to contain the galaxies. Her head swelled on the end of a long slender neck. Her upper body symbolized the night sky with moon and her lower body represented daylight, supporting the sun.

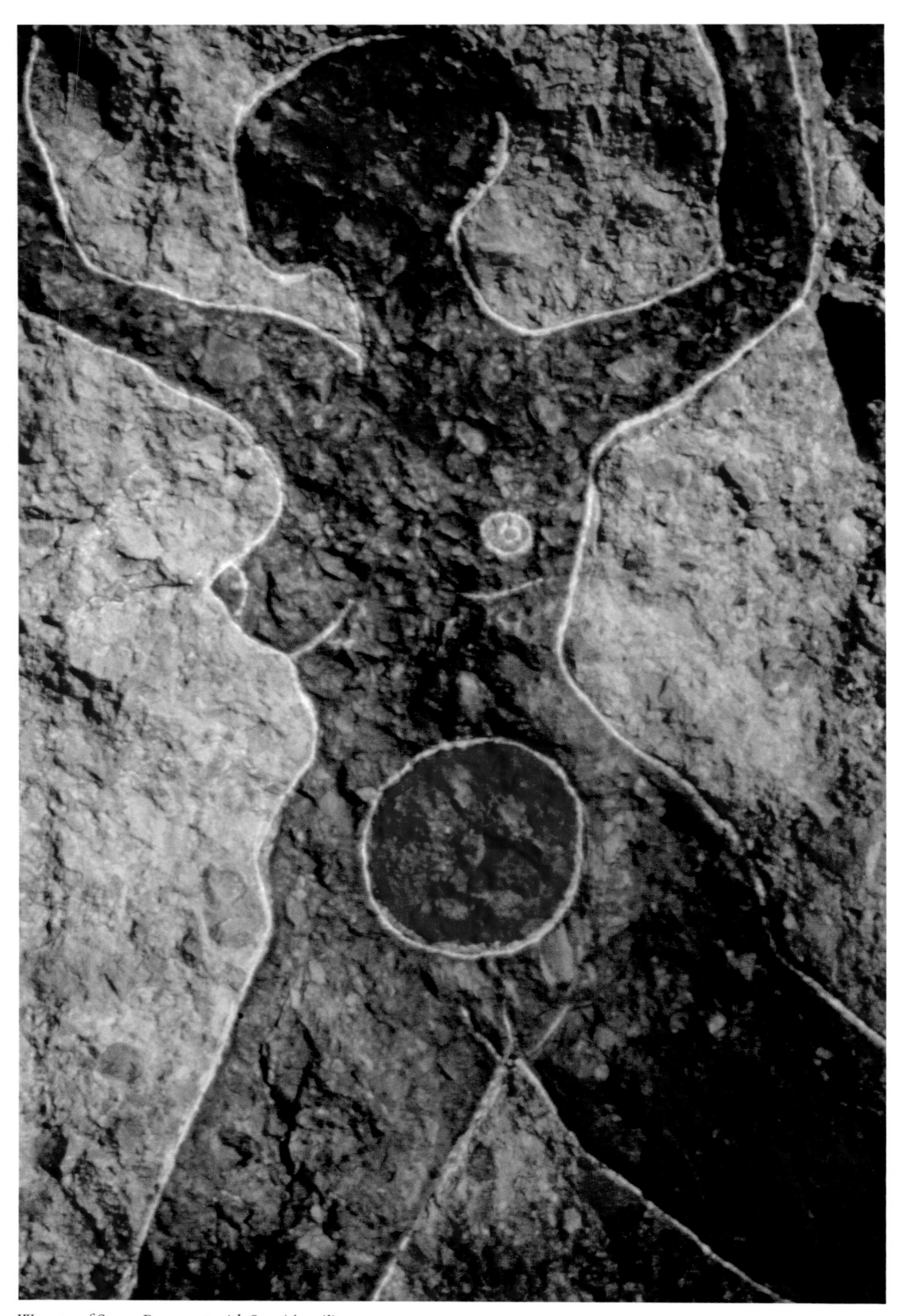

Woman of Space Pregnant with Sun (detail)

She had been growing within me ever since I had seen a photograph nine years ago of a cave painting in Africa. She grew further when I arrived in this area and saw cave paintings of the Indalo Man with upraised arms that meet as a rainbow. I had been looking for years for a stone that would contain her essence and here she was, already in the stone.

Early on New Year's Day, Jan, the owner of the land, arrived with friends from Madrid. Six men and six women gathered for the ceremony. It was a joyous moment for me when they arrived. The number of people was as fulfilling to me as if there were six hundred. The atmosphere was luminous, unearthly. One by one I brought each person into the circle of the earth wheel, and smudged him or her with sage smoke and feather. The children of our guests stood at each of the four cardinal directions with branches from the sacred trees of the area, giving one to each person as they entered our sacred space and sat in a circle around the Earth Wheel. Earlier, we all had carved and painted a stick that nature had twisted into the shape of a serpent, and this became our talking stick.

I presented the questions that provided form to all these performances: *What is our essence? What is our sickness? What can bring the world and us into harmony?* The talking stick was passed around the circle. Each person held it until they were moved to speak from the honesty of their hearts. The feelings expressed can be summarized in two sentences: *We are tied to our past in arrogance. We want to let go and jump into the future with a new freedom born of thought and action.*

Afterwards, everyone commented on the light. It was as if the objects, indeed space itself, had begun to glow. Everyone experienced a sense of weightlessness, as if we were at some great altitude. People lingered in a semi-silence they hesitated to break.

Two of the participants, Juan and Maribelle, invited me to live in their second home, a desert cottage outside of Lorca, while I worked on a World Wheel newsletter. Their generosity provided me with time to connect with people in the next countries—Italy and Greece—and with old friends in our growing World Wheel family. While there, in gratitude for the silent space, I also completed twenty-five small alabaster sculptures representing the Viking runes and an environmental sculpture for Juan and Maribelle's cottage. Joaquin came and assisted with the sculptures, creating three of his own. Since I had been unable to raise money for the projects in Italy and Greece, selling the small sculptures allowed me to continue the World Wheel.

Juan came early each morning, and we would meditate and walk together over the desert floor, grown luxurious with spring flowers and blooming almond trees. The cottage sat in the center of a desert valley, surrounded by mountains. Juan, in his determination to carve a spiritual life for himself amidst business and family, had started building a Zen-like temple. He said he wanted the cottage to be a retreat for the World Wheel Family.

When the October Gallery in London invited me to present my work on the World Wheel, I decided that the project in Spain was complete. Joaquin drove me to Valencia where I would catch a bus to London. We stepped out of the car for only a few moments, but when we returned, half an hour before I was to take the bus to London, all my bags had been stolen. Camera and money, even my treasured eagle feather that had belonged to Black Elk were gone. Most importantly, my writing, original slides, and photos had vanished—everything I needed for the presentation at the October Gallery. I was in shock, but I took the bus anyway, determined that my time had come to an end in Spain. I was ready to experience London. Again, I left, as I had left the States, with a feeling of jumping off a cliff into the unknown, not knowing where I was or how I would land.

I had been living at the October Gallery for a month in residences provided for visiting artists. The date of my presentation was drawing close when I received a call from Joaquin. He told me that a writer in Valencia had found my suitcase in a parking lot. The man lived in a tall building looking down on the lot, and for an entire day he had observed a bag sitting isolated and abandoned. When curiosity overcame him, he looked inside, and, realizing the importance of the materials, had managed to track me down. Through Spanish addresses and telephone numbers in my journal, he had called a friend of Joaquin's in Valencia, who called Joaquin. By the end of the week, the luggage was on its way to London via air. I had been sick all that week and had found it difficult to sleep, wondering how to present my talk without my treasured slides. Reluctantly, I had prepared myself to speak without them. The announcements were out, and people I ran into spoke of coming. I trembled with relief when I received the call from Joaquin that the baggage was on its way, but what was still in it?

With nervousness over a route I had never traveled before, I caught a bus to the central station and then transferred to another bus that took me to Heathrow Airport. After a little searching, I found the administrative office where my suitcase awaited me, tagged with my name. I held my breath as I opened my bag and felt around. Money, camera, and my eagle feathers were gone, but the irreplaceable address book, writing, and slides were intact. I could feel myself breathing almost normally again as I rode the bus back to the city. I arrived at the London gallery only fifteen minutes before my slide lecture was to begin.

The Mediterranean earth and people, the richness and simplicity of each day, had infiltrated my blood. Sometimes I look upon the World Wheel with awe. It has a life of its own, each spoke infusing the environment, as well as my personal life, with its own particular flavor. The time in Spain had not been a time of public performance or articles in magazines, but a personal initiation into a more direct relationship with the spirit of the earth and with people—for me and for each person who came into the Wheel's orbit.

CHAPTER SIX

Into the World

Montreal, Canada
1964–1972

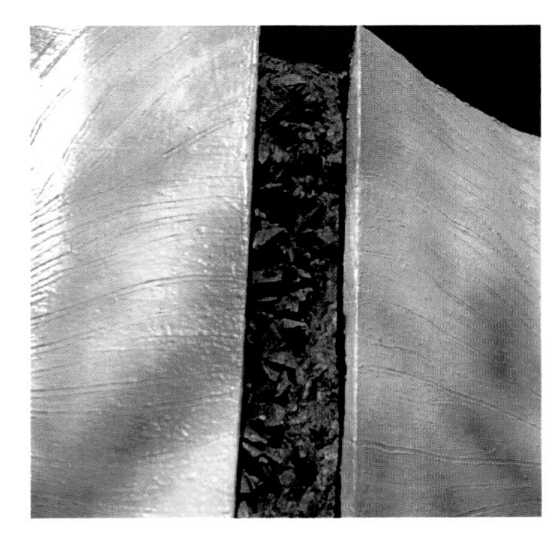

90% Bliss (detail)

IN 1964, I LEFT THE CONVENT and boarded a bus to Canada. I had chosen Ottawa because of John. The year before, while still in the convent, I had made a trip to Dallas to nurse my aging grandmother, and there I had met John, a Canadian student from British Columbia. He was in Texas for a summer job, earning money to continue his studies toward a Ph.D. in Economics in Ottawa—but he also planned to go to Africa to help people in underdeveloped countries. His idealism attracted me and I envied his opportunity to study. We corresponded while I waited in the convent for my Canadian Green Card. For an entire year we wrote of our great plans for the future and a mutual desire to hone our skills and be of service to the planet. The love between us grew and I dreamed of joining him in his studies and of our possible work in Africa.

Three days on a Greyhound landed me on the Canadian border at midnight, my work permit in one hand and all my possessions in the other. But my possessions weren't weighty enough. A beady-eyed official invoked an obscure regulation: *The alien must have two hundred dollars worth of "assets" in order to enter this country—no drifters allowed.* I bundled myself up and sat through the cold night, not knowing what else to do. I would not turn back. Finally, after dawn, a second official took pity, or maybe just wearied of this quietly defiant bundle, and let me through customs.

"All right, young lady," he said, "we won't detain you any longer—you can go on through. But be careful."

I leapt up, wanting to hug him, then found an early morning bus to Ottawa, John's address clutched in my hand

I contacted John, and to save our pennies for our studies, we moved in together. I was with my very own boyfriend in his small, dingy city apartment. Right away I got a job at a life insurance office. My first paycheck went to John for his university fees. At age twenty-five, my first priority was to fall in love with John and finish losing my virginity. Although I had been with Swami for three years, he had never entered me, and because of our age difference, there was always a daughter/father feeling mixed with my love. I was more than eager to be with John, yet my first intercourse hurt more than I could have imagined.

In only three weeks, with dizzying speed, I discovered a whole new world. I found myself amid many foreign students—sons and daughters of government officials and ambassadors from Nigeria, Kenya, and Sierra Leone. I met their families and got involved with international politics and hopes for world peace. We were devastated by the assassination of John F. Kennedy and the death of Pandit Nehru, and elated that Martin Luther King, Jr., had been nominated for the Nobel Peace Prize.

What exuberance, what ecstatic abandon in experiencing this unwalled environment! Life force flooded inside and out—whoosh!—energy, energy everywhere. New sights, new sounds, new people, new places everywhere. I embraced each situation. I welcomed every challenge. Come on, whatever is out there! No difficulty could approach the contradictions and

Ghosts from the Past

depression of the last three years of convent life. Then, one day, I arrived home from work to find no John, no note, and all his things gone. A week later, on a torn scrap of paper in an envelope, the words: "I am sorry, honey. On my way to Africa."

Outwardly I showed little emotion. I must get on with life, I told myself. I won't be tossed off like that torn scrap of paper! But aching memories of my mother filled me, so beautiful, seductively loving me, taking me to unknown places, and then disappearing without a word.

Meanwhile, the rent was overdue. I had already gone two days without eating when I came home from work to find the lock on my apartment changed and a note from the manager. I went to talk things over with him, but he summoned the police. I had to phone my new friends. Foreign students understood what it's like to be stranded. One lent me money for the rent and a Rhodesian couple invited me to move in with them.

Later, John asked me to come to Edinburgh to marry him. He had ended up there instead of Africa, working to finish his Ph.D. But I was already married—to Shiva, the unmanifest, the eternal, the companion who doesn't take the rent money and disappear without explanation. Also, in the brief time I'd spent with John, I'd seen no way to share my inner life with him. I had continued my habitual meditation schedule alone. But something in John was ignited—years later he went to Swami Prabhavananda for initiation and even spent a year as a monk in the Vedanta Society's monastery.

I decided to go full-speed ahead with my education in art. After only a couple of months at the life insurance office, I already had trouble keeping an attentive eye on the never-ending whirligig of meaningless paper. I jumped at a chance to work on a forthcoming publication for the National Research Council, where I would interview various scientists and make silkscreen and pen-and-ink illustrations of their discoveries and theories.

A few painting commissions brought in some money, enough to relocate to Montreal and enroll in an art program at Sir George Williams College, which I learned had the best art department in Canada. I worked days and attended evening classes. For a California girl, the winters were dreadful—sometimes fifty degrees below zero—but by the next year I had a scholarship and could study without hindrance.

I maintained correspondence with one of the young Vedanta nuns, Mangala, with whom I had enjoyed exchanging ideas. She kept me informed of the details of the convent, and we continued the conversations we had started when I was there.

I don't remember my father ever writing, although I think he must have. I have no memory of any contact with him except for a phone call about my mother. He said that she had had a craniotomy—an exploration of the brain in which the skull is opened up. Evidently the doctors felt nothing could be done about the brain tumor she had developed and closed the skull again. She died shortly afterward.

"Honey," my father said simply, "your mother has passed away."

I stayed in my room and wept. Then I went down the street to a florist and ordered two dozen roses sent to the convent and given to Sarada Devi, Ramakrishna's spouse, for our little shrine. I called the hospital wanting to know whether it had been a fast- or slow-growing tumor, if it had been malignant, and the details about her life and her death. But the state mental hospital would tell me nothing.

I received letters from Swami regularly. Occasionally, I would send him a little something. For his birthday I sent him twenty-five dollars—I had hardly any money, but I wanted to do it. He wrote back honoring my gesture, "It is like someone else sending me five hundred dollars." In one letter he wrote: "We all miss you. My heart sometimes weeps for you. Whatever is the will of the Divine Mother, my only prayer is that She may always keep you under Her protection. With much love, Yours in Sri Ramakrishna, Swami."

In the first year of college, I took mostly general courses: composition, literature, anthropology, science. In the second year, I added the arts. I found that only my literature teacher encouraged us to question, marvel, speculate, experience. I still remember her insights. Why weren't more students and teachers interested in the whys and hows of life? Maybe my head needed this "headucation," but I felt out of sorts, unsatisfied. And the approach to art was to imitate the work of the famous professor who had shown in all the important places—New York, Paris, Rome, London, Buenos Aires. No instructor mentioned meditation or insight or nature as sources of inspiration for artwork. Gradually it became clear to me that my reasons for becoming an artist were different from these other people, students and teachers alike.

Toward the end of my third year, after a long winter and with the snow melted, bright blue light suddenly pierced dark, overcast skies. Knife-sharp, ice-forming winds transformed into soothing breezes. Spring at last! My enthusiasm for life returned, but my longing for total openness, embracing whatever came, wasn't working out so well in practice.

I remembered Swami's words, "The sexual act itself is not harmful to spiritual life. It is the complications arising from the involvement that distract you from your path." In the convent with Swami, I intuitively understood the fusion of spirituality and sexuality, even though I didn't experience my sexuality fully. Now my sexuality was developing, but was I any closer to integration? Not yet, but I knew I was born to find it.

The college year ended. It was 1967, and I read in the paper that Christopher Isherwood's *A Meeting by the River* had been published. My mind went back to the convent. I wanted to head west. I also read that Dr. Christian Barnard had performed the world's first human heart transplant operation. Yes, I thought, I need a heart transplant badly. I would go to California for the summer. For three years I had been away, living the worldly life. I would head back to my old environment to see if I could integrate my old life with what I had learned.

I planned to return to an educational environment after the summer break. Since I wasn't getting what I wanted out of my present university, I had looked into other colleges. After winters in Canada, I dreamed of the sun in Mexico, the Instituto Allende in San Miguel was a school with a good reputation. I decided to investigate after my visit with my convent family.

I set off hitchhiking from Montreal through the maple woods of Vermont, the monuments of Manhattan, and further south into gentler accents and faces, then westward over the Rockies and across endless spaces and wide-open vistas to California, where I ate my first good enchiladas in three years.

One day, while visiting my old friends at the convent, Prabha and Mangala said, "We want you to meet an artist who lives down the street." And so, on the temple steps after the Sunday lecture, they introduced me to Dale Clark, a small rugged man with thick graying hair and dancing blue eyes. His skin was lined and tanned from living on his sixty-foot boat. The nuns piqued my interest by telling me that he had built the boat himself, and had cruised for nearly a decade between Terminal Island off San Diego, California and Puerto Vallarta, Mexico.

Dale walked me down the road to his property on a street just below the convent grounds. On this two-acre piece of land studded with boulders and chaparral, with a perennial stream running through, Dale was building a studio. Constructed of Mexican adobe bricks, it had a high ceiling with thick wooden beams and Mexican Saltillo tiles on the floor. He had equipped the space with foundry, kiln, smelter, heliarc welder, and carpentry tools.

Dale showed me a little cabin with a wooden deck hanging out over the stream. We stood together on the deck, the water splashing and murmuring below us as it lapped over stones and pushed through fallen trees. Looking up, I saw the same Santa Ynez Mountains I had watched through my ten years of convent life. In the other direction, the Santa Barbara Channel Islands rose from the ocean. Dale walked me back to the entrance of the convent property.

As I said goodbye, he asked, "When can I see you again?"

"Soon," I said.

Over dessert, during a dinner date a week later, he again asked, "When can I see you?"

Ten days later, at the end of our third date, he said, "Vijali, will you marry me?"

I had already planned a trip to Mexico to explore the possibility of attending art school in San Miguel; we decided that Dale would join me. We would get married in Mexico and make the trip our honeymoon.

Every so often, as Dale drove, he chanted, "I love thee, I love thee."

I did not know if he addressed me or God, and I did not care. But as the miles passed and I had time to think, I wondered why I had said yes. I reassured myself: he could provide the spiritual and creative companionship I craved. I also wanted to complete my education, a frustration I carried from my convent days when I was not allowed to go to college. He assured me that he had no problem with my continuing studies.

At the border, a man shoved a card through the window while the officer checked us. The card read *Marriage License* and provided an address. Dale and I looked at each other: "Why not?"

We passed through customs, parked behind the customs building and followed the man to a tiny closet of a room in the back of a nearby shack. "Do you take theese woooman to be your lawful wedded wife?"

"I do."

"Do you take theese man to be your lawful wedded hus-ban?"

"I do."

"Now it ees time for da reeng."

Dale and I burst out laughing. It was two a.m. and a ring was the last thing we had on our minds. As we paid the twenty-five dollars, Dale asked, "But where is the witness?"

"Oh, my friend will sign in the morning. He is asleep right now."

We flew to Mazatlan and rented a room in a motel overlooking the bay where we immediately fell asleep on the twin beds. Half an hour later, I woke myself up with a blood-chilling scream.

Dale leapt off his bed and rushed over to me. "What is it, honey?"

"Oh, I forgot to tell you. I sometimes wake up in a panic, screaming."

He gave me a funny look.

"It started when I was in my late teens at the convent. I'm so sorry—there are so many things we haven't had a chance to tell each other."

This at least got us into a bed together, and we made love for the first time.

When Dale and I returned from our month-long honeymoon in Mexico, I met his two teenaged sons—Danny and Gregy, fifteen and sixteen years old. They would live with us, along with his eighteen-year-old daughter, Serena, whom I had already met at a Temple lecture. Dale's youngest daughter, nine-year-old Lori, lived with her mother in San Diego, and she would visit on her vacations.

The boys teased me, and Serena would not come home from school in the afternoons. She had been the mistress of the house for the last few years, and I was closer to her age then I was to Dale's. I could see that she was in a struggle to find her relationship with me so I went out of my way to talk with her. "You look hungry as an owl, Serena. What would you like for supper?"

"Spaghetti," Serena and Danny shouted. "Spaghetti," Gregy chimed in.

"It will be ready in half an hour," I promptly assured them.

"We'll be back in half an hour, Turkey Legs," the boys said with a twinkle in their eyes as they ran out the door, pushing each other down the steps.

Serena slumped down in a chair as I began cooking. "I love that ceramic plate you made. How did you cut into the surface to get the design?," I prompted her.

Her eyes lit up, "Oh, that's my secret."

We never received our marriage license from Mexico, but two months later we had a civil ceremony in the Santa Barbara courthouse. My correct convent language was broadened in the coming year, and I learned not to take myself too seriously. I jumped right into cooking three meals a day, cleaning, doing the laundry, and assisting Dale with his fight against time on an architectural sculpture commission.

We worked together to cast aluminum shapes and fit them together to form a magnificent tower symbolizing Mt. Sinai for the Beth El Synagogue in Arizona. The tower rotated on ball bearings with the push of a hand to face east, and aluminum doors opened to expose the Torah. We rented some land near the ocean and erected a large furnace and crucible. We used the lost styrofoam technique of casting, which is a modern version of the traditional lost wax method in which molten metal is poured into a plaster cast that surrounds an image made in wax. The wax burns out and the metal fills the cavity. In this technique, the heat burns out the styrofoam that is buried in sand, and the sand holds the shape of the sculpture. At the same time, I made small castings of my own sculptures, and created a mural for the Carousel restaurant in Phoenix.

In my early years of painting, I had grown frustrated with the flat surface of the canvas and had experimented with all kinds of extenders in paint and glued-on materials to give more texture and dimension to a surface. Now, with access to Dale's studio-shop, I developed a new medium—a marble composition that consisted of ground marble and other fillers mixed in a polyester resin that hardened chemically. I chiseled, ground, polished, and painted forms made of this material. The acrylic paint bonded permanently to the surface and enabled me to produce work that was an amalgam of painting and sculpture, and which allowed me to make large murals that had texture and dimension.

Vijali in her and Dale's home with the sculptured marble painting, *Sailing Free*

Dale and I took these sculptural paintings to the Renaissance Fair and other outdoor festivals and art exhibitions, and they sold well. When Dale saw that I made a good living from them, he began turning down commissions offered to him, saying he wanted a simpler life without deadlines.

At that time, he was in the midst of five lawsuits brought by workers he could not pay because he had underestimated his budget. He still owed money for the land we lived on, and our studio home was unfinished. He was thousands of dollars in debt, and he wanted a change in his work. By supporting him and the children with the sales of my artwork, I was able to give him time and space to experiment and make

The Great Mother

that change. So we worked together to find outlets for my work, and, eventually, with Dale's support of my work, I paid off all his debts. Friends remarked that we were the ideal couple, able to meditate, create, and live together in the beautiful mountain home we eventually finished together.

If on the surface we looked more compatible than we actually were, in one area everything clicked: sexually. We had read about a tantric practice in a book given to us by a friend. One afternoon when no one was in the studio, we went to the cabin over the creek and took the positions we had heard about. We lay on our sides intertwined, and for four hours kept each other close to climax, but never actually climaxed. We parted deeply satisfied, and continued our work. For days afterwards we both experienced heightened energy and clear minds unlike anything we had ever experienced before. We resolved our creative problems easily and remained calm.

But another problem remained unsolved. I tried to enroll at the University of California in Santa Barbara, to fulfill the desire I had when we first married. But Dale had changed his tune. "How can you go? We have to make money."

I audited classes and took extension courses, but I did not attend university full time. By the second year, I had sole responsibility for our income, and any study was out of the question. I had no time to read a book or to make a friend outside of the working and selling environment.

In addition to earning our living, I did all the cooking and household chores, and kept the household running smoothly. It never occurred to Dale to make a cup of tea or to pick up a dishtowel and dry a dish. Nor did it occur to me to ask or tell him to. I simply fell into bed each night exhausted. We had been married for three years, and I longed to create without pressure, to have time to meditate as we did in the beginning of our marriage, to take a walk, or to spend time with another person. I felt the way Dale had when we met—overwhelmed, wanting no more pressure, wishing someone else would carry some of the burden. But when I told him I wanted a shift in our marriage midway toward what I needed creatively and spiritually, Dale resisted.

For two years I lived like this, but during this period, I had a recurring dream that helped nourish my inner life. In this dream, a brown-skinned, motherly woman draped in white garments embraced me lovingly and enveloped me in her voluptuous body. I could feel her breath against my skin. I could feel the warmth of her body, and her heartbeat becoming one with mine. I drew and wrote about her in my journal, and I began to create large sculptural paintings of "Earth Mother," as I called her.

One evening we went to a meditation at the home of two friends, and as I walked down their hallway, I found on the wall a photo of the woman of my dreams. I immediately asked our hostess, Markell Brooks, about the woman in the photograph.

"That is Anandamayi Ma, who lives in India," Markell said. "She is one of the greatest saints of the twentieth century."

I left the house with a handful of books about her. I gazed at Ma's beauty in photographs I placed by our bed. I went to sleep and woke up with the image of her face before me. I had the feeling that if I went to India, I would not tear myself away from her.

My work had paid off the mortgage on the property and I had taken care of Dale's debts. Now I felt that my turn had come. Dale, however, fought more stubbornly to maintain our status quo. Nevertheless, I was determined. I did not know how I would get to India—I just knew I would. At the next art show, I sold the sculptural painting, *Inner Space,* for three thousand dollars and earned another three thousand from selling smaller works—more than enough money for two people to go to India. The children were now on their own, except Lori, the youngest, who still lived with her mother, so I saw no reason not to go. After some initial resistance, I finally convinced Dale to join me, and within a month we flew to India to visit Anandamayi Ma's ashram in Varanasi.

CHAPTER SEVEN

World Wheel-Spoke Four

Umbrian Forest, Italy
1989

Rainbow Seeing

I ARRIVED IN ITALY ON May 26, 1989, and followed a friend's sketchy directions to Etain Addey's summer community, nestled in the Apennine foothills between Perugia and the ancient town of Gubbio. This region of the Umbrian forest was at the time home to a number of "intentional families" and land-based cooperatives in which people pooled their resources, lived close to the earth, and practiced voluntary simplicity.

I had read about Etain's commune, Pratale, a few months earlier in a magazine about alternative schooling. Pratale advertised itself as a place open to travelers from all over the world. People could drop by and stay a few days, weeks, or months while participating in the activities of the farm. This interested me so I decided to visit.

After a long trek by bus, train, and foot from London, I found Etain's rural location by asking neighbors in the general vicinity for her whereabouts. She welcomed me as I wandered into her patio, hot and dusty after walking several miles from the end of the bus line. A plump woman in her mid-forties with brown hair and dark, soulful eyes, Etain stood about my height and spoke English with a distinct British accent. As she showed me around the premises, she introduced me to her partner, Martin Lanz, who was busy taking care of twenty Sardinian sheep. I also met their three children who were playing hooky from home schooling in the shade of a large oak tree. Etain scolded them for shirking their studies.

The farm consisted of fifty acres of forest and rolling pasture in a green valley. A country road cut through fields surrounded by maple trees, oak, juniper, hornbeam, wild rose, and dogwood. After an earthquake in 1984, Etain and Martin had rebuilt their old farmhouse with stables, storerooms, a cellar, and a workshop. The new house also contained several small bedrooms, each accommodating two people. But on summer nights, everyone congregated on the central patio where we slept on mattresses under the stars.

Given the opportunity, country people in Italy often leave their farms and move to the city. In the 1970s, however, a growing number of young city-born Italians had done just the opposite. They had fled from urban sprawl and had taken up residence in abandoned farms and old half-ruined country houses. Intelligent and well read, Etain had left her job in Rome and had joined this fledgling back-to-the-land movement. Calling themselves "New Peasants," they prided themselves on not having a car, phone, freezer, or other electrical gadgets.

"It is more laborious to walk, write, make our own entertainment, and do things from scratch," Etain said, "but it's simpler. Of course, sometimes it's exhausting and frustrating. But most of the time, it feels good."

To my delight, Etain had been researching the early rituals of the area and she told me about the Eugubbine Tablets, which comprise the most important ritual text of local antiquity. Created approximately two centuries before Christ, they describe ancient ceremonies involving stone and geometric calculations.

What I found most intriguing about the tablets was that they spoke of mathematical and spiritual configurations derived from the relationships between direction, stone, and the angle of mountains. The center of this geomantic configuration became a place of observation. The tablets say: "The ceremony must begin with the observation of the birds." A qualified person would sit in a central place and observe the flight of birds, noting which kind of birds flew by and their formation and trajectory as a flock, all of which were deemed an important message.

But the idea for several sculptures and a theatrical ritual began to crystallize in my mind when Etain put into my hands *The Descent of Inanna-Ishtar*, a book describing the Sumerian myth of Inanna-Ishtar's descent into the Underworld.

"In the beginning of time, Inanna visited the dark realm where her sister Ekreshkigal lived. As Inanna entered the first gate, hidden hands reached down and plucked a golden crown off her head. As she passed successive gates, other hands stripped her of every article of clothing and every aspect of her identity until she no longer knew whether she was a man or woman. At the final portal she stood naked and trembling, her spirit completely humbled. She dissolved into the womb of the earth, into the womb of her dark sister, and only her body remained, left to shrivel on a meat hook. But winged spirits came to rescue her rotting corpse and she was miraculously reborn. Upon her lips, they laid the food of life. Upon her cold heart, they sprinkled the water of life. . . . She arose, and returned to the land of the living, filling the hearts of her people with joy and amazement, for she had gone where none had gone before. Since the Paleolithic era, people in Mesopotamia have called upon Inanna for guidance when they confronted the travails of the unknown, their own progression through life and death, through time and eternity."[10]

Toward the beginning of my stay in Pratale, I visited another commune comprised of about fifty people residing at the top of a mountain in the northern part of the Umbrian forest. I was thinking of involving other communities in the World Wheel project and this group sounded interesting to me. A friend of Etain's drove me there through acres of thickly wooded landscape, followed by miles of washed-out dirt track which was rarely, if ever, used. When we pulled up in the car, their founder, Mario, was milking a cow. An energetic man in his early forties, Mario had led this group and a number of other cooperatives in the Umbrian Forest for ten years. He visited each of these enclaves, giving advice and support while articulating the Confucian ideals he studied and strove to live by.

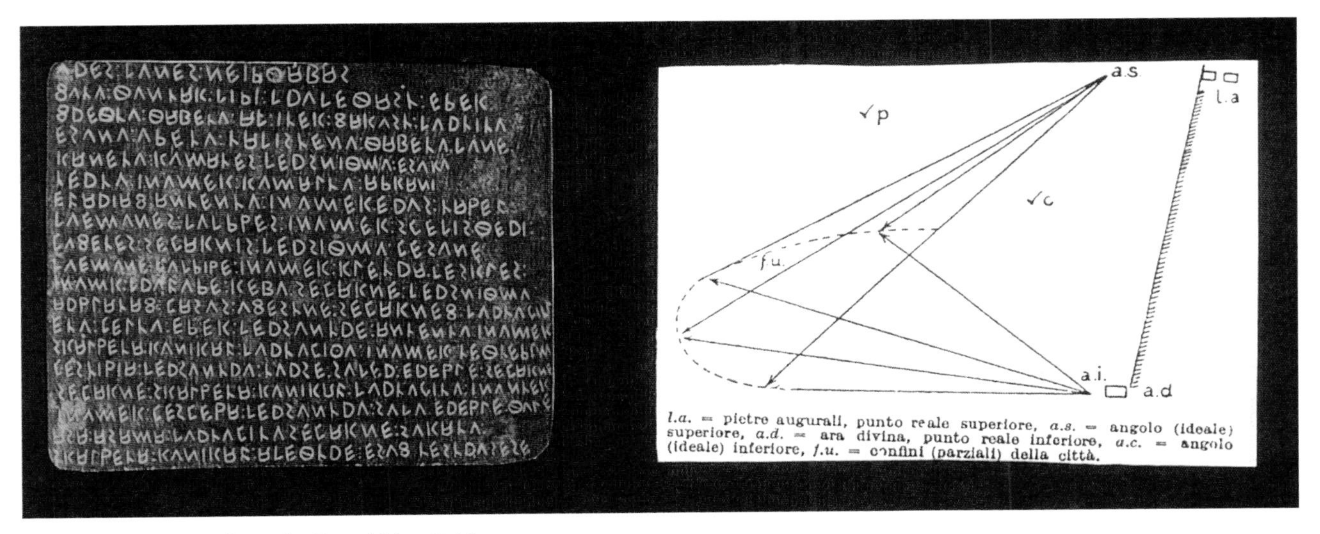

Script and diagram from the Eugubbine Tablets

The young men and women who gravitated to Mario's network thirsted for a sense of community. These urban refugees, mostly in their twenties, lived self-sufficiently, buying only the salt and tobacco which they could not produce themselves. They had already delivered sixteen babies in this mountain enclave, and they seemed genuinely happy living without electricity, making their own music, and dancing in the evenings—a life they deemed in harmony with themselves and nature.

Angelo, a small, olive-skinned, balding man in his early forties, made a point of befriending me. An artist, he kept an extensive journal of drawings and writings that delineated his philosophy. He was born a Catholic, but had pulled away from the church and the control of the Pope to find his own beliefs in community, love, and spiritual self-reliance. As we talked, I visualized him as one of the characters in the performance. "Angelo," I asked, "would you like to come to Pratale and become involved in the performance of the World Wheel?"

His face lit up, "I was just thinking the same thing when you were describing your work." We parted with the idea that he would hitchhike down in a couple of weeks.

Back at Pratale, I settled into a routine. I rose in the early morning and strolled up a hill to feed the weaning lambs, then made sheep's cheese, swept the patio, cleaned bathrooms, and washed dishes. We were fifteen people in all, including the children. Others tended the orchards—plums, cherries, apricots, pears, peaches, persimmons, pomegranates, various nuts, and about a hundred olive trees. They also kept horses, donkeys, and poultry on the farm.

In between chores, I wrote in my notebook and hiked the land where St. Francis had walked, refreshing myself by drinking water from the stream on the far hill. "The earth feels alive under my feet as I think of him and of his relationship with the animals," I observed in my diary. "It was in Gubbio that St. Francis tamed the wolf."

But when several wolves had been spotted in the area a few weeks before my visit, local farmers had shot them on sight, causing some of the young people to protest the needless killing and the irony of killing wolves in the very place where St. Francis had protected them.

On June 4, shortly after this incident, we received news of the student massacre in Tiananmen Square in Beijing. I reflected with despair on the dark underworld of our times.

In mid-June, I found the site to use for the World Wheel: a deep hollow in the middle of the forest. This enchanted thicket had walls of stone draped with ivy. "This is the Underworld!" I thought. The ivy assumed the shape of people and animals as my eyes adjusted to the darkness.

At first I felt a need for stillness. I lay on the ground soaking up energy from leaves, insects, and earth, while I looked up at trees and sky. It was a thirst that took time to quench. As I meditated, the whole performance played before my eyes: A man and woman emerge from over the hill, as if coming from some unknown place, and pass the first gate, the entrance to the forest. The winding pathway between the trees takes on different characteristics with the changing light and becomes the seven gates of the Inanna myth, through which she must pass on her journey to the Underworld. I see myself as stone, then wolf, then woman.

Inspired by the Eugubbine Tablets, I sat quietly in the forest and watched for birds. Three hours must have passed. The first bird came very close, looked into my eyes, fluffed its rust-colored breast and wings, and flew away. It felt like an acknowledgment that this was the right place and right time for the performance and sculptures to develop. Next I noticed a small, delicate black bird sitting on a branch a short distance away. Then a hawk, considered a sign of power and foresight in Native American cultures, flew across the sky from the east.

On the summer solstice, Joaquin and his friend, Fina, arrived from Spain in the ten-year-old Citroën. Joaquin wanted to continue learning sculpture as my apprentice. He was also eager to have his first experience as a performer in a World Wheel ritual. The renewal of friendship called for a celebration, and Joaquin and Fina cooked a paella—my first in three months.

Joaquin joined me regularly at the sculpture site, his company soothing and his work steady. Many

Ancient Roots
Umbrian Forest,
Italy

faces peered out of the stone wall waiting for us to carve them. The body of a giant woman goddess lay nascent on a ledge formed by mud washed from the land. Using my hands and a shovel, I molded the earth which already hinted at a female form. But where was her head?

I found a large stone in a canyon above the wooded hollow. With a tree for a lever, Joaquin and I tried to ease the stone down to the ledge and position it on top of her sculpted body, but the rope broke and the stone fell to the ground below. We got more rope and recruited three others to help lift the heavy weight up onto the ledge and turn it around. The stone already looked like a face. A strange archaic smile appeared when shadows fell across her eyes and nose. I called her *Goddess of the Underworld.*

A seasonal waterfall had eroded the surface of much of the local limestone known as *pietra viva*, or living stone, so it carved extremely well. I carved faces out of three of the stones and Joaquin carved one. Each was approximately three feet tall and two feet wide. These were faces of the Underworld, vital with the energy of our primal selves, unscathed by society, by parents, schools, or by our cluttered schedules and Walt Disney endings. I named one of the faces *Ancient Roots.* Her lips were already semi-formed when I began to chip away at the stone, and I left parts of it untouched. I carefully worked around vines on her head—they were her primitive hair, tangled and writhing like snakes. Mother Nature was my collaborator, and I respected the exquisite forms and textures she had sculpted over the millennia.

One weekend Joaquin and I made a trip to Pietrasanta and the Carrara quarries on Italy's northwestern coast to gather marble. The atmosphere there was the same as it had been in 1971 when I first came to Italy with Dale and had worked the stone for a month. I had shared a courtyard with Henry Moore, Noguchi, and many great Italian sculptors. Everyone I met had "marble fever." I certainly did! All I could think of was marble, marble, marble; carving marble with a passion, as if the earth might stop producing it tomorrow.

Joaquin and I returned to Pratale with six wonderful marble slabs which we immediately began to carve into a sculpture that symbolized one of the seven gates of the Sumerian underworld. The seven gates also correspond to the seven chakras, or energy centers, in the human body, discussed in tantric teachings. Placed at intervals along the forest path, the seven stone portals ushered us downward into the dark wooded recess—our version of the Netherworld.

Each gate sculpture was carved from a different type of stone that corresponded to the nature of the portal. I told Joaquin as we worked what a medicine woman had taught me about stone when I lived with her on the Hopi Reservation in Arizona. She said that for healing there were certain stones that take away pain, headache, a bad feeling, or a bad mood. If you take a lava stone in your hand and meditate with it, your bad feeling goes into the stone and you feel better. You must then take the stone outside, pour water over it to moisten it, and place it away from people where the sun can dry it out. She told me that sandstone is nice to work with for healing. It is a happy stone and more yielding. It is a love stone. Granite is hard and bold. Marble is cool and proud like the Greeks. She said she worked with red stone a lot. It doesn't have to be any particular type of stone as long as the stone is red. Red stone gives instead of receives, and is a healing stone.

One of the sculptures in this series, a marble hand, rose out of the earth. Another, a sandstone pillar, I painted with a doorway of sky on the surface. Inspired by the rusts and greens of lichen on stone, I painted small portions of each carving. A chemist had helped me to develop an ultraviolet-resistant acrylic paint that withstood the elements, so I was able to leave the painted sections of the sculpture in the sun and rain without the color bleaching.

As we worked under the tall oak trees, all the children came begging to carve, too. We gave them light tools with which to play. Sheep wandered by, put their heads under our benches, and dozed. Two chickens poked around, and the ever-curious donkeys put their faces right on the sculptures while we worked.

I named one of my sculptures *Trinity*. It had three faces emerging out of alabaster. I could see them before I started to work the stone. As I carved with my smaller and more delicate hammer and chisel, I simply released their presence in a more tangible form. This was one of my favorite pieces, but we did not include it in the performance. A couple in London had asked me to create some sculptures for them after they saw my slide show about the World Wheel, and when they came to Pratale they chose that one and four others.

Some people in Pratale expressed surprise when I sold these sculptures. They had difficulty believing that I did not have limitless money, given that I was from the United States. In fact, most of my money had been stolen in Spain; I had arrived in Italy with less than I needed to live.

As the summer advanced, fifty newcomers camped at the farm, and Joaquin fell for a fiery Irish woman who joined us. A dance couple from Australia appeared, and two backpackers came from the United States. Several Italians also joined the mix, including Silvana, a young woman who took the lead alongside Angelo in the performance. I was overjoyed when six more friends trouped in from Spain, four of whom had participated in the ceremony near Alicante. A world family was growing!

Nonetheless, these visitors, combined with the time Etain and I spent together working on the performance, began to wear on Etain's husband, Martin. He was a man of the land, a workaholic who showed little interest in the performance. He felt that practical tasks took precedence over art. Etain withdrew from me somewhat as more visitors arrived and Martin became increasingly uncomfortable with the amount of time his wife and I spent together. I

Trinity, Umbrian Forest, Italy

heard them arguing about this. She had made the huge transition from being a city sophisticate to the country life, but Martin criticized her literary tastes and artistic inclinations.

Because of this, I moved away from my sleeping quarters in the farmhouse and pitched a tent in the forest. When I heard the howl of wolves and the squeal of wild boar at night, I asked myself, "What is this hunger for wilderness, this thirst for primal life that persists like a whispered reminder of something forgotten, irresistably drawing me to our roots, strengthening the present?"

At night, when I found time to be quiet and still, new dimensions of understanding emerged. Sometimes I saw lattices of light extending from stones, luminous patterns rising into space, as I had often seen during my five-year retreat on Boney Mountain. Initially, I had experienced this light as a sensual pulse running through my body, growing more intense until the pulse throbbed all around, in every object and in space, reaching out into the universe, vibrant streams of light, like a multidimensional spider's web.

Angelo, Silvana, Joaquin, and I rose at six every morning to meet on the edge of the forest for yoga, performance and voice exercises, and to organize our daily activities. In the evenings, we met under an old oak tree and I solicited their responses to my three questions. We discussed, wrote, acted, and sang their answers. *Where have you come from?,* I asked. Angelo answered, "Our spirit and our soul is a drop in the great lake of God. These invisible bodies have incarnated in a material, physical body, male and female, birthed by our one mother, the Earth." To the second question, *What is your sickness, your imbalance?,* he responded: "The sickness of the Italian people comes from delegating individual power to authorities as if they were supreme arbiters of the great spiritual questions." As to what can heal and bring harmony, Angelo answered, "We must stop relinquishing our own power to the church and outside authorities. Gather the good tribe and harmonize lovingly with the life that surrounds us."

Word of the World Wheel ritual had spread throughout the region and many people gathered in the forest for the commencement of the ceremony on August 15, 1989. The community in the Umbrian forest that I had visited when I first came was there. My friends from Spain arrived, and it felt as if the work was beginning to draw together the global community that I had first seen in my dream. It was one of those days when the earth smells rich with soil and leaf mold after a rain, when new grass springs up overnight, and the sky is startlingly blue behind white sculptured clouds.

The performance began with the slow emergence of Silvana and Angelo over the crests of opposite hills, representing the women and men of Umbria. As they descended to the edge of the forest, Sabrina Sannipoli, an opera diva, sang her own response to my three questions in Italian. She became a bird and lamented that her home had been taken away. Her ethereal song

Gate Guardian, *Voices of the Umbrian Forest* performance

Vijali as Stone next to sculpture *Goddess of the Underworld*

prophesied man's alienation from the earth and the loss of our own homes.

Then three hundred people walked through the seven gates along the forest pathway leading into the Underworld, where the jutting crags of limestone shape-shifted into archetypes from our collective psyche. At first it looked as if nothing existed there. But as our eyes became accustomed to the dark, the stones appeared as humans, trees began to move, and animals emerged from the shadows.

I emerged from the belly of the sculpture *Goddess of the Underworld* with my stone-looking mask and my body and sarong covered in grey mud that had dried, leaving cracks in the cloth and on the surface of my skin. I moved slowly as if I were a stone dislodging itself from the earth.

Then, as I lowered myself from the ledge where the *Goddess of the Underworld* lay, I turned my back and donned a wolf mask. Walking on all fours, I looked into the eyes of the audience and described how my wolf children had been killed.

Within the dark earthy recess, I ripped off my wolf mask and became Gaia as we re-enacted the story of Adam and Eve and the fall from grace. But our rendition differed significantly from most Sunday school interpretations. We portrayed it without the implication that knowledge or awareness is evil. In our version, man and woman took equal responsibility for their change of consciousness. The Divine was recast as an inner, rather than an outer voice, and the Serpent symbolized a positive force, the transformative energy necessary for the awakening of

Vijali as Wolf speaking to the community in the *Voices of the Umbrian Forest* performance

knowledge. The voice of God was the voice of Gaia, the Earth herself.

The ascending journey out of this dark enclave into the dappled light of the path that lead us out of the forest took on a new character. Each quality personified at the seven gates manifested its mythic counterpart. Instead of appearing menacing, the performers at each of the seven gates brimmed with life energy, offering milk, honey, wine, and fruit to all the participants as they passed. Musicians played while everyone made their way back to the courtyard for food, dance, and celebration; different languages and accents echoing in the crowd.

People had come from all over the world for this event, and many stayed at Pratale for several more days in tents erected on the green grazing slopes surrounding the housing complex. People radiated goodwill. They saw their future arising out of a profound yet practical relationship with their immediate habitat and their bio-region. Imagery created in the performance helped local participants from Umbria develop a unique community voice. Such imagery is the beginning of a fresh and revitalized contemporary mythology, something badly needed in our times.

Among those who pitched tents on the land were some of the local farm neighbors who had taught Martin and Etain to grow food and raise animals when they first moved to Pratale. They now drew up plans to help each other with sheep shearing, grape picking, and harvesting the wheat. These practical developments pleased Martin immensely, and in the glow of his gratification, Etain blossomed. Everyone seemed to feel better about themselves and their lives.

A few days after the performance, I left Pratale and my Umbrian colleagues. Joaquin and I drove south for a long stretch. We spent a day by a stream in a mountain forest and slept under the full moon at night. It got very hot as we resumed driving toward the port town of Brindisi where I planned to catch a boat for Greece. Along the way we stopped at blue lakes and running rivers, intending to drink and swim to cool ourselves. Repeatedly, however, locals warned us not to touch the polluted water. I heard stories about sickness, even death, from toxins in the watershed. At the seashore I heard the same story: Don't touch the water. A deep sadness shrouded me. What can we do? We are the earth, the universe, and we are poisoning the blood of our own body.

Drinking milk and honey on the ascent in the *Voices of the Unbrian Forest* performance

CHAPTER EIGHT

A Room of My Own

Benares, India
1972

The Room Inside

MARKELL BROOKS, from whom I had first learned about Anandamayi Ma, had arrived in Benares a few days before Dale and me, and she had arranged for us to have a private meeting with Anandamayi Ma.[11] We entered her small room. A white sheet covered her narrow bed and she sat cross-legged upon it as if she expected us. Although Anandamayi Ma was in her seventies, her hair flowed long and dark over a white sari, a radiant smile was on her lips still full and youthful, and her large almond eyes glowed. She seemed to me the essence of beauty and grace. The hair on my arms stood on end. Here was the face of my dreams, in flesh and blood!

We took our places at Ma's feet. Without any greeting she continued looking into my eyes, her smile ecstatic. For ten minutes I stayed within this first embrace. Her penetrating gaze continued, and my whole life lay bare to her. I knew instantly that she loved and accepted me without question. Eventually, Ma indicated we could ask what was on our minds. She had not spoken for two years, but she communicated to us by writing with her finger on the palm of her attendant's hand who translated for us.

I had one burning question. "I was a nun for many years in the Vedanta Society convent, and I have also followed Self-Realization and Buddhism and other traditions. But what is my real path?"

"Do what comes spontaneously," Ma replied immediately.

Twice each day, we went to the ashram to see Ma or to participate in devotional chanting. Ma had abandoned conversation, but often sang devotionals or shouted out the names of Gods and Goddesses, "Hari, Narayan, Narayan, Narayan."

After three days with Anandamayi Ma, a strong and completely unexpected feeling swept over me. Before I came to India and after I had arrived, I had been doing a lot of *japa,* the practice of chanting mantras, and *puja*, ancient Hindu rituals. I now felt ready to give them all up! This came as a shock to me. I had aspired to become an illumined person and thought I knew what I must do. I wrote in my journal: *Because of Ma's comment, I feel I am ready to drop all the prescribed rituals and practices, all the spiritual paraphernalia.*

The next day we went to the ashram for afternoon singing. We stood around for some time with a group of devotees in the main hall, waiting for Anandamayi Ma to arrive. Unaware that Ma had come in behind me and was now passing toward the front of the room, I shifted my weight and stepped back into her. Her large body felt lithe and as light as a feather as her arms steadied me.

She continued on to the front dais as the singing began. As Ma's voice leapt out above the throng, I remembered my dreams of her and how her voluptuous "Great Mother" body had surrounded me from the back as she had held me close. In awe, I thought how the cosmos repeats patterns that seem to us like accidents.

Dale and I walked out of the temple after singing and sat on the front steps of the ashram that led down into Mother Ganga, the sacred river Ganges. We watched crowds of people pass, and a beautiful little

Anandamayi Ma

girl, perhaps a year old, played at my feet. Her mother came over and held the child up in front of me and gave me what seemed like a formal lecture. Markell stood nearby. She had studied Hindi and she translated for me as the woman talked. "I am very poor. I have a large family and cannot take care of all my children. I know you will give my child a good home. Please keep her and be her mother." She placed her lovely child on my lap and disappeared into the crowd.

I had never seen a child with so much beauty, one who delighted my eyes and touched my heart so deeply. Unlike babies I had known in the United States, she was extremely delicate. As she looked up at me from under long swooping lashes, she seemed fascinated with me also. Her tiny fingers pulled at my sari. I had desired a baby of my own, but was uncertain about the responsibility and about how parenting might conflict with the life I had chosen as an artist. Well, here was this little girl on my lap! I did not ask "should I" nor "should I not." Here she was. My mind was already thinking about the details of obtaining her papers. But her grandfather, who had watched this scene, came over and snatched the child away.

As I walked with Dale from Anandamayi Ma's compound by the Ganges to our room in another ashram, I marveled at the unexpected situations that arise in India. On the day we arrived I had seen a man in the street with his skin draped over his bones, so weak he could not move. He was choking and couldn't breathe. While Dale stayed with him, I ran to hunt for a rickshaw to take him to the hospital, but when I returned he was dead, and his belongings, a water pot and a blanket, had already disappeared.

In India it seemed that all life was on the streets, unlike our own compartmentalized society where the old, the insane, and the dying are isolated, shut away in separate boxes. I saw people in the streets that would be institutionalized in the United States, and I often thought of my own mother. One man stood in his rags at the edge of the crowd, giving a speech. Another man passed by and put food down in front of him. A wandering monk passed, a *shaivite*, a follower of Shiva. He had smeared his nude body with ash, and his hair was matted above his penetrating eyes. He held a trident in one hand. Later, a procession made its way down the street to the crematorium, carrying a colorfully wrapped body garlanded with flowers. Joyous singing and cymbals accompanied them, and the *shenai,* a wind instrument, sounded like the voice of the deceased spirit. In Benares, locals believe that the soul is liberated upon death. At all hours of the day and night, we heard *Om Shiva, Shiva, Shiva.* Benares, the city of Shiva, the holy place where people come to die. It became my favorite city in the world.

Returning home, on the day of our departure from New Delhi, we learned that Anandamayi Ma had arrived in that city. We quickly packed our bags, hopped in a cab, and drove to where she was staying.

When we arrived at her ashram, an attendant said, "Ma is ill and is not seeing anyone." The attendant went to Ma's room, but in two minutes came back saying, "Ma wants to see you." As soon as we entered her room, Ma threw a garland around my neck and said, "Parvati." Then she threw a garland around Dale's neck and said, "Shiva," the consort of Parvati.

As Dale and I sat down, Ma started to laugh a raucous belly laugh. She shook all over and tears streamed from her eyes as her arms danced uncontrollably by her sides. I did not know exactly why she laughed, but soon we could not help but join her.

People in the ashram heard us and came running into the room, only to be caught up in the laughter themselves. I rolled on the floor, holding my stomach unable to catch my breath. We knew we had to leave or we would miss our plane, but we could scarcely stand! We backed down the stairs, looking at Anandamayi Ma, waving and laughing. Even after she was out of sight, we could hear her laughter following us.

When I returned to the United States from India, I chose not to do all the typical things devotees often do, like taking on Indian mannerisms and dress or meditating before pictures of gurus. Instead, I went into a deep depression. I longed more than ever to give up any preconceived ideas of a spiritual path or life. And though somewhat mystified at the time, I realized eventually that Ma's, "Do what comes spontaneously," was the most helpful spiritual suggestion I had ever received.

I had learned I could not liberate myself by sitting at the feet of Anandamayi Ma or other gurus. I had to acknowledge the guru already within. I had to find the answers in my own country, in a modern world. This was liberating, yet I felt blocked. Sometimes I felt I had exchanged the convent walls for the walls of marriage. I could never experience the spontaneity that Anandamayi Ma suggested when I had to cook three meals a day, clean up after us all, and support the household financially, all with a smile on my face.

Again I tried to talk to Dale, but he made jokes or said he was too busy. A heavy, dark bubble seemed to hang over my head, until one night it broke open in the form of a wish—the wish to live alone, away from the "shoulds" of marriage.

On a trip to Los Angeles, I found a room for rent

Anaïs Nin

on the second story of a quaint house near the beach in Venice. Though I still lived with Dale, I rented it as that longed-for luxury—a room of my own. The second story bay windows looked out over the ocean and framed the evening sunsets. All variations of life flowed through Venice, while Santa Barbara had begun to seem sterile even in its beauty. I spent a few days a month in "my room."

Dale went to Mexico for three weeks, and I spent the whole time in my Venice room, which had been freshly painted white. I ate simple food, whatever I could manage on an electric plate, and I left the room only to walk, get groceries, and use the shared bathroom. Whatever feelings and thoughts moved through me, I immediately wrote down as a journal entry or as a poem, then I drew them or I danced them.

At some point during this time, a friend put the first volume of Anaïs Nin's diaries in my hand. I devoured it. I sent her a letter through her publisher and enclosed a photo of one of my sculptural paintings. She responded immediately and invited me for tea at her home near Los Angeles.

Anaïs greeted me warmly at the door. I found her very pretty, feminine, and attractive in an old-fashioned way, with her eyebrows plucked thin and her lips painted into a bright red bow. She was then in her seventies. She led me into a living room filled with art, where windows invited the sun and garden inside. We sat on her golden couch and spoke as if we

25% Bliss

had long been intimate friends while the afternoon sun streamed through the window.

I asked her, "Do you remember the statement in your fourth diary, 'The story of complete freedom does not appear yet in this volume—the hero of this book is the malady which makes our lives a drama of compulsion instead of freedom'?"

She nodded with a smile.

"How do you feel now after so many years?"

She looked into my questioning eyes and said, "Free!"

I visited Anaïs every other week at her home.

"Publishers would not publish my work," she said once as she brought in tea on a Japanese tray. "But I was determined. I bought a press, learned the printing trade, and printed my own novellas." She filled our porcelain cups with steaming black tea, and the lingering sunlight shone through her long cotton dress, revealing a youthful body.

She sat down next to me and as she talked about her life, I could see that through persistence she had raised her own voice to the world. "Yes!" I thought. "I also want to raise my voice."

I gave up looking outside myself for the answers. I gave up teachers and scriptures, and I began to experience what was within me and around me. I started spending time alone in the Santa Ynez Mountains behind Santa Barbara, listening, listening.

One day a friend came by and I decided it would be nice to go for a walk with him, to take my sketchbook and draw, and so I did. Dale went unglued. If I wanted to be alone or read a book or happened to show an interest in something outside our routine life, he interpreted this as a lack of commitment to him. If I did work that he felt would not sell in an art show, he got upset.

Finally Dale loosened up enough to allow new activities to enter our marriage, but they were still within his control. I found it hard to breathe and would wake up in the middle of the night from dreams of my old struggle to leave the convent. Finally I stopped all compromise. I had to leave.

One day I felt my conviction strong enough to say, "Dale, I want a divorce. I feel our life has boxed me in. I struggle to find myself within our marriage, and there's no space to develop my own potential."

After seven years of marriage, Dale and I divorced. With shaking hands, he came to me with the papers for our property and house to sign over to him. I did.

I moved into an old warehouse by the ocean in Santa Barbara. I repaired, painted, and made the warehouse livable. I created a makeshift kitchen, and used a bright yellow tub left by the former tenant for my bath. My studio was a large open space lined with rows of windows. Pillars supported the ceiling. The open space invited dancing, and I often found myself whirling and leaping between the green potted plants hanging from the ceiling. An old piano with its stringed insides exposed sat at one end of this space, shielding a view of pipes and a water heater. Sometimes late at night, I would put my hands on the strings and play until the space was vibrating with sound.

Toward the back of this large area, I placed tables and a hefty wooden easel that held a sculptured painting of synthetic stone. A former storage room became my meditation room. I covered its floor with a goatskin rug and set a *tambura*—an Indian stringed instrument—in one corner and tabla drums in the other. In another tiny storage room I put a foam mattress on the floor for my bed and a folding cot, which I eventually used to give acupressure treatments. I covered the walls with massive sculptured marble paintings, products of the past nine years—female figures twisting, floating, moving out of the surfaces.

The black cat of the neighborhood, Midnight, believed that this was his home, too, and he often crawled in through open windows. This was an industrial area only a few yards from the beach, so sometimes I could hear the waves over the hum of the gas-run blowers used by the sculptor next door. At last, my own personal sanctuary!

I lived here alone for three years, giving weekly poetry readings, "Art from Within" workshops, and art exhibitions of my work. Soon I had more commissions than I could handle and many new friends. Finally, I lived a "normal" life. But the art scene still felt too commercial. My art had become a commodity, packaged and no longer grounded in real life. My spirit was still bound.

One quiet evening, while sitting in the small meditation room, I had a profound experience. Slow heat rose from my heart. It burned its way up through my spine and seemed to explode out the top of my head. I had the sensation that my body, the goatskin rug, the wooden floor beneath me, the drums and *tambura*, even the granite stone, were all melting into a great ocean of breathing, pulsating light. Sweat poured from me and I thought I must be dying. Nine interminable hours later, when the energy subsided, my world had changed forever.

95% Bliss

CHAPTER NINE

World Wheel-Spoke Five

Tinos, Greece

1989

Serpent, Tinos, Greece

I SAILED FROM ITALY to Greece in wind and tempestuous water. In the boat, I held onto the railing with all my strength, as enormous swells of the Adriatic Sea rolled our vessel from side to side. Waves splashed against my face, and chairs and tables screeched as they slid across the deck. A sailor ordered me below, taking my hand to half guide, half drag me across the pitching deck. I hated to separate myself from nature's testy spirit, and I pulled back to catch a glimpse of purple clouds rimmed in orange, the last light of day.

By the next morning the storm had passed, and I caught my first view of Greece. Powerful shapes of earth and stone rose from the sea and then disappeared as the waves crashed into the rugged coastline.

We entered the Gulf of Corinth surrounded by Hellenic land. After we docked, I took the bus to Athens. Gasoline fumes and the constant honking of cars in Athens assaulted me after the morning's soothing sea ride. As the sky darkened, I still had no place to spend the night. A Greek woman who had attended my lecture at the October Gallery in London had given me the telephone number of Ingrid Fragantoni, an architect living in Athens. I dialed her number and she soon invited me—a stranger on the telephone—to her home. What sweet relief!

A vivacious woman with long brown hair, tanned skin, and penetrating blue grey eyes, Ingrid welcomed me and led me into the living room, where the stark black and white decor reflected her taste as a designer. Born in Austria, Ingrid considered herself Greek after having lived for fifteen years in Athens. We sat on a black leather sofa and she looked at photos of my sculptures while I explained my peace project. She immediately suggested possible sites and people to contact.

The next day, Ingrid introduced me to two strong Greek women who were part of her circle of friends—Paula, an artist and dancer, and Maya, a musician.

As the evening progressed, I asked my three questions. To the first, *What are our origins?,* they replied, "We come from the elements of nature." To the second, *What is our sickness, our imbalance?,* they answered, "We have a Greek arrogance that often leads to rivalry and jealousy. We try to hinder someone who gets a break and becomes famous. We cut them down instead of supporting them." To my third question, *What can heal this sickness?,* they responded, "We need to love and support one other." Many times in Greece, I asked these questions and many times received similar responses.

My new friends suggested several sacred spots to visit, as well as possible sites for the World Wheel sculpture and performance. But first I wanted to make my own pilgrimage to Delphi, Greece's most sacred ancient site. I took a bus from Athens to Delphi and arrived in the late afternoon. On the slopes of Mt. Parnassus, I sought out the ancient Castalian Spring that flowed through a narrow gorge of vertical rock walls. Laurel trees grew at the entrance, and to the right votives burned in four niches cut into the cliff to mark the sacredness of the spot. I drank deeply, intuitively, and dipped my head into the water as a purification of my body and mind in preparation for my work in Greece. Later, I learned that this bathing of the hair was a ceremony of purification in ancient Greek times.

Hiking back along the road, up a steep hill still paved with stones, I arrived at the ruins of the Apollo temple, built over an ancient sanctuary of Gaia, one of the chthonic deities that predated the Olympian gods. The myth of Apollo's slaughter of the gigantic serpent Python, representing the feminine power, tells of Gaia's dethroning. The ascension of Apollo and the killing of a sacred earth creature symbolized not only the triumph of the Olympians, but also the patriarchy which subdued and eventually destroyed the older matriarchal society.

I turned back and looked out over a sea of olive trees that followed the slope toward the Gulf of Itea. Then, as I walked around the temple, my body became more and more sensitive, as if it had soaked up the wisdom stored within the rocks and earth. I knelt and gathered small stones and soil as I asked permission of Gaia to take her spirit with me in these forms.

I recalled the story of how the oracular priestess, Pythia, spoke the words of the Goddess, muttering her prophecies in verse after inhaling the trance-inducing fumes from a nearby chasm. I could imagine her chewing laurel leaves, pausing from time to time to drink water drawn from the Castalian Spring.

Robert Graves tells us in *The Greek Myths* that Pythia represents the power of prophecy, the only magical power left to women who had been reduced to the status of chattel.[12] After the conquest of Apollo she retained her ancient role, but became a mouthpiece for the God rather than the Goddess herself.

As it grew late, guards closed the area, so I found my way down to the sea. On a private sandy bay, I set up my tent and in my dreams a priestess sang to me. The tones of her voice gave me energy and inspired me to fly. I flew above a crowd of people and my body whirled and danced in the air. I awoke in the middle of the night, went back to sleep, and entered the same dream. It was almost as if the energy from Gaia's sanctuary had triggered the ecstasy of the ancient Pythia.

In the morning I sat outside my tent and read the ancient Greek prophecies in Edith Hamilton's *Mythology*.[13]

> "The fifth race is that which is now upon the earth, the iron race. They live in evil times and their nature, too, has much of evil, so that they never have rest from toil and sorrow. As the generations pass, they grow worse; sons are always inferior to their fathers. A time will come when they have grown so wicked that they will worship power; might will be right to them, and reverence for the good will cease to be. At last when no man is angry any more at wrong-doing or feels shame in the presence of the miserable, Zeus will destroy them too. *And yet even then something might be done, if only the common people would arise and put down rulers that oppress them.*" [My emphasis]

After my pilgrimage to Delphi, I sought out a site for my work. My friends in Athens had cottages at Epidauros, an ancient healing place, and at Tyros along the east Peloponnesian coast. I visited these places, yet as beautiful as they were, they did not enter my dreams or resonate within me.

I returned to Athens and there met Xenophon Giatagama. He told me about the beauty of Tinos, one of the northernmost islands of the Cyclades, an archipelago of some fifty-six islands, southeast of Athens in the Aegean Sea. These ancient islands were inhabited as early as the Mesolithic period, seventh millennium BCE. He owned three cottages there and offered to let me use one. Several days later, I left on the ferry from Rafina for the four and a half hour trip to Tinos.

The boat was loaded with Greek pilgrims. The moment I stepped off the boat at Tinos, the passion of the eager pilgrims swept me along. I set off to see the famous miracle-working icon of the Virgin, Megalokhari, whose name means "Great Joy." Megalokhari, once buried for centuries, had been recovered in 1822 as a result of the visions of a nun named Pelagia.

A huge crowd of Sunday worshippers, some walking, some crawling, surged up a broad avenue leading to the Greek Orthodox Church of the Annunciation. These throngs arrived here every week from all over the world to receive blessing or hoping for a miracle through their connection with the icon.

Worshipers and hopefuls packed the church. Ordinarily I would avoid such a crowd, but the priest's singing drew me like a magnet, inch by inch through the throng and into the Panayia Evanghelistra, as the locals called the church. Something sounded familiar to me and I remembered my dream, in which a priestess chanted a similar penetrating refrain with the same fervor as the priest high in his pulpit.

People milled around, kissing the ancient icons on the walls and in the shrines, lighting tall beeswax candles. They deposited *ex-votos*—small objects shaped like the part of the body they wanted healed—praying, weeping, all with passionate intensity. The air grew thick with smoke and the scent of incense and burning wax. Filigree marble carvings covered the window like lacy blinds. I saw evidence of the pilgrims' devotion by the icons that were so covered by silver, jewels, and pearls—added by those who had been healed by the images—that the painted faces and hands had become barely visible.

Beneath the church, I joined other pilgrims to collect water from the ancient spring and soil from the spot where archeologists had found the icon. Something about this spot had drawn the people of Tinos here for centuries. To honor this sacred spot they had built, in Hellenic times, a Dionysian temple, and, later, a church. The hands of many pilgrims, likely unaware of the temple's ancient origins, had rubbed the stones smooth.

I left the church and temple behind and found my way to the nearby village in search of my friend's cottage. My love of stone warmed me to this bare and rugged island, where rocks studded the fields and bordered them in walls. Tiny stone houses sheltered goats and sheep in stormy weather. In the villages, the islanders had built simple cottages of stone which they painted a pristine white so that they gleamed brightly against the sea. Blue doors and sometimes blue window frames corresponded naturally with the environment. Even the narrow village streets, too small for cars, had been whitewashed and painted gaily with flowers. Along these pathways farmers brought fresh vegetables from the fields on the backs of donkeys.

Arriving at Ktikados, I followed Xenophon's instructions to go to the local taverna and find someone to take me to his home. The thick stone walls of Xenophon's traditional cottage immediately charmed me, and I noted with pleasure the marble insets carved with floral and animal designs over doors and windows. From the second floor I had a spectacular view of the sea and of fields with grazing goats. I met my neighbor, an elderly Greek man who came home from his fields every day and led his donkey into the ground floor of his house. This harmonious living arrangement between people and animals is typical of the island, providing shelter for the animals and warmth for the human inhabitants above. As I got to know the people of the village, it touched me that they did not treat me like a tourist, but allowed me to move about my day as one of them.

I hiked to a hill near the cottage and followed a dirt path to a ridge where I discovered a tiny white chapel. These small shrines could be found in the most inspiring places, often built on top of ancient pagan sanctuaries. A gust of wind almost knocked me off the ridge as I approached the shrine. The door had to be pried open, but once inside I felt protected from the elements. I lay down on a wooden bench, overwhelmed by the forces of earth and the heightened current of energy running through me. After some time, I rose, dropped a few coins in the offering box, and lit the incense and candles that lay on the windowsill. As their fragrance filled the chapel, I slowly circled the icon from which the Virgin, Protectress of Foreigners, smiled down on me.

The wind died down for a moment and I hiked farther along the path, toward a canyon sloping to the sea. Not far from the chapel the cry of a young goat caught my attention, so I walked over to investigate. She staggered around, looking for her mother, still wet with membranes from the afterbirth. I held her in my arms until her bleating subsided, then laid the kid in the grass close to her grazing mother and returned to the path.

On my left I saw a massive grey-green rock formation pierced by oval window-like openings that framed magnificent vistas of the azure sea. As I crawled through one of these holes, I realized that the wind had carved them, a wind so strong I could barely catch my breath. I had to lie flat on my belly to avoid being knocked off my feet.

I continued my descent down the trail, the sun warming my back. I felt as if I floated over the land and touched the sea on all sides simultaneously until I reached the bottom of the hill and, with feet firmly planted on the ground, watched the locals farmers move about with their flocks of goats and wandering cows.

Though I scouted other places for the World Wheel sculpture and ceremony, I always felt a thread connecting me to Tinos, pulling me back when I visited anywhere else in Greece. Finally, against the warnings of my friends in Athens who said the inhabitants would neither understand the World Wheel nor attend an unorthodox ceremony, I settled upon Tinos as the fifth spoke of the World Wheel.

Tinos had captured my heart. I felt strength in the land, something intrinsic there that accounted for the island's reputation as a healing place. Besides the miracle-working spring and icon, snakes once abounded on Tinos. They were used in ancient healing practices and so gave the island its original name, Phidusa, the Place of the Snakes. I felt tied to Tinos by an umbilical cord. I could stray, but I could not stay away.

Returning to Tinos felt like returning home, and I found my way back to the guesthouse Xenophon had offered me. The first morning I awoke in my new home, I wrote in my journal:

Today I organized my house: writing space, meditation space, painting space, and sculpting space, while the radio sang out popular Greek music and made me want to dance and make love and weep for the beloved.

A journalist friend of Ingrid's published an article about me and the World Wheel in a prominent magazine in Athens. As a result, I received a call from a Greek artist who gave me the name of a woman on Tinos who might help me.

Maria impressed me immediately with her warm heart and willingness to translate for me on an island where *no one* spoke English. Through her I met Polyxeni, who would be one of the performers in the final performance, and other islanders who suggested possible locations for the work. Things went so well in those first weeks that I half awaited some difficult moment to arise.

I spent a few days exploring the island, traveling to all the quarries and gathering the green, white, and gray marble for which Tinos had became known through the millennia. In the town of Pirgos I talked with artists and artisans in their studios as they carved the local marble. In the tradition of the island, they created statues and window inserts with intricate bird and flower designs.

Around the island, in the numerous tiny bays unaltered by humans, I gathered marble tumbled by the hand of the sea, smooth flat pieces of the sort once carved into the goddess images during the early Bronze Age (now referred to as "plank idols"). The carvings are highly schematized images of the Neolithic Mother Goddess and her descendants. Most of these marble statuettes found on the Cycladic islands stem from the Early Minoan period and represent females, givers of life, with arms folded across their abdomens.

From my journal, October 19, 1989:

Today I found the site! It has been here all the time, waiting. It is everything and more than I have always dreamed for a sacred site: fresh water running into a tiny bay where the sea has eroded caves and mythical forms into granite. The choice reflects my feeling about Greece—the harmonious relationship between water and stone, the unconscious and the manifest. The granite has high iron content, and the sea and air have oxidized it, giving it an orange tint. The warm color of its forms flows into the deep Mediterranean blue of the sea as if it has captured a sunset and frozen it in time. Immediately, I saw Aphrodite rising out of the sea and Gaia stirring slowly in the cave. The wind blew and wave hands beat against stone as Poseidon created his sea music. I built a fire in the cave and gave thanks to this place. On leaving, I cried out into the winds, efharisto. *Thank you.*

Raphael, a friend of Xenophon, agreed to help me get permission to sculpt and perform at the site, Livada Bay. He took me to the tiny village of Mircini, the town next to Livada Bay, to meet Antonis Darmie, the mayor of the town that owned the property where I wished to work. I took my portfolio, anticipating a quiet meeting with a venerable gentleman. As it turned out, we sat in the local tavern and men drifted in from work, drinking round after round of *raki*, the fiery biting liquor distilled from local grain, grapes, and plums. Many of the men worked as goat herders, and carried the smell of their charges on their clothes. As the evening wore on, I began to feel as though I were in a Fellini movie. The weather-beaten faces, squint-eyed and gap-toothed, the gnarled hands and twisted bodies combined with the *raki* to place me in a surreal dream. With talk all around and no idea of what anyone said, I could only watch as more and more men converged on our table to consume more and more rounds of liquor. At midnight when we left, Raphael turned to me and said, "You have permission."

The next day, now having permission, I wandered around Livada looking with new eyes. On the ridge I saw giant stone eggs, broken open to release new life toward the sea—giant stone fish, tortoises, and dolphins, all carved into smooth shapes by the wind. The Greek myth of the Universal Egg laid by the first goddess Eurynome, creator of all things, had materialized in this place! After coupling with her creatures, the serpent Ophion and the North Wind, Eurynome took the form of a dove and laid the egg that hatched all heavenly and earthly things.

I found a path through boulders down to the sea. A light green snake, descendent of Ophion, slithered under a bush and a dove flew up from the same bush into the sky. After I had explored the entire area, I chose to work where sea fingers pressed into eroded folds of stone, creating sea music, groaning, clapping against the stone, biting into stone flesh, shaping rock as rock shaped the sea. A natural amphitheater for the performance already existed here, and any voice or instrument would have to honor this natural "instrument" first.

As I sat on a boulder overlooking the expanse of water, I reflected on my decision to remain celibate until I completed the World Wheel. In my youth I had sought sexuality, and I remembered how I had longed for a soul mate. Even though I had married, I felt I had not yet found my true companion. Back then I saw friends around me find life partners and marry, and I wondered if something was wrong with me, if I was an outcast from that process of life. In the night I would cry out, "Where are you?"

But now I did not long for anything. I felt free to experience something more intense and sensual, not connected to a single person. The beloved accompanied me all the time, in different clothes than my earlier fantasies had conjured—in the warmth of the earth caressing my feet, in the hardness of stone pressing against my thigh, in the howling wind that wrapped its arms around me, in the eyes of children as I took my morning walk, in everything I saw or felt or touched.

The sun sank into the earth, turning both the sky and me orange like the stone I stood on. Darkness fell and I gathered my belongings, slid down from my stone seat, and found my way home through the shadowy maze of boulders.

The next morning, I arose early and cooked a rice and vegetable casserole for my lunch at Livada Bay. With my sketchbook and carving tools, I walked four miles on the narrow road that wound past waking villages, through valleys pungent with herbs. As I neared Livada, I looked down on the sparkling bay with its fresh stream flowing over tumbled red, black, green, and white stone toward the sea. Antonis sat on the far hill with his youngest son, tending their herd of goats. He waved as I passed.

I hiked over the hill and as I descended my eye caught a prominent stone by the edge of the water. Its swelling shape suggested a giant serpent rising out of the surface, like the sacred Python rising from the mud after the Deucalion deluge. In Ancient Greece the snake symbolized life's renewal. Asclepius, the physician healer, kept snakes at his sanctuary in Epidauros.

I drew the image of the serpent I had seen in the granite and then began to carve its outline. A few days earlier I had removed a small test stone from the area and had learned that the stone on this site was *hard!* The first pound of the hammer blunted my chisel point beyond use. I had bought the chisel two days earlier from an islander who said he had made it for granite. I didn't believe him, but bought it optimistically hoping he was right. My carbide chisels from New York would hold up for awhile, but even they did not last for the completion of this piece, which was so large I had to view it from the adjoining cliff to gain the correct perspective. Antonis walked over from tending his sheep, watched me for awhile, and then, with hand gestures, indicated a slight change in the curve of the snake's tail. I immediately made the correction and drew the new curve on the boulder where I would begin work the next day.

Serpent sculpture, Tinos, Greece

November 2, 1989:

> *The serpent is alive, moving in the stone as I release her form day by day with my chisels. I carry my tools to the site in my backpack: two sizes of hammers, one for the initial work of removing stone and a lighter hammer for details. I use two chisels, a flat head and point, a carborundum stone for sanding the surface smooth if I wish, and paint. These simple tools have allowed me to work without electricity. They have made the entire world my studio.*

The work on the stone was very slow. Day by day I released the natural serpent from the top of the boulder with carbide-tipped chisels I sharpened twice a day. I had never worked on harder granite. It ate away at my tools and resisted any carving at all. My body felt strained and the joints in my fingers, wrists, and elbows ached.

While I worked with hammer and chisel, the performance came to me. I saw characters moving across the landscape, from under rocks and out of caves, speaking into the wind, moving with the rhythm of the sea.

After lunch, I visited one of the caves and sat inside, as if within the bowels of an animal, looking out through its open mouth. This earth-house resonated as "home." As I sat there, I felt a burning sadness, the feeling that I had not yet fully communicated through my life and work the borderless view that was my constant reality. What else is the artist's moral obligation, if not to show a vision

Vijali with *Serpent* sculpture

of life, some fresh opening into the opaqueness of our conditioned experience?

In the mornings I worked on the serpent, and in the afternoons I prepared the ceiling and a wall of the cave which I called *Gaia's Laboratory*. I smoothed six natural recesses into organic shapes and then painted the spirits of the elements—water, air, earth, and fire—in bright, enamel-like colors. With more somber tones I painted what I termed *The Matrix Web*, showing a human head within a web that connected us to the earth and universe.

Friends arrived to help me with the project. Paula Lakah, who I had met in Athens, was in her thirties, with light brown hair and voluptuous features and figure. Everything she touched became artistic. Joaquin came from Spain with his yellow two-cylinder Citroën. He had become a skilled sculptor and budding performer in the process of creating the last two World Wheel spokes in Spain and Italy, and he

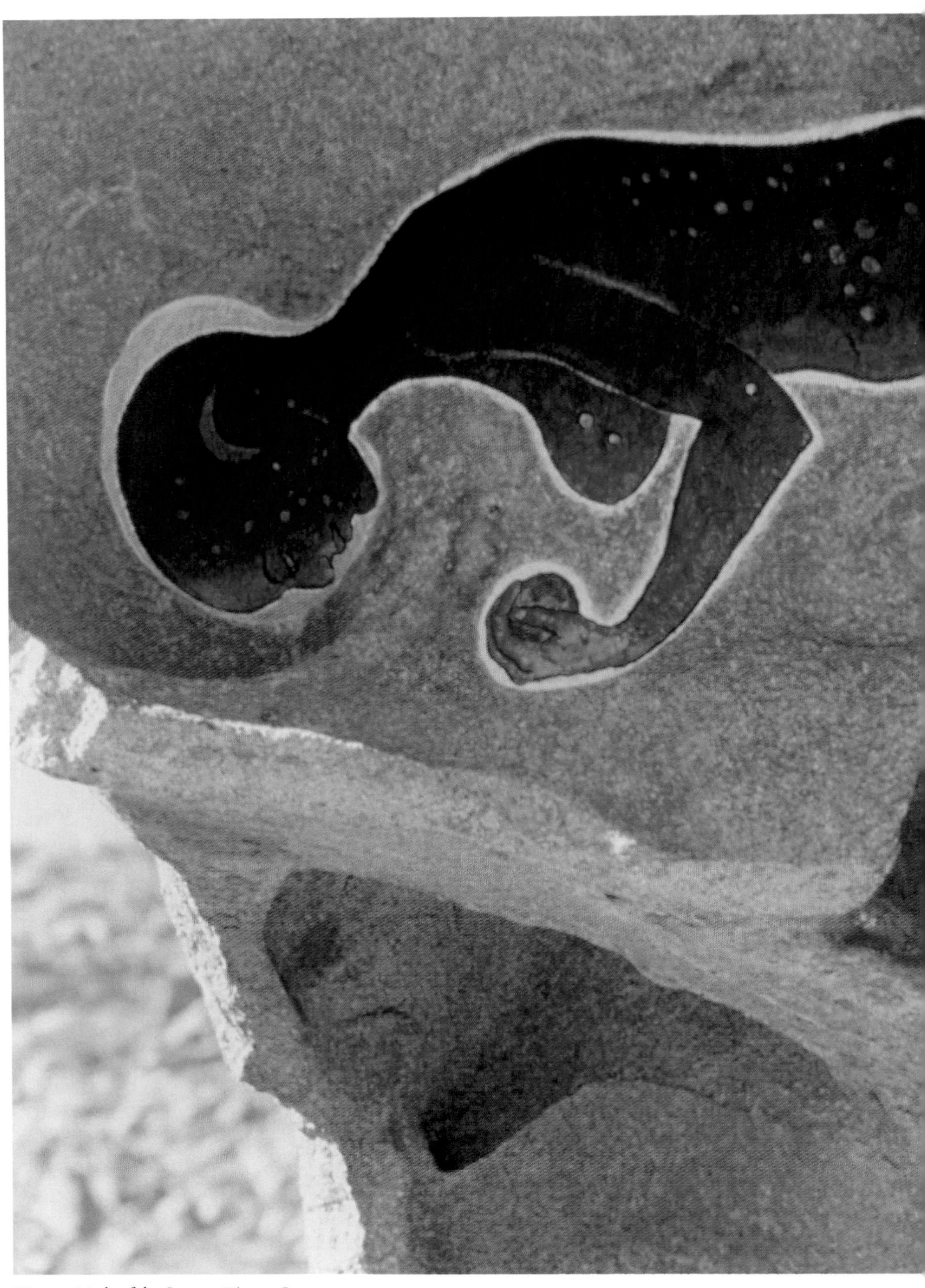

Woman Made of the Cosmos, Tinos, Greece

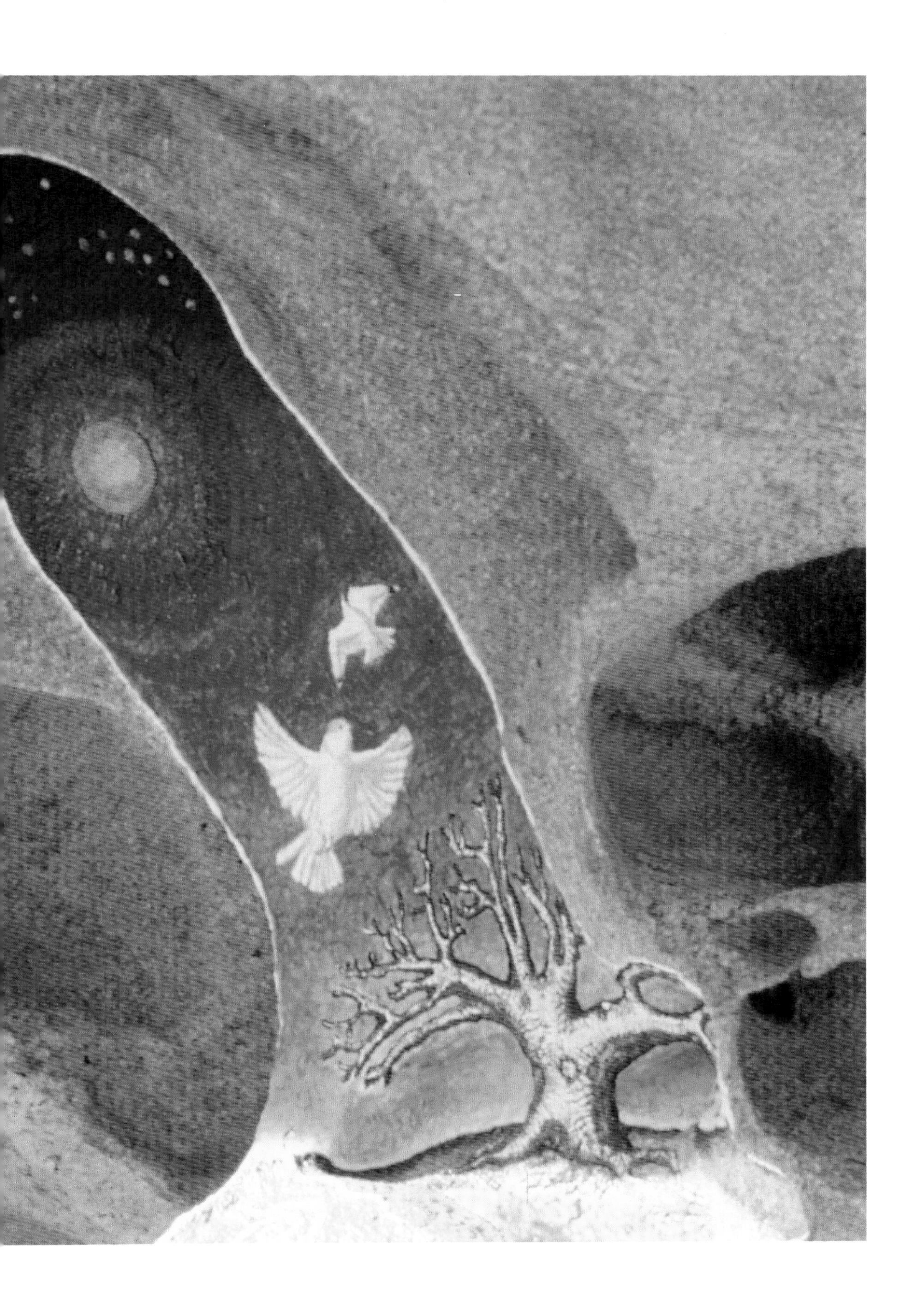

wanted to participate in as many of the events as he could. The three of us drove to Livada each day to work. Joaquin helped carve the serpent, and together we gathered pebbles from the surf for a medicine wheel on the floor of Gaia's cave. We pressed the colored stones into the earth, like a pebble mosaic. On four sides we dug holes and filled them with small red, yellow, white and black stones to represent the cardinal directions.

In Athens, I hunted for a lead actress for the performance. I had the name of a woman, Katarini Razelou, whom I called and asked to meet at Ingrid's apartment. She was in her early forties, of medium height with long jet-black hair, penetrating blue eyes, and the features of a classical Greek goddess. Her voice and gestures were dramatic. She had acted in ancient Greek and Shakespearian plays, in Greek films, and also read literature on her weekly radio program.

Katarini brimmed with enthusiasm and ideas. On learning that I intended for the story to present the archetypal contemporary woman from a Greek perspective, she went home to ponder the questions quietly and to write the life story of this woman in diary form. After she left, I danced in Ingrid's living room expressing the joy I felt from our meeting.

The next day, Katerini returned with me by boat to Tinos, and we began to script the performance. As an actress, her great fear was the loss of youth. The solution, she thought, was to find beauty in each moment. She wanted her performance to reflect that.

I also wanted to acknowledge the strength of women and the need to balance feminine and masculine power. I began to work with Polyxeni Evangelatou, a young art student living on Tinos. She and Joaquin would play the roles of the internal feminine and masculine within Katerini. We decided to call the performance *Phidusa Snake Woman,* recalling the ancient name for Tinos.

I had located a second cave, which would be Phidusa's cave, at the crest of a ridge overlooking the sea. I worked there every day, often in terrible winds. I had already smoothed the stone walls of the cave and was working on a figure I called *Woman Made of the Cosmos,*

Woman Made of the Cosmos (detail)

who represented our true nature as part of the cosmos. The upper part of her body was the starry sky, while her lower half contained a Tinos landscape with tree, pond, snake, and doves, representing all of the earth. In her hand, she held the world globe. This image emerged out of my own fleeting memories of birth, of Nut, the Egyptian goddess whose body formed the vast sky, and of Kali, who contained the whole process of life, birth and death, preservation and destruction within her form. An image of who we really are!

It was freezing cold on the last day of my work on the painting. I built a fire, but got mostly smoke, as this was the windiest point of the site. I stuck my paintbrush into the holes I had cut in my gloves for my finger tips. With stiff, frozen joints, I painted the last strokes of earth for Phidusa's feet. The wind carried paint from my brush and streaked the stone with yellow and blue that I would have to chisel off the next day.

While I was working, Antonis came by and watched for an hour. He seemed impressed by how I continued to work in the relentless winds and cold, just like the shepherds and farmers of the island. He spread the word and my dedication seemed to earn me the respect of the islanders.

Katarini arrived with a draft of the script. At Livada Bay, in the freezing cold, we worked together to develop the choreography so she could rehearse portions of the script in different locations. Polyxeni developed her part as Phidusa Woman's spirit.

A great freeze with snow arrived on the performance day, and I had to postpone the performance until the following weekend. Almost everyone had the flu—Katarini and my other friends from Athens, many of whom had planned to be part of the performance. I had taken a six-hour hike to center myself, and the icy wind—its breath piercing nostrils, eyes, and ears—had brought on a sore throat and bronchitis.

To my great joy, Shirley Graham, a friend from California, arrived. And then Jan Semmel, friend and owner of the World Wheel site in Spain, came with a couple of his friends. Together we created a scroll to commemorate the performance and our time on Tinos, including in it some of the sculpture images and words from the script. We sealed the scroll in a waterproof container and ceremonially buried it deep in the earth of Gaia's cave.

My friends had told me not to feel hurt if the islanders didn't come to the performance. "They only go to church festivals, family dinners, and the yearly killing of the pig," they said.

But to my surprise, the whole island stirred over the World Wheel event. The mayor came and even the priests from both the Catholic and Greek Orthodox churches came. Their congregations, who were usually locked in conflict, arrived and mingled—a rare event. The children and teenagers of the island came, as well as the elders. Altogether, about three hundred people gathered in Livada Bay.

The storm had lifted, leaving a magnificent day with just enough wind to make the water sing and to play with the the hair and the clothes of the performers. The story was about a Greek woman named Phidusa, played by Katarini, who brought the voices of the past into harmony with the present. She asked herself the questions of life: *Where do I come from? Who am I? Where do I go?* She recounted the history of Greece and how she came finally to Livada to find herself and become healed. Polyxeni, as her spirit, stood silhouetted against the sky as the people of the island gathered at the bay.

Phidusa leaned against a giant boulder and spoke. "I come from time. At a specific moment in time I was born. *He* bore me. Time. In this country called Greece, ancient and modern, mystical and bright, pagan and Christian Orthodox, I carry in my cells Homer's poems. I carry the philosophical conception of Ephessos, and yet I am here. The flourishing explosion of arts and science of ancient Greece are married to the severe spiritualism of Byzantium. The twelve Gods of Olympus and the Greek Orthodox Christianity are both here under this sun, the Mediterranean sun, at this sea, the Aegean Sea, Aegean, *mare nostrum*."

She wandered through the forest of boulders and came to the first cave, where she touched the plants which formed the cape of Gaia, in which I was costumed. She talked to the earth, and asked for her help and wisdom. The cave represented Gaia's laboratory in which she mixed the elements for creation.

Vijali as Seaweed Gaia in the *Phidusa Woman* performance

As Phidusa talked to the earth, the earth rose and became the figure of Gaia. Phidusa sat in amazement as I lit sage by the fire and blew smoke over her with a feather. From one of the four piles of stones in front of me, I picked a white stone for wisdom and gave it to Phidusa. Phidusa then caught sight of the cave paintings, and she rose to explore the rest of the cave.

The audience followed her, each one entering the cave. I, as Gaia, picked one stone to contain a seed of wisdom for each individual and placed it in his or her hand. I remember the look of childlike innocence and awe on their faces as they came to me and received a stone. They held it with great love; some cried. Each then continued their own journey through the wilderness of boulders. At the top of a hill, Phidusa entered another cave and fell down in prayer. As she wept, she raised her head and saw a vision of herself represented in an immense cave painting, *Woman Made of the Cosmos.*

In the painting, the island—with its waters and snakes—represented Phidusa's feet. From a tree, the white pigeons of Tinos rose. In Phidusa's cosmic body, she held the sun and moon and the stars. Around her head glowed a halo, and in her hand she held the earth.

Now Phidusa rose, carrying this vision of herself in her heart, and continued her journey toward the sea. She descended to a rock jutting out over the water, where she was drawn irresistibly to the giant yellow serpent carved in the granite stone. She stood on the rock and gazed pensively out to sea. The audience gathered on the boulders around her. Poseidon's music—the sound of waves breaking against eroded granite—filled the air.

Finally, Phidusa spoke. "I look at the sea, this sea, immense, blue, omnipotent, and at these rocks, gnawed, chiseled by her, but still solid and resisting, and I think how this landscape will change. Little by little the sea will eat the rocks—even this stable, immovable rock that I stand on now, after thousands of years, will no longer exist!"

Greek musicians playing in the *Phidusa Woman* performance

Sea the Unconscious, dancer Shirley Graham, in the *Phidusa Woman* performance

After saying this, Phidusa sank down into the stone and fell asleep with the serpent to dream of Gaia. I appeared as Gaia on the horizon, then descended dreamlike to the stone where Phidusa slept and touched her. Gaia plucked some berries from her cape and left them by Phidusa's side. Then she faded away as in a dream. Phidusa stirred, conscious of some strange new life in her. She awoke with the wisdom of the earth, cured of her agony. Then the sea drew Phidusa, and she baptized herself with the seawater that remained in a natural basin in the stone.

"But there is beauty in each separate moment," Phidusa continued, "in this exact moment while we are alive and healthy under this sun, at this amazing bay. We can see, feel, taste. And if we feel the vividness of each moment, we abolish time because each minute becomes an eternity. This is the secret of happiness."

Next, Shirley, as "The Sea" (I had painted her face blue and white as a seascape) representing the unconscious, danced as waves with each person in the audience as they passed through the unconscious on their way to the second bay, "Consciousness."

The participants climbed over a high ridge and descended into a mysterious bay of black stone. Phidusa sat on a jutting section of the gigantic black wall of stone, looking out into the sea, and seemed at peace. From the black wall emerged her inner form of man and woman. Joaquin and Polyxeni ran towards each other, leapt into the air, and found each other in an embrace as the sea gathered around their feet. Joyfully, they ran toward a tall tower of driftwood and set it ablaze.

Phidusa rose and musicians from the island played Greek island music while she drew the audience into her circle to dance.

That evening, after the performance, Mircini, the closest village to Livada, gave a festival to honor the World Wheel event. In between Greek music, dance, and food, the people of the island gave speeches to me, and read poetry they had written expressing their gratitude, their love of the sculptures and the performance, and their pleasure at being given this connection to a larger spiritual family. Many of them said that we had shown them the beauty of their own land and had reconnected them with its spiritual force.

One elderly woman, the mother of Rigos, the postman, had tears in her eyes as she held my hand and said, "The young ones here have lost connection with the church. Your sculptures and ceremony have given them a spiritual form with which they can relate."

This is exactly what I had hoped for—an emerging mythology that was relevant to our difficult modern times.

At the end of the festival the villagers danced. Danced? No, they *became* gods and goddesses. Their earthly faces and work-worn bodies became radiant, transfused with light and joy. Of all the gifts they offered me, this was the greatest.

Vijali as Seaweed Gaia at the Aegean Sea

CHAPTER TEN

Kundalini

Santa Barbara, California
1976

Within (detail)

MORNING FINALLY CAME and with it, exhaustion. I leaned into the large rust-colored pillows on the rattan-covered floor in my studio, pulled a Peruvian llama blanket up over my shoulders, and closed my eyes. I wanted to sleep, but the images and feelings from the night's tremendous experience haunted me and struggled to take shape again. I reached for my leather-bound journal and recorded the experience as if it were happening all over again.

July 8, 1976:

> *I am siting on the floor of my studio with a cup of freshly picked sage tea, relaxing after supper and studying the sculptural painting I completed this afternoon. An intense and foreign feeling suddenly radiates from my chest and grows as hot as the sun as it slowly rises up my spine. Each breath becomes more difficult. I try to hold on, but my sense of self is no longer confined to my body—it expands outward. My point of observation is now from a great distance. I look through a billion eyes in every direction. I must stop this force that has taken hold of me, but I can't. I am propelled by some energy beyond my control. My body is rigid. I am unable to move. I cannot speak, yet I am excruciatingly conscious. To pass out now would be a great relief! Every detail of both the studio and my body is painfully clear. My fear and panic increase in proportion to the heat and energy rising within. I think that I am surely going insane. Am I dying? The flaming sun-force moves up through my neck and into the center of my head. I see blinding light. This blasting force moves through the crown of my head out into the space above my body. My perception changes—everything becomes radiant light. My body, the pillows, the floor I sit on, the space itself, all of it—the table, cushions, and hanging plants—breathe, quiver, and melt into one boiling, pulsating ocean of light. The world I am accustomed to dissolves into open space. The world continues in a new frequency, pulsing, merging, uniting.*
>
> *I have lost sense of time. Hours may have passed. I have no way of knowing. The energy moves downward, my body becomes heavy again. The heat subsides. The hardness of the floor returns and brings me back into a world of separations. But this knowing stays with me: This world of seeming divisions is really one endless buoyant sea of light. Dawn slowly emerges. The light in the sky becomes brighter as my own light recedes, cools, dims to apparent, solid boundaries.*

I put down my journal and buried my face in the voluptuous pillows in an attempt to get some early morning rest. But thoughts kept hounding me. The sensations that moved up my spine, the light, was this the Kundalini energy I had read about? Why the panic? Was something wrong with me? And the deeper fear: was I schizophrenic like my mother?

I pulled a book from my shelves and read: "The word 'Kundalini' means 'That which is coiled up,' like a serpent, traditionally explained as an energy lying dormant at the base of the spine. When

Roots of Consciousness

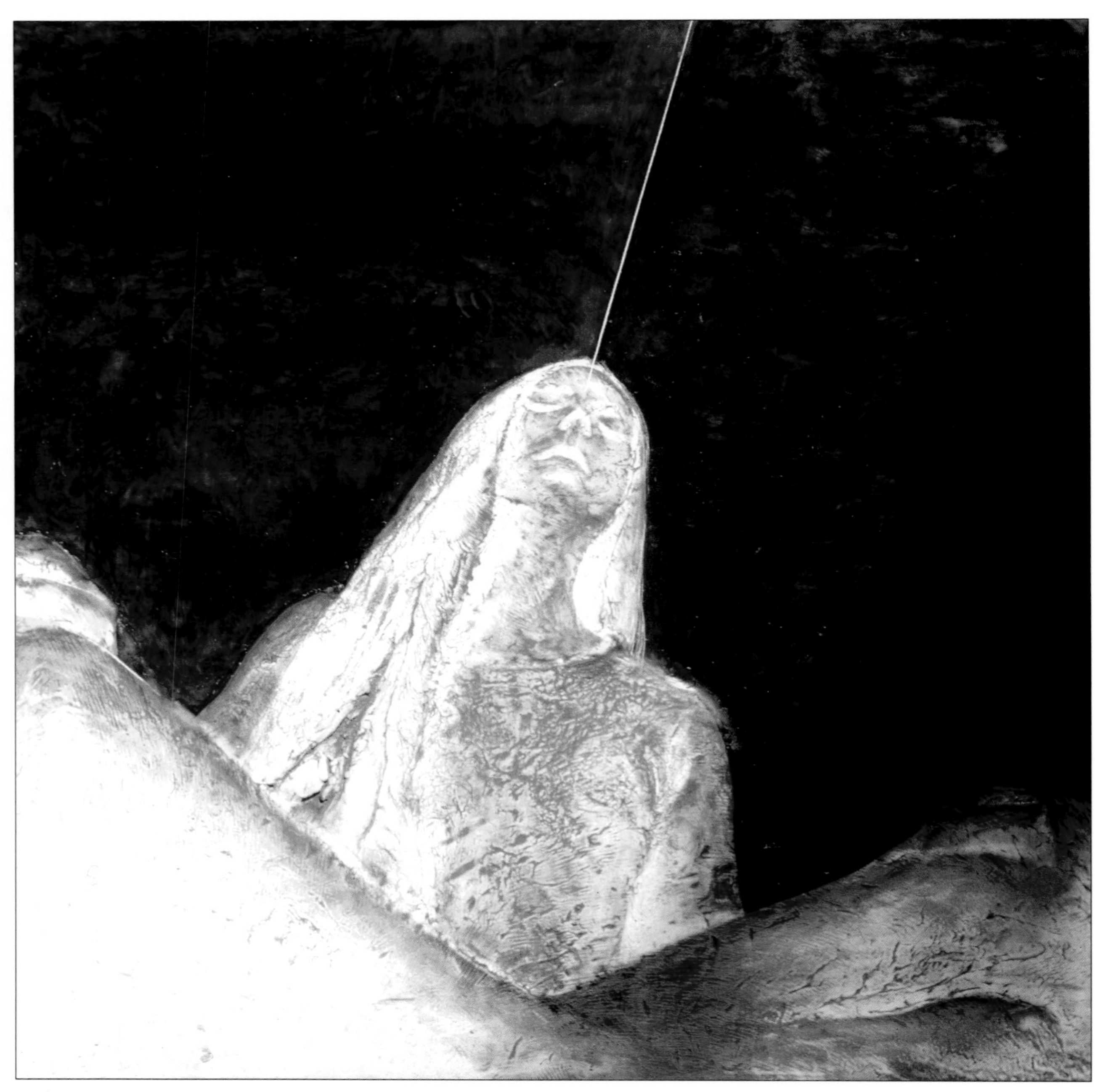

Within

aroused, it rises, moving upward through the spinal column, touching six main centers, or chakras, as it ascends to the crown of the head. These chakras, although located in specific anatomical areas, exist on a subtle plane. As the Kundalini energy passes through each center, the chakra becomes vitalized and its specific characteristics are experienced on the physical, mental, and emotional levels as well as the spiritual."[14]

I heard a knock. A voice penetrated the thick wooden door. "Vijali, are you there?" I was jarred out of my reverie. I rose with trembling body and slipped into a paint-splattered smock, stiff at the cuffs with polyester resin. The bolts slid back easily and I swung the heavy door open. Jeff, the sculptor from next door, stood silhouetted against the morning sky, lean and tall, his hair already ruffled from work. He held a wrench.

"Vijali, you look like a ghost!"

The light hurt my eyes, and it took me a moment to understand what he was talking about—something about replacing a gas line for his kiln. "Oh, yes, the lines." Speaking was difficult, and I struggled to continue the conversation.

The day advanced, people came and went. The studio—my sanctuary—now confined me and walled me in painfully. The people, the studio, the work with the synthetic marble material I had developed, all of it repulsed me. Everything seemed of the past and no longer valid in the new world of light and energy I had glimpsed. I felt like a stranger in my own life. Who could I speak to about what I had seen?

Ron Levy, an art collector who had been buying my work for many years, arrived from Los Angeles. He browsed through the studio. His small, well-built body was tense with shyness, but his genuine support and love for my work broke through. He always conveyed a feeling of warmth, and usually left with a sculptural painting under his arm or sometimes a large one that we carried out with the help of my neighbors.

I felt listless as I showed him the piece I had completed the day before.

"That's marvelous," he said.

I smiled, but the work no longer had importance. My thoughts drew me in one direction, my actions in another. I felt dizzy. Then the same current I experienced the night before shot through me again, less extreme, but in the same pattern.

"I'm going to take a walk on the beach," I said. "Make yourself at home." I pushed the teapot across the counter. "Here, have a cup of sage tea."

Instead, Ron wrote me a check for $4,500—half payment for the mural *Exit into Life* that I was working on, still unfinished. He took the sculptured painting I had just completed to show to a friend. We lifted it off the dolly and struggled to fit it into the back of his station wagon. He drove off with a big smile and I walked down to the ocean, relieved to be alone, my feet sinking deep into the wet sand as the tide rose around my ankles.

A few days passed and I wondered how I would finish the sculptural mural for Ron. I knew I must complete this piece before I could begin my new cycle, but felt distaste even touching the work. I needed to be out in the mountains, amongst stone and nature.

The phone rang. I answered and heard Mangala, the young nun at the convent who had corresponded with me while I was in Canada.

"I wanted to let you know that Swami is dying."

I immediately called the Hollywood Center. "I want to see him," I told the nun who answered the telephone.

"Only the monastics are seeing him now," she answered.

I hung up with that same old feeling of being shut out. Could Swami's imminent death have anything to do with the changes I felt?

The desire to be in the hills consumed me that afternoon. I grabbed my Peruvian poncho, jumped in my VW bug, and drove to my secret spot in the Santa Ynez Mountains overlooking the coast. I had found this site when Dale and I returned from India, and it gave me comfort—the power spot I turned to in times of stress for strength and clarity. The hills were strewn with huge boulders, and I sat at the foot of one that resembled a female deity. The round stone body seemed ready to give birth to a child of ancient wisdom. Holes that formed eyes looked benignly down on me as I wrote in my journal and wept.

A lizard established its territory on the far side of the hip-shaped boulder that we shared. We stared at each other, curious and respectful, until an idea formed as strong and clear as if it had lived with me always: I would work in harmony with the organic forms of these special areas, to carve and paint these boulder outcroppings as our earliest ancestors once did. I drove down the winding road off the mountain, carrying a little of the mountain's peace within me.

I gave away the rosary Swami Prabhavananda had given to me at the time of my initiation. Though I had dearly loved it, recently it had become a hindrance, not a help. And though I didn't yet understand what had happened, I became convinced that the changes I felt were the Kundalini transformations described by Indian yogis.

Borderless

I wrote in my journal:

If I start jumping up and doing the crazy movements my body wants to do, I fear people will put me in a psychiatric hospital. But the vision persists: the understanding of myself as pure energy, as the world.

I tried to work with the roller-coaster energy and realized that two things were happening one after the other: The arousal of the Kundalini energy in my body had changed my consciousness, and then the change had created panic. I knew that panic did not initiate the experience; it only distorted the energy. I felt deeply that I had experienced a borderless reality, and that the tension and fear came from living in a society that denies that reality.

As I worked in my studio, a recurring image haunted me. I saw myself standing in a wilderness area carving boulders with a simple hammer and chisel, releasing some aspect of the feminine spirit from its encumbrance. I saw myself transcending the conditioning of the artist in a commercial world. Then I saw myself leaving the sculptured boulders for whoever came across them.

The need to close my studio in Santa Barbara consumed me. I decided to give away everything I didn't need: clothing, the sophisticated power tools for my artwork, and an enormous commercial dough mixer I had used for mixing my marble composition. I needed only simple hand tools—hammer and chisel and a few paints. I gave away the library that I had collected over thirty years. The giving was joyous, not desperate. To each person, I gave what I felt would be of benefit. I saved only what I would need for survival: backpacking equipment, art supplies, and a few pieces of clothing.

In September of 1976, I had an art exhibition in which I gave away my art. It was amusing to observe how people responded to this event. If someone came up to a piece and admired it, I lifted it off the hangers and said, "It's yours!"

Some people freaked out. One man backed off when I tried to give him a sculpture, saying, "I'd like this, but I'm sure there's something wrong. What's going on here? Is this some kind of joke?" He left the studio quickly.

Another man stood admiring a sculptural painting on the wall. When I said, "You can take anything you like," he began to grab everything in sight. A friend of mine had just entered the studio. He put a hand on the man's shoulder and said, "Why don't you leave a few things for someone else?"

As the day ended, more friends arrived and I opened the large portfolio of drawings I had left for last.

Alone after the show, I thumbed through my journal and read a dream I had written the year before:

A blasting, roaring fire sweeps over the mountains, burning houses—everything in sight. I can see it coming and have only a few minutes to take what I can carry in my hands. I go into each room, start to take some books, then put each book back and say to myself, I don't need the books of the gurus anymore. I start to take a piece of clothing and realize I don't need it. I can't find anything that seems important enough to take. I end up taking only my toothbrush! I walk away feeling total relief, lightness, and joy. I don't look back at the consuming flames.

On December 5, 1976, I removed the passenger seat of my Volkswagen bug and fit in a piece of wood so that I could sleep full-length. I made the other half of the back seat a table for my typewriter. My camera, paints, hammer, and chisel fit into a box underneath the table. I put a few clothes in the back along with my guitar. A friend had made me a tiny ceramic plate and cup that fit neatly in the glove compartment.

I had saved a little money from the sales of my artwork and I thought I might survive for a year or two if I lived simply. I didn't know where I would go, but I drove off in my VW bug singing.

The first night I fell asleep in my car at Gaviota Park after watching the sun set over the ocean. The next morning I woke early to take a long walk barefoot along the shallows of the Pacific. Having turned myself inside out, I now found that my internal life resided on the outside. I had walked into a new life with no division between the inside and outside—a vast world.

As I sat on a boulder watching the sky turn pink and the ocean become opalescent, I remembered the words from my dream the night before: *The answers are simple; they come from the Earth. The answers are simple; they come from the Earth. They come from the Earth.*

This feeling of living on the edge of the unknown became a spiritual practice for me. From that day forward, I ceased making choices based on past habits, patterns, or the need for security or religious tradition. Instead, my choices were based on intuition—what my spirit responded to and the feeling of love. I experienced life as an unfolding ritual of returning to the moment, to my breath, to Earth. Living this way, I might find what I had known in childhood when I sat in my circles of stones in my grass hideaways, where I listened to silence, and felt joy in the messages of clouds.

Om bhur bhuvah svaha
tat saviture varenyam
bhargo devasya dhimahi
dhiyo yo nah pracodayat

Earth, Atmosphere, Heavens,
Body, Mind, Spirit,
we meditate with an unwavering mind
on the radiant light of our source
from whom the universe has sprung.
May we live and move
with illumined consciousness.

Vedic Gayatry Mantra

CHAPTER ELEVEN

World Wheel~Spoke Six

South Gallala Plateau, Egypt
1990

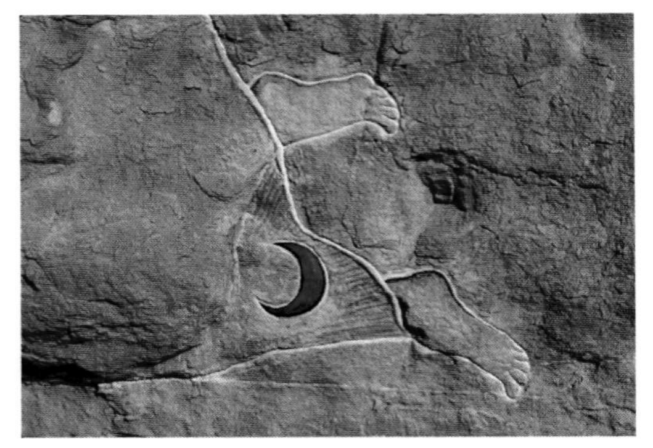

Woman with the Wings of an Eagle, Sun at Her Forhead, Moon at Her Feet (detail)

OMNEYA GOMAA invited me on the telephone to come and stay at her elegant Cairo apartment overlooking the Nile until I found my footing in Egypt. I had been given her number while in Greece by one of my new friends. Omneya, an Egyptian woman about my age, had worked for the United Nations for twenty years setting up recruitment programs throughout Africa. She had beautiful black hair and golden skin, and the sculptured lips and large eyes of the classical Egyptian statues I had always admired. She dressed in modern clothes, not the *purdah* and long dresses of the women I saw in the streets.

On my second day in Egypt, Omneya's closest girlfriend joined us. She had the same chiseled features as Omneya. She brought her husband and the two of them took me to their farm in the desert oasis Wadi El Natrum. From there we walked into the surrounding desert, to Saint Bishoy's Monastery. Built in the fourth century, the domed adobe buildings had a wonderful simplicity about them, reflecting the lives of their inhabitants, monks of the Coptic order.

Although Omneya and her friends were Muslim, they had a fondness for the Coptic monasteries, where I found the original spirit of Jesus and the essential ideology of Christianity untainted by the power politics of the modern church. The Coptic monks based their practices on their direct experience of God, and embraced all forms of mysticism and the love of humanity. Some of the monks spoke English, and among these were doctoral scholars, writers of books on Coptic subjects. I had read about the Egyptian desert hermits as a child, but I had assumed the tradition was dead. Instead it was flourishing. I longed for a closer look.

Of the eighty monks in this monastery, five lived in caves as hermits. I told them about my ten years as a member of the Vedanta monastic order and my five years as a hermit on Boney Mountain in California. One of the monks told my story to an elder who had been a hermit for thirty-five years. Father Elias rarely spoke with anyone and especially not with people outside the monastic order, but he expressed an interest in talking with me.

One of the monks led me to a private corner of the monastery and introduced me to Father Elias. He sat in a chair and gave me a warm smile when I entered the courtyard. He gestured for me to sit close to him and immediately welcomed me as a kindred soul. A grandfatherly man, complete with white beard against olive skin, he spoke English well.

"I understand you love caves also," he said. "I used to live in a cave attached to another monastery, but they worried that I'd lead the monks away from agricultural labor and toward mysticism instead, so they asked me to leave." He chuckled. "Now I'm seeking permission from the Coptic Pope to return to my cave life at another monastery. I live here in St. Bishoy's as close to isolation as possible. I have to stay here because I have problems with my digestion."

He leaned back in his chair and we sat silent for a while. Tears filled his eyes and he said, "In my life as a hermit, I experienced uninterrupted communion with God. It's different here in the monastery." Then he leaned forward and spoke softly, "Please pray for me, and I will pray for you to find the right place for your retreat and for the World Wheel work."

I put my hand on his. "I *will* pray for you." I felt so close to him. We took comfort in our silences and watched the clouds gather above us, then break up into tiny cotton balls.

I broke the stillness with a question. "Can you share your spiritual practices with me, the ones you use alone in your cave?"

I adjusted the shawl that I kept over my head and shoulders in respect for the women's traditional dress of the country. My long skirt covered my legs and I settled back in my chair.

"In the hermit life," he began, "one must keep changing routines, going from one activity to another—from reading scriptures, to prayer, to work with the hands. Make a list and start with the things you like most. End with those you like least. Then begin the day with what interests you least, because that is when you have the most energy. End the day with the things you like most, because that is when you have the least energy." He had such a twinkle in his eyes, I almost believed he was about to wink at me. "Also, protect your life from external pressures so you're free to live spontaneously."

"I try to keep my life simple for that very reason," I said. Then, after a pause, I asked him, "Have you seen God?"

Tears sprang to his eyes and he nodded his head, his white beard spreading over his chest. "Yes, my daughter!"

When his breath deepened, I stood. He had given me so much. I didn't want to take away more of his precious silence with God.

As we stood together, tears rolled down his aging cheeks and mine became moist, too. He said, "Come any time, my daughter, you are always welcome."

I left, wondering whether it is possible to live such an intense inner life with God amid the activities, deadlines, and pressures of the outside world.

After my talk with Father Elias, I took a walk in the desert to savor my time with him. But in the middle of a sea of golden sand, a small, wiry, dark-skinned Egyptian man appeared from nowhere and stood on a pyramid-shaped dune. He greeted me in broken English, punctuated by Arabic. He must have registered my shock at seeing someone else when I believed I was alone in this endless stretch of sand and sky, but for some reason I felt no fear, only surprise.

He raised an arm, thin and blackened by the sun, and he pointed to a nearby sand dune. I got his message: he lived just over the next hill. He beckoned me to follow. Intrigued, I walked in his footprints across the dune until we both disappeared over its ridge and entered a tiny one-room structure buried in the side of the hill.

He lived alone, with no donkey or means of transport, but he had painted the walls of his tiny shack with primitive pictures of eagles in all stages of flight. From one corner he pulled out a strange contraption. Using gestures, he showed me how the cord trap would catch hold of a large bird by the feet. I realized that he trapped eagles.

I surveyed his environment. "What do you do with them?" I asked.

"I transport them on foot—and—sell—them." He stumbled with the English. "In local Arab markets." He pointed south.

We left the shack and climbed to the top of the dune where we gazed out over the horizon. With the sun almost kissing the edge of his desert, he pointed to the open sky and said, "All I love and need is right here, the open sky, the barren sands."

Although he had only a few words of English, I understood him well. Tears shone in his eyes as he spoke about the stars at night and of his love of this world. His wife and children, it seemed, did not share his love for the desert, and they lived in the nearest town. I understood—*how* I understood—and I wept with him over the agony and ecstasy of a life so close to my own in its sentiments.

Although Omneya's friends had invited me to stay at their desert farm and to create the World Wheel sculpture and ritual there, I felt I needed to experience more of Egypt. Filled to the brim with the love I had experienced, I returned to Cairo and visited an Egyptian museum where visitors can touch the art as well as look at it. Since childhood, I had a special love for Egyptian art. When I was sick or sleepless, I used to curl up with art books depicting the artifacts I now saw and held. They soothed me then and they nourished me now.

That evening, Omneya held a United Nations party in her flat and I watched my first Egyptian belly dance. Later we sat and talked about Islamic practices. The practice of Ramadan, an annual month-long fast, appealed to me in particular, and I planned to fast with the locals. I also marveled that the traditional dance of this culture, which so emphatically emphasized the covering of a woman's body, would be belly dancing, which exposed it in such a delightful, sensual way!

I felt the need to walk from Cairo to the Pyramids as a pilgrimage, so on my fourth morning I set out before sunrise. By mid-morning I was lost. I found myself in a section of Giza devoid of western dress or influence. I pulled my scarf down over my forehead and checked to see if my skirt covered my ankles. Then I consciously drew my energy in, becoming as invisible as possible. In the maze of streets new smells and sounds transported me, and the crowds dressed in traditional Muslim clothing fascinated me. I looked at each face as if it were my own and warmth filled my body: "Yes, you are my family, my very own."

In a mosque, I entered the section for women and prayed as a Muslim. Egyptian children begged me for "pounds," and squeezed and pushed up against me. As I bowed and touched my head to the ground, other women's bodies pressed against me. I prayed for our world family, my only family, for the freeing of women's lives all over the world, and for the earth, our common mother.

Finally, I reached the pyramids. With other tourists I entered corridors and chambers so cool and dark that I felt as if I were deep in a cave, an experience which always brings me back to the roots of my being. I longed for time there alone, but the guides hurried us through, anticipating the moment when they would ask for a tip.

A few days later I took a bus across the Suez Canal, down the west side of Sinai to the tip that juts into the Red Sea. At Sharam al Sheikh, I found a campsite at the water's edge and set up my tent. The next day I swam in the clear blue sea among coral reefs. Unaware that I had set up camp near a tourist site, I found the tourist environment jarring. I hated the constant pressure, the nagging for money, and the endless questions: "Are you married? Are you alone? Where do you sleep?" American music blasted into the night, and the next day a bulldozer gnawed into the earth next to my camp site, adding its thunderous voice to the blare of American rock. I wanted to be with Egyptians in their normal setting, so I was happy to leave.

An American couple from the Midwest gave me a ride to Mount Sinai. Here the desert floor swelled into sculptured mounds touched with salmon, yellow, and green. We occasionally saw Bedouins among these dunes, traveling with their camel trains. The women wore black veils and brightly embroidered dresses. Some tended flocks of goats.

The bone-bare granite of Mt. Sinai rose red out of the desert. This was one of those places where I felt how the power of stone could transform consciousness. Shape, size, and chemical composition, all united to become a conduit between the core of the earth, ourselves, and the heavens.

From the base of the mountain we hiked for over two hours, straight to the top without stopping. I felt the 7,000-foot ascent in my legs and lungs. The temperature dropped to freezing and it began to snow. When we reached the summit, the view was staggering—range after range of red and salmon granite, twisted by the movement and eruption of the earth. Here Moses had received the Ten Commandments from God. Who would not hear the voice of God in this place?

The ancient Greek Orthodox monastery of Saint Catherine, built at the beginning of the sixth century A.D., sat at the base of the mountain. They had guest accommodations, so I spent the night.

The next morning I hiked on the mountain again, and found my own sacred spot among enormous granite boulders dislodged from the top over the centuries. As I sat in the rays of the rising sun, the first day after the dark of the moon, I felt a deep unspoken knowledge of what God is and what our relationship is to the Whole.

Vijali standing in the desert of Egypt

I left the next day with an American family returning to Cairo. What a shock to leave the silent and pristine beauty of the desert and enter that hectic city again, with its garbage and the unceasing honking of car horns! I took a tiny room on the thirteenth floor of the Everest Hotel at a cost of six and three-quarter Egyptian pounds per day, a little more than an American dollar, with breakfast. The noise rose from the streets below, but even that and the grimy windows and doorsills couldn't decrease my joy at having a space of my own: bed, coffee table, even a sink. The manager seemed nice, but not *too* nice, a refreshing change in a city where Americans represented dollars and sex.

I met a couple from Europe who wanted to visit Saint Anthony's, another Coptic monastery, so we hitchhiked together, catching three rides. The last, a large truck with a rough-looking Egyptian man as driver, dropped us off at the start of the fourteen-kilometer road to the monastery. When he saw us beginning to walk down that road, however, he called us back, and, to our amazement, unhitched the large bed of the truck and drove us in the cab right to the monastery.

The Coptic father who greeted us at the entrance said warmly, "It is God who has brought you to this place."

He wore a black tunic and a black embroidered hood. Behind him the monastery buildings rose with ancient ambiance—a grouping of beautifully sculpted adobe domes, topped with crosses. The father guided us to the dining room where he offered us bread, honey, and tea.

I developed an immediate rapport with a monk whose name was Father Dioskouros. We shared the stories of our lives and spiritual experiences. Eventually, I asked permission to spend four days of retreat in one of their caves. Typically, outsiders are not told the location of the caves, but he argued my case with the Bishop who happened to be at the monastery and the Bishop granted permission.

"St. Paul lived in his cave and every day birds brought him bread for food," Father Dioskouros said in cultured English, as we sat drinking tea in the dining room.

In my short stay at St. Anthony's, the kind friendship of this monk and the desert fed me. Father Dioskouros took me to St. Anthony's cave where a long narrow tunnel opened up into a fairly large room. "The temperature is always perfect inside," he told me. "Cool when it is hot outside and warm when it is cold."

Large frescos covered the walls, and he explained that the hermits often painted their visions, though few were artists. Even so, the strength and passion of their visions came through.

When Father Dioskouros left me at my own small cave for retreat—more of an overhang, really—I explored further up the mountain and found a perfect two-room natural formation with a flat floor. The stone walls of the cave had been carved by nature into an abstract mural with swirls of rust and yellow. From an artistic perspective, the textures and design were so exquisite it would have been an intrusion on perfection to alter them in any way. A black bird perched near the mouth of the cave seemed to welcome me. Just as it became dark, I laid out my blue sleeping bag on the natural floor.

Every day of my retreat a black bird came and circled above me and one day, close by, I saw a lion. My heart raced. We stood transfixed, staring at each other until I took a few steps forward and then realized that my "lion" was no more than the shadow of a stone on the ground. Nevertheless, throughout my stay in the cave, whenever I turned my head in that direction, my body would still remember that "lion" and adrenaline would rush through me again.

Beginning on the third day, a strong wind kicked up and howled through the canyons and across the desert for an entire day and night. I crawled into my sleeping bag and covered myself completely for protection. As I lay there, I thought about caves as portals into heaven. The light that shines through the doorway into the darkness of the cave is the doorway into spiritual knowing. The caves are locks, and the mind of the hermit is the key that opens the doorway to divine consciousness on earth. Every time I drifted into sleep with the wind still howling, I felt the presence of the sage with me, until I finally awoke with the rising sun and the wind had quieted.

I left my cave retreat in the morning and returned to the monastery. Father Dioskouros had arranged a ride for me back to Cairo with a young French couple. During the ride, they asked me if I would like to stay in their second-floor flat in a quiet suburb of Cairo while they went on a two-week sabbatical from teaching at the university. I was delighted and accepted eagerly.

The first day alone, as I stood at the door to the flat with groceries from the local market in my arms searching my purse for the keys, I heard a man come up the stairs behind me. I assumed he was another tenant going to the third floor, but, as I put my key in the lock, he grabbed my buttocks and pushed me up against the door. I wheeled around and yelled, "*Le! Le!* No! No" He hurriedly ran down the stairs, but when I stopped screaming to fiddle with the key in the door again, he returned. I kept screaming at the top of my lungs until he actually left the building. The cave lion came out of my mouth, a voice I had never heard before.

At the beginning of April, thinking I would stop at the sea before I entered the desert again, I went to Hotel Mary's Beach, seven kilometers south of Ain Sokna on the Suez Gulf. I planned to spend a month writing and meditating, much relieved to get out of Cairo, to touch the water and absorb the silence of this place. I had a tiny closet-like room with a view of the hills and the sound of surf twenty feet from my door. A table, a chair, a good bed—what more could one ask for?

Just as the sun set there was a knock on the door. I had to show my passport to the local police. Ah, well. The police wondered why I was here, an American alone in a hotel with only the manager present.

"Are you leaving tomorrow?" one of the policemen asked.

"No."

He responded with a questioning expression. "Are you on the way to Luxor?"

"No."

"You cannot stay here," he replied.

Finally, I remembered the Coptic cross Father Dioskouros had given me and drew it out from under three layers of T-shirts. "I'm on my way to the Coptic monasteries," I told them. They seemed to accept that and they released me.

I didn't mention that I wanted to stay a month because very few women travel alone in Arab countries. Every few seconds, wherever I was, on the street or at a restaurant or shop, I encountered the same questions in more or less the same order: "Where are you from? Are you married? Where do you sleep? Do you want to have sex? (With the accompanying finger gesture.) Do you want to buy hashish? Can I spend your money?"

The people at the hotel were sweet by comparison. It took them six hours to start asking questions and they stopped after the second one. Naively, I believed this place was my haven, and very tired, I entered my room, locked the door, and fell asleep.

In the middle of the night, someone came to my door and knocked. When I didn't answer, a man yelled, "Open, open, open!"

I screamed back, "No, *le, le!*"

He tried to pry the door open with a metal object and then pick the lock.

I leapt out of bed with my arms raised and my long hair tangled and flying in the air, and I screamed at the top of my lungs.

I heard his footsteps as he left. Silence. A few moments later the same footsteps returned with another person. Rasping, scraping sounds of a screwdriver against metal filled the night silence. The door shook and the hinges loosened. I quickly put on another layer of clothes, grabbed my scissors, and screamed like a wild animal for as long as I possibly could. Eventually they left. I returned to my bed, fully dressed, with my scissors still clutched in my hand. I thought I would spend the whole night in vigil, but eventually my body gave in to sleep.

The next morning I woke before the sun rose and I felt a wail like a great wave crash through my whole body. As sunlight streaked through my window, I thought about women in the Arab world and sadness filled me. One step into the wilderness and I would have a trail of Muslim men snorting behind me, making sucking noises. Even the modern monastic community treated women with disdain. I had visited a Coptic convent in Cairo and had found conditions there appalling. While monasteries for men erected new buildings, these women struggled

Saint Paul's Coptic Monastery, Egypt

together in a tiny apartment with no apparent means of financial support.

Despite this, women in the Coptic Church have an extensive and surprising history, and the Church has a number of well-respected female saints. This is partly due to their cleverness and wile because, although some lived in convents, many disguised themselves as males and entered the monasteries, even becoming cave hermits. A life of disguise allowed them access to knowledge and equality they otherwise would not have enjoyed, and some interesting stories having resulted. Saint Hilaria, for example, was the daughter of the Emperor Zeno. In a monk's disguise she healed her sister, thought to be possessed of evil spirits, by holding her and kissing her throughout one night. But such unusual behavior on the part of a monk caused the parents to ask questions. Only after they promised to honor her secrecy, did Saint Hilaria reveal herself to them as their daughter. Through her intercession, the Coptic monasteries began to receive food and support from their rulers.[15]

I left the Hotel Mary's Beach the next day and headed back into the desert, to Saint Paul's Coptic Monastery. I had heard the Coptic Pope speak in Cairo and, although I hadn't understood his Arabic language, I had found his presence awe-inspiring. I requested his permission to create the World Wheel sculpture at Saint Paul's Monastery. In a letter given to him by an attendant, I explained that the World Wheel was a pilgrimage for peace, an effort to create a world family, and that the sculpture I left behind would represent the spirit of the desert. He thrilled me by sending his blessings in response.

To reach Saint Paul's Coptic Monastery, I took a bus along the Red Sea. The bus driver dropped me off and pointed into the desert. "Hike three hours and you will run into the Monastery."

As I walked through an endless and stunning vista of sand dunes, I wondered if I had heard him right. I kept checking my water, worried that it would run out. The desert seemed so barren and so vast—and after three hours of hiking without seeing a plant or any sign of a person, I found it difficult to believe that anything else existed there. Blisters formed on both heels and sweat poured down my neck, caused by both the sun and the rising fear that I might have misunderstood the driver.

Just when I thought I must have walked in the wrong direction, the monastery popped up out of nowhere, with palm trees and adobe domes rising out of the desert floor. Hot and tired, I nearly crumpled in relief.

When I arrived at the front gate, Father Mati greeted me in his traditional Coptic black tunic and embroidered hood. He took me into the refectory and offered their mainstay: bread, honey, and tea.

"Where have you been staying in Egypt?" he asked.

I told him about my trouble at the hotel and he laughed, then he looked concerned. "That's a dangerous place, a drug center."

My eyes must have grown wide with understanding, and then I handed him the note of permission from their Pope.

"We're happy to have you," Father Mati said. "You'll stay with us in the guest quarters."

Over the next days and weeks, he shared his time and knowledge with me, giving me the *Philokalia* to read, a collection of texts by monks that concern the practice of spiritual living, particularly in a monastery. I had wanted to read these texts ever since I had read the journal *Way of the Pilgrim* as a teenager, because the *Philokalia* had inspired the Russian pilgrim. These texts became my inspiration during my stay at the monastery.

The next day I rose at 3:00 a.m., when the bell rang for the monks. For the first time, I heard Coptic chanting in the ancient Egyptian language used before Islam swept through Egypt and forced the Copts at sword point to become Muslims. Tension and intrigue still existed between these two religious groups, and although the ancient language is thought to be dead, one of the fathers said he knew of two families who spoke it at home and taught it to their children.

Later, I sat for hours in the cave of Saint Paul, where he is rumored to have lived for ninety years with two lions for companions, and where the birds fed him. During the day, I observed that when male visitors arrived at the monastery, Father Mati washed their feet in the tradition of Jesus.

Every morning and afternoon, I hiked the terrain surrounding the monastery. When I chose my site for carving at Saint Paul's, I deliberately chose it close to the monastery, only a thirty-minute hike

Woman with the Wings of an Eagle, Sun at Her Forehead, Moon at Her Feet, desert of Egypt

from the buildings. I believed that the sacredness of the mountain and the presence of the monks would protect me.

The site first attracted me because of a cave I saw at the very top. As I came near, however, the cave revealed itself as shadows leading up to a plateau. On top of the plateau I discovered a natural medicine wheel with a back wall formed from a limestone outcropping, all with swells and twists and interesting textures. As soon as I reached this spot, a heavy sleepiness came over me and I lay down at its base. This often happens when I reach the right place, as though my body knows and relaxes.

While I was there, three cranes greeted me. When I returned and told the monks, one monk said, "The cranes are a sign for you. It means you are home."

I developed tremendous love for the monks. It is rare to meet people who are unconditionally open, but with the monks I could be present without manipulation or demand. To have this experience struck me as an immense gift, particularly in a culture where strangers of the opposite sex rarely met.

In my room at the guesthouse, I had been reading the Bible, Revelation 12:1-17, which inspired the sculpture I wanted to create:

> *And there appeared a great wonder in heaven; a woman clothed with the sun and the moon under her feet and upon her head a crown of twelve stars. And she being with child cried, travailing in birth . . . . to be delivered . . . .And after she gave birth the woman fled into the wilderness where she hath a place prepared of God. That they should feed her there a thousand two hundred and threescore days . . . . And when the dragon saw that he was cast unto the earth, he persecuted the woman which brought forth the man child . . . . And to the woman were given two wings of a great eagle, that she might fly into the wilderness, into her place, where she is nourished for a time, and times, and half a time, from the face of the serpent . . . . And the earth helped the woman.*

In Christian mythology the winged woman is the Virgin and also the Church, and we, as individuals, retain part of that body of God while the pattern of God is also our pattern in our individual lives. The flight of this woman into the wilderness, to be nourished and protected by God, was also my flight and my nourishment.

Except for wandering Bedouins, I saw no one as I worked. The sculpture became my only companion, and her eyes watched me from out of the limestone. She was alive and breathing. Late one afternoon, I laid my tools down after completing the wings of what I now called *Woman with the Wings of an Eagle, Sun at Her Forehead, Moon at Her Feet.* The sun disappeared behind the highest range. Peace came over me. I felt I could die that very moment and I would be perfectly at peace with death. I would become air, the warmth of my body would fade with the sun. I would sink into the sand and become earth, stone, stillness, and silence.

Egypt had been a time of retreat for me, so when I finished the sculpture, I created my own ceremony alone in the desert and answered my own questions. I carried bread from the monastery in my backpack and broke it with a stone, leaving half for the earth. Standing on the ridge, I spoke my answers to the wind with my arms raised and my hair flying.

What is our essence? "We come from the great void and are of that matrix of life that runs through all creation." "Our ailment is our own misunderstanding of who we are. We think we are separate from the earth and the life around us." "The solution and healing is to realize that we breathe with all life as one organism."

I created *Woman with the Wings of an Eagle, Sun at her Forehead, Moon at her Feet* to represent the spirit of life that is dying in our industrial lives. She would live wherever nature was left intact. My connection with the spirit of Egypt came from the tremendous silence of the desert—not from the pyramids and the powerful civilization that Egypt represents—but from their source.

Woman with the Wings of an Eagle, Sun at Her Forehead, Moon at Her Feet (detail)

CHAPTER TWELVE

Winged Woman

Simi Hills, California
1976

Vijali carving on *Winged Woman*

AFTER A WEEK OF wandering in Los Angeles in my new VW bug home, I headed for the mountains. I turned off the freeway at the Topanga Canyon Road exit and headed inland. Twenty minutes later, I made another turn onto a narrow, winding road that led me into the Chatsworth area in the Simi Hills. Houses grew sparse. As I drove toward the summit, I could almost believe I was in total isolation. My shoulders relaxed. My breath deepened. In front of me rose the highest point of the hills.

As I parked on the side of the road, my dream of carving stone in wild areas leapt into my mind. Could it be now? Should I take my tools? I stepped out of the car, put on my blue windbreaker, laced my hiking boots, and placed my hammer and chisel in my backpack. A deer trail led me into the boulder-studded hills.

Each footstep in the December morning dew brought out the fragrance of the earth and the scent of sage. After about thirty minutes, I reached a small clearing in the brush. In front of me rose giant sandstone boulders—whales, dolphins, turtles, manatees. Lichen spotted their craggy surfaces—chartreuse, orange, green. When I touched them, the society of boulders drew me into their world. The tension of Los Angeles left me completely and I breathed easily in the silence, broken only by the chatter of a jay and a lizard's scratching on stone. This was *my* place.

Something caught my eye on the crest of the next hill and two protruding shapes pulled me closer. My artist's eye saw a female form rising from the earth with a male form lying by her side—the only two human forms among the sea creatures. I hiked through the brush until I stood quietly in front of them. I felt an almost imperceptible vibration and then a hum that became an *Om* rising through my feet and legs and moving through every cell in my body to make my own energy dance. I looked around to make sure I wasn't experiencing an earthquake.

As I touched the female stone, I heard a voice say, "I am the *Winged Woman*."

"Do I have permission to touch your forms?" I asked. The presence of the woman in the boulder was so haunting, her call for release so strong, and my body's response so immediate, that I felt certain of her approval.

I returned to my car, then hiked back to the site with fruit, nuts, cheese, a mat, and my sleeping bag. I had seen some mugwort in the ravine and I wanted to make a dream pillow in the tradition of the Chumash people who used this herb on vision quests. The scent from the leaves induced prophetic dreams, and answers to questions were translated into dream imagery. Sliding down into the ravine, I made an offering of water and prayers to the mugwort and drew my knife from my back pocket. I cut a few fresh leaves from the silvery green plant and wrapped them in purple silk.

Beside the *Winged Woman* and the boulder I named *Reclining Man,* I rested my head on the dream pillow and watched the sun disappear into the stillness of twilight. I lay in my sleeping bag and listened to the sounds of my breath and the hoot of an owl on the far hill. The noise of crickets grew louder, like strains of conversation from my last month in Santa Barbara: *You're a fool to abandon the style of your past artwork. It has taken years to develop a good clientele, and now you're throwing it all away! You have every artist's dream, a warehouse by the ocean. Why leave it?* The crickets stopped suddenly, as if a conductor had given them a sign, and my mind returned to the present moment and the scent of mugwort surrounding me.

The moon rose, changing the boulders into liquid silver light. Eyelids grew heavy, the weight of my tired legs and arms pulled me down into the luminous space between grains of sandstone. I slept soundly until the first morning rays touched the stone and turned her gold. I awoke with the resolve to work in harmony with the organic forms of these special areas, much as I imagined our earliest ancestors might have done.

I sat in front of the *Winged Woman* to eat my breakfast of fruit and nuts, and I touched the rock surface, textured like the sprouting of wings. Her presence was so strong in the boulder, so compelling, that again I felt sure she had something to say and wanted me to free her voice by carving. A breeze blew through the chaparral. The sound of bees, busy with their day's activities, carried me into my own work.

Rose-colored bans streaked through the sandstone. I ran my hands along these ribbons and touched the lichen scattered over the surface of the rock. From the top of the prostrate male form, I leapt onto the upper part of the twelve-foot female stone. I felt her face with my hands—she looked radiantly out toward a distant valley—so I scratched lines into her surface with my chisel, outlining her eyes, nose, and lips. I took the hammer tucked under my belt and released her eyes, her high cheekbones, and brow. The hammer's tap, tap, tap, and the flying chips revived some ancient memory of primal urge and motion. My hands and the swing of my arms moved on their own. And for the first time in months, my mind rested.

Tools for carving

Three hours passed as a moment. Then I stopped chiseling and sat on a boulder across from the emerging sculpture. I munched an apple and cheese, and watched a lizard do push-ups in the warmth of the sun, establishing his territory on the far side of the rounded rock we shared. I pulled off my shirt and stretched out on the boulder, my back against the warm stone, while cumulus clouds formed in the cerulean sky.

Across from me I felt the penetrating eyes of the *Winged Woman* and her gaze drew me back to my work. As I chiseled, a mound of sand grew around the boulder. I felt drawn into timelessness, carving just as an unknown ancestor did about 23,000 years ago in Austria, creating the *Venus of Willendorf.* She could be held in the hand with her voluminous thighs, breasts, and stomach her predominant features. Yet her eyes had not been carved. Why? What were the thoughts of the person who created that little figure? Why did I feel so compelled to carve *Winged Woman?*

On the curve of *Winged Woman's* body, I saw again the suggestion of wings. The protruding part of the stone looked like a hand ready to thrust through the stony membrane and touch the world. First, I drew the emerging form on the sandstone, and then, with hammer and pointed chisel, I incised the contours of the outreaching hand. With the forked chisel I removed rock fragments, freeing finger after finger until the entire hand stood revealed and seemed to touch me with warmth.

The sun dropped and shadows lengthened—an entire day had passed. I put my tools into my backpack and sat across from *Winged Woman.* Her emerging eyes looked benignly upon me and her sumptuous stone body seemed ready to give birth to some child of ancient wisdom. Out of nowhere I heard the words from my dream of the previous week: *The answers are simple; they come from the Earth. They come from the Earth.*

Stone before carving

Winged Woman, work in progress

Winged Woman and *Reclining Man*, Simi Hills, Southern California

With my new mantra, I hiked back to the car, tucked my sleeping bag and backpack away, and drove off toward a friend's home in Beverly Hills. As I turned off Topanga Canyon Road onto the Ventura Freeway, traffic slowed and rush hour halted me.

The next morning I examined maps, made telephone calls to the Chatsworth County office, and finally located a telephone number for the people who owned the property where I had seen my sculpture. I called the number, and a woman's voice answered. Nervous about what she and her husband would think, I told her how I had found the site and had fallen in love with the boulders and the view.

"Please, go ahead," she said, clearly delighted with the idea of a sculpture on their land. "Bring friends if you like, and let us know when you've completed the sculpture. We want to see it."

Through the next six months, I carved on the *Winged Woman* and she worked on me. Sometimes I slept in my car, sometimes by the boulders, and sometimes at a friend's home in Los Angeles. Nothing felt more important than going to the mountains to work alone with this stone.

Meanwhile, the heightened energy in my body and the experience of light continued after that night in Santa Barbara when my world opened up. I had a lot of pain on the surface of my body as a result. Sometimes, with a surge of energy, my body shook and I

Winged Woman (detail)

Reclining Man (detail)

wrestled with shifts of consciousness that occurred two or three times a day while I tried to look and behave like a "normal" person.

Sometimes objects around me seemed to breathe with me. Sometimes I felt as heavy as rock or as light as a hummingbird. Other times I experienced the earth shaking, and needed to ask others if we were having an earthquake. Sometimes I reached such deep, peaceful knowing and connectedness that no fear could possibly exist; while at other times I lost the familiar altogether and experienced my old terror about going crazy like my dear mother.

But instead of going insane, I felt I was acutely sane, though I had no way of sharing or communicating this with others who struck me as living in a conjured, unreal world. Carving stone grounded me, and only the wilderness felt comfortable, like home. The wilder the area, the more peace I felt.

In my early years as an artist, I had formed images in my mind and then projected those images outside myself onto the medium. But my process had changed radically during this period. I waited until I understood what lived in the stone so that I could be instrumental in releasing its innate form. In turn, the stone encouraged movement in me. It became a reciprocal dance. As I worked, the boulder became my altar, the hammer and chisel my instruments of worship. As the *Winged Woman*'s face came alive, I remembered that ancient stone was a deity, the first object of worship. In this sense, the site was my true church, and I needed no other.

As my carving progressed, I understood why the church used stones to shape idols or statues, why the water of streams became holy water, why the church took the colors from the sun shining through flowers and leaves as inspiration for stained-glass windows. All of nature's elements were incorporated symbolically into the church, yet distanced from direct experience. While in church, I missed smelling the earth, feeling the sun on my back, hearing the wind dance

Winged Woman and *Reclining Man* (detail)

through leaves. I missed the fragrance of sage and wildflowers anointing the moment with their presence. I wanted my hands in the earth—becoming "dirty," as my grandmother would have said. Touching the warm sandstone felt like a return to the beginnings of art, of ceremony, of spirituality.

One morning, as I worked, I realized that the tapping of my chisel against sandstone was my mantra, and my work had became prayer. By noon I stopped work and laid my tools on the ground before the sculpture, stretched out on the big flat rock across from *Winged Woman,* and gazed at the sky above me. My friends in Los Angeles thought that I was in the mountains "doing art," but they would not have understood if I had said I was going to look at clouds for the day! My calves and back pressed against the rough sandstone surface, absorbing the warmth while I drank in the expanse of sky. Hawks circled overhead, evoking my own movement of spirit, and the day passed as if only a second.

One morning I drove over to the Vedanta Center in Hollywood to pick up my father, who still worked there as the general manager, to take him to the mountains to carve with me. I found him in the office inundated with papers, telephone calls, and people coming in and out to ask questions. He suggested that I go and talk with the new Swami until he was ready to leave.

Swami Swahananda had come from India after Swami Prabhavananda's death. I didn't know him well, but this seemed like a good opportunity to ask him about the panics that swept over me. I felt strange entering Swami Prabhavananda's old room to find a new Swami there. He asked me to take a seat.

"Swami," I said. "I've been experiencing a rise of energy that changes my perception. Everything becomes light. My body feels as if it is dissolving and sometimes I panic."

"It will pass—just pray to the Lord and say your mantra."

I blinked. He stared. Clearly, he hadn't experienced what I was going through.

Soon my father came looking for me and we drove out into the hills. I showed my father how to hold the hammer and chisel and where to carve on *Reclining Man,* the boulder lying next to *Winged Woman.*

We carved together throughout the day, stopping now and then to talk or eat. As my father worked on the wings, I finished details on the face. We stopped for lunch and I pulled out our sandwiches. I handed him the ham sandwich that I knew he liked. "Tell me more about my mother, about my childhood," I said as I poured him a cup of apple juice.

Tears filled his eyes, "I feel so bad about what happened. But I'm proud of the way you turned out. I'm lucky to have you as a daughter."

I laid my hand on his shoulder. "Tell me about *your* childhood." The question unleashed a stream of stories I will always remember.

"Dad was a salesman." He handed me his empty cup and I filled it with more apple juice. "He was away from the family a good part of the time. When he was home, he used to beat me. He'd take out the leather strap he used to sharpen his razor and would give me a wallop. Mom would often lie in bed after he left

Winged Woman (detail)

for a trip and cry. She didn't have an easy time." He shifted his seat on the rock and looked thoughtful for a moment. "I remember an experience that changed my life. One evening when I was about twenty years old, I was coming home from visiting a friend. I'd been depressed about my home life. I actually hated my father. I was walking absentmindedly, kicking a stone—and all of a sudden, my mood totally changed. I experienced joy, for no reason. Everything became positive—I felt love for everyone and everything."

"Did that feeling last?"

"Yes, for years afterward. Because of that shift I decided to go into the ministry. I went to Texas and entered theological studies, but by my third year I'd become totally disillusioned. I wanted to know what had caused the shift in my viewpoint and they didn't have the answers. I looked into other religious groups, but only found the answer when I was introduced to Vedanta.

"Vedanta taught me that the purpose of life is to know our inherent divine nature. It's possible for this shift of consciousness to come about through meditation. Through quieting the mind and letting our real nature surface."

I nodded. Then I gathered our lunch remains and stuck them in my backpack. For the first time, I felt as though I had begun to know my father.

My last day of work arrived. I put the finishing chisel marks on the wing of *Winged Woman* and laid down my tools. As the sun fell, I stood transfixed by the golden hillside and the boulder sculptures set like jewels against the darkening sky. I knew that, through rain and wind and time, nature would continue to change her.

I climbed onto the far boulder and sat quietly as the salmon colors of sunset washed over the world. I suddenly remembered the image that kept coming to me the last few years, when studio life exhausted me. Precisely this scene had come into my mind—a female presence radiating through a completed boulder sculpture as the evening air wrapped around us. Gratitude and awe were in my heart.

Here I felt I had finally met some intrinsic part of life, an essence that pervaded everything. As I looked at *Winged Woman*, I saw her flying, entering the world more fully. I saw *Reclining Man* by her side in repose, drawn into his inner world. In their gestures they said to me, "This shift of roles is needed for new balance to take place between men and women in the world. The *Winged Woman* is a moment of transition, of movement essential to a new kind of partnership. It is not yet the balanced partnership that is eventually possible."

I walked down the slope and drove away as the birds of night emerged.

That evening I felt drawn to the silence of a campground near Santa Barbara, on the ocean sands of Summerland. Instead of returning to Los Angeles, that night I slept by the sea and in the morning I located the campground host. He lived in a trailer at the edge of the blacktop designated for parking. I knocked on the door and a short, sleepy-headed man said, "What do you want?"

"Sir," I said, "I would like permission to carve a sculpture down by the ocean."

"I guess it's all right" he replied. "Those boulders are tumbled by the tide anyway. If anyone complains, just send them to me."

I hiked down the beach a couple of miles, enjoying the early morning light on the water and the ocean breeze on my skin. The curved shape of a smooth boulder sitting at the edge of the tide caught my eye. I stood in the wet sand, feeling the coolness of the water, listening to the seagulls chatter, and watched shadows creep slowly from behind rocks.

The next day I returned with my hammer and chisels. I thought of the high tide each day carving into the concave womb of this boulder. With each of my hammer strokes, I felt myself a part of the steady, relentless rhythm of the cutting waves.

The sun lowered and the tide rose around my feet, tugging at me with each receding wave. My toes burrowed into the moist sand. When one big, teasing wave doused my back, I realized it was time to leave my labor to the waves again. Gathering my tools, I quickly threw them into my soaked backpack and hiked up toward the campsite.

After a few weeks' work, I put the last touches of

rust-colored paint on three profiles carved in the concave shape. Rising from the sand, the profiles caught the rhythm of waves. A name for the sculpture came to me: *Continuum.* I put each tool in a cloth, folded them carefully, then packed them in my bag, and swung them over my shoulders—leaving the destiny of the sculpture to the tide.

We had a week of torrential rain and I wanted to return to *Winged Woman* to see how she had fared. As I walked the uphill path I heard voices and I arrived to find a group of people standing near the sculptures. I approached them and inquired about their visit to the mountain.

A tall man in blue jeans and a hat turned to me. "A friend of ours accidentally discovered these figures," he responded, "and told us we *had* to see them."

A woman was photographing the piece. She said, "We're eager to share it. We're coming back with friends next Sunday to meditate."

They all had a sense of reverence and great seriousness. I asked, "What do you think it is? What does it mean?" because I wondered if they had made up fantastic stories or explanations for its existence.

"We love it," someone said. "It seems to have some sort of spiritual meaning. Perhaps it represents an angel, but we don't know. We're just here to enjoy it."

I have continued to leave the sculptures I carve in their native homes. I have learned to focus my work not on a product or its exploitation, but on the experience of creation itself. Not just on the act of carving, but on the total experience—the process of getting permission to work, contact with the earth, the vagaries of wind and weather, and then sharing the experience with friends and family and sojourners.

Continuum, Summerland tide, California

CHAPTER THIRTEEN

World Wheel–Spoke Seven

Dead Sea, Palestine and Israel

1990

The banks of the Dead Sea

"Do THESE ARAB ADDRESSES belong to your friends?" The security officer at the Cairo airport gazed at me steadily, looking for some flicker of information.

A bead of sweat rolled down my temple and I looked to where his finger pointed. "Elias Jabbour started the House of Hope, a center for peace through education. I've been corresponding with him for a year." I flipped to the next page of my address book and added, "And this is my Israeli friend, Revital Arieli, who has invited me to Israel."

"Wait here." He disappeared into an office.

I shifted from foot to foot for more than half an hour, growing more nervous with each moment, until he returned with another officer and introduced me.

"Mr. Mustapha is our head manager. He wants to ask you a few questions before you board the plane for Israel."

They both peered into the bottom compartment of my backpack, and the first officer pulled out my hammer, chisels, and dust mask. They both gave me piercing looks, and Mr. Mustapha spoke gruffly. "What are these?"

I swallowed hard. "My tools."

They found my portfolio with photos of my sculptures. I opened the portfolio for them and pointed. "These tools are for my sculpting work." I flipped through the images. "This one was on the Seneca Reservation and this one I carved in Spain. This one is in Italy, and this one I sculpted on a granite stone on an island in Greece. I have just completed a stone sculpture here in Egypt, out in the desert behind Saint Paul's Monastery. Here is the photo."

The two officers looked a little baffled and left me for a few moments. Again I shifted from one foot to the other. I needed a drink of water, but was reluctant to leave the spot where they had left me. Finally the two returned with a third officer.

"What is this?" He snatched up a little book that was in my handbag and held it defiantly in front of my face.

"Mahmoud Darwish," I said. "My favorite Palestinian poet." I tried to explain: "I use my art work and community theater to bring understanding between people and communities. I've been on a project for four years. I call it the World Wheel." I explained that Israel and Palestine were the seventh location in which I had planned to create sculpture, and that I still had five more countries to complete the circle.

"Stay here," Mr. Mustapha said, his tone still rough.

He and the three officers disappeared into an office and, as time dragged, I imagined the possible outcomes of this interrogation. Perspiration ran down my forehead and nose, and I kept wiping it away with my hand.

It must have been an hour before the manager returned. "OK," he said. "Your plane is about to take off. You can go, but you'll have to leave your laptop computer here in Cairo. I'll give you a number and you can pick it up when you return." He tore it from my hands before I had a chance to let go. (When I returned six weeks later on my way to India, the customs officers couldn't find my computer. I had to miss my flight and stay an extra four days, hounding the office before they located it.) The interrogation had taken four hours. As I walked toward the plane, escorted by the pilot, I scanned every face that I passed. I had begun to feel that perhaps they were right—I must be guilty of something—and I suspected every person I passed of being a plainclothes intelligence officer watching my movements.

When we finally boarded the El Al flight, the pilot pointed to a seat in the back of the plane. "You'll have to sit back here with the stewardesses."

I fell into my seat and dropped off to sleep even before the plane departed. But, with every sudden movement, I awoke with a start, thinking someone had jabbed a gun into my side. Each time, I fell back into nightmarish dreams.

When we arrived in Tel Aviv and I walked down the ramp, I could see my Israeli girlfriend, Revital, standing behind the wire fence waving and beaming a welcoming smile. I had first met Revital on the Seneca Reservation in 1988. We shared such similar goals that we had vowed to work together when I came to Israel. Long, dark hair almost touched her waist and framed an attractive face and dark eyes. We hugged warmly, jumped into her friend's car, and drove to Revital's parents' house. I breathed a sigh of relief as we stepped inside the front door.

Revital's mother, Hya, originally from Poland, chopped vegetables in the kitchen. She was short and a little plump, with very fair skin, brown hair, and a loving expression. She wiped her hands on her apron and hugged me warmly. Revital's father, Nissim, read in the living room. He rose, looking wiry and intense.

"Sit, please," he said. He inquired about my trip.

Laughingly, I told him about my experience with the airline.

He nodded and did not seem surprised.

Later, Revital took me to my quarters, a small room that was once her bedroom. We sat on her bed and chatted like childhood buddies about this and that, and then about more serious topics. It was 1990, and the U.S. was preparing for the Gulf War.

"My father escaped from Iraq when he was sixteen years old," Revital said. "He walked for weeks through the desert to reach Israel, so my parents are grateful to be here, but I've grown up with war. Yesterday there were shootings at the Wailing Wall, and we're all depressed and afraid even to go out in the streets. Reprisal killings have started. Innocent people are dying on both sides. I'm sorry to say that we distrust anyone from a different ethnic background, including friends and business partners. To add to the tension, America and Iraq are in a face-off. The government has made gas masks and we fear a full-scale war."

Revital seemed to be constantly holding her breath, but then she relaxed into a smile. "Let's call my friends. They've been waiting for you."

The next evening we met with nine women friends of Revital. As each woman arrived, she presented an object sacred to her and laid it in the center of the room to form an altar. One woman brought a crystal, one a black stone, one a cup that had been in her family for generations. I placed my journal on the altar, together with an eagle's feather that had recently been given to me by an American Indian friend. Next to them I placed a bag of earth that I had gathered from the previous six sites of the World Wheel. We sat in a circle and addressed our feelings of despair, each contributing her solutions to create a ceremony of hope. As each woman spoke about the object she had brought, there emerged the common belief that we must discover the feminine, the receptive voice, in these cultures so dominated by male aggression.

Revital and I had earlier decided that we would create the World Wheel sculpture and hold the final ceremony at the Dead Sea, the lowest point of land in the world, 1,290 feet below sea level. We invited the group's participation in the World Wheel event, and the women were tremendously committed. We parted feeling a great bond among us.

The next day I wanted to visit the House of Hope. Elias Jabbour, its founder, lived in Shefar'Am, the second largest community of Palestinians in Israel. Revital and a friend from the evening before drove me north from Tel Aviv through the desert.

We finally arrived at Elias' home, a building of ancient stone, which had been transformed into the House of Hope. Through speaking tours, exchange programs, and mailings, Elias had expanded his dream far beyond resolving the Israel/Palestine conflict. His home had become not only a community center, but also an international center for peace.

Elias and his wife, Hevam, greeted us warmly. He had dark, graying hair and soft eyes. His wife wore a brown dress; she had short dark hair and olive skin. They were both in their fifties. They took us through the center, stopping proudly in their international library which was filled with books on peace in many languages. We settled in the dining room, where Hevam served us a delicious Palestinian meal.

After dinner we met with a group of twenty Palestinian, Israeli, and Druze children from Shefar'Am, aged between eight and eleven. The Druze call themselves *muwahhidun* (monotheists) and are a group that regard themselves as carriers of the core of Islam. We sat in a circle on the patio surrounded by ancient stone walls and olive trees. I held my eagle feather and asked the children to respond to the three questions I had asked in every country of the World Wheel: *Where do you come from? What is the problem in your life, in your family, in your community? What is the solution?*

Responses came from the childrens' open hearts as we passed the feather: "We come from God. Our problems arise from a feeling that a person from another culture is not our brother or sister, but an enemy. We can look through others' eyes and understand. If we understand, we can love each other as brothers and sisters."

Tears came as I experienced the wisdom of these children who had grown up with continual war, but now were under the wing of Elias.

The shadows of late afternoon reminded us that we must go.

"Elias," Revital said. "May we ask your son to represent the Palestinian people in the World Wheel ceremony?"

Elias and his wife glanced at each other. "We would be delighted!" he said. "You have our unconditional support."

Revital and I spent a few days making telephone calls, meeting people and organizing; then we traveled to the Dead Sea. At Mitzpe Shalem Kibbutz—a nature preserve and home to tigers, wolves, porcupines, and many other animals—we walked out onto the bluff overlooking the Dead Sea, the saltiest body of water in the world. People travel here for the healing properties of the sea. According to the Bible, the cities of Sodom and Gomorrah are hidden under it. Across this incredible expanse of water, we saw the desert plateau of Jordan, two thousand feet high.

We walked the same earth that the Essenes had walked, the ascetics who inscribed the Dead Sea Scrolls found in caves not far from here. Water and wind had cut into the mountainsides, carving them into rivulets and sculptural shapes, exposing the golds, purples, and greens of the eroded earth—a desolate and mystic land.

One particular spot drew me—a natural circle half enclosed by boulders, but still open to the eastern expanse of sea. Two stone sentinels marked the pathway to the rising sun. Some of the people from the kibbutz helped us move stones into the circle to form a twelve-pointed *Earth Wheel.* We placed the four largest at the four cardinal directions, and dug a hole in the center in preparation for the planting of the *Tree of Peace.* As we gathered the stones, we found nine bullets, which I later buried in the hole as a gesture of peace before we planted the tree.

That evening we prepared for the next day's ceremony. While Revital and our friends worked in the cabin preparing their special clothes for the ritual, I went to the site alone and walked around the great spools of barbed wire fencing placed to keep out Palestinians. These closed one side of the *Earth Wheel* off from the Dead Sea. On the other side, a great stone cliff loomed. An owl hooted from the top of a pole when I lay my sleeping bag down at the edge of the stone circle, and the wind blew fiercely across the Dead Sea, whipping dust over the land. I pulled my head inside and zipped myself into my cocoon. As I lay there reviewing the events that had transpired, I could hardly believe we had been at the site for only one day.

As I slipped into sleep, I wept and dreamed I was a Palestinian mother, head bent, face veiled in black. President Bush drowned out my sobs. "I'll take care of everything," he said. His voice grew louder and louder until my weeping could not be heard at all.

I woke with the first rays of light and continued work on the *Earth Wheel*, raking, clearing, and putting the finishing touches on the circle before the ceremony. I had not been able to come to the site earlier to carve the stones as I usually do, but we planned to return to the site after the ceremony and carve symbols into the twelve stones. The caretaker of the nature preserve,

Ceremony at the Dead Sea with a Palestinian boy and Israeli girl planting the *Tree of Peace* in the *Earth Wheel*

Oren, whose name means "pine" in Hebrew, arrived with the pine tree, the *Tree of Peace*. A crowd gathered—people from many different ethnic backgrounds, with their children and musical instruments.

Elias and his family arrived. As we gathered in the stone circle, we saw eagles flying overhead. Revital and I lit the sage together and ritually smudged everyone with its smoke. This signified a purification, a release of the past confusion of body and mind, and made space for the present moment with its possibilities of a new future. Revital prayed in Hebrew and I repeated the same prayer in English. Everyone there echoed the words in their own languages: Arabic, Yiddish, German, Dutch, French, and Spanish. The children—Mamet, the son of my Palestinian friends Elias and Hevam, and Yael, the daughter of an Israeli friend, both twelve years old—came forward and lowered the *Tree of Peace* into the hole in the center of the *Earth Wheel*.

We all took turns laying a handful of earth at the base of the tree and we each said a prayer for peace. Revital and I danced in a circle around the *Earth Wheel* and everyone joined in. Soon the hundred people who had gathered all danced and sang together, adding their Israeli, Palestinian, and Christian songs and dances to the ones that Revital and I had learned from Yehwehnode on the Seneca reservation.

Two days later we returned to the site. Revital, two of her friends, and I completed the twelve stone sculptures that formed the *Earth Wheel* around the *Tree of Peace*. We each worked on three stones in the circle as I showed each person how to carve, following the designs that Yehwehnode had given us. The tap, tap, tap—music to my ears—continued throughout the day. At the completion, I gave instructions on how to put color on the stone, then how to polish it with wax. The circle came alive.

On the drive back to Revital's house that evening, we sang the entire way. When we passed through Jerusalem, I asked to go up to the Mount of Olives to find a man named Jammal Sheik, a Sufi master and peace activist known as the "Peace Keeper." As we drove through the streets, we were met with angry and hostile stares. Revital and her friends became frightened. We left quickly and learned shortly after that there had been shooting that night on those very streets.

Palestinian boy and Israeli girl planting the *Tree of Peace*

Carving stones for the *Earth Wheel* on the banks of the Dead Sea

Revital soon left Israel and returned to the States, and I went to stay with Tamar Meir, an artist who helped organize weekly protests against human rights violations. Her group, "Women in Black," put on black hoods and stood outside public buildings in downtown Jerusalem. She introduced me to her Palestinian artist friend, Abdul, who lived on the Mount of Olives. I wanted to find someone to take me into East Jerusalem to meet the Sheik. When I asked Tamar to come with me, she declined. Only the week before, close to the Mount of Olives, someone had shot her daughter in the leg on her way home from school.

I went alone to meet Abdul at his jewelry store in downtown Jerusalem. A handsome, bearded man with an air of sadness and intelligence, he invited me to his home in the Palestinian section of the Mount, certain we could find someone who knew of the Sufi Sheik.

As we drove to the Mount of Olives, Abdul told me stories of how he regularly endured stonings and the jeering of his neighbors as he commuted to his store downtown. As we entered the Mount of Olives, he grabbed his keffiyeh, the Palestinian scarf, and put it on the dashboard where it would be broadly visible as a statement that he was Palestinian. We stopped at a taxi stand on the Mount and a driver gave us directions to Jammal Sheik's house.

The Sheik greeted us at the door as if he had been expecting us and as if we were his dearest friends. Elderly, with gray beard and hair, and a sad, kind face, he wore a long white tunic over his heavy body. After he seated us, his wife came in and served us food and drink on elegant trays. Incense burned and I could hear soft Palestinian music coming from an adjacent room.

While we ate, Jammal Sheik spoke with tears in his eyes. "Yesterday a young Palestinian boy, my neighbor, was tortured brutally and then murdered in the Mosque by an Israeli. Blood flowed like a river and covered the floor of our sacred shrine. I heard his screams even from here." He turned to me from time to time while he narrated this sad event, and he asked me, "Beloved, what are you doing? What are you doing to stop this river of blood?"

I felt guilty by association because I am an American and America supports and funds Israel.

Jammal Sheik said, "I'm in jail frequently for my protests for human rights. My life is so much in the public eye, I'm at risk for assassination."

As we departed, he said, "Sister, my death is very near. Beloved friends, be very careful when you leave. You will, for sure, be followed."

Outside the Sheik's house the night was magic; the full moon drew Abdul and me in the direction of the Old City. At the Wailing Wall, orthodox Jews rocked back and forth in prayer. I wrote a prayer for peace on a paper and stuck it between the cracks in the stone where thousands of other pieces of paper were lodged. I ran my hands over the ancient stones and wept for the sorrow I had witnessed that night, my tears mingling with the tears of centuries.

As we walked through the streets of the Old City, the stones spoke their long history to me, laid down as they were and traveled by a multitude of God's devotees—Christians, Muslims, Jews, Baha'is, Druze—all drawn to this Holy City for worship. Then we walked across fields to Mount Calvary, the site of Jesus' crucifixion, to the Garden of Gethsemane, and to the Mount of Olives where Jesus prayed and cried out in his pain.

Returning to Abdul's house that same night, we smelled tear gas in the air. Close by we heard gunfire. Abdul said in an agitated voice, "Come quickly! Get in the house!" Inside, he hurriedly closed all the doors and shutters. My eyes stung from the tear gas and I drew out my handkerchief. When I had a chance to look around, there was welcome in the grace of his home, a grace I had not suspected from the outside. His parents had lived there before him and I recognized the depth of feeling in the placement of art objects and the atmosphere of culture and elegance. He served me Palestinian food and wine, his hospitality unparalleled.

As we lounged after dinner in the living room, Abdul shared the frustrations of his life and the great sorrows of his people. I began to sing and this seemed to lift his spirits as the moon shone through the window and touched his shoulder. Because it was late, I asked Abdul if I could spend the night in his home. He hesitated and then agreed. Curious about this hesitation, I learned later that even though Israelis and Palestinians may be personal friends, they rarely visit each others' homes. Tamar, in her fifteen years of friendship with Abdul, had never been inside his house.

Abdul and I talked about plans to turn the Old City into a neutral city for peace, where everyone could come freely and worship. I wanted to stay in Israel to help Abdul in his work—but if I did, it would be a commitment of years. I had planted a seed with the ceremony at the Dead Sea, and that seed would grow with time. However, I resolved that my role was not to stay physically. I needed to continue the World Wheel and to connect other people and other countries to this new family.

When I returned to Tel Aviv, the papers recalled new killings on the Mount of Olives. Saddam Hussein's name seemed always in the background, on television or in conversation. The United States had already occupied the Gulf and was on the verge of officially declaring war. If I didn't leave soon, events would force me to stay at least for the duration of the war. I had already purchased my ticket for India, the next country on the World Wheel. My flight departed on an Arab airline with a layover in Baghdad.

Elias telephoned with a question in his voice. He had seen a television program on the World Wheel and had read the interviews with Revital and myself. The coverage made no mention of the Palestinians. Since the reporting was all in Hebrew, I had had no way of knowing what had been reported. I could only promise that when I finished my own writing about Israel, I would send him a copy. I assured him that I would represent all I had seen as faithfully as I could.

Eventually, I learned that the Israeli government had ordered blanket suppression in the media of any information about the Palestinians and their situation. They even censored the word "Palestinian" for its political charge. The press had eliminated all mention of the Palestinian involvement in the World Wheel and the planting of the *Tree of Peace* by Palestinian and Israeli children together. Individuals in this country, like Tamar Meir, Jammal Sheik, and Elias Jabbour would give their lives for peace and resolution, but did so without support and at great risk to themselves.

So although the ceremony itself was powerful and brought hope to the people who attended, I left the country contemplating the slowness of change and the long struggle ahead. But seeds planted eventually grow when the right conditions arise. The power of a circle of stone, the voices of the children, their answers to my questions—those were the seeds for me. Exactly one year from the day of the completion of the stone circle, Palestinians and Israelis came together in Spain for the very first peace talks.

My heart weeps for the unresolved conflict, but I feel hope when I recall the answers of the children. As the Palestinian, Israeli, and Druze children said in the House of Hope, "If we can look through the eyes of people who live and think in a different way, we can understand them. And if we can understand them, we can love them as our brothers and sisters."

CHAPTER FOURTEEN

The Amazon Jungle

Peru

1976

Don Hildé, with termites nest in Amazon Jungle

LOS ANGELES GREW MORE and more uncomfortable. Although I spent much of my time living simply in my VW bug in the hills outside the city, I had also accepted the use of a guest room in the home of a psychiatrist friend, Dr. Oscar Janiger, in Beverly Hills. I became a walking paradox. At Oscar's home I tried to fit in to the social norm, but the baby steps that I had made toward a border less consciousness clearly led me in the opposite direction. My body hurt.

I was now thirty-eight years old and still having my ongoing panics. I had consulted an L.A. psychiatrist, the Swami at the Hollywood Vedanta Society center, and my friend Oscar Janiger, to no avail. None of them knew what to suggest. But one day Oscar invited me to join him and some friends for tea.

I had met Oscar through my former husband, Dale, when we lived in Santa Barbara. Now in his sixties, Oscar was of Russian Jewish descent with thick, dark hair, graying at his temples. He had a kind face and a twinkle in his dark eyes as he introduced me to his friends. Marlene de Rios was an anthropologist and the author of a book on *ayahuasca,* a hallucinogenic vine that grows in the Amazon of Peru. Her husband, Yando, was a painter and the son of a Peruvian *curandero*, the equivalent of a Native American medicine man.

After we had visited for a while, Oscar said, "Come upstairs. I want to show you some artwork."

We walked upstairs and he pulled out a painting. "In the fifties, I had a grant to research the effect of hallucinogens like LSD on the creative process.[16] Anaïs Nin painted this for me." The painting was a swirl of color. Oscar selected another canvas. "This one was done by Clark Gable. It looks like an explosion." He showed us several other paintings, done by celebrities under the influence of LSD, and then we returned to the living room.

Yando and I exchanged ideas on art, and I said, "One time my perception changed so that everything around me filled with light, with no divisions between objects, similar to an LSD experience, except that I hadn't taken anything."

Yando seemed interested. "You should go visit my father, Don Hildé, in the Amazon. He lives in that sort of consciousness."

That invitation was all I needed. In the next days after our tea party, I bought a ticket with the small amount of money still left from the sale of my sculptures, gathered my tools and a few clothes—only what I could easily carry in a small backpack—and boarded a plane bound for Peru.

When I stepped off the plane in Pulcalpa, a frontier jungle town in the Peruvian Amazon, I stood mesmerized by the faces of the people. Their features and angular bone structure resembled those of the Incas, known to me only through the stone sculptures in my childhood art books and *National Geographic* magazine. All around me, people had skin the color of honey. I could recognize the Shipibo Indians because the women wore their skirts made of traditional woven cloth with rectangular white designs against a black background. The men wore white loose pants. Other Peruvians wore standard western dress.

Following Yando's instructions, I found my way about a mile down a red earth path that led from the outskirts of the airport to Don Hildé's home, a wooden shack of rough-hewn boards in various shades and textures. Don Hildé greeted me at the door. He had just received Yando's letter telling of my arrival and was expecting me. He was in his sixties, although his sun-shriveled face and thin hair made him appear older. His short, lean body, on the other hand, looked strong and wiry through his white cotton shirt and loose pants. Dark eyes looked at me with concern as he led me into his house. Several patients sat on a wooden plank bench in the main room. I learned that they often waited all day for his attention.[17]

Don Hildé showed me to a tiny, windowless room not much bigger than a closet. His wife, Beatrice, sat in the kitchen, crippled by painful arthritis. She looked young enough to be his daughte; she pretty with long black hair, honey skin, high cheekbones, and the lovely almond eyes of the Shipibo Indians.

I fell asleep quickly that first night, and woke in the morning to the sounds of chickens, ducks, and dogs. Don Hildé, in his quiet manner, moved unselfconsciously amid the cooking, washing, and animals in the simple house. There was no electricity, running water, or sewage system. We all wore few clothes, simple cottons, because of the heat and humidity of the jungle. Privacy was unknown except for brief moments in the outhouse. An enema bag hung over the picture of Jesus in the kitchen.

On the second day, Don Hildé motioned for me to join him in the jungle as he gathered herbs for his work. This was the first time I had been in a jungle, and I saw layer upon layer of vines curling tender green tips around dying stalks. Out of the decaying humus grew red and pink orchids. Strange birdcalls pierced the silence. We walked along a narrow trail of red mud that wound into the dense jungle. The rainy season had begun and every once in a while the swollen cloud bellies burst, clearing the hot, humid air with cool, wet, musical beats, leaving behind the pungent fragrance of earth. The river by our side changed from sky blue to silver jewels as the rain hit its surface. Shipibo Indians bathed nude along its banks as we passed, unveiling childlike smiles in adult faces. A grandmother sat in the shade rocking a newborn baby. The red adobe mud soon stained us.

Don Hildé entered a dense mass of foliage and I followed. He had spotted a termite nest. With a long pole picked up from alongside the path, he loosened the gnarly nest and it fell to the ground. I ran to pick it up, but felt squeamish when I saw it alive with termites. He stuffed the tangled nest into his backpack and swung the huge bundle over his shoulders, assuring me that termites helped with the treatment of arthritis. I followed behind him as he pushed his way back to the path, looking even more shriveled and tiny under the bulk of his cargo.

We walked deeper into the jungle and gathered the *ayahuasca* vine for a ceremony to be held by the *curanderos* in a few days, then turned back in the direction of his home, stopping now and then to pick herbs along the path. Don Hildé showed me which part of each plant to pick and how to wrap the ends in jungle vines to hold them together. I finished one bundle and then ventured to ask, "Yando told me you used to be a carpenter. What led you to become a *curandero?*"

"I was a carpenter for many years," Don Hildé said, "and at that time I used my powers improperly to control people for my own benefit. But nine years ago, I had a vision of Jesus. In this revelation, I experienced the compassion of Christ. I saw how my actions harmed other people and myself, and that completely changed my life. Instead of thinking only about Don Hildé, I became concerned with the people around me. I brought a dying neighbor back to life with herbs and prayer. After that, people started coming to me."

We sloshed through puddles along the path. I enjoyed the feel of red mud squishing beneath my feet. "How do you go about working with people?" I asked.

"The important thing is to 'see.' I enter a trance and see the person's disease by color: liver conditions are black; cancer is a dark, muddy red. My own body feels heavy in the corresponding region. Knowing the cause of the disorder is the most important element. Some are physical problems from birth and others arise through chronic malnutrition or infection or trauma. Some are in the spiritual realm—maybe the lack of a guide, a protector, or a companion—and some are mental distortions caused by a *doño,* a person sending negative thoughts. There are negative and positive forces that you can attract or repel, and which you can direct for good or evil. Everything is energy."

In my excitement on hearing his ideas about energy, I almost tripped over a rotting log. "Don Hildé, I have come all this way to ask you something," my words rushed out. "At times my perception changes. I see everything as light and my body seems to dissolve into an ocean of energy. When I'm going through this, I panic because my mother was declared medically insane. I'm terrified that I'm like her."

Don Hildé stopped on the path and turned to me, his small black eyes penetrating. I was fortunate that a Peruvian student happened by and helped with the translations. "We don't have the idea of insanity as you do in your country. We are more concerned with negative and positive energy. I've worked with other people having this same difficulty. The physical being has to be strengthened to create balance and a spiritual protector is absolutely essential."

"Yes!" I said. "I'm going through a period where I don't feel the presence of Jesus or Ramakrishna. Their forms disappear into a void of light. I used to feel secure in their presence."

Don Hildé walked on. "Without their protection you're lost in the cosmic forces. This energy is too strong. Prepare your body with diet, exercise, and meditation, and then you can draw in and incorporate the universal spirit. And will power is very important—to take responsibility for your own life. You must follow your individual path, not with a deity to worship, but with a protector that shields you from negative forces."

We reached Don Hildé's home where people still waited on the wooden bench for his services. He instructed me to boil the termites and the termite nest into a compote for Beatrice's arthritis while he attended to the first patient.

As I stood over the stove, a young woman arrived, completely hysterical. In the United States they would have called her manic, given her tranquilizers, and taken her to a psychiatric hospital. Don Hildé came in from the meditation room with a glass of water. The young woman stood shaking in her simple cotton dress, waving her arms, and talking rapidly in a high-pitched voice.

Don Hildé put his hand over the glass of water, prayed, and gave it to her. She drank it all and, to my amazement, settled into a perfect calm. She sat with Don Hildé and they talked.

"This water has been energized and has already neutralized the negative energy sent from a *doño,* your jealous cousin. He has affected your digestion. You must change and strengthen your own life, but you are safe right now. I'll give you a prayer to say continually. This prayer is the only continual protection you'll need. Know that Jesus will protect you and guide you to change the way you are living." Don Hildé stood up and led the woman into the meditation room to impart her prayer.

After a few moments they walked out of the room and she left the house stepping onto the earthen path in perfect peace. I stood mute with a mixture of admiration of this natural healing and anger at western medicine. Images of the Metropolitan State Hospital, Dewitt State Hospital, and the Camarillo State Hospital flashed through my mind. I recalled my mother sitting in the waiting room, suffering the effects of long-term residence in these institutions, her body red and swollen from drugs, her mind damaged from shock treatments. She had lost all her teeth due to lack of care during years of catatonia. Hair had grown over her chin, her face was pasty and puffy, and her blank stare bore through me. The beautiful bright mother of my childhood had turned into an unrecognizable hag.

Two weeks before this trip to Peru, I had seen her hospital records: *Lillian Melba Hamilton ran away from the hospital ward for the second time. After a series of shock treatments, she shows signs of severe brain damage. She is now cooperative and sleeps and eats well.* It was powerful to realize that this didn't need to have happened.

I stirred the termite compote with new strength. It splashed out of the pan onto the stove.

The day advanced as Don Hildé worked with one patient after another. The termite nest boiled down to a thick, murky brew. Beatrice and I started supper. After the three of us finished our fried bananas and rice, Beatrice played cards with Don Hildé at the kitchen table, while the termite compress on her knees gave her temporary relief from her arthritis.

A week after my arrival, Don Hildé said, "We will have an *ayahuasca* ceremony this evening." During the previous days, I had seen him brew the hallucinogenic vines we had gathered in the jungle. He had asked me to keep this quiet lest we have prying eyes. As darkness approached, Don Hildé made the rounds of his yard and house to make sure that all his patients had left, and then he securely locked the doors and windows. A few moments later, he went around again and double-checked.

I heard a knock on the front door and Don Hildé opened it to greet another *curandero* and two of his friends. Yando and Marlene had arrived from the States and we all sat in a circle in the main room in total darkness. The *ayahuasca* brew was passed around. I was the only one who did not sip. In the past I had smoked marijuana a few times and taken LSD once, but I found that my creativity shriveled, so I had decided not to use any drugs or plant hallucinogens as aids for transformation. Through meditation and the creative process, however, I had had similar consciousness-altering experiences without the use of hallucinogenic substances.

One by one, everyone vomited into a bucket passed around the room, including Don Hildé and Beatrice. Don Hildé started a breathing exercise similar to the yogic *pranayama* exercises I had learned in India. He pushed air out of his lungs as he moved his torso and arms and then he inhaled deeply. But the environment lacked the color of India where they had incorporated flowers and bright materials, candles, and singing in their ceremonies. We sat in darkness inside Don Hildé's old wooden house where no decoration of any kind, not even paint, embellished our surroundings.

After the vomiting everyone got sleepy and sank down into their internal journeys. We sat quietly for over an hour with no sound or movement from our group. I drew inward into my own meditations, then I let myself slip into the void that had so frightened me. This time the silence and darkness allowed me to feel at home in my borderless world of energy. The darkness grew luminous and alive.

Eventually Don Hildé began humming softly, and a tune slowly emerged followed by words. Earlier he had told me, "When the song comes, the spirit is contacted and moves through you." He chanted and sang for a long time, then started talking in a strange voice as Yando translated. "An entity has come and wants to contact you, Vijali, and help you. He sees that you are a good, kind-hearted person. But someone wants to harm you, to veil you, to make you uneasy and bring you confusion. You have begun your own inner development, and that person can't obtain what you have, so he wants to eliminate what you are.

"You drew inside for natural protection while this person took your energy, but you have to attend to your inner work properly, which takes *all* of your energy. This person works with drugs and is in an unhealthy environment. He makes a show that he is good and loving, but it is only a decoy to attract the bees. What is true is that he works with negative forces and puts things into your body to prevent you from succeeding at your mission."

I shook all over as I listened. I knew he referred to Oscar Janiger. For a month, I had taken the anxiety medication Oscar had given me for my panic, until I decided it was not the route I wanted to take. I had also noticed his ambivalence toward my spirituality. Oscar displayed a certain reverence for the spiritual when we were alone, but then would jovially shut me up when I tried to express myself in front of his friends.

Don Hildé called for me to come and stand by him. The wooden floor yielded and creaked as I walked to his side. I sensed reverence from the people sitting in our circle, though I couldn't see their faces in the dark.

Don Hildé spoke again. "My teacher and others have felt your heart and seen your situation. They've come in spirit and have asked me to make a formal presentation to you in this room, a benediction. They want to hear your voice. Please say something to them."

I stood there with a completely blank mind. I could think of nothing to say.

Don Hildé prompted,"They're waiting to hear your voice."

I spoke softly and shyly what I felt in my heart. "Thank you for coming and caring about me and wanting to heal me."

Don Hildé kept saying, "Speak louder, speak louder."

"Thank you for coming! Thank you for wanting to help me!" I spoke as loudly as I could.

They seemed satisfied because Don Hildé went on to say, "This moment I have gone back a thousand years and am a reincarnation in Mexico. Roscal Necoks, a Toltec, has asked me to protect you so this force cannot get you. I put a new life in you and from now on, your only duty is to take care of the light. Think only of the light and the beliefs you have, the yoga, and how you used to pray and direct yourself. You have a new body. Take care of it and live only for that force, for God. Always, always remember this room, no matter how far away you are. Call my name and I will be with you and will protect you. Every day keep the light in mind and do your work."

I retreated to my place on the floor, my mind and body vibrating. The effects of the *ayahuasca* gradually wore off the others and the morning light crept through the cracks in the wooden shutters. The other *curandero* and his friends left silently. Don Hildé, Beatrice, Yando, Marlene, and I went to our respective bedrooms.

In the afternoon we emerged from our rooms and Don Hildé prepared herbs for a ceremonial bath to cleanse and protect me. I took the bucket of warm brewed herbs to the bathing area in the back yard amidst the chickens and ducks. Planks of wood nailed together formed a four-sided stall with an entrance that faced away from the house. Wooden slats formed the floor and the cracks between them allowed the water to run to the ground. I took off my clothes and hung them on a nail, then from the bucket poured the warm water and herbs over my head and body, saying aloud as Don Hildé had instructed, "I am cleansed and protected from all negative forces."

After I dried off, I put on a white cotton dress which I had brought with me and had saved for a special occasion. Then I joined Don Hildé in the meditation room. A small platform in the middle of the room formed an altar, with three candles on it and a bowl of water in the center. Don Hildé prayed, holding his hands over the water and energizing it.

We sat in silence and meditated for a long time, until Don Hildé broke the silence with a prayer he wanted me to chant throughout my life: *May Jesus Christ always be with me and protect me from the evil forces attempting to enter my life and body.*

"Jesus as your protector will guide you through the infinite space that has opened to you. Without this guide, you're vulnerable to the negative forces." He described the shield I was to visualize in front of my solar plexus as a disk of radiant white light. "Know that nothing negative can penetrate and enter your energy field. There will be a time when power will come through you. Use it wisely and always remember this time of vulnerability."

I wanted to accept Don Hildé's suggestions, yet as thankful as I was for his help and guidance, I questioned his perception of negative forces. Is there not a place or a view of existence beyond the duality of good and evil? Beyond negative and positive forces? It seemed to me that my experience of a borderless world might *be* that place, and perhaps only when I experienced separation did I also experience fear and the need to protect myself.

During my stay at Don Hildé's, I had hoped to find a site to carve at the Marina Coshe lagoon, located a half hour away at the headwaters of the Amazon River. While I explored, I saw the Shipibo Indians bathing along the river's edges, but I noticed that they never swam out into the lagoon. Early one morning, I swam to its center, diving and surfacing like a fish in its warm waters. As I swam, I felt something gently touch my thigh, perhaps the most sensitive touch I have ever experienced, and then a twelve-foot sweet-water dolphin leapt out of the water at my side! After my initial fright, I relaxed and swam underwater, turning and playing like a dolphin in response to her presence.

As I turned, turned, turned in this warm, wet-green world, I lost sight of inside or outside, up or

Shipibo children bathing in the Amazon of Peru

down. The water carried my weight as if the universe had reached out to cradle me.

Back on shore, I asked why no one swam in the lagoon. The women and children along the banks said, "There are piranhas in the water."

The towering Peruvian Andes with their granite outcroppings loomed in my mind. When my search for a stone to carve in the Peruvian jungle led to nothing, I knew I had to leave. Yet I hesitated to leave the only environment that supported my perception of a spacious world of luminosity. While I couldn't accept Don Hildé's beliefs completely, when I was with him I no longer experienced the panic attacks that had plagued me daily in Los Angeles, surrounded by its pervasive "This is mine and all else is separate" attitude. When I lived in Don Hildé's world—where he saw everything as energy and understood every being and every action as coming from the universal source—all my physical and mental pain vanished.

But my desire to create art from the Peruvian earth pulled me away from my jungle family. Yando and Marlene had scheduled me to give a slide show talk to a religious group in Lima. After the presentation I planned to go into the mountains in search of stone. So with great thanksgiving for my two-month stay, I said goodbye to my new family and boarded a bus headed for the Andes.

I was lucky to get a seat. Squawking chickens, pineapples, and mothers with nursing babies jammed the aisles. The twenty-two hour bus ride over a fifteen thousand-foot pass took me through the jungle along the Brazilian border to Lima on the Pacific Ocean side of the Andes.

The tattered old bus, with its dusty shrine of the Virgin Mary, often teetered toward the edge of the eroded earthen road where the mountainside dropped thousands of feet into the canyons of the Andes below. The driver regularly stopped to examine the road, move a few rocks, check the tires, and peer into the steaming motor before he drove off again.

We also stopped every two hours to relieve ourselves—women behind the bus, men in front. The other women had no trouble; they squatted down on the ground with their colorful, voluminous skirts flared around them. My jeans, however, were a real problem. Many times I returned to the bus with a full bladder, having been unable to find a private space away from the prying eyes of the men.

As we rose higher in altitude nearing the fifteen thousand-foot pass, people brought out lemons and held them to their noses, sniffing. Someone vomited. I asked about the lemons. No one seemed to know exactly why, but they helped with altitude sickness.

Every few hours we passed through a village and more people boarded the bus. Each group wore a different style of clothing, spoke another dialect, and played different forms of music that I had not heard before. My favorites were the Highland Huayno songs (pronounced "wino"). Sometimes described as Andean hillbilly music, these songs reflect the deepest emotions of the village people.

When we stopped for supper at a roadside cafe in the coca fields, our waitress had a flask hanging from a chain around her neck. She took customers aside and sold cocaine from the flask. The locals called it "lettuce" and said that coca leaf tea "adjusts the blood to the altitude." Then, as the cold night came, we slept as we could between the stops, the aisles of the bus packed with snoring bodies.

In the morning we arrived in Lima, the grayest city I had ever experienced. My first impression was of the shanty towns on Lima's outskirts where thousands of people lived in unbelievably poor conditions. Inside the city the buildings were a dingy gray and the people wore grave expressions. Even the earth itself was gray. When I stepped from the bus, the odor of stale urine and overripe fruit overwhelmed me. I missed my green jungle, red earth, and Amazon family.

My spirits picked up, however, when my slide presentation, "Art as a Spiritual Process," was enthusiastically received both at the Brahmananica Organization and at the University of Lima. Many women approached me afterward with their addresses and telephone numbers and asked to stay in contact with me. One woman whom I would see again, Maria, particularly touched my heart with eager questions and her life story which she briefly shared with me. The next day, still thinking of these encounters, I gathered twelve dark stones from the river to carve.

Although the women captured my heart in Lima, I chose to return to Chosica in the Andes, a small and beautiful town on the Rio Rimac. I had seen it from the bus window passing through, and Yando and Marlene gave me the name of an innkeeper there before they returned to the United States. When I arrived at this little town, I looked him up. The innkeeper and his wife graciously rented me a tiny room on the second floor with a view of the church across the street.

On the morning after my arrival, I walked over the bridge and down to the river. There I sat on a rock in the sun and watched the children pass on their way to school. I eyed a massive granite boulder rising from the river and waded out to this stone through the chilly water. My hands wandered over it, touching a surface polished smooth by centuries of fast moving currents. I felt the life inside as if I had touched the belly of a pregnant woman. I found her back, then her slightly bent head and embracing arm. "Here you are," I said aloud. "I've been looking for you and I think perhaps you've been waiting for me."

I ran back across the bridge to my room, threw my hammer and chisels and a portfolio of photos of my sculptures into my backpack and then returned to the river. A young woman stood on the path leading to the schoolhouse.

"Do you know who owns this property?" I asked.

"I'm a teacher at the school," she said. "This area is the property of the school district."

I asked her to introduce me to the school principal. We walked side by side to the school, where the young woman knocked on the principal's door. Looking more than a little curious, he invited me into his office.

"I'm a sculptor," I explained, "and I'd like permission to carve on a beautiful granite boulder in the river. I understand it's on the school's property?" I showed him my photos of *Winged Woman* and *Continuum*.

"Yes," he said, immediately in broken English. "We're fortunate to have you!"

I returned to the boulder where I crushed a few leaves of California sage and sprinkled them in the four directions. The remainder I burned, smudging the boulder, my tools, and myself. As the smoke rose into the clean air, I prayed that I might carve and release the woman in the stone. The river splashed and chuckled, a sound I took for its happy consent.

I stood in the cold, ankle-deep water and carved, incising the outline of a woman's face and shoulders. Then, sitting on the boulder, my feet out of the water, I carved her arm. The work absorbed me, and I didn't realize that the school day had ended until I looked up and saw that I had attracted an audience. Five boys and girls stood with their arms around each other watching. I stopped in surprise, and then motioned for them to come closer and try their hand at carving. They giggled and ran off down the path that bordered the bounding river.

I carved on the stone each day with my simple hammer and chisels, allowing the boulder's innate female form to emerge. At night, exhausted and happy, I crossed the bridge to the inn and to my tiny room on the other side of the river.

I had wondered how the Peruvian people would react to a lone American woman doing this strange thing. Would I be ridiculed, laughed at as crazy? To the contrary, the people who passed by and entered my life seemed to understand my work better than people did in the U.S. I did not speak Spanish well, or the Indian languages at all, but that made no difference. When I showed each person I met the photographs of my work, I felt an immediate rapport with them. Lines of communication opened through the art, more intimate perhaps than if I had been fluent speaking in words to them.

The women were especially enthusiastic. One day I received a message at the inn. Maria, the woman who had attended my talk in Lima, would arrive at noon the next day. At my lunch break the following day, I found her waiting in the small lobby at the inn. We embraced as long lost friends and then we walked together to the site, carrying the lunch she had brought. On the river bank, we spread rice, a fish dish, bread, and wine out on a cloth that Maria pulled from her basket.

"May the Lord bless this food and our meeting," she said with great reverence.

The food tasted so sweet that it must have been imbued with the love she carried. The sun warmed our hands in the cool mountain air and our hearts filled with the camaraderie of women friends.

After we ate I showed her how to carve with the hammer and chisel, but she preferred to sit and watch, singing me a song in her sweet, passionate voice. Then she told me more of her story, the story of many women in Peru.

"My husband was very handsome," she said. "We were very much in love until we had our first child. Then he started going to the bars after work instead of coming home. One night, he never returned at all. A week later I ran into him and another woman at the center square." Maria stopped to take a deep breath. "They walked arm in arm down the street and we didn't see each other until we almost collided. When I started crying, he hit me and ran off in a rage, the other woman's hand in his." Her eyebrows furrowed and she set her mouth, "I haven't seen him since. I had to find work to raise my daughter and the baby I was expecting at the time. I've opened a stall on the street at the bazaar where I sell clothes that I make."

The next day a woman from the village, Theresa, stopped by with some sweets. An Andean Indian woman in her fifties, she held her head high and wore patched, but beautifully woven clothes. I stopped work and we sat on the stone by the river where we ate the sweet bread and drank the tea from her thermos. Before long she told me a story very similar to Maria's, though set in a different time and place.

I was a symbol of freedom for these women. They were fascinated that a woman could manage alone, doing what she loved, and they often came to visit me at the site bringing food or friends. My heart wept for them as they struggled to make a life for themselves in a society where women are seen as second-class workers or sex objects.

I felt this firsthand myself in Lima. Marlene and Yando had introduced me to the owner of one of the best galleries in Peru and he had arranged a show for me. As the date of the exhibition approached, I went to the gallery to check the size of the rooms and see how my twelve stone sculptures would fit into the space. The owner asked me to dinner and we walked to a nearby restaurant that played the Highland Huayno music I loved.

At the end of our meal he said, "Please, Vijali, come to my house tonight and we will make love."

"Of course I won't," I said.

"Then I will cancel the show. Every woman who has a show in my gallery sleeps with me and you are a California woman." Unable to deal with my continued refusal, he canceled the exhibition.

As enraging as this was, fortunately I had other options. But for abandoned Peruvian women, the only answer open is to go into the streets to sell food or sometimes sell themselves in order to support their children alone. Unsure of how to help them, I continued to sculpt and offer my friendship.

The last day of work arrived as the sculpture reached completion. The children who had been coming every day after school wore sad faces. The teacher who had introduced me to the principal that first day came with one of her fellow teachers. Maria traveled from Lima and brought a friend. Theresa arrived from the village. We all waded out into the river to hold hands around the sculpture. The women had tears in their eyes and could not find words. Finally, one woman started a song and the children joined in.

Homage to Andean Woman, Chosica, Andes of Peru

The Indian woman rose out of the stone, her body still embedded in the bulk of gray granite, her head bent from the weight of an invisible load. We named her *Homage to Andean Woman*. After the song, silence returned but for the river splashing over stone, speaking the words that eluded us.

I soon returned to the United States to face and resolve the problem of how to live in my new "borderless world" within my own culture. I needed to go back and stay in the pain and confusion until I found an avenue out. I had a sense that if I found a way for myself, I might also find a way for others.

CHAPTER FIFTEEN

World Wheel-Spoke Eight

West Bengal, India
1991

Vijali and Shivashundar Baul

BEFORE I LEFT THE UNITED STATES to go to Spain I had attended a retreat given by Lama Wangdor, a Tibetan lama, who had invited me to visit his community in Rewalsar, India in the foothills of the Himalayas. There a group of Tibetan refugees lived in caves, and I was eager to meet them.

I took a bus from New Delhi to Rewalsar, over rough earth roads that wound through the foothills. The trip took two days. I arrived under a full moon that illuminated pine forests on steep mountain slopes. I went immediately in search of my old friend, who greeted me with obvious pleasure.

Lama Wangdor was a small man, less than five feet tall, yet when he had fled Tibet after the Chinese invaded in the 1950s, he had carried his teacher, a large man, on his back over the Himalayas because the teacher could not walk. Many who made that journey died of starvation or froze to death, but Lama Wangdor's group reached Rewalsar safely and settled into the natural caves situated above a clear mountain lake. It was here at Tso Pema (Lotus Lake), that Padmasambhava, the great Buddhist saint normally considered to be the father of Tibetan Buddhism and Princess Mandarava, his consort, were burned alive by Mandarava's enraged father. According to legend, they changed the fire into a lake and emerged unscathed from the flames in union on a lotus in the water. In a group of caves above the lake the tiny community lived in seclusion, speaking only Tibetan. Unexposed to other cultures, they lived life as they might have in Tibet.

When I expressed my desire to live in one of the caves, Lama Wangdor gave me directions for the two-hour hike that would take me straight up the mountain. In the morning I gathered cooking pots and food, stuffed them into my backpack on top of my sleeping bag and started out.

Sweat poured off me by the time I arrived at the cave. Two giant granite boulders had lodged together to form the main room and a small place of level ground formed a veranda outside the entrance. I had to bend low to enter the very small door wedged into its entrance. An elderly monk, who lived in a nearby cave, had already laid a cotton rug on the wooden pallet that would serve as my bed. He had also repaired a tiny glassless opening in the wall with mud. I was unable to stand up inside, but I didn't care. It had been my heart's desire to retreat into a cave, to meditate within a supportive environment of nature and community, and there I stood, peering through the opening onto the vast snow-covered Himalayan range.

In the silence of the cave, with its earthen floor and walls of bulging stone, I spent the rest of the day cleaning and repairing, making it my own. The rickety and ill-fitting door looked as if it might fall apart at any moment, so I strengthened it, and in one corner I created a shrine. I placed on the altar a stone that had caught my attention on my trek up the mountain, and also a print of Milarepa which Lama Wangdor had given me when I arrived.

Milarepa is perhaps the most beloved saint of Tibet, an ascetic who lived in caves in this rugged

Himalayan country in complete awareness of our borderless nature. He is believed to have flown through the air and to have lifted an enormous boulder with one hand. My picture depicted him in front of a cave with a pot simmering over a wood fire. The snow-covered Himalaya Mountains rose around him, and a hunter with his weapon beside him kissed the hem of Milarepa's clothing.

After I arranged my cave, I cooked my first meal on a fire I made outside its entrance—a bowl of vegetable soup—and I reflected on the blessings that had been bestowed on me in each country. Afterwards, I explored the mountain for a possible World Wheel site.

The snow-capped peaks of the Himalayas stretched as far as I could see. I hiked to the cave where Padmasambhava, or Guru Pema as the Tibetans call him, allegedly attained enlightenment. Followers had turned the cave into a shrine with statues of Padmasambhava and his disciple Yeshe Tsogyal in its pyramid-shaped chamber and the adjoining room. Coming back from the cave, I found the World Wheel site I was searching for in the cluster of boulders that formed my own cave.

Days passed in a continual meditation on each simple act. When the weather turned cold, my gentle neighbor brought me a blanket and a candle. My only difficulty came with my roommates, the rats. My first night in the cave I didn't sleep much. I kept the candle burning all night. I kept a pot in one hand and a lid in the other to bang, making a great noise and shouting, "Out! Out!" every time I saw a rat. The next night I did better. Still with pot and lid in hands, shouting every time I heard a scampering sound, I grew so tired that I fell sound asleep between visits. On the third night I had an early visitor. I did all my clanging and shouting, and then fell soundly asleep with no candles, only a flashlight in hand, just in case. The next night I heard no sound from the rats, so I put rice and a butter candle on one side of the cave for them. A reward and a treaty: that is your side and this is mine.

One day all the monks and nuns of the community gathered in a big cave for a ceremony, or *puja,* for Padmasambhava. Everyone came out of the caves and I was delighted to see the whole community of sixteen people for the first time. We were together all day in a large room dug into the side of the mountain and adorned with figures of the Buddha and other deities. We looked each other over thoroughly as the day progressed, with acceptance on both sides. All ages were represented, from seven to eighty. Everyone was a Tibetan monk, nun, or lama except me.

I sat the whole day silently chanting a portion of the seven hundred thousand *Om Ah Hung*s I had undertaken as a prayer for the freedom of Tibet. When I first met him in at a retreat in the United States, Lama Wangdor had given me this mantra with instructions to chant it seven hundred thousand times as purification for the mind. I made the commitment, and silently dedicated the effects of this effort to Tibet's release from Chinese occupation.

The *puja* continued, and now the monks and nuns performed the Chöd ceremony. This consisted of a meditation on the dissolution of the body and ego accompanied by chanting, drums, bells, and horns made from human thigh bones. The music sounded like thunder. In fact, all the ceremonies and chanting sounded like the elemental forces of nature—water flowing, boulders crashing, rain, wind, thunder, and fire. I felt at home with their sounds even though they were new and strange to me.

No one spoke English, and I had learned only a few words of Tibetan: *Nam* which means "sky" and *Thujeche* which means both "thank you" and "hello."

After the ceremony, the weather turned very cold and snow fell in the night with much lightning and thunder. My cave leaked by the window. To add to my discomfort, the many cups of Tibetan tea with rancid butter that I had drunk upset my stomach. After two days, the strong winds eventually blew the storm away and once again I could sit on the stone outside. I had lived in my cave for eight days now and, for the first time since I arrived, my thoughts turned to the Gulf War and to my friends in Israel and Palestine. I prayed for their safety.

My own "storm" had cleared, too, as a result of chanting *Om Ah Hung* while keeping count with a rosary. I completed three hundred thousand mantras, but the thought of chanting four hundred thousand more somehow repelled me, even though

Lama Wangdor at Rewalsar (Tso Pema), India

I would ultimately finish them at a later time. In the night I reconnected with my own energy and inner voice, the nameless path that comes from inside. Where it leads is always correct for me. I woke with Anandamayi Ma's voice ringing in my ears: *Do what comes spontaneously*.

So I sat in meditation, under a radiant sun, feeling content. I always feel like a mountain when I meditate—still, with life moving around me, and nothing more to do but be. The silence filled me so beautifully and exquisitely that any manipulation of the moment would be a distraction. The little spot on the ground where my eyes rested in meditation became a luminous mandala radiating out until an entire latticework of light surrounded me. I switched back and forth from ordinary sight to this luminous sight, and at some point I thought about making a cooking fire. I didn't push the thought away, but followed it back to its source—the void containing all, even as my stomach rumbled. Another image came to me of my Israeli friends in Tel Aviv with Scud missiles flying through the air, hitting their house, and causing it to burst into flames—my fears presenting themselves to my imagination.

I left my meditation seat and built a fire for cooking breakfast, anxiety over my friends in Israel and Palestine mixing with the stillness and beauty of my snowy surroundings. I realized that a shift had occurred in this middle part of my life. Instead of feeling thrown back and forth between the great expanse of consciousness and the separate, small Vijali, I saw both relationships existing simultaneously. The individual Vijali is a ripple on this vast ocean of consciousness. They function together as Kali and Shiva, the dancing forms of creation rising out of the infinite. I remembered the Vietnamese Buddhist monk, Thich Nhat Hanh, learned not to turn away from suffering by personally removing the putrifying bodies of his people after U.S. helicopters had bombed his village.[18] The impact of this act became the foundation of his spiritual practice—breathing, smiling inwardly, bringing seeds of peace into the confused world.

Night came and stars illuminated the void. I stood on my veranda of earth and gazed into the blackness. Somehow the black void entered me, and my body took the position of the *Burning Blue Vajra Mudra*, a practice that Lama Wangdor had taught me. The practice of body stance and meditation brings the *tumo*, or heat. Then metabolism is stimulated and the body raises its temperature. I stood in the cold night air, snow covering the ground, with my arms and legs forming the double diamond shape of the *Vajra* symbol, my eyes lowered, my mind in meditation—and I began to sweat. Lama Wangdor said *tumo* burns away impurities, and it immediately burned away my discursive thoughts, so that energy flowed through me.

During my stay in Tso Pema, storms raged around the slopes and brought more snow. I couldn't protect myself from the cold by making a fire inside my cave because there was no outlet for smoke. So each night before I went to bed, I would go outside my cave and stand in the snow using the *Burning Blue Vajra* mudra stance to kindle the *tumo* heat within me.

Lama Wangdor eagerly wanted me to create the sculpture and ceremony for the World Wheel, but because Tibetans have no legal rights in India, he had asked me to seek permission from the local Hindu authorities. The timing was unfortunate. The Indians had just made a big issue about the Tibetans carving the mantra *Om Mani Padme Hung* on stones in the mountains and they wanted to curtail this, as well as Tibetan activities in general. So permission never came. After a month of political wrangling, I left Tso Pema in a thunder storm.

The bus swayed so much on the mountain curves that my luggage fell from the top of the bus. A month later, I learned that some Tibetans, following behind in a taxi, had rescued my belongings. Eventually, remarkably, they located me and returned my luggage with its contents intact even though it had not been locked.

I went on to Dharamsala to see His Holiness the Dalai Lama and attended a class he was giving to the monks. I am always touched by his humble presence and by the work he is doing throughout the world to bring peace and understanding, a peace that is so far not manifesting in his own country, Tibet. I left with the tears in my eyes that his presence always brings—a feeling of coming home to myself.

I decided to travel to Shantiniketan in West Bengal, home of the late poet Rabindranath Tagore, a Nobel Prize laureate whose poetry and idealism had always inspired me. Perhaps there I would find a site for the World Wheel.

I caught a bus, then an eastbound train that took three days to take me to Calcutta. There I intended to change trains and go north to Shantiniketan, but Dakshineswar, on the banks of the Ganga just outside Calcutta, drew me before I could travel farther. Ramakrishna, the saint, the inspiring figure for Vedanta centers and the convent where I had lived for ten years as a nun, had spent most of his life at the Kali temple in Dakshineswar. I hadn't been there since my first visit in 1972. I just had to go!

A family I had met on the bus led me to the temple, and I followed their ritual of worship. Leaving my shoes at a flower stall, I first dipped my feet in the sacred Ganga, then carried my flower and incense offerings to the back of the long line waiting to have a glimpse of Kali, the Hindu Goddess revered by Ramakrishna and worshiped in the Kali Temple.

As the line of people slowly moved, the air crackled with excitement. Three people waited ahead of me. Now two, now one. I stepped up to the railing and the priest ushered me to the side where I could have a closer look at Kali's piercing eyes, her red protruding tongue, and her black basalt body covered in fine silks and garlands of flowers. At my first glimpse of her fierce dark beauty, I experienced what Ramakrishna must have felt when he saw her. A shiver went up my spine. Tears filled my eyes.[19]

The officiating priest gave me offerings that had been made to Kali that I could take with me—a small toy of Kali's knife with blood on its edge, a container of the red powder that the women use to mark the third eye at their forehead, a sweet called *sandesh*, a few flowers, and two coins—all in a basket made of leaves.

I left the pushing crowd, which shouted, "*Jai Ma! Jai Ma!* Hail, Mother." I visited the room where Ramakrishna had lived for most of his life, enjoying

Vijali in meditation in front of her cave at Tso Pema, India

the quiet inside. Verandas surrounded the room and one looked out onto the sacred river Ganga.

I sat in one corner and meditated and then rose to leave, remembering an incident from my first visit here in 1972. Back then, in gratitude for Ramakrishna's presence in my life, I had given small coins to the beggars and lepers who were at that time allowed into the courtyard of the Kali Temple. Word got out that I had coins to give, and the beggars surged upon me grabbing at my clothes and hands. Immediately, a guard saw what was happening. He quickly extricated me from the beggars and led me out of the courtyard.

Sternly he said to me, "You have to leave the area immediately. You can't do that. This is dangerous. You can't give them money."

I left shaken. Not by the beggars, but by what the guard had said. "What is it that I *can* do?" I prayed. That prayer has stayed with me through the years and the work of the World Wheel has answered it. I couldn't do the work of a philanthropist or of a doctor or politician, but I could do what I did best—art. My prayer became, "Allow my art to grow until it touches people, touches the globe, and helps to change our consciousness so that we all can come closer to living in harmony with each other and with our environment."

This time I left Ramakrishna's room and looked in the Nahabat, a tiny building across the courtyard where Sarada Devi, his wife, had lived in a small space under the stairs. There she cooked his meals, and would often peek through the screen to have a glimpse of Ramakrishna in his room across the way as he danced and sang in ecstasy with the devotees. I couldn't believe that she had lived for so long in this tiny space. I could see her now, bringing the food to his room after the devotees left, serving him with great love. Nevertheless, Ramakrishna had worshipped her as a goddess, as his true spiritual partner and equal. And although the Vedanta Society regards her as his equal, she lived her life in the *purdha* tradition where a woman must remain unseen.

When I left Sarada Devi's room, I went to the dining area of the temple, where Ramakrishna sent his devotees to have a meal prepared by the temple cooks. I sat on the floor in a long line of devotees and ate sumptuously of the curried vegetables and chicken, dhal, and rice that volunteers ladled from a bucket onto our palm leaf plates. We ate with our right hand which is the custom, although I am left handed, because Indians use the left for cleaning themselves with water after going to the bathroom. I departed feeling satisfied in all dimensions.

As I walked out, I caught sight of myself in a mirror in one of the stalls and thought, "The real Kali Temple is my own body. Should I not walk with my head high, my shoulders back, and my breasts bare, like the statues of goddesses in India? Or at least with my shoulders back?"

When I arrived in Calcutta, I found a room near Mother Teresa's Mission of the Sisters of Charity. I felt an urgent need to visit Mother Teresa. After all, how much longer would she be with us? A nun I had met on the train to Calcutta had told me what I needed to do to be able to talk privately with Mother Teresa. So I rose before dawn and walked to the Mission for mass at 5:45 a.m. The Mission building had an unassuming presence with a wooden sign over the double front doors. I found the chapel up a flight of stairs overlooking an inner courtyard.

I entered this very stark room. There was a simple cross as an altarpiece and no chairs. Only thin straw mats covered the floor. As I knelt, I saw Mother Teresa enter and take her place among the young novices toward the back. Occasionally she appeared to nod off.

When the mass ended, I slipped out first and stood, as the nun had instructed me, outside Mother Teresa's room by the balcony. As she came out of the chapel, she talked to the various people who waited for her. Looking down from the balcony into the courtyard as I waited, I could see about one hundred young Indian girls who were novices, washing their clothes, each with her own wash pan. Later, I learned that many of these girls were orphans, outcasts, or young widows. I marveled at the joy Mother Teresa provided them through a simple life of service. Here these girls, who had no place in Indian society, had escaped from otherwise miserable lives.

When she turned to go to her room, I stepped forward and stooped to touch Mother Teresa's feet with my right hand. I then touched my forehead, symbolically taking the dust of the feet, the least regarded area of the body, to place on my forehead, the most highly regarded area. In India, this is a gesture of great respect. I asked to speak with her for a moment and she graciously accepted. She walked hunched over and her aged face showed signs of recent illness. Her eyes, however, exuded light and inner strength.

When we stood before the door of her room, I said, "I was called to be a nun in my early years and now, through a dream, I've been called to take this pilgrimage of the World Wheel for world peace." Then I told her a little about the process of my work.

She seemed touched and held my hands and prayed, "You have heard the call of God to do His work and He will guide you. Blessings on your life and your pilgrimage for peace."

I spent that day and the next as a volunteer. I played with the children in the nursery and assisted the nuns in whatever ways they needed me. The small babies stayed in a room that had been partitioned into tiny units with individual beds. Many of the babies had been rescued from trash cans. Others had been abandoned on Mother Teresa's doorstep shortly after birth. Some of them had suffered severe starvation, almost to death, or were extremely deformed. As I looked at each child, I couldn't keep the tears back. One baby had an unbelievably skinny body, her skeleton showing through a thin layer of skin, and she stared as if in shock. I picked her up and held her for a long while, and then a faint smile came to her face and a tiny light entered her staring eyes. Her gaze still haunts me now. Looking back, I see this child's smile as my greatest accomplishment on the pilgrimage.

The next day I entered the streets of Calcutta. As an American in India, one doesn't need to find a guru to be changed. One only has to walk in the streets of Calcutta for a moment to wash off a sheltered life of privilege and façade. I bowed in awe and admired the ingenuity born from suffering. One boy beckoned me to look in his address book. When I did, he peered into my ears, brought out a Q-tip, then offered to clean them for a rupee. As I walked farther, I looked for a little girl I had seen begging on the corner the day before. I wanted to ask her, "Why don't you make something beautiful with your hands and sell it in the streets?" I wanted to ask her to create a doll that resembled her, with her wide black eyes, that I could buy from her. But she wasn't there. Instead, I saw a puppy with no hair in the road with watery eyes beseeching me—and a dead horse. Yesterday, I had seen the horse's driver beat him to move a cart piled with wood and the puppy had sat on the cart. The horse, ribs protruding, could not move. I saw his legs buckle beneath him as he fell, crumpling like a garbage bag of bones cracking on cement, and I heard his neighing in the road, lost among the sounds of other cries as his master beat his fleshless body. This was Calcutta.

The next day, I took the train to Shantiniketan, birthplace and home of the Nobel poet Rabindranath Tagore. It was my hope that some surprise in Shantiniketan might lead me to the right site for the World Wheel event. Before long I heard music in a distant train car, a wonderfully rhythmic, earthy, bluesy sound. I hoped fervently that the musicians would come my way.

Finally they arrived, the Bauls, folk musicians of Bengal. The men and women were dressed in plain cottons, all different shades of ochre (the color of

Baul minstrel singing, West Bengal, India

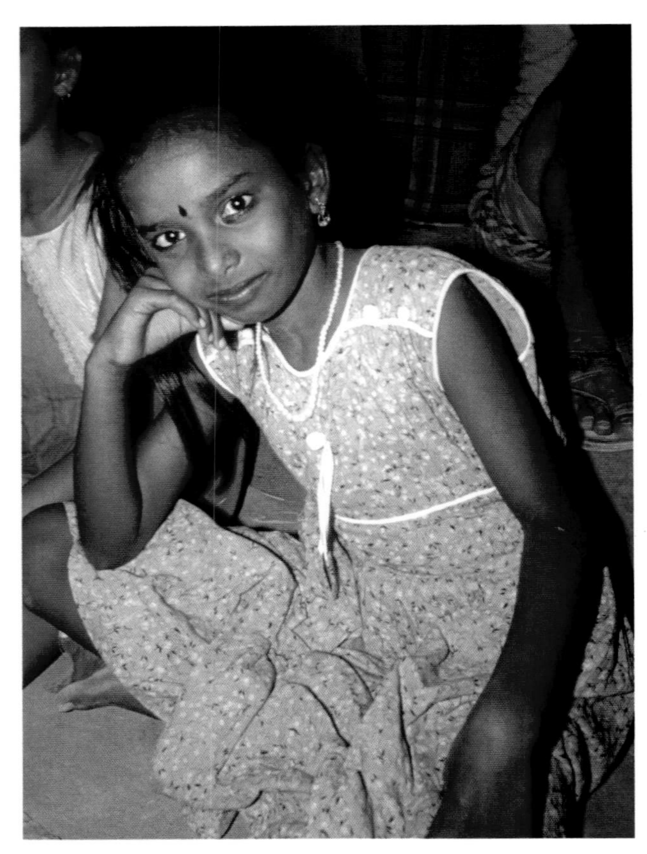

Village child in West Bengal, India

renunciates), bedecked with bracelets and beads. Their long hair was pulled into topknots and a few had their foreheads streaked with the white sandal paste of their worship. They sang for money as they played their one-string *ektaras,* and I kept giving them little coins so they would stay and sing in my compartment. We had so much fun together that they invited me to their village outside of Shantiniketan.

The village consisted of a few houses and some palm and banana trees surrounded by communally owned rice fields. The villagers were very poor; they each owned only two pieces of cloth, one to wear and one to wash. Although they were not traditional renunciates because they married and had some personal possessions, the Bauls wore ochre to signify their renunciation of caste distinctions. They accepted all people as their equals. In the eleventh century, when the Muslims overthrew the Hindu and Buddhist rulers of Bengal, all the Sufi, Buddhist, and Tantric groups went underground. Over time, they merged into one group, the Bauls, which means "mad." Because they ignored caste distinctions, Indian society regarded them as outcasts. At the beginning of the twentieth century, Rabindranath Tagore hailed them as the poets and mystics of India. Since that time their music and dance have been widely accepted, although they are still considered social outcasts.[20]

Their tiny, one-room houses were made with mud floors and thatched roofs. Inside, their homes remained bare except for a few spices, cooking pots, a rope bed, and one change of clothes. But the inhabitants received me like royalty. They spread a mat beneath a banyan tree, and a woman named Urmala brought spiced tea from her hut. Young Mara, a neighbor's child, hung a jasmine garland around my neck, and her eyes blazed as she danced barefoot on the ground.

Under the banyon tree, Basudev, Urmala's husband, played the one-string *ektara* I had seen on the train coming to their village. He was small, dressed in ochre clothes with a shining face. One delicate hand held the gourd instrument while the other kept rhythm by squeezing the split bamboo that fastened the single string. He stopped playing and explained to me in Bengali, while a student who had just arrived practiced her English by translating. "The *ektara* is symbolic of our philosophy. All life is One, like the one string of the *ektara.* Bhagavan, God, and Goddess are in everything. We don't abide by the caste system because all people are equal."

Then Basudev picked up the instrument again and began to sing and play with a passion I had not seen before:

> *Shabloke kai Lalon kejat shong share*
> Everyone is asking what caste am I?
> Are you Muslim or Hindu, none can tell.
> What difference is there,
> Hindu or Muslim, Man or Woman?
> When we sleep we breathe the same,
> When we die we leave the same.[21]

The word went out that a guest had arrived. Baul singers came from many villages, bringing the *ektara,* cymbals, drums, and flutes. They danced and sang into the heart of night as the full moon emerged and lodged in the branches of the tree above our heads.

Vijali and villagers building a communal round house for the village

I asked their permission to stay, and these people, for all their poverty, shared everything they had with me. Within a few days, my Baul friends had located a hut for me in the village next to theirs, the village of the Shantili, one of the indigenous tribes of India.

My first day in this tiny village among the Shantili thrilled me. They had a culture completely different from the Bauls or the Bengalis, with their own music, dance, and language. Their mud houses and thatched roofs were sculptures in themselves, very neat and clean, with geometric designs painted around the base of each house in black or white. The most important feature of the village was a pond where everyone bathed and where the women washed their dishes and clothes. They kept the ground sprinkled with water and swept every day. Palm, coconut, banana, and mango trees gave the village a tropical look and were a source of shade and nourishment. The banyan tree, with its many hanging pendants and gnarly roots, had the presence of an ancient *sadhu,* or "holy one." The Brahman cattle roamed freely and looked well fed and content, unlike the emaciated cows in the streets of Calcutta.

I lived in a complex of mud huts owned by one Shantili family. My hut was behind the others. I lived in one half, with a young Indian man living on the other side of a flimsy partition. Children played outside the back window while I sat and stared for hours at the mud walls, their fine texture hand-smoothed into large swells. The walls, supported by a central pole of natural wood, were about two feet thick with soft molded corners and recessed windows. The roof, supported by wooden beams, was made of ceramic tiles. A courtyard garden connected us with the other huts. The front cottage was home to the family, which spanned four generations, from elders to babies.

Living there, I realized how poor the families in the area really were. Many times they did not know from where the next day's food would come. Although I wanted to create something for them, I didn't feel right creating a sculpture when they already had such beautiful sculptures in their villages.

They took me an hour's bus ride away to the village which had been the birthplace of Basudev Das Baul, the young man who sang for me on my first evening. There many Bauls lived, including Basudev's brother Shivasundar, his young wife, their new baby, and his elderly mother in a tiny one-room mud hut. When night came, the whole family insisted that they move out so that I could sleep inside. Instead, I slept on a raised mat outside. I wept for them and for the barred gates to homes in Beverly Hills, each one protecting luxuries that would support three of these villages for a lifetime.

One night the Bauls celebrated *Purnima*, the full moon, with singing and dancing. The whole village had engaged in preparing food and setting up

Vijali singing with the Bauls at the construction site

a temporary platform for the occasion. We joyously ate and sang into the night. At one point the villagers tried to coax a beautiful, but very shy, young girl of the Shantili tribe to sing. When she finally agreed, the song was exquisite. Afterwards they asked me to sing, so I sang "That Lucky Old Sun" over crackling speakers. The next morning we returned to their village near Shantiniketan on the local bus and, because it was jammed full, I sat on top of the bus with my Baul friends and enjoyed a great view.

One evening, I asked my three questions. Besudav's response to my first question, *Where do you come from?* was: "We come from love, the love between our mothers and fathers, and out of the womb of our mother. We come from the Mother Earth and we are part of the Great Goddess Kali." To my second question, *What is your sickness, your imbalance?* Shivashundar responded, "We are under such strain all the time because we don't have enough money. Every day we have to go to another town to make money. We sing and sing until we are exhausted, and when we come back we worry that we still don't have enough money to feed our families. So the problem is the anxiety connected with our work." To my third question, *What could heal that problem? What could bring the balance, the solution?* they both chimed in, "To really love our singing and work and not to worry about the future. To keep on doing what we are doing, but give up the anxiety and be fully present with every moment of our day. We would probably have even more abundance," they said, "if we could let go of that anxiety."

As I got to know the village, I saw that they desperately needed housing. Some of the Bauls lived like beggar minstrels wandering from village to village without a place to stay. And the children had no schoolhouse. Instead they had to gather under the tree where they had entertained me that first evening. This worked well in the dry season, but became a problem in the rainy season. Even those with houses had problems. The rice grass used to thatch their roofs had become weakened from pesticides so that their roofs didn't last long and they didn't always have the rupees to re-thatch them.

Finally, I knew what I could give them. I would build a sculptural house that would be a *Baul Kutir*, meaning Heart of the Bauls. It would be a place for the Bauls to practice, perform, and sleep, as well as a place for the children to have classes and for the community to gather.

Vijali and Basudev Baul (right) gather materials for the construction of the communal house

The suggestion, however, was more complicated than it sounded, because the Shantilis, the Bauls, and the Bengalis each maintained their own customs, even though they live together in the same villages. The Bengalis and the Shantilis follow the caste system, and consider the Bauls outcasts. As the caste system prescribes not only social status, but also occupation, the Bauls earn their keep only by begging with their singing. However, I envisioned all three groups sitting together in a circle.

In these villages, land is passed down from generation to generation. As a result, three or four generations might live in one small room. Extra space was almost impossible to find. Basudev and his wife, Urmala, owned some land in front of their house. They offered this for my use, the very spot where the Bauls had entertained me under a Banyan tree on my first evening in the village. Basudev and other Bauls from the surrounding villages had a meeting and decided that this was the best place for me to work. Since the land was Urmala's private property, I needed no further permission.

So, one morning in late April, at sunrise, Basudev, Urmala, and I broke ground for the Baul ashram.

Constructing the thatch roof for the communal house

Constructing the thatch roof of *Baul Kutir*

Ceiling of the communal house, *Baul Kutir*

Urmala and I removed a pile of bricks half buried in the earth, struggling while the men watched. We measured with string to find the center of this area. Then, stretching the string taut with a stick tied on the other end, I inscribed a circle. I proceeded to dig a trench outside of this line, one foot wide and one foot deep.

I hired two Sudras, experienced builders of the lowest caste, to work with me. They were eager to work and walked three hours every morning to come from their village. They taught me how to mix mud together with straw to build the walls. I also bought a load of broken bricks and bamboo, and had them delivered by water buffalo.

At first, the Bauls just watched as I worked in the mud. After a while, a man came to help. Soon his brother came, and then his father. Then someone from another village on his way to work would stop and say, "Oh, my goodness, you don't do it that way. You do it this way." Then he would work for an hour, and that is how we built the ashram.

The villagers found the idea of a round house very strange. As we built, they kept talking about where the partitions would go to make a place for the priest and a place for the different castes. I firmly countered with, "No, we won't have any walls. It will be a circle."

They kept bringing this up and I kept reminding them "no walls." Then, after the men finally understood, the women started, "Where will the priest sit?"

Change happened gradually, but from the day I drew the circle on the ground, whenever we needed to meet we sat in a circle, so they grew accustomed to the idea. In part, they went along with me because of my background as a Vedanta nun, which meant that I was versed in their religion and knew many of their practices. This provided common ground and a basis for mutual respect.

Baul Kutir completed

One Baul told me of a problem with the roof of his house and asked for some money to fix it. I said "yes" and always said "yes" when someone asked, but this was the second time this man had asked, which left me wondering, "Am I really a friend for the Bauls or simply a foreign woman who can give them money which, indeed, they do need?" Perhaps I was both.

By the first of May, my birthday, the weather had become excruciatingly hot, so hot—our bodies didn't want to move. Working outside one day, I suffered a sunstroke. I became so dizzy and feverish I had to go back to my room, my entire body in pain. I had no appetite, and I could only wash clothes and draw water from the well for my bath with great effort. At the well, I fainted. Later, I vomited up any food that I ate.

Joaquin arrived from Spain to help complete the house while my condition remained shaky. Slowly the Shantili mother nursed me back to health. The rice grass arrived allowing us to build and thatch the roof. The ashram was completed, and we were ready for the final ceremony.

I had enjoyed working with the two Sudra builders. They were great fun, always joking and laughing, but when they completed the building, they wouldn't enter it because they were both from a low caste. When the day came for the *puja* for the house, they hovered timidly outside and had to be coerced to come inside, even though they had put so much work into the construction.

On the day of the consecration, five hundred people came and feasted on food cooked over a pit fire in front of the *Baul Kutir.* The Brahmin priest, the Bauls, the Sudras, and all the people in the village sat together in a circle. The Bauls sang the songs they had prepared as responses to the three questions. Rather than have the Brahmin priest preside over the rituals,

I asked that we all sit in a circle and offer the mantras, flowers, incense, and *ghee (*clarified butter) into the *dhuni*, the sacred fire in the center of the room. We buried soil from the other World Wheel countries in a hole in the floor of the house, and Urmala covered it over with handfuls of earth.

That night the Bauls who had come from other villages slept in the communal house. The next day, the children gathered in the *Baul Kutir* and Urmala held the first class. My World Wheel vision of this little mud house had come true!

Leaving my Baul friends, I took the two-day, two-night bus ride to Katmandu, Nepal, where I intended to get a visa and make arrangements for entering Tibet, the next country of the World Wheel. But I picked up giardia drinking unfiltered water at the hotel where I stayed in Katmandu. That, on top of my weakness from sunstroke and a bout of bronchitis in India, left me with little strength. I laughed at my fate. I had contracted this intestinal bug in a hotel, though I ate and drank all the food and beverages offered to me in the villages of India and never suffered an ill effect. Then when I visited a travel agency in Katmandu about my pilgrimage into Tibet, I found out that there was a special price on plane fare to the United States. My body leapt with joy at the thought of flying home to regain my strength!

Baul singing at ceremony of completion of *Baul Kutir*

CHAPTER SIXTEEN

Freedom

Beverly Hills, California
1977

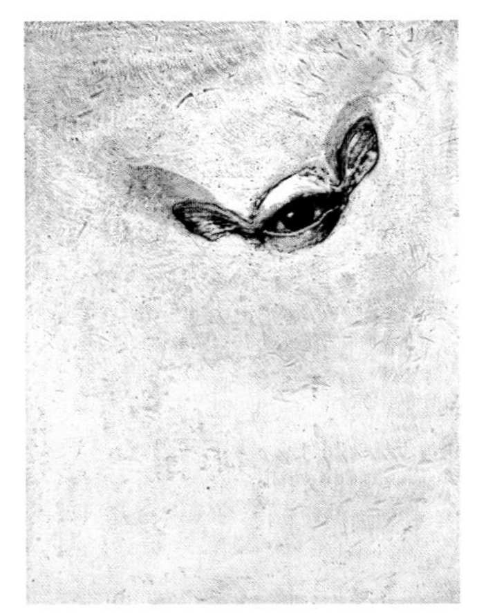

Eye of Freedom

I HAD JUST RETURNED from three months in the Amazon and the Andes, and southern California greeted me with car exhaust, honking horns, and screeching tires. The cars on the freeway appeared rippled as heat rose around them. I exited the freeway and parked at a shop on a side road to pick up photos of my trip: Don Hildé, my sculpture *Homage to Andean Woman,* the Amazon jungle, and the Rio Rimac in the Andes. Only five days back in Los Angeles and already I felt the same old panic. How would I survive?

I returned to my friend Oscar's house and entered the quiet of his guest room. I lay on the bed and watched the tops of the sycamore trees bend to the wind outside the window, their leaves silvery through the smog. With each scrape of the branches against the side of the house, my mind spun with old voices and my body became painful again, as it had before I left for the Amazon. For what seemed like hours, I swung from one emotion to another—anger, confusion, hatred, and a grasping, egotistical need to be a success one moment, a desire to let go of my ego the next. Then I would experience moments of profound clarity and ecstasy. I realized that the inner voice of truth, of divinity, came from a still place in the center that was unaffected by the emotional extremes. This "knowing" felt familiar, as if it had always existed in me.

I looked at the clock—only ten minutes had passed. I rose and walked through Oscar's house, passing his beautiful antique furniture and rows and rows of books from floor to ceiling. Large mirrors cloned everything and chandeliers hung in the hallways—the closest thing to stars in Los Angeles' polluted air. What was I doing here?

I sat in the dining room and looked at my reflection in the polished wooden table. I mused about the budding love between Oscar and me. I thought of Don Hildé's psychic reading of Oscar, his jealous poisoning. I knew Don Hildé was referring to the medication that Oscar had suggested that I take for my panics. I had taken it for a month. The panics had left, but so had my dreams and what seemed to be a large part of myself. I had made the decision to stop the medication and follow my own way—meditation, introspection, time in nature alone listening deeply to all around me and within me, and carving the spirit of the earth in stone.

Once again I felt the desire to leave everything behind me. But I had already gone to so many places and experienced so much. I had been a Vedanta nun for ten years. I had practiced spiritual exercises diligently for thirty years. The mantra given to me by my guru, Swami Prabhavananda, when I was thirteen years old was still with me constantly—during my dreams, waking me in the morning, continuing with me throughout the day. I had been to India and had stayed in many ashrams. I had participated in numerous groups and retreats in the United States, and had worked with medicine people both here and in the Amazon.

However, I recognized the limitations in the perspective and environment of each path. Each teacher had taught me a partial truth, although each thought that his or her view was the greatest path, if not the only way. Often I saw that people around these teachers lacked freedom and sometimes even seemed less loving than the ordinary people of the secular world.

I knew that if I returned to the . they would accept neither my questioning nor the validity of my experience of the Kundalini energy. They accepted only Ramakrishna—*he* could go into a state of ecstasy, but anyone else claiming to do so was a fake or crazy. Normally those who had such experiences took their begging bowls and left the normal householder world, but I already had tried that.

"Okay," I said aloud. "I've been married and I left the marriage, so becoming single isn't the answer." Again I considered the growing love between Oscar and me. Getting married a second time was no answer either.

I had studied for years with the most evolved spiritual teachers I could find and still I felt bound by fear. What else could I do? I got up from the table and went out to the back patio where I touched the leaves of a little potted orange tree. I bent over and smelled the pungent orange fruit that hung on a branch. Then, with a sudden burst of energy, I went back up to my room, opened my closet door, and started removing my art supplies and the few clothes that I had stored there. In minutes I had emptied the closet completely of my belongings. I took them in cartons to the garage, where I found a gallon of white paint and some brushes. I spent the rest of the day painting the dirty green closet a pure white. By late afternoon the sun streamed through the tiny closet window and filled the little room with light. After finishing, I showered and changed into fresh clothes.

Re-entering the bedroom, I saw a stone that I had brought from the Rio Rimac in the Andes. I traced the smooth granite shape with my fingers. A combination of water and time had rounded the stone and thrust one side upward where it swelled forth as if to release its contents. I placed it on the closet floor, then gravitated to a small Indian grinding stone I had found in the San Ynez Mountains near Santa Barbara. This I set in front of the Peruvian stone, and I filled its hollow with water. I went downstairs and carefully picked the orange leaf that I had touched earlier, brought it back to the closet and set it afloat in the water. As a final touch, I spread a black and white Peruvian cloth woven by the Shipibo Indians in front of the stones.

I lit a candle, closed the closet door from the inside, and sat down on the cloth. With relief I realized, "This is it. There is no one to see. There is nowhere else to go. There is nothing else I need."

I sat quietly for a few moments, noticing the rise and fall of my chest as I breathed, enjoying the textures on the stone, and the green of the leaf

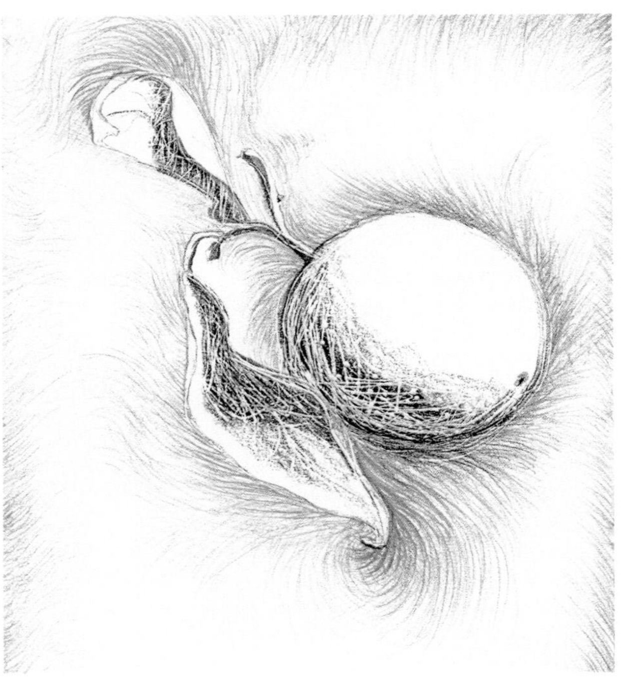

Orange

against the surface of water. I sipped a little of the water and gave thanks for my time with Don Hildé in the jungle.

Soon I felt the presence of Ramakrishna, Jesus, and Buddha, and of Kali, who contains all cycles of creation and destruction. I envisioned myself placing my fears in the body of Kali, in her all-encompassing form beyond good and evil, creation and destruction, dark and light. I picked up the orange leaf as if it were my ego and all the trappings that I so easily identified with—including even the spiritual trappings that subtly kept the old patterns alive. I held the leaf in the flame of the candle until it became ash. I knew that Kali did not protect me from evil forces—she swallowed them up in her vastness, in her completeness. One half of her body is nourishing, protecting, granting life, while the other half holds a sword and a severed head, ready to cut our illusions asunder.

Before long a tingling sensation began in my feet. Soon after, a burning energy erupted at the base of my spine, intensifying until it became an excruciatingly strong sexual urge and I felt ready to climax. But instead the energy burst upward toward my navel. The sexual feeling disappeared, replaced instantly by the need to throw up. This also passed as the force continued upward, its heat penetrating my heart. My chest ached and then exploded into something far more intense than a sexual climax.

Waves of love flooded me and radiated outward. I longed to melt into all beings, to join all beings in this wave of ecstasy. But this too passed, and my tongue pulled back in my throat and my breath seemed to stop until I worried I would lose consciousness. I started to panic and gasp for breath, but this time I inhaled long and deep and touched the floor with my fingertips, touched the river stone and my belly with both hands, and came back into the present moment.

I knew then that there was no help outside myself. All is within. To my amazement, my panic evaporated with my outgoing breath. I felt a tangible shift into my own center. I looked around me—at the stones, the water, the wall, at space itself—and saw that everything was filled with light. Light and energy moved freely around me in pulsing waves that left me feeling consciously loved, full of love.

What surprised me most was that I knew how to help myself! For so long I had believed that the knowledge to overcome my physical discomfort and panic lay outside me, and that I needed someone else to do it for me or to show me how. Now I knew that knowledge was inherent within me.

Every day after that, I went into the white closet, with its tiny window framing a patch of blue sky, and sat on my Peruvian cloth. I learned how to know when I had too much energy in my head and how to move it down into my belly and release it. With my opening heart I sent that extra energy out into the world to those I knew who needed it and to others I didn't know. It was so simple. And from that time on, I never panicked again. The physical pain that I had experienced for two years did not return. Gone too were the doubts about my sanity and the fear that my identity would dissolve and leave me without moorings, because I knew without a doubt that I *was* consciousness, unchanging, undying.

I could survive in California, or anywhere else, by being in the "radiant present," aware of each moment, aware of that inner feeling of love and joy, a feeling of rightness, which to this day guides my responses.

CHAPTER SEVENTEEN

World Wheel-Spoke Nine

Shoto Terdrom, Tibet
1992

Vijali in cave with *Rainbow Bodhisattva*

I REGAINED MY HEALTH in the United States and raised a little money by giving slide show talks about the World Wheel. Andrew Beath, who had helped dig trenches on the first site in Malibu, matched my thousand dollars through his foundation, enabling me to return to Tibet and continue my pilgrimage.

I flew to Calcutta with Karil Daniels, a videographer from San Francisco who wanted to film the World Wheel. In Katmandu we met Beth Robinson, a vice president at J.P. Morgan & Co. and an experienced trekker. The three of us hired a van to drive us four and a half hours into the Himalayas to the Tibetan border. The road frequently turned into a muddy trail, and on the slopes below these treacherous stretches lay the remains of overturned vehicles not so fortunate.

At the Tibetan border, officials asked us to complete seemingly endless paperwork. While doing so, we saw a Chinese border guard launch an unprovoked attack on a group of young women standing on the Tibetan side. The guard threw sticks at them, kicked them, and spat at them until they ran away.

At that time, all foreign visitors to Tibet were required to hire a tour crew—a driver and a guide. I was grateful that the tourist company had assigned us a Tibetan one. Chinese law in Tibet forbids foreigners to make friends with the local Tibetans. But my feeling was that a Tibetan guide would be far more lax about this than a Chinese one. Also, I had illegal possessions in my backpack—pictures of the Dalai Lama and Tibetan prayer flags for a "free Tibet."

We crossed the border in a Land Rover provided by our travel agency with Tashi driving us as Tsedor guided. In a half hour we arrived at Khasa, or Zhangmu, as the Chinese now call it. We spent our first night in a multi-storied hotel, a 1950s relic of Chinese imperialism. The hotel had rooms with high ceilings, elegant wallpaper, and heavy drapes, all stained and grimy from years without cleaning. The plumbing was nonexistent.

In the streets, a Chinese movie theater broadcast its soundtrack through an outdoor speaker, drowning out the prayers in the Tibetan temple next door. When we ventured out, children took our hands and shouted, "Hello, hello."

The next day as we drove, the mountains shot upward, dramatically changing in character as we left the softer landscape of Nepal behind. Granite peaks rose almost vertically for mile after rugged mile. The earlier people of Tibet, the Bons, practice a shamanistic religion similar to that of American Indian cultures comfortable with these elemental forces. As we drove higher and higher, I could feel this original wild spirit of the land. The Bons worshiped the *dakinis*, feminine deities whom I was certain were making themselves felt. As we drove higher, Mount Everest's snow-capped peaks grew visible on the horizon. Despite fierce winds, Tibetan men and women worked in their fields, plowing with yaks adorned with red tassels. Barley is the only grain which grows at this altitude. It is the main crop and main diet of Tibet, ground into flour for storage, then wet and rolled into edible balls called *tsampa*.

The next day, we stopped to visit the cave of Milarepa, one of the early Buddhist saints. We hiked down the slope incised with stone steps, and children ran out to ask for safety pins and pictures of the Dalai Lama. A temple erected in front of the cave had been torn down by the Chinese in the 1960s during the Cultural Revolution, but the local people had reconstructed it stone by stone. In the cave, we found the giant stone that Milarepa had purportedly raised in one hand when he was challenged while teaching on the illusion of form.

I asked if we could sit and meditate and chant. The monk attendant brought a rug and, as we sat to face an image of Milarepa, the gathered crowd grew quiet and respectful.

Back in our Land Rover, on our way to the hermitage of Tibetan nuns at Shoto Terdrom, we began the arduous climb over the seventeen-thousand-foot Thang La pass. Beth joined me in chanting the last hundred thousand repetitions of the *Om Ah Hung* mantra that I had committed to do for the freedom and welfare of Tibet. Each of us kept count on bone rosaries we found in Nepal, one hundred and eight beads on each, made from the bones of one hundred and eight different skulls.

We bounced along on the rocky road until we reached the pass. Beth and Karil got out of the car, but quickly returned as the cold wind battered them. I stepped out too, walking over to the most sacred point, honored by a pile of ceremonial stones. I called our Tibetan guide, Tsedor, to come and lead me in a tradition ritual. He said a prayer and we placed our stones with those of other pilgrims. I managed to circle the plateau with its spectacular view of the high snow-covered Himalayan peaks—Shishapangma at twenty-six thousand feet and Mount Everest on the far horizon. Tibetan prayer flags snapped in the wind. Back in the car, I wept. For the first time, I had experienced the spaciousness for which my spirit had longed.

The Chinese hostels in which we were required to stay en route to Lhasa had neither plumbing nor heat. By morning, we needed hats and gloves in bed. That night while I lay awake, a great pageant of deities and demons passed before my eyes, whether open or closed. Perhaps the change in altitude caused these visions, but every inch of the room filled with spirits pressing around me. Buddhas in bubbles exploded into light. Now I understood the imagery of the Tibetan Tankas with their swirls and curlicues of vibrant color.

At Shigatse, the second largest city in Tibet, we stopped at Tashilhumpo Monastery built in the 15th century by the First Dalai Lama and the seat of the late Panchen Lama, the second most important figure in Tibetan culture. Tibetans believe that religious leaders such as the Dalai Lama and the Panchen Lama are reincarnated. In 1995, Chinese officials kidnapped the Panchen Lama's latest incarnation, a six-year-old Tibetan boy, only days after the Dalai Lama recognized him as the eleventh Panchen Lama. Although he is now believed safe, his whereabouts remain secret to protect him from the Chinese government. We visited an enormous, two-story high statue of the Buddha, and then went on to Gyantse and Tsedang to see the monasteries there. However, none of them moved me as much as the simple cave of Milarepa.

After our stops, we drove nine hours to Lhasa, where we would pick up our cook, Karma, along with his cooking tent and our supplies. We passed through the stark Yarlung Valley where the blue ribbon of the Yarlung Tsampo River, birthed by the faraway melting snows and streams of Mount Kailash, marks its winding way across the earth. The Tibetans have another name for this mountain. They call it "Kang Rinpoche."

When we arrived in Lhasa, the mountains surrounding the city glittered with fresh snowfall, creating a cheerful, picturesque scene. But I was saddened to see that almost every business was run by Chinese, with Tibetans relegated to the low-paying jobs at the bottom of the economic ladder.

Our guide, Tsedor, our driver, Tashi, and our cook, Karma, had all experienced first-hand the destruction and lack of peace. Each had seen his relatives killed, and the land and religion they so dearly loved torn apart. They understood the purpose of the World Wheel—personal and world peace. Perhaps because of this they allowed us to bypass the required tourist route of hotels and monasteries to camp in Shoto Terdrom, one of the most sacred areas of Tibet.

Vijali at Shoto Terdrom, Tibet

Moreover, they told us that they wanted to participate in the culminating ceremony, even though it meant that they would risk their jobs.

The drive from Lhasa to Drigung Valley and Shoto Terdrom was magnificent. I had heard about this valley from an American friend, Tsultrum Allione, who had visited there the year before. The topography was as beautiful as she had described it. It had rained and snowed throughout the night and off and on all the next day, but this only intensified the beauty. A stream flowed along the floor of the canyon, which narrowed dramatically as we approached our destination. Stone outcroppings and caves dotted the canyon walls, and yellow and purple wildflowers covered the ground. On the stones, mossy growths bloomed with tiny white flowers.

When we reached the Shoto Terdrom valley, sixteen thousand feet above sea level, the road stopped short of the hermitage. Nevertheless, as soon as we stepped out of the Land Rover, young nuns with beautiful round faces and open smiles swarmed around us, asking for a picture of the Dalai Lama. A few minutes later, they helped us with our bags and tents and followed us to our campfire site. We overlooked the river from a precipice that was holy ground, as evidenced by the many prayer flags and the two fire pits used for burning sacred cedar as an offering.

As we set up our tents, an unusual-looking Lama suddenly appeared and observed us. I found him exceptionally beautiful. He appeared to be about thirty-five years old, with great light and energy radiating from his handsome face. His hair grew long and wild and he wore a tattered silk tunic, but he had the bearing of a prince and was clearly a powerful spiritual practitioner. He watched in silence and then quickly left. I called to him, intrigued, but he had disappeared into the mountainside.

Other people passed by continually, performing a sacred walk of the valley known as a *kora*. Tsedor, Tashi, and Karma set up the cooking tent some distance away while Karil, Beth, and I also made a *kora* around the *stupa*, a structure that represented the enlightened mind and body of Buddha in abstract form. We also went to the main *gompa*, or temple, and made our three full-length prostrations, a gesture of respect for the *gompa* and nuns.

Tibetan nun practicing Chöd at our campsite

When a nun gave us a tour of the statues in the *gompa*, it saddened me to find the image of Yeshe Tsogyal shoved into an obscure corner. Her consort, Padmasambhava, known as "Guru Rinpoche" in Tibetan, is one of the most revered figures in Tibetan Buddhism, and Yeshe Tsogyal is one of the most prominent holy women. Here in Shoto Terdrom, she had opened a convent after her full spiritual awakening in a cave in this valley. She had blessed the valley and promised she would remain here throughout all her reincarnations. During our stay, we met her current incarnation, Khandro, a dark, vigorous woman of great presence. I longed to see the statue of Yeshe Tsogyal, representing her as an equal beside her spiritual mate Guru Rimposhe, both reflecting the harmony and balance of male and female that is so necessary for the health and continuation of our planet.

It snowed the first night in our camp, and I rasped and rattled with bronchitis in our tiny backpacking tent. I slept with all my clothes on, including my down jacket, and even then I would have been cold if not for the warmth of Beth's body in the tent.

Karma made porridge and eggs for our first breakfast. Karil and I discussed the need to begin filming. How would we find a senior nun to whom I could address my three questions? We had no sooner voiced this concern when three wizened old nuns came by to inspect us. We were set! Karma asked them the questions, which delighted them, and then he sat on their right side translating while I sat on their left.

They explained, "We have been here since adolescence. Our ages are sixty-nine, seventy-seven, and eighty-nine. After 1959, the Chinese invasion forced us to hide in the mountains and to wait out the Cultural Revolution. Many of us died of starvation. But now we are happy to be back on our sacred land."

They answered my questions in a very practical way. Their problem was inadequate food and clothing, and the solution was to get more donations. Throughout our talk, they never stopped smiling. Afterwards, whenever they passed our tents, they always stopped to "chat," miming everything they wished to communicate.

After the interview, we three Americans went exploring in the area. On the other side of the hermitage was a narrow gorge with a small stream that trickled out from under a cover of thick ice. Up in the canyon I discovered a small shelf-of-a-cave in a limestone wall. It was perfectly formed with a flat, sandy floor and recessed just enough to provide a feeling of being part of the earth. Beth and I crawled into the cave and sat with our backs against the stone. At first glance, I didn't notice that tiny plants flowered in every crack and corner that their roots could penetrate. Soon after I noticed this, I went into a deep and powerful meditation. Karil sat by the stream, happy to use this short period of sunlight to film the scenery for the first time.

After supper, I excused myself and went up to the cliff on the far side of the tent to lie down. I closed my eyes and once again felt pulled into the same deep meditative state I had experienced that morning. I shared my experience with Beth when I returned to our tent. I learned that Shoto Terdrom was not sacred just because Yeshe Tsogyal and Guru Rinposhe had once lived there. They had come because it was a place of incredible power where they could deepen their practice.

To visit Guru Rinpoche's cave, we started up a steep trail and walked for an hour, very slowly because of the altitude. We looked back down, gasping for breath, and we noticed how the canyon below our camp was etched deeply into a much broader valley formed by even higher peaks. The higher we hiked, the more the snow-covered mountain ranges were revealed, until the entire valley came into view below us, cut through by streams and encircled by the inner and middle *koras.* The outer *kora* was a strenuous five-day hike I would like to have walked, had it not been inaccessible because of ice.

Two nuns joined us for the last stretch up the trail. One of them had retrieved my woolen glove that I had dropped along the way. When we reached Guru Rinpoche's cave around noon, Doltse, the keeper, greeted us. An imprint in the cave showed the body of Padmasambhava in meditation, the stone indented with the impression of his back and head and with the top crown, supposing he always wore his regalia, poking into the ceiling. On his right lay an impression of his Khatavanga staff, adorned with three skulls and representing the inner consort. On his left, was another indentation. It was the hole he had made when he had grabbed a *vajra*, the Buddhist symbol representing the lightning bolt of illumination, out of the stone and had hurled it into a poisonous lake below, making a tunnel through which its demons were expelled. The cave is named "Expelling the Demons."

Also, to the left of the sitting figure lay a pool of water, created when he threw a spear. Doltse gave us some of this water, and I sipped and splashed myself with as much joy as any Tibetan. We asked if we could meditate in the cave, and Doltse instructed us to meditate with our backs touching the stone. This was precisely what we had done spontaneously on the ledge the day before when I had felt such a powerful connection. I believed that this earlier response to the canyon was the earth's way of giving me permission to stay here and work.

Karil and Doltse went on to the temple built above the cave, while Beth and I stayed in Guru Rimpoche's cave to meditate. It was a very still and powerful place and we meditated long and deep. Though we felt the cold through our hats, gloves, and down jackets, we didn't want to leave. Nevertheless, we eventually left our meditation seats and joined the other two upstairs. They were still conversing in, what we later learned, was actually Khandro's room, the room of the current incarnation of Yeshe Tsogyal whom we wanted to meet. The keeper told us that she was in Lhasa and would return in a few days. We found the two-room building lovely and simple. As we sat on low benches we admired a large prayer wheel in the center and a 1986 calendar on the wall. Over many cups of butter tea served by the gap-toothed, very friendly Doltse, we told stories and asked questions.

When we finished our tea, Doltse introduced us to his ailing yak. "This black and white yak was given to me by a Lama who made full body prostrations from Kham to Padmasambhava's cave here, his yak by his side. It took him seven years. When he finally arrived, he gave me his only possession, his yak."

Doltse also showed us a shortcut to the valley, a steep path that led into the snow-filled ravine we had explored the day before. We walked over the icy ceiling of a streambed, the stream flowing beneath, and then down toward the entrance of the gorge.

Just before we reached the shelf-cave I had found

the day before, I saw another cave, wonderfully framed in stone and lined with eroded deposits in the shape of stalagmites. Inside, I discovered a flat back wall. As I sat in the stone rubble looking out, I knew that this was the World Wheel site. The cave was in an unused area and was not part of the traditional *kora*. It was exactly the sort of place I had hoped to find, as I didn't want to disturb the traditional ceremonies of the valley.

Back at camp, I prepared for the next day's work and talked to Karma about getting permission from the head nun of the Kagyu nunnery. He assured me that, because of the cave's location, I did not need permission. Before bedtime, Beth and I hiked from our tent down a steep precipice to the roaring stream below. Just as we started back, large hailstones fell and within five minutes white jewels covered the ground.

The next morning, as we ate breakfast, the sun peeked over the ridge on a cloudless day—a fine day to begin work. We packed our tools and lunches and left with Tsedor for the cave. Karil filmed, Beth lit sage and cedar, and I smudged the cave, pledging that I would do nothing to harm or change it. I would only bring out the spirit already existing in it.

Beth prayed, "We ask to experience an inner connection with this land and people, so that we may mirror them in the outer world."

Tsedor added his prayer in Tibetan and we joined hands, each with a big smile.

Beth, Tsedor, and I removed piles of stones to level the cave. Then we knocked down any dangerous rocks that hung overhead. After that, we donned gloves and cleared the cave floor of its debris, down to its rich-smelling earth. In the process we discovered a tablet of stone with Tibetan characters carved into it.

Tsedor read: *"Om Ah Hung Bendza Gurur Pema Siddhi Hung."*

Beth and I had both been taught this mantra of Guru Rinpoche, and now we recited it as we worked. I knew of mantras carved on stone from my experience at Tso Pema in India, and I wondered how long this tablet had been in this seemingly unused cave. Below the cavern, we found a second stone inscribed with the same mantra, which we moved to the altar we had created above. We made steps with the rubble and marked the entrance.

Our work complete for the day, I asked Tsedor to sit with his back to the stone wall in the meditation posture. I drew his outline on the back of the cave with chalk in preparation for the sculpture I wanted to start. Then we feasted on boiled potatoes, hard-cooked eggs, and oranges.

While Beth and Karil walked back to camp, I stayed and meditated alone in the cave, allowing myself to become receptive to the stillness of the canyon. The cave became luminous as I faced the back stone wall and rainbow colors bled into the seemingly solid stone. I picked up my tools and incised the stone where I had drawn the outline around Tsedor's form. The outline of the Bodhisattva took a predominantly female character as the light shifted and changed. I became completely engrossed in work, as an organic non-linear process of color, outline, and carving all proceeded together to form an image, almost like cells dividing.

My spine lengthened and straightened as I saw my own understanding of myself mirrored on the stone in front of me, rainbow-colored, prism-like, faceted and dazzling, all colors moving, filling this space called body, and spilling out into the sky above and earth below—one substance alive and connected.

I stayed for some hours, barely noticing that the sun had dipped over the canyon wall and a chilly wind swept through the ravine. The camp expected me for supper and the light had almost faded, yet I felt no incentive to move. Finally, Beth's footsteps punctuated the silence.

"I was afraid you wouldn't return," she said.

Slowly I rose and, carrying myself as space undivided by boundaries, pulled by Beth's will, I returned to camp.

During supper, Karma said, referring to the Six Realms of Buddhism, "You Americans live in the God realm with all your material comforts, but I don't envy you. There is sadness in your hearts. We Tibetans are only human and we suffer basic wants. We are ignorant, but we are happy in our lives."

After supper, Tashi, Tsedor, and Karma played a popular Tibetan game accompanied by howls of victory.

As I carved the next day, I heard within me the mantra *Om Ah Hung. Om:* the absolute, source of everything.

Ah: the joyous wonder. *Hung:* us, the here and now. Each word rang out in my cells with every blow of the hammer on my chisel. Tap, tap, tap—*Om, Ah, Hung.* I dug out the earth from the lower part of the image and revealed a stone penis. A female breast and arm were already clearly visible in the stone. The limestone broke and split as I tried to modify the shapes, and I realized I was not to touch the intrinsic meaning in the stone.

I became more receptive, listening and learning from the form in front of me as I incised the granite much as I imagined ancient peoples had incised their pictographs. The colors of the stone became vivid again. I tried to capture the light by using an ancient Greek technique of pigments and wax I had brought with me from the United States. I applied them with toothbrushes supplied for guests in the Chinese hotels, and then buffed them with a scarf that Beth had donated for the cause. I felt strongly about not using the Chinese-made acrylic paints in Tibet. I had shopped in Lhasa to extend my pigment range with wax shoe polish, nail polish, make up, and even some green sparkles.

Little by little, the fractured stone reflected prisms of light. The outlined face had no features, but a white point of light shone at the position of the third eye, a red triangle at the throat, and a blue square at the heart. I chiseled strands of hair on one side and on the other an ear with a long lobe protruding. As I added color to the hair, it transformed into vibrant, radiant streams of energy. The day passed as a flash of lightning.

That night, I bathed in the nearby hot springs. Chinese workers were building a guesthouse there for the pilgrims who come for its healing waters, and they peered over the stone wall that separated the sections for men and women. A nun also bathed in the water, her lips moving in silent recitation of her mantra. I quickly removed my clothes in the cold air and submerged myself, head and all, into the hot bubbling waters.

During the next few days that I worked in the cave, the cold made carving difficult. I had to wear all of my clothes with a windbreaker on top. The sun didn't enter the back of the cave, so from time to time I came outside to thaw myself in its rays. Beth periodically worked on a sculpture of her own, a patch of ice into which she carved the sun-moon sign that Tibetans paint on their doors. She also tidied the sides of the cave, cleaned the *mani* stones (the stones with mantras carved into them), and arranged candles and incense. The cave felt alive!

At breakfast one morning, Doltse appeared to tell us that Khandro, the incarnation of Yeshe Tsogyal, stood at the road above. We rushed up the hill to meet her. She held our hands tightly and smiled broadly at us, her long hair swept into an impish ponytail at the nape. We didn't visit long, but before we parted she said, "Shoes and warm boots are the biggest need of the nuns." We felt the imprint of her vitality long after she had gone.

At last I completed the figure I named *Rainbow Bodhisattva.* I had hoped to create a piece traditional enough that the nuns and hermits living in the valley could identify with it, but I also wanted to embody a universal image, unlimited by any one concept of spirituality. I didn't know whether anyone here would consider my creation sacred, but as I packed my tools, two nuns who had been gathering herbs in the canyon came by. When they saw my carved figure, tears came to their eyes, their faces blushed red, and they threw themselves on the ground three times in full-length prostrations. I had succeeded in creating a sacred site.

These nuns invited me to their home, a shack built onto the front of a cave not far from our camp. The inside was cold and dark, much closer to a cave than a house, but for three hours they shared with me their most precious possessions—sacred objects they brought out from silk wrappings, and bits of herbs that different Lamas had given them. For hours they went through their daily chants and practices, the jewels of their lives. We became very close even without a common language.

The nuns had spoken earlier about Lama Pema Somdup, a high Lama who had left his monastery in Kham. He had been living in a cave in this valley for eighteen years, practicing Chöd, a ritual that dissolves the ego through meditating on the impermanence of the body. Beth and I had asked the nuns if

Two Tibetan Buddhist nuns in the cave with *Rainbow Bodhisattva*

we could receive the Chöd "empowerment." Now we were informed that the Lama had come just to give us the initiation and was waiting. When we entered the temple, we were accompanied by several young nuns who wanted the Lama's blessing. To our surprise, the Lama was the same radiant hermit who had watched us set up camp when we first arrived. We couldn't take our eyes off of his magnetic smile. A yogi, he had not shaved his head (as most of the monks do), and he wore his long black hair held back by a twisted red cloth.

He performed the Chöd ceremony with great shouts and thigh-bone trumpeting. It was quite wild! After the ceremony, and instructions for practice and meditation, we offered him a one hundred-yuan bill, about ten American dollars, and the traditional scarf, but he would not take them. I sometimes weep when I think of this, of his tattered clothes and barest of foods gathered from the mountains and pilgrims' offerings. I find myself comparing him with the spiritual teachers who regularly raise money to build ashrams and centers in the United States. I know that one moment in his radiant presence affected me more than any organized retreat, and made me reflect on what is happening in the U.S.—religion with a price.

One time, when I was attempting to practice the Chöd with the drum and thigh-bone trumpet I had bought in Lhasa, the two nuns who had come to the cave and had prostrated before my *Rainbow Bodhisattva* sculpure, arrived. Among much giggling, laughter, and teasing, they showed me how to play the thigh-bone horn, the bell, and the drum. Every time I tried to blow the thigh-bone horn, it only emitted a dying cow sound, and they burst into sidesplitting laughter.

After they left, I went to the cooking tent to discuss the World Wheel ceremony that we were planning for the next day. I badly wanted to invite the nuns to participate, but Karma said that politically it was impossible. To do so would endanger the nuns, who might be arrested and beaten for mingling with tourists. To involve the nuns in the ceremony would, in fact, put us all under suspicion. Even in this isolated place,

Karma said, informers did their job. Unfortunately, he was right. Only two days earlier, German tourists had picked up a hitchhiker who later announced he was a Chinese official.

I had learned where Lama Pema Somdup stayed when he was not in his cave, and I wanted to extend him the courtesy of an invitation to our ceremony. Beth and I went up the mountain to the area where the Lama had a shelter built on the outside of an old nun's hut. When he came into the hermitage from his cave, the Lama meditated in this tiny space, a space so small that he could not even lie down in it. When we arrived, a black-faced nun greeted us with grunts and gestures. This was her time of silence and meditation. We talked to a nun in the next hut who told us that Pema Somdup had been away for a day or two. If he had returned, he would be below in a room close to the temple. We descended the mountain and entered the tiny room pointed out to us by one of the elderly nuns I had earlier interviewed.

We were startled to find that Pema Somdup was actually there. He beckoned for us to sit close to him. With Karma translating, I told him about the World Wheel project, first showing him pictures from my portfolio, and then describing the cave and the Rainbow Bodhisattva. "This is us," I said, "our real nature," and I closed the portfolio on my lap.

He looked delighted and said through Karma's translation, "I think the World Wheel pilgrimage and the sculpture in the cave are marvelous. I will go and see the sculpture and meditate in the cave."

After a morning of preparation, Karil, Beth, and I hiked with Karma and Tashi through the canyon and across the ice to the cave entrance. I had never adjusted to the altitude and lagged behind the Tibetans and Beth. Tsedor had come down with the flu and couldn't come, but we were joined by Mimba, the seventeen-year-old brother of one of the nuns. Karma, Tashi and Mimba took twigs and wedged them into the rocks above the entrance so that we could hang the prayer flags that I had brought from the States. A slight breeze picked up the ends of these illegal flags and whispered their presence.

Karil filmed while I laid a container in the red clay base of *Rainbow Bodhisattva*. We each gave a prayer of thanks and hope for this sacred land. Then I placed a number of articles in a waterproof capsule—soil from the other World Wheel sites, and a scroll we had created that morning to commemorate the power of this place and moment. Karma buried the capsule in the cave, and then we sat, three Westerners and three Tibetans, in meditation. I experienced the moment as a completion and a fulfillment of the spiritual practices I had engaged in since the age of nine, a moment of dissolving the ego self into the luminosity of the larger Self, the *Rainbow Bodhisattva* filled with rainbow emptiness.

The next morning, we packed up our tents and said good-bye to the smiling young nuns who helped carry our bags to the Land Rover. As we departed, my new friends and family pressed their faces against the window of the Land Rover with tears in their eyes. I opened the door, took off my hiking boots and down jacket, and passed them into the crowd. Whoever received them would need them more than I would.

As we drove off on the unpaved stony road, I gave thanks for the time I had spent in this sacred valley. I mused on the answers I had received to my three questions, which I had asked of the nuns in the valley and also of our guides. I had been puzzled by the seeming superficiality of their answers: they came from the place where they were born; their suffering was lack of food; the solution was more donations. It had taken me a while to realize that these questions had no relevance to them. They lived in a vast landscape at the top of the world. Everything around them was already a spiritual environment which expanded consciousness.

As we flew out of Lhasa, we saw the snow-capped Himalayas fading into the distance. My heart had lodged in these mountains and with the Tibetan people. Their enduring spirit had grown out of this fierce beauty and I carried it with me, as the very ground of my being, the physical spaciousness of the earth and sky. Just before we arrived in China, Beth and I completed the last few *Om Ah Hung*s for Tibet's welfare.

Rainbow Bodhisattva, Shoto Terdrom, Tibet

CHAPTER EIGHTEEN

Marriage

Santa Monica, California
1978

Oscar

ONE EVENING, OSCAR took me to dinner at one of his old haunts, the Brown Derby restaurant on Hollywood Boulevard. His hand warm in mine, we waited for our Caesar salad and lamb chops. The atmosphere was dark and filled with smoke, and it felt like the world of another generation. After dinner we walked on the Boulevard, peeking into tattoo parlors and adult shops to entertain ourselves. Prostitutes, the homeless, and teenagers with brightly dyed hair and leather pants swarmed the streets. Through the glitz I remembered the innocence and romance of Hollywood in the 1940s when my father first brought me and my grandparents to California.

In this nostalgic state, I drove back to the house with Oscar and lounged on the overstuffed couch in the living room. We held hands and enjoyed the environment he had created. He had lined an entire wall with books, only a fraction of his library of ten thousand or more volumes. I tucked my legs under me as we listened to Brahms' *Concerto for Horn*. Flames writhed upward in the fireplace, and Oscar's hand warmed my back. I practically purred.

When Oscar retired for the night, I stayed downstairs playing on the upright Steinway late into the night, improvising on the piano and with my voice. I wished he had touched my breasts. I wished that I had my arms around him. The music poured out of me, racing with excitement. Then strains of sadness surfaced and pulled with them memories of misconnections, of others who had not been there for me—Dale, my mother, my father, the nuns, sometimes Swami. And I thought about the warning words of Don Hildé about Oscar. My fingers danced on the keyboard and the full range of my voice bathed the room with my heart's music and my pent-up feelings—from high piercing melodies to the vibrations of my lowest tones—until they culminated and resolved. I would open to Oscar's love.

Oscar was tired of the commute to his office and I longed to be closer to nature. As a result, we moved to a cottage by the ocean in Santa Monica. I painted and redecorated our new home. Oscar had a room upstairs to receive his patients and he relinquished his Beverly Hills office. I made the extra bedroom, lined with his books, into a meditation room. We shared a bedroom that looked through sliding glass doors into a garden splashed with purple flags, gardenias, naked lilies, white jasmine, and pink oleanders. Through lush trees, we had a view of the ocean and I could smell fresh salty air. Over the pounding of the surf, we agreed to begin our new life.

In the course of the next month, Oscar asked me to marry him and I said "yes." While I had struggled to find harmony between the silence of the hills and the noise of Los Angeles, the love between Oscar and me had grown. The disturbing doubts about Oscar that Don Hildé had brought to light during our *ayahuasca* ceremony had died away when I realized that I didn't

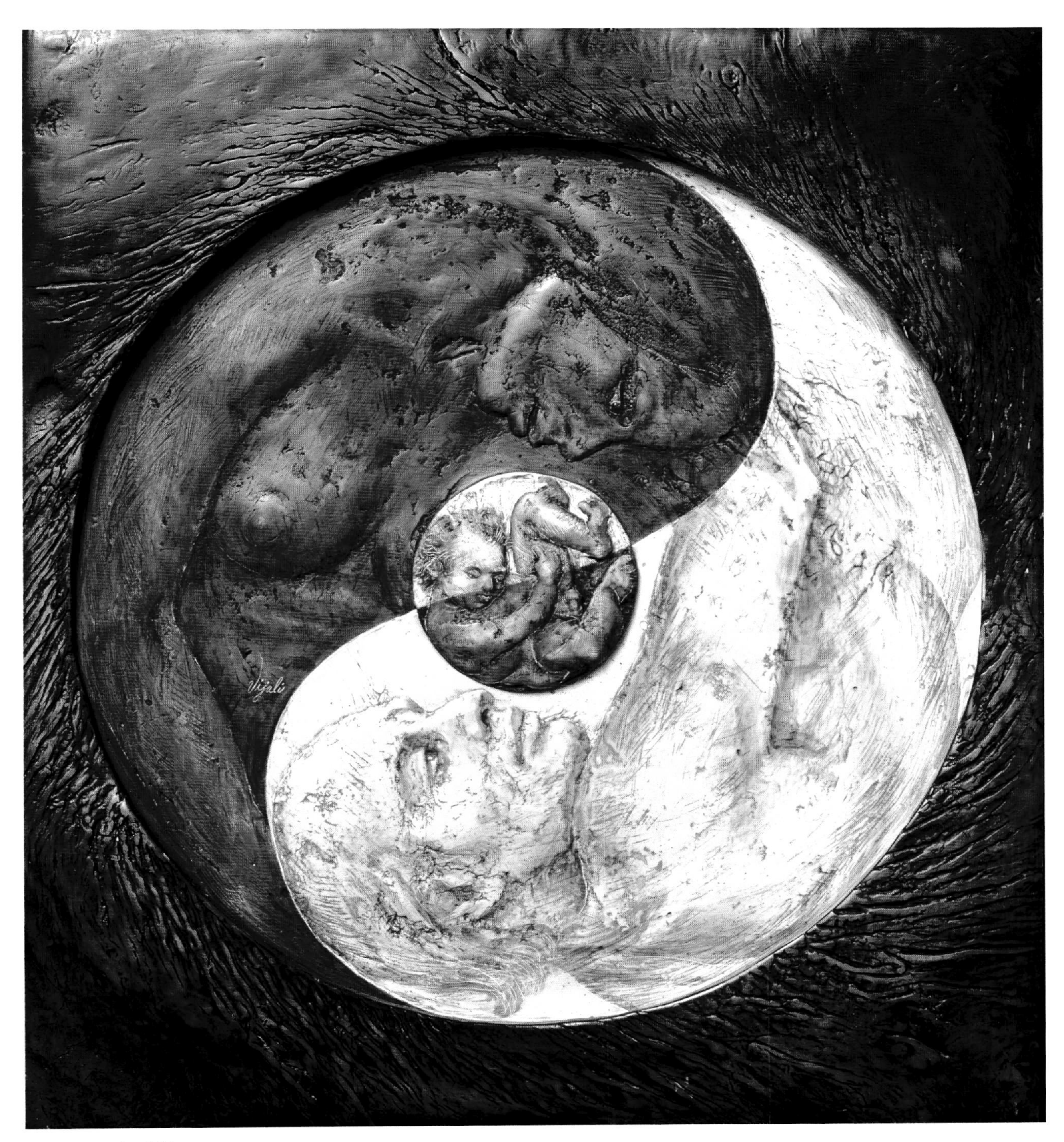

Yin Yang with Child

have to take the medication that he had suggested for my panic attacks and that it was all .right to love someone who had different ideas about healing. I was able to draw upon the strength of my own convictions about what was right for me. Secretly, I hoped that his comfort in the city and his full social life would provide a base for integration in my own struggle—my love of wilderness and my need for companionship in the city. And I thought that perhaps I could contribute a spiritual dimension to the life of someone I loved. Perhaps a new kind of child, a new consciousness, could grow out of this mating.

We wanted a simple wedding. We scheduled the Justice of the Peace from the Malibu courthouse to come on the appointed day. As I had no need for my friends to share this intimate moment, only four others attended—Oscar's sons, Robi and Dave, both in their early twenties, and Oscar's two closest friends.

I grew anxious five minutes before our wedding ceremony and asked Oscar for a few moments alone with him.

We sat on our bed holding hands. "Oz," I said, "I know we've talked about this before many times, but I have to say it again. I'm worried that you'll be uncomfortable with my creative side and with my need to leave sometimes and explore. Do you understand that this is the way I learn?"

Oscar held me close. "Your creativity and spiritual insight drew me to you. That's no problem. But I have to ask you again because of *my* nervousness: I'm twenty-two years older than you are. You're only thirty-nine years old. Are you sure this isn't a problem for you?"

"Of course, I'm sure."

We both felt better with this affirmation and walked out into the garden still holding hands. Under the palm tree in the backyard, the Justice of the Peace read the simple marriage vows I had taken from Kahlil Gibran:

Ay, you shall be together even in the silent
memory of God.
But let there be spaces in your togetherness,
And let the winds of the heavens dance between you.

Love one another, but make not a bond of love:
Let it rather be a moving sea between
the shores of your souls.
Fill each other's cup but drink not from one cup.
Give one another of your bread but eat not
from the same loaf.
Sing and dance together and be joyous,
but let each one of you be alone,
Even as the strings of a lute are alone though
they quiver with the same music.

Give your hearts, but not into each other's keeping.
For only the hand of Life can contain your hearts.
And stand together yet not too near together:
For the pillars of the temple stand apart,
And the oak tree and the cypress grow not in
each other's shadow.[22]

Afterwards we celebrated with champagne and took our favorite walk down the Santa Monica beach. The wind blew through our hair and waves washed over the footprints we left in the sand.

CHAPTER NINETEEN

World Wheel-Spoke Ten

Kunming, China
1992

Kuan Yin of the People I,
Kunming, China

OUR FLIGHT FROM LHASA arrived at the Chengdu airport in western China. Beth caught a plane back to the United States and Karil stayed with me for the first month in China to film the next site of the World Wheel. I had only the name and telephone number of a librarian at the Kunming Teachers College in Kunming, given to me by Allen Ginsberg, Oscar's cousin, before I left the States. I found a taxi to the train station and we drove through the streets of Chengdu, which were wide and lined with tall, modern buildings. The city looked affluent, its people stylish. Even the women on bicycles wore high heels and flowing dresses.

I carried a certain wariness arising out of my recent journey in Tibet. I saw the Chinese occupation there as brutal and oppressive. I felt deeply for my Tibetan friends in their struggle against China, and those impressions had stayed with me.

At the Chengdu train station, I learned that train tickets were hard to come by, so we found an inexpensive hotel overlooking the river. The Minjiang River, exquisite by night, was a sluggish soup of trash by day, thick with bacteria. But the hotel was clean and friendly, home for the few days it took us to get train tickets on the black market for a "hard sleeper" to Kunming.

The twenty-five-hour train ride to Kunming passed in a flash. I slept well at night and during the day watched the landscape roll by—dark red terraces, rich and luxurious; bright green rice fields; picturesque villages—all in exquisite harmony with the earth.

On my first day in Kunming, I visited the Yunnan Art Institute where I showed photos of my artwork to the vice-president. He received my work warmly and invited me to give my slide show the next day. Then he took me to an exhibit of works by the directors and teachers of the Institute.

At Kunming Teachers College, I was greeted by Li Juan Yang, the librarian whose name and telephone number I had brought with me to China. She was exquisite, beautiful and delicate. She wore a green silk dress with high heels and stockings, and she had twisted her long black hair into a bun with white fragrant flowers. In a small sitting room, I showed her the photos of my work. Although we communicated primarily through gestures and smiles, we nevertheless arranged for her to come to my hotel the following week with a translator.

In the afternoon, I browsed through a bookstore and picked up a Chinese propaganda booklet on Tibet called *The Friendship Bridge to Tibet.* In brief, the booklet reported that China had given Tibet better roads, and had saved the Tibetans from feudal lords, superstition, and infanticide. I had just experienced the real situation in Tibet, but how many others would believe what they read?

That night, new Chinese friends invited me to dinner and we talked about life in modern China. At this time, Chinese law forbade families to have more than one child, and a woman at the table related a story from one village.

"In the villages, a husband often chooses another wife if his current one can't bear him a son. The government doesn't permit divorce, so a man I knew killed his wife because she couldn't have a child so that he could take a new wife. Egged on by his mother, he refused to give her food, and then he dug a hole and buried her alive. Wife beating used to be common, too, until the government outlawed it. These days the violent husband is punished. I have a daughter, the only child I'll ever have. And I'm determined," she said, "to educate my daughter well so she'll have some choices in life."

The next morning, I returned to the Yunnan Art Institute to give my talk. I showed slides of the countries I had visited so far, but when I asked the students my three questions, they responded with stunned silence. The teacher explained that the students were unused to answering such questions and were shy. When they did talk, they showed an interest in the World Wheel, but firmly said I shouldn't waste my time trying to get permission to work in a public area. They were sure that the government would never agree to the project. They said that administrative red tape would prevent me from getting even a negative answer for three years or more. Their sweetness and support touched me.

My new librarian friend, Li Juan Yang, arrived at my hotel the following Tuesday with her friend Steven, an English teacher from the college. They were keen to help me create the World Wheel and suggested that I look for a site in an area not publicly known. Steven confirmed what the art students had said, that the red tape connected with famous national parks was horrendous.

While I explored the possibilities for private sites, I looked for a Tai Chi teacher in Kunming. In every country of the World Wheel I had participated in the local religious practices of that culture to better understand the people. Because it was ancient and had survived through the wild turbulence of China's history, Tai Chi represented something immortal in the Chinese character, like a deep root running through the culture. It took me a while to find my way to the Sports Center and then to the right gymnasium. I had only a piece of paper with "Sports Center, I want a Tai Chi instructor" written in Chinese script.

The Sports Center, surrounded by student and faculty apartments, housed a full-sized stadium and several gymnasiums. I made my arrangements with the Tai Chi teacher, and the following Monday morning at eight-thirty had my first lesson observed by a throng of onlookers who had come to see "the American" learn Tai Chi.

The instructor's name was Gangping Zhu, a Muslim Chinese. We became great friends. Small and in his middle thirties, he customarily wore a childlike expression on his handsome face. I enjoyed the lesson immensely. On my way out, one of the observers informed me that my teacher was a nationally known gold and silver medal champion of Woo Shu and Sword, two forms of Chinese martial arts.

Two friends arrived from California, and we decided that Lijiang, in the foothills of the perpetually snow capped Yutong Mountains, seemed like it would be a good place for the World Wheel project. The area was also home to the Naxi people, a matriarchal minority culture with roots in Tibet.

Shortly before we were to leave for Lijiang, however, I received a call that an official from the National Parks Bureau wanted to meet with me. I immediately assumed that I was in trouble and imagined that I might have been too outspoken in my talk at the art college. My heart remained with the Tibetan people and I presumed those feelings had shown.

On the appointed day, the representative came to my hotel dressed in a suit with white shirt and tie. In a friendly manner, with a heavy Chinese accent, he said, "We have heard about your World Wheel for Peace and the world family you are creating."

My heart sank. I knew what would come next. He would ask me to leave the country. I offered him tea.

"We have permission for you to create your sculptures in any of our parks. The director feels this is what China needs at this time—an exchange with the outside world."

I could only stare at him in astonishment. My visitor, Ke Shaw Song, worked for the Park and Garden Bureau as a landscape architect, and his department had instructed him to assist me in any way he could. I was to choose a park, make a drawing of my plan, and submit it to the director. We would stay in Kunming.

The next day a government official took me in his chauffeur-driven car to the zoo so I could meet with experts to discuss China's endangered species and the ecological problems of the area. I wanted to integrate these issues into the World Wheel performance. We went to the tiger cage and watched the magnificent tiger pace back and forth.

The scientist with us said, "Dangerous! Dangerous!"

I nodded. "Oh, yes."

Then we went to the panda cage, and as we watched the panda, lodged in the branch of a tree behind the fence, he said, "Dangerous! Dangerous!"

Then I got it. He meant "endangered species."

I moved from the hotel to the Yunnan University guesthouse in a picturesque old section of town where dilapidated houses of stone or brick lined narrow lanes, and began to explore the parks in Yunnan Province. Eventually I decided on Shisan Forest Park as the site for the World Wheel sculpture and performance. I chose this park not only because of its proximity to Kunming, as I wanted my friends to participate in the ceremony, but also because the site had attracted me from the beginning. I had come to learn that my initial heartfelt response was usually the right one.

I made several exploratory trips into Shisan to find the exact location. I hiked through a series of tunnels carved into the rock face of the mountain, emerging now and then to expansive views of Dianchi Laake. Shrines to Kuan Yin, the ancient and widely revered Chinese Goddess of Compassion, and other Taoist deities already existed, carved out of the living rock in natural cave shelters. So I was in my element, touching the shiny smooth stone that had been rubbed by devotees for centuries.

On a remote hill I explored the forests and met an occasional cow or goat feeding on the luxurious undergrowth covered with buds and flowers. Kunming means "eternal spring," and the lush vegetation of the park—always in bud and flower—lent veracity to the name.

One day my feet led me straight to the site, up on a hill with a 360-degree view of the mountain range and Lake Deanchi. Forty-five minutes from the park gates, the site was silent and secluded and far off the tourist track. Any images I created here would not impose on anyone, would be visible only at the site itself, and the vigorous hike necessary to get there would afford physical and mental preparation for entering sacred space. The stone formations suggested twisting, dancing people, and stone tiers would provide perfect seating for an audience. Flat ground around the main clump of stones would allow Gangping to perform Woo Shu, one of the marshal art forms for which he had won his medals, and would provide space for the other performers whom I hoped to draw into the event.

Here ferns and flowers already grew out of the stones and the place seemed alive with potential birth. I meditated in front of the limestone outcroppings with the warm sun on my back and asked the earth and stone for permission to carve here. As I touched the stones, I felt welcomed by them.

When I submitted drawings of my intended sculpture to the park authorities, they were delighted at the faces of the people and animals of China emerging from stone. The sculpture was to represent the harmony of life. I chose the title *Return to Harmony* for the performance, set a date, and began to work.

On one unusually sunny day, I returned to Shishan Park, intending to work. But when I arrived at the site, I discovered that my tools had been stolen, every one, including the carbide-tipped chisels I had borrowed from a professor at the Art Institute, as well as all my paints and brushes. The week before, a cow herder had been hanging around the site and had been much too aggressive for my comfort. He had breathed down my neck with his alcohol breath and had tried to take the hammer and chisel out of my hands.

At the end of my workday, I had hidden my tools under a bush behind the sculptures, so I wouldn't need to hike up the hill with them. I had a feeling that the cow herder came back for the tools, but without evidence I couldn't accuse him. Unsure about whether to tell the park authorities about the theft or not, I did nothing.

Vijali sculpting at the World Wheel site, Shisan Forest Park, Kunming, China

A few days later at the Art Institute, I ran into the teacher who had lent me his tools. I felt horribly embarrassed because he had been so generous in giving them to me. I felt even worse when I learned that carbide-tipped chisels were not available in China. He had made everything himself, even the special masonry hammer. He was completely good-humored about the news and offered me the rest of his tools to complete my work, saying that my work was most important. He took me to his studio where I chose three more chisels, the last of his supply.

We arranged for a graduate student to assist me when I needed him, and I agreed to pay fifteen yuan plus lunch per day. At the Art Institute supply store I discovered, to my surprise and delight, that I could buy acrylics very similar in quality to those I used in the States.

The next time I went to my Tai Chi lesson at the Sports Center, I saw tanks rolling into the large stadium and the compound teemed with armed officials. Gangping explained that once a month the government held public executions in the stadiums. "Good citizens" attended the executions of rapists and murderers, but Gangping refused to go.

He told me that every three months he and everyone else took a mandatory government examination in which they had to answer questions about their political and social attitudes. The answers went into a permanent file that the government kept on each individual for life. Such a heavy bureaucratic hand crushed his boyish spirit, and I wondered how long he would be able to keep his playfulness alive.

I had been working alone at the sculptural site for some time over the objections of my friends, who claimed that the park was dangerous. One day, as I hiked to the site a local man pulled a knife on a tourist only a few feet from me and robbed him. After the attacker bounded into the forest, I had to admit that I could be targeted as well. I was perhaps especially vulnerable while I worked alone at my isolated site, a forty-five minute hike from the tourist trail. So I decided, to everyone's relief, to have someone along with me from that time onward. On days when friends were unavailable, I took the graduate student.

Each day as I went to the park I also became better and better acquainted with the beggars along the entrance leading to the caves tourists visit. One young man traveled the one-hour bus ride with me every day. He looked very bright on the bus and clean cut, perhaps a university student, and he used crutches for his twisted leg. But, when he got to the entrance of the park, he rolled his pant legs up to make his deformed leg visible and scooted himself along the road with his arms, his legs twisted and dragging so that it looked as if his whole body was deformed. He put on a strange face and grunted when tourists passed. Then, returning home, he once again became a nice looking young man riding on the bus. All the beggars became familiar with my presence there and, when friends came to find me, they would point out the path to the site.

While I worked on the sculpture, I thought about the local ecological problems to address in the performance. The rivers and lakes in China were so badly polluted that I couldn't eat the fish. While I saw articles in the China Daily about attempts to clean up and control pollution, I didn't see the results around me in practice. Each morning, black coal smoke billowed into the Kunming air, and cars and trucks spit exhaust in my face as I rode my bike the thirty minutes to the bus stop. On the train, I carefully kept my trash to put in a bin at the station, but the men who cleaned the train swept the other trash, piled with styrofoam containers, out onto the tracks as we sped along. I wondered if they realized how long this material stayed with them, dotting the countryside in unyielding white.

Paradoxically, amidst the pollution and garbage, the Chinese love of beauty showed through. People were exquisitely groomed and they took great pride in the appearance of their children (although the women envied white skin and sometimes used white face powder in the traditional way). All around I felt a strong sense of morality. Many people in western China, despite the rules of Communism, considered themselves Taoists, if not by attending temples then through culture and history.

Kuan Yin of the People II, Shisan Forest Park, Kunming, China

Nyland Nido, who had studied sculpture with me in Yelapa, Mexico, came from California to help me at Shisan. I appreciated his help on this project of six large sculptures, and his intelligent and creative company delighted me. Unfortunately, we both came down with bronchitis, and often spat and coughed on our long forty-five minute trek to the site. Most of the time it rained, so we learned to work with our raincoats on. Sometimes, when I arrived at the site, I felt so tired I only wanted to rest, but I kept going, knowing that the performance needed to take place before winter.

It was now October. Day by day the faces of the local ethnic groups of Yunnan Province emerged from the stone. But I had problems with the most prominent face—the stone kept breaking, losing part of the face, but, as in life, the areas with which we have

Woman of the Sky Holding a Lotus, Shisan Forest Park, Kunming, China

the most difficulty eventually become the strongest and most developed.

I succumbed to the familiar stress leading up to a performance. Continual rain prevented my work—more rain than in the rainy season. Bronchitis continued to plague me. It took days to reach people on the phone, and I needed to make contact with the Naxi minority culture whom I wanted to bring from Lijiang, with their music for the performance. I still waited for the Park Department to keep their eternal promise to move the plants from around the sculptures, and I worried that friends would soon arrive from America to find nothing ready. But I had learned that each ritual performance takes on its own design and brings its own set of surprises. These surprises always seemed to work in the end.

Plants sparkled with health after weeks of rain followed by sun, and even more wildflowers grew in this place of eternal spring. Kuan Yin had emerged from the stone. She represented the people of today and reflected the divine beauty in ordinary humans. Earth and moss grew out of the crown of her head and her feet of stone buried deep in the ground. I had painted one side of her face and body blue to represent space and spirit, while her natural stone side anchored her to the earth as matter. I called her *Kuan Yin of the People.*

The sculptures and painting at Shishan expressed my complete philosophical view of a borderless reality. Space itself was represented by the side of a large stone painted with shades of blue, evoking the feeling of open sky. Emerging from it was the profile of a woman, her hand holding a lotus, the Chinese symbol for unity of the sexes. Three other sculpted faces peered out of twisting limestone outcroppings. Both form and formlessness existed side by side, symbolizing openness to all customs, religions, and attitudes.

I wrote in my journal:

> *The worship of ancestors makes as much sense to me as any other worship. From some viewpoint it is all correct and useful. From the outside, I may seem fickle, performing prostrations and mantras in Tibet and now Tai Chi in China. But from my own perspective, I am consistent. My love is for the space that encompasses all. All views and practices lead to this point, the window of unity.*

On the day of the performance, a large crowd gathered. I had brought fifteen Naxi musicians eighteen hours by bus from their village of Lijiang, close to the Tibetan border. Naxi society is matriarchal, so that wealth and surname pass on through the women who take care of business. The men are musicians and for the performance they played their ancient instruments. A Beijing Opera director painted the faces of Gangping's martial arts students as traditional opera characters. Musicians from the Yunnan University also arrived to accompany the performance.

I based the performance ceremony on the three questions that I had been asking people all along. I decided to answer the first question in the perfor-

Naxi musicians at the *Return to Harmony* performance, Shisan Forest Park, Kunming, China

A Naxi musician with his ancient instrument at the *Return to Harmony* performance

Group prepared for the *Return to Harmony* performance

Vijali emerging out of *Emptiness* painting in the *Return to Harmony* performance
Shisan Forest Park, Kunming, China

mance by representing emptiness or the void with my face painted as an open sky. I emerged out of the *Woman of the Sky* sculpture and danced, while Xuan Ke, leader of the Naxi musical group, read their creation myth.

In answer to the second question, Gangping's students, along with a live snake, slid through my legs, taking birth as they performed the classical animal forms of the martial arts—the snake, monkey, eagle, and crane. Then Gangping and his students moved into the sword forms to show the conflict that peasants had suffered at the hands of royalty.

In answer to the third question, the audience and performers joined hands in a circle, embodying the name of the performance, *Return to Harmony*. In the

Gangping Zhu, martial arts champion
performing in park

center, I buried a stone blessed by the Dalai Lama when I received the Kalachakra empowerment from him a few years earlier, as well as earth from the previous World Wheel countries. I invited the children to write their answers to my three questions on a long scroll, for which I had provided brushes and bottles of ink. One young girl wrote: "I think since God created us human beings on this beautiful earth, we should treat each other and the environment honestly and peacefully. I believe that this world will be full of love if each one gives their love, even a little, to this world."

Television crews recorded the performance for both local and national distribution. I hoped that my work might contribute to a process whereby China would open its doors to a world family. Imagine—all this had blossomed from one telephone number!

Leaving China, I had a stopover in Beijing, where a Chinese friend of a friend came to meet me. We went together to Tiananmen Square. As we stood by one of the underground corridors, my friend began to cry.

"I stood right here," he told me in English, "when the tanks rolled into the square. The troops, just young boys the age of my students, had been given "medicine" and it made them mad. That was the only way they could have killed these young people, their own kith and kin. I knew some of the soldiers, and I could look into their faces from where I stood and see their eyes glazed from drugs. After the killings, the soldiers disappeared without a trace. In the Square, the blood was so profuse that nothing could wash it away. Some of the flagstones had to be pulled up and replaced. Before the killings, the government had sent out trucks of guns parked in the city so that civilians would take the weapons. That gave the troops an excuse to fire into the crowd, because some people held guns, even though they had only one or two bullets in them."

He paused. "It's extremely dangerous for me to talk about this. Everything is reported to the authorities

Chinese children writing their answers to my three questions after the *Return to Harmony* performance

Chinese child in the *Return to Harmony* performance

and it's not unusual for rooms to be bugged. You can't talk about anything, especially in Beijing."

My friend grieved for the young people of China, who he felt had no guidance and no vision for the future. "Their lives," he said, "have no meaning and no purpose, because their choices are so limited." He thought that the best they could do was study to become teachers like himself so they could make decent money. But the political situation prohibited writing or publishing anything of interest.

"Some day," he confessed, "I hope to write a book about the underground student movement and smuggle it out of China."

Another Chinese friend knew some of the students involved in the Tiananmen Square incident. "The ones who were not put in prison," he said, "are leading a life of living death, wasted lives. Many bright young scientists are stuck with manual jobs like street sweeping, and can't get housing because they are blacklisted. To hire them means losing your own job. And to help them means a blot on your own record, one that will follow you to the grave.

"There is a joke," he said, "that in China when people die, the paperwork on them could fuel their cremation, there is so much of it."

He had attended some of the underground meetings, even though he was against the student demonstration at the Square. Because of this blight on his record, his salary was fixed at eighty-nine yuan, approximately seventeen dollars a month, for the rest of his life, regardless of his success as a teacher or the number of years he would work at the university.

He said, "The blacklisted students heard about you and the work of the World Wheel. They asked me to bring you to them. They were excited that someone had found a way to help China, a way that the government accepts, and that has the potential to create positive change. They send support and encouragement through me, but I wouldn't let them meet you. The authorities would have found out and put a stop to your work."

Later, when I returned to the United States, he wrote to me, "I want to dedicate the rest of my life to the World Wheel for peace and environmental protection. Usually I do not believe in fate. But this time I believe it is with fate that we met and shared the same thoughts and ideas. I hope fate will lead us to our destination and realize our dreams in our lifetimes."

Kuan Yin of the People III,
Shisan Forest Park,
Kunming, China

Kuan Yin of the People II

CHAPTER TWENTY

Spirit Within Matter

Santa Monica Mountains, California
1977

She Who Opens the Doors of the Earth (detail), Yelapa, Mexico

NATURE DREW ME OUT of Santa Monica, where Oscar and I had moved, and, every chance I had, I roamed the secret crevices of the Santa Monica Mountains. For a month, I explored a particular canyon, drawn by a protruding stone I had glimpsed in the distance. This monolithic boulder jutted from the chaparral and stuck in my thoughts—its persistent, penetrating shape, rising like an erect *lingam*, parted the sky. Beyond it I could see what looked like a waterfall, something rare in these usually dry canyons. Each day that I returned to the canyon, I searched for a way through the ridges of stone and the thick chaparral—the scrub oak thickets and thorny bushes that grow in the semi-arid coastal region of Southern California. I crawled on hands and knees through nearly impenetrable tunnels made by the blacktail deer through the dense growth. I felt as if I were a child again, moving through tunnels of dried prairie grasses—except that as a child, I had known where the tunnel would lead.

One morning, I accompanied the Art Director of Pepperdine University on a drive into the mountains behind the campus, part of the school's wilderness property. The Art Department had agreed to my request to create environmental art in one of the canyons, and as we drove, the Director pointed out the extent of this land. To my great surprise and delight, it covered the area I had been exploring! We drove back toward campus and he let me out at the entrance to Winter Canyon, the gateway to the area that so intrigued me.

I had packed my backpack that morning with sleeping bag, water, hammer and chisels, and dried fruits and nuts. I shouldered the pack, entered Winter Canyon, and walked until I came to a wild ravine where I faced a sheer rock wall. I managed to skirt the rock by climbing up the precipitous bank to the right, then worked my way down to the stream behind the falls. I squirmed through its narrow canyon, barely squeezing through with my backpack, searching for an opening in the dense growth that grew on the steep slopes of the stream. But a massive patch of deceptively lovely poison oak blocked my way, its shining leaves burnished with corrosive oils. I pushed it aside with a dead limb, but one branch swung back and whacked me across the face. I took another stick and pinned the poison oak back again, but the voice of Kote, a Chumash medicine man I had known in Santa Barbara, rang in my ear: "You must always ask permission from the Earth before entering her caves and canyons."

I released the poison oak, sat down on the ground, and plunged my hands into the moist soil. "Earth, may I enter the folds of your skin and learn how to walk in harmony?"

I noticed velvety, silver leaves growing beside me—mugwort—and I remembered that mugwort was the antidote for poison oak. "May I take a few of your leaves and remove the poisonous foils from my face?" I sprinkled water on the plants and carefully tore off four leaves. With these I wiped my face. Then I was able to freely pass.

The canyon pulled me farther into its recesses. As I hiked, I heard the squish of my boots in the red mud and noticed occasional deer tracks. I saw a cat print almost five inches in diameter, and I remembered a ranger telling me that he had recently spotted a mountain lion in the vicinity. When the poison oak receded, it gave way to a clearing with the decomposing carcass of a deer. I held my breath because of the stench, bent over it, and looked into its face. The exposed skull bore a peaceful expression as it lay there becoming part of the earth once again.

A wall of tall reeds blocked my path. I pushed through on my hands and knees and followed a narrow passage made by deer. The tall grass closed behind me, shutting out the sun as I wriggled through, now on my belly. Finally, I emerged from this dark tunnel into the light. When I looked up, I saw the rock *lingam* towering in the distance.

Soil had collected in the ravine, and a few scraggly plants of chamois and spiky yucca grew there. I moved through the yucca spikes in a smooth, fluid way, then stopped with a jerk as one of their points stung me. I uttered a few words of prayer and gently glided forward again until I found myself standing before the two-story tall sandstone tower.

I sat in front of the boulder to meditate. The wind had stopped, a red-tailed hawk circled above, and perfect silence enveloped me. I felt the warm hands of the sun on my back. My body and mind relaxed. As I looked at the stone, its solid form dissolved and became luminous as if a doorway had opened in the stone to reveal its spacious nature. I sat in front of this radiant space, and my body had the sensation of expanding until I felt no-boundary between "Vijali" and "stone."

I felt that I was the essence of stone and of all life—where light and energy move without restraint—and where all physical distinctions are illusions. Fear was non-existent, even impossible. Carried by waves of bliss, I stayed in that state of no boundaries until the dark elongating shadow of the boulder finally pulled me back into time and place. As the sun went down, the hillside turned amber. Using a round stone for a pillow, I stretched out inside my sleeping bag and watched the light fade into darkness.

Sandstone boulder before carving

The next morning, I sat at the base of the *lingam* and studied the upright boulder. An indentation at the very top formed a circle about four feet in diameter. I knew that circle would be the doorway into the nature of the stone. I took my hammer and chisel from my pack and tucked them into my belt.

The back of the stone rose out of the hillside. A few ferns grew in the shade of the boulder where eroding earth had piled up against the stone to form a natural incline to the upper part of the rock. I added a few stones and made a stairway that allowed me to reach the natural impression of the circle I had seen from below. I started to carve.

At noon, I moved into the shade of the *lingam* and stopped to eat the dried fruit and nuts I had brought with me. When I finished, I sat in silence and observed small details around me—the green of leaves turning brown, dried twigs, and sand that had succumbed to millions of years of pressure becoming sandstone. I noticed a sense of composition everywhere I looked—as if a little switch inside me had flicked on and created a shift of consciousness. Everything became more beautiful and settled into its rightful place.

In this tranquil state, I returned to the sculpture and followed the natural lines of the strata in the stone as I carved. The tapping of my hammer created music, and the gusts of wind, occasional cries of hawk and raven, scurry of lizards, and scratching of birds in the fallen leaves under the scrub oaks joined in the symphony. The rhythm of this music carried me to a place beyond time.

Every day returning to work, I hiked through the canyon with my tools in my backpack. I had purposely searched for a stone in a place that required me to hike, gratefully purifying my body and lungs each day as I sweated and panted through the brush and up the ravine.

The path grew easier with each trip, and the brush slowly gave way, welcoming me into the canyon. When I arrived at the stone, I laid my tools—my articles of worship—in front of the towering form. Then I sat in silence, entering the space of stone that I had experienced that first day. After a time I would feel drawn into work and, with my hammer and chisel placed in a new pouch I had made, I climbed up the earth-stone stairway on the back of the boulder and began to work steadily away, shaping and deepening the circle. The rough chisel marks in the rock and the pattern they created pleased me.

As I worked, I thought of the upright stones across the continent of Europe, where early civilizations had worshipped since the Neolithic age. In the seventh century, the Catholic Church had issued the "Edict of Nantes," which condemned the worship of stone as a rite of paganism. Then, in the eleventh century, many majestic cathedrals, including the Vatican, were purposely built over sites where stones had been the previous objects of worship.

In South America, people had transported stones of gigantic proportions across rugged mountain ranges. In Bolivia and Peru, immense monuments exist that were made of stone from Ecuador, fifteen hundred miles distant. The largest known monolith transported, was fifty feet long, twelve feet in diameter, and weighed approximately sixty tons. Nevertheless, the Jesuits, in their crusades against paganism, had it destroyed in the sixteenth century. It took eighty men three days to reduce it to fragments.

The shadow of my own stone of worship lengthened and a dark cloud of bees swarmed over my head, sounding like a high-voltage electric current. I stuck my hammer back in my work pouch, astounded that the day had passed. As I climbed back down the boulder, touching its rough surface, love for that stone poured through me. I paused before the sculpture to study the form that had emerged after three months of work. Nature had taken centuries to carve this monolith; I had only accentuated its natural form with my chisel. I could see space within the rock juxtaposed with the rock, affirming the emptiness of mass, the fullness of space. The sculpture's name emerged: *Spirit Within Matter.*

From the beginning, this rock had exerted a strong magnetic pull on me. As my feet touched the ground, I thought, *I want to know.* I want to know *why* a place is holy, *why* the Infinite reveals itself in a particular location, and *why* we have worshipped stone monoliths since the days of the earliest people.

Spirit Within Matter [23]

I thought of Stonehenge, Easter Island, and the many cathedrals and other stone-circles located directly over magnetic anomalies. I remembered that the Earth is made of three distinct layers: the crust, the mantle lying just below the continents and oceans, and the core at the very center of the Earth. I had read that the density of the core may be identical to that of compressed metals such as iron and nickel. It behaves like an electromagnetic engine as it rotates on its axis, generating powerful electric currents that surge upward through the mantle and the crust toward the sky. This highly convective molten core, physicists now say, is the origin of the earth's magnetic field.

I crawled through the dark tunnel of grass and emerged into the western light, the sun heating my face. From the sun, another gigantic molten magnet, electrons and protons stream toward the earth in ionized hydrogen gas called plasma. This is the solar wind. As one side of earth faces the sun, the earth's magnetic field compresses and flattens out, forming a cavity called the magnetosphere. This action deflects the solar wind which moves through space at two hundred to eight hundred kilometers per second. The solar wind would otherwise bombard the surface of the planet with streams of charged particles, rendering it barren and creating a lifeless surface like that of the moon, which has no magnetic field. The earth's magnetic field is critical to the existence and survival of all life.

As I hiked homeward, the rays of the sun made me sweat. I felt the sun's power enter my body in the same way that it enters the scrub oak along the canyon walls and all biotic life. Imagine rising lines of force from inside the earth, powerful enough to hold at bay another force equal in strength, the solar wind! What stands in between? Everything on the planet—water, plants, insects, fish, birds, ourselves. And stone.

Electromagnetic vibrations from the magnetic field constantly move through the earth. As they rise, they penetrate its crust, which varies radically in thickness. Thus, certain areas of the earth's surface have less resistance than others. Also, certain ore deposits have a high magnetite content, which allows the conduction of extremely low-frequency electromagnetic waves. Locations with dominant ore deposits have strong magnetic fields, and low frequency waves pulse through them with greater intensity.

Physicists hypothesize that Stonehenge, Easter Island, and many cathedrals and other stone-circles are located directly over such magnetic anomalies. These "holy" places, places that "work miracles," create changes within the mind and body because of specific physical effects. Perhaps the thinness of the earth's crust exposes the body more directly to the magnetism and the greatest source of low-frequency waves, creating minute cellular changes to the body. Perhaps early humans discovered this and used these forces in their lives. I noticed that each day after I carved on the stone, I felt alive and joyous, but once I entered a house and stayed for a while that vitality subsided. Could my monolith stone be one of these places?

I continued my work on the stone. Sometimes, as with *Winged Woman,* I invited people to come with me to the site. Once a week, nineteen-year-old Thomas, the son of one of Oscar's close friends, came with me to the mountain. Thomas was tall and handsome with thoughtful blue eyes, light brown hair, and an intelligent, childlike expression on his face. We had hit it off the first day Thomas's father had brought him to my house. We read our latest poems to each other, and as I showed Thomas the photos of my sculptures, the idea came—why not take him to the mountains with me?

His father looked delighted when I told him my idea. He confided to me that Thomas had been diagnosed as paranoid schizophrenic. My heart raced when I heard this, and I thought of my mother and all she had gone through. Silently I prayed that Thomas would find a kinder world to live in than she had.

On our first hike to the sculpture site, as we skirted the waterfall, he spotted a bird spiraling above. "Look!" he said, and added, "The flat angle of the wings, not flapping but gliding, shows that it is a raptor."

When we arrived at the stone, he immediately headed for a large flat rock where I sometimes slept.

He lay down and promptly fell asleep as I unpacked my tools in front of the *lingam*. Fifteen minutes later he woke, perfectly calm and clear, and climbed up the earthen stairway to where I worked. There was just enough room for the two of us, so I put a hammer and chisel in his hands and showed him how to deepen the lines that I had already begun.

Yet often, when I picked Thomas up at his mother's house, I found him agitated, disturbed, sometimes in the midst of a full-blown panic attack. Once on our way to the site, as we emerged from the tunnel of dry grass, Thomas turned grave, informing me, "This week the police put LSD in my water and arsenic in my food." I could feel him on the verge of panic.

The panic subsided as he carved alongside me. Our energies transformed as the hammer and chisel sang out the rhythm of our work, slowing our minds to the pace of our bodies. Within an hour, we could feel perfectly balanced within ourselves, with each other, and with the environment.

I wondered about the changes that occurred again and again at these power spots when people touched these stones. I had been reading James Beal's article in the book *Biologic and Clinical Effects of Low Frequency Magnetic and Electric Fields.*[24] In it, he discusses how the natural electromagnetic field is walled off in autos, aircraft, buildings with metal frames, and other metal structures, and how extensive use of plastic materials inside buildings and vehicles creates highly positive electrostatic charges that augment fatigue, irritability, and apathy. I thought about the energy changes I had observed in Thomas and so often in myself when I left the city to work on the stone. I wondered how many modern ailments might be prevented by the use of natural materials.

One day, Thomas and I sat on a stone at the site, watching insects and enjoying the breeze. A hummingbird hovered briefly in front of us. Then Thomas pointed. "Look at the spider building a web at the base of the sculpture."

We watched the spider weave the same circular image we had been carving. I took off my hiking boots and adjusting myself on the stone, took a better look.

Spirit Within Matter (detail)

After a few minutes, I slid off the rock and walked over to the sandstone sculpture. I climbed barefoot to the top with my paints and brushes. Thomas stood at the base and watched. Shading the blue to become lighter as I worked toward the bottom of the circle, my brush seemed to penetrate the stone, my paint to open the form into limitless space.

I glanced at Thomas. Only the wind broke the silence, and even our individual forms seemed part of a larger design, a much greater image. I looked up and gazed out over the stone ridges and chaparral growth. The solid substrate struck me as illusory. The stones, our bodies, the sage, and the space around us all united in a web of light, a web like that of the spider.

Thomas broke the silence as he pointed toward the painted circle in the boulder. "It's as if there was a little window through which we can look and see what's really inside the stone."

To me, this stone was the perfect symbol of basic matter, basic form. When I began my sculpture work years ago, I looked only at the external form, but as the work continued, it moved me to understand the essence of matter and of ourselves. My first boulder carvings like *Winged Woman* and *Reclining Man* were influenced by my earlier figurative style. Even though I had transitioned my work from the studio to the wilderness, my approach had remained largely representational, often showing women struggling to free themselves from the stone. Now I embraced simple abstract forms and concepts. My evolving vision was one of the world as moving, flowing energy rather than the crystallized, static forms we are taught to see and psychologically validate.

While I worked at resolving the creative problems of working with stone, I was also working to resolve the conflicts within my own life. I saw the blue space within the stone as my personal confrontation with the *void*, the borderless reality thrust upon me. The choice of stone for my medium represented the seemingly solid—my body and other material objects—trees and houses and chairs and cars. I realized that the feeling of being bound originated in my own mind. I had to break a pattern of blaming or leaving a situation. When I sought help inside myself rather than externally through others, I gained inner knowing and confidence, which allowed the answers and wisdom within me to surface.

Thomas clasped his hands loosely behind his head and looked up into space. The panic that he felt when I picked him up was gone. He watched as I put the final touches on the circle, rubbing clear wax over the surface. I climbed down the sculpture to where my backpack lay next to him.

A snake slithered into the chaparral, catching my attention. Thomas sat up with a start when I said, "Look at the rattlesnake." It coiled and rattled when Thomas moved, tongue darting back and forth. When we became still, the snake relaxed and continued its way through the chaparral.

The lengthening shadows reminded me of the late hour, and I moved to leave. But Thomas said, "Aren't you going to sign the sculpture?"

"Nature was the original sculptor," I said. "I only assisted in bringing the stone's spirit out a step further. Now nature will continue the process of change." As we packed the tools, I added, "With these earth sculptures, I want to develop a language that doesn't reflect any particular culture—Eastern, American Indian, or Christian—but which conveys the essence of all religions, a wisdom that speaks to everyone."

As we entered the freeway, Thomas' hands drew up into fists and his bright eyes narrowed and darkened. I could feel my own shoulders tighten as we merged into the traffic. What would it take, I wondered, to keep these doors of consciousness open into this space? They closed so easily each time I returned to the city, where a life of appointments and deadlines pulled me into an unnaturally fast pace. I witnessed Thomas going through this too, right before me. I pictured a new environment, one created from a different kind of relationship with everything around. *Spirit Within Matter*—the spirit *within* the world, not separate from it. When we can identify with every flower, stone, animal, and person as part of our own being, we will be enlightened.

When we arrived at Thomas' house, his mother stood at the front door. I gave him a big hug and left him, feeling the walls of the house and the darkness of his own mind swallow him up.

Shortly after we completed the sculpture, Thomas' parents committed him permanently to the Metropolitan State Mental Hospital. He resisted the best he could—he ran away twice to visit me, but the Hospital notified his father, who found him and took him back to the ward. The next time I saw him, I recognized that puffy red body and dazed look in his eyes—the result of medication and an institutionalized life. My heart still weeps for Thomas, for my mother, and for all the other precious, unusual souls like theirs. I pray they may find comfort and joy in nature instead of cement walls and medication. What would happen if they lived within the healing arms of stone, under a ceiling of sky, a carpet of grass stretched out before them, animals nurturing them, fresh spring water baptizing them, dolphins swimming with them for at least a part of each day? What would happen to us all in such a life?

My own fear of being or becoming insane like my mother had vanished when I saw Thomas adapt so happily in a natural environment. I realized that separation from nature, fostered by society, creates an isolation that accelerates as the extended family of people and nature deteriorates. Then we develop a sense of separate identity, of ego-based life—the root of the form of "insanity" most of us suffer.

In 1976, before I worked in Winter Canyon, the Park Service had given me permission to carve *Seed of Space* on a peak in the Santa Monica Mountains. Then, in

Shelter Sculpture, Winter Canyon, Pepperdine University, Malibu, California

She Who Opens the Doors of the Earth, Yelapa, Mexico

Seed of Space, Santa Monica Mountains, California

the jungles of Mexico in Yelapa, I had carved *She Who Opens the Doors of the Earth* with the help of the community, integrating elements of the void, abstract form, and my personal life.

After this, friends started asking me to carve sculptures for them, and I began creating meditation gardens, bringing a touch of what I experienced in the wilderness into people's urban lives.

When Pepperdine University gave me permission to create two more environmental sculptures in Winter Canyon, I carved *The Shelter Sculpture,* which you could crawl into, and the *Sculptural Amphitheater,* which had two caves and three levels that formed a natural seating area. The University scheduled a one-woman show in their gallery. There I documented the process of my environmental work and, on the day of the opening, I took people on a trek into Winter Canyon to experience the sculptures first hand. This event initiated the integration of theater and music into my work.

All the while, I used the same process. First, I asked permission from the earth, from the stones, and from the owners of the land. Then, in ceremony, I listened for the heartbeat of the stone. In each site I was drawn not only by the stone, but also by the quality of the air and water, the characteristics of plants, the shape of the mountains and the canyons, and finally the shape of our planet. All of it became my canvas. I often invited others to carve alongside me as I taught them the skills involved.

The world became my studio and all people, animals, plants, and stones became my family, an earth family. I changed with each sculpture and with each site, and as the sculptures took new shape, my own consciousness took new form. I learned patience. I learned to listen to the wind and to the changing seasons. People found their way to the sculptural sites to experience the sacredness of the earth, to hear the stories of wind and storms and rattlesnakes and mountain lions, and to tell their own stories and childhood memories. Sometimes my story simply became everyone's story.

Spirit Within Matter III & IV, garden pieces in Santa Monica, California

CHAPTER TWENTY-ONE

World Wheel-Spoke Eleven

Lake Baikal, Siberia, Russia
1993

Vijali in Siberia with Buryat woman

WHEN I LANDED IN ULAN UDE, Siberia, I immediately contacted a family known by a Buddhist friend in the United States. The man on the other end of the phone line spoke English and offered me a space in his house with his family. They were in the process of moving.

Alexander, his wife, Tonya, and their two children made me feel completely at home. They introduced me to their wide circle of friends, many of whom were minority Buryatians of Mongolian descent who practice a religion based in shamanism and Buddhism. The Buryatians had suffered severe repression under the Soviet regime which had disallowed their religion, but in the 1990s, Buryat culture was seeing a resurgence in the region.

Alexander's family had a tiny apartment filled with boxes ready for their return to their native St. Petersburg. They had no money, and the financial crisis in Siberia and all over Russia forced them to go where they could find work. So, when Alexander and his family left Ulan Ude, I moved to the home of Vladimir Volodia, a prominent Buryat architect, with his wife, Dolzitma, and his eighty-eight year old mother.

A recent flood had necessitated the evacuation of 1,300 homes in the immediate area of Ulan Ude. Some families had moved to barracks, but many had camped on their roofs to prevent vandalism. The flood had contaminated the city's water supply and typhoid was rampant. We lived in the upper story of Vladamir's house, with neither cooking facilities nor electricity. His mother couldn't remember that she must not drink the tap water, and she fell sick with dysentery. I spent many days cleaning her up and washing out her clothes and linens. Eventually, the family took her to the hospital where she died.

In the street markets, women sold their wedding rings or furniture for food at a price so inflated that it exceeded the average income. I wondered what would happen to these women when they ran out of things to sell. The stores carried few supplies, and the general atmosphere was one of grayness and depression—and rampant alcoholism.

At the table in Vladamir's home, the three of us sometimes shared two small boiled potatoes and some pickled cabbage, not even quite enough for one. I held back even when I felt as if I would starve at one point. I gave them a hundred dollar bill to buy more food, but they were so enamored with their first American bill that they framed it and put it up on the wall. Vladamir had only one leg, and the only artificial limb available to him was very heavy and cumbersome. They wanted me to find a way for them to come to America so that he could get a more comfortable prosthetic. Others also requested that I connect them with some rich person in America who could help them with some particular problem.

Everyone presented their problems to me and sometimes I went to bed very depressed and sad. I wanted to help every person, but I did not know what I could or should do. Even with food so scarce and a lack of soap, toilet paper, and other personal items, the poverty in Siberia was less severe than what I had witnessed in India, Tibet and China. Siberia had two great advantages—space and its untouched forests.

Dolzitma and a young Russian woman named Oxana planned a weekend trip to Lake Baikal for me. We were driven by a young Buryat couple whom I had never met before. The sky was still light when we left the city at nine on a Friday evening. On the outskirts of town, we passed log cabins with brightly painted doors and shutters scattered among the trees, but the farther we drove from the city, the denser and darker the forest became. I felt pulled into its mystery, and such longing arose in me that I imagined myself leaping out of the car and running until I fell to the ground exhausted—submerging myself in the forest's dark denseness.

When we reached Lake Baikal, the waters reflected the sky, calm and clear, and the forest grew right to the water's edge. I walked for the first time into the Siberian forest, feeling its life around me unaltered by human imprint. A Buryat monk had told me that many forested areas were still virgin. "No foot has ever touched their soil," he said. Here I found ripe blueberries, currants, cow cherries, and varieties of ferns and plants that I had never seen before. This confirmed what I had heard—that over two hundred species of plants and animals are unique to this forest.

The first day we ate local fish called *omal* straight out of the lake, cooking them on the beach. I rowed Oxana to an island and back as clouds gathered in the sky. We stayed with the young Buryat couple, both of whom were in the computer business. In my honor they had brought a sheep in the trunk of the car. The morning after our arrival at the lake, the men killed and butchered it. Fathers traditionally pass their method of slaughtering sheep down to their sons, and the technique varies according to the area of Buryatia in which a family lived. They killed this sheep by slitting its stomach, putting a hand up inside, and twisting the valve to the heart.

If I was going to eat this sheep, I wanted to observe the whole process of preparing it. I helped the women clean the intestines, their traditional chore. Then we wrapped the intestines around strips of heart and lung, so that the end result looked like a fat coral necklace. They mixed the blood with herbs in the intestines to make blood sausage. Finally, they made sheep soup from salty hot water with the sheep's fat floating in it. Every part of the sheep was used. For the next three days, we ate nothing but sheep with bread three times a day (although for our first meal, we also had pickled cucumber which quickly disappeared).

And vodka! All day long, everything provided an excuse to have a shot. Before they drank, the Buryat made a libation by dipping the ring finger (considered to be the clean finger) into the glass and flicked drops of vodka to the four directions, sprinkling the plants, trees, and the earth. At meals they replaced this ritual with a toast every few minutes. Unaccustomed to drinking, I dipped my finger in my tumbler after each toast and dotted the vodka between my eyebrows, at the third eye.

The Buryat used the toast as a sort of talking stick, giving each person the opportunity to express their deepest feelings, or whatever struck them as important in the moment. I loved the Russian expressiveness and vivaciousness, the sense that feelings should be communicated, but I was not taken with the drunkenness it engendered as the day or evening advanced. Often heated discussions followed the toast, verging on fist fights.

The drunkenness was pervasive. On the buses at night, both men and women regularly passed out on the floor. Often, as we drove back, our host would stop the car and vomit, or the man sitting next to me might crumple over onto my lap, passed out for the rest of the journey. On our way to Lake Baikal, ritual stops along the road had punctuated the drive. We would get out of the car and walk a short distance to a view, or to a significant tree, and make our vodka offerings and toast. The young Buryats who took us to the lake were between the ages of twenty-five and thirty. The young man named Misha was a mathematician and physicist, tall and handsome. He drank all night and passed out during the day, but was sober and reliable when the time came for the three-hour drive back to Ulan Ude.

While I waited for the arrival of Laura Hoffman, a videographer from the States, Dolzitma showed me around the museums in Ulan Ude. In the Geological Exhibition of the Archeological Museum, an ancient stone circle inspired me. At its center was a human body, positioned east to west. Although I hadn't found a site for the World Wheel yet, I decided to recreate this design for the sculpture, and to carve patterns found in nature, such as the spiral and the circle, on the stones. We also visited the Childrens Theater, once an underground theater and art gallery, now operating with government approval. We watched singing and folk dancing, Buryat style. When we spoke to the performers, we saw their pride in contributing to the revival of Buryatian culture. There was a sense of newness and excitement in the air after the long oppression of Communism.

One afternoon, we met with the Chief Ecological Scientist, a man who had dedicated his life to saving Lake Baikal. The lake holds twenty percent of the world's fresh water supply, and while 335 rivers feed into the lake, only one drains out—the Angara River. Seventy percent of the fish, mammals, and plant species found in this region exist nowhere else in the world. This includes the *nerpa*, an earless freshwater mammal that migrated from the arctic a million years ago. Lake Baikal is the oldest lake in the world, estimated to be from twenty-five to fifty million years old. It is more than a mile deep and lies over a geologic fault that grows an inch in width each year. The growing fault prevents the lake from filling with sediment.

The diversity of plant and animal life in and around the lake makes it as valuable to modern-day scientists as the Galapagos Islands were to Charles Darwin more than a century ago. But pollution is choking Lake Baikal. The primary source of this pollution is a pulp mill which the government has officially closed, but which continues to run because no one enforces the closure order. A second source of pollution is the phosphorus mining carried out on the Mongolian Plateau. The run-off from these activities flows into the lake. The resulting contamination has already caused the fish to shrink in size, and about 200 species of indigenous plants have become extinct.[25]

After our trip to the lake, I moved to the dormitory at the Agricultural Institute, delighted to have my own private space and to have a moment of separation from the tragedies of the lives around me. Friends told me that any room on the ground floor was susceptible to looting, so I chose one on the fifth. On the first night, as I prepared for bed, I admitted to myself that my personal depression was mixing with the tension I was feeling around me. I longed to chant, to meditate, and enjoy every moment in contemplation. "I can," I said aloud. "So why be sad?"

I went to sleep with a prayer on my lips, "Show me how to have in my life and in each moment, no matter how stressful, a continual contemplation of the whole."

My unconventional life entertained the people I met, as did the novelty of a woman alone creating the World Wheel. But what of my real gift—the vision of our borderless nature and the manifestation of a life expressing that state? Was no one interested in that?

That night I wrote in my journal:

> *Now that this seven-year journey has almost come to an end, I think perhaps I have failed. Each day I have prayed for tools to awaken us more directly and clearly to the great truth of who we really are. I have used the tools of my art and theater to show that it is not necessary to step in the footsteps of Buddha. He simply showed us by the example of his life to not be caught in schools of thought and sects, but to sit naked in spirit under the tree that drew* him *until he found that connecting thread of oneness. May we each find the courage to follow our own footsteps, ringing with the clarity of who we truly are—as different from one another as each snowflake pattern is different, but equally beautiful. We are, each one of us, luminous beings, only for a moment clothed in the misunderstanding of our true nature that our upbringing has encouraged in us. Tonight I shake off the depression that eats into our lives. I shake off the darkness, this view of separation and isolation, in order to know again that our true nature is one with every child, every creature, every plant, every stone, and every atom of the universe.*

Organizers of a UNESCO conference in Ulan Ude, held to address the ecological problems of Lake Baikal, invited me to show my slides of the World Wheel project. There I met Lena, the head of the Administration of Science and Culture of the province of Buryat, who became interested in the World

Wheel work and invited me to meet with her. Despite her busy schedule, she brought in a TV crew and some very interesting women journalists with whom we had a round-table discussion. I had the opportunity to ask Lena my three questions, live on television, and her answers were profound. She ended by saying, "In all religions, the key message is to develop love as the solution to our problems. For what is love other than uniting with the other? It is a recognition and consummation of that union."

After the meeting, Lena lent me her car and driver and we went to the main center of Buddhism in Russia named Ivolginsky Datsan. There I spoke with the head lama. For this meeting I chose to wear the traditional Mongolian dress that Ojunbulig, a young Mongolian girl, had given me. Others told me that no Russian woman would wear such a costume, so in this way, I expressed my solidarity with, and support for, the Mongolian/Buryatian people. I wore it for the duration of my stay in Siberia. The lamas at Ivolginsky Datsan loved the idea that I would create a sculpture in Buryatia. They treated me with great respect, and honored my work and my spirituality by giving me their blessings and by agreeing to attend the celebration ceremony. They asked me to create a giant Buddha on a cliff next to one of their monasteries. When I made it clear that I intended to sculpt a contemporary image, not a traditional one—the Buddha *now*, that consciousness dwelling in each of us—they responded with fascination and accepted my decline.

Laura Hoffman, the videographer I was waiting for, arrived from the States to film the World Wheel project and stayed with me in my room. By the time of her arrival, I had made up my mind to create the World Wheel site on the shores of Lake Baikal because I wanted to draw attention to the ecological problems of this important lake. Olga, a Buryat teenager and part of a women's group that had asked me to speak, came with Laura and me to be our translator. We took a six-and-a-half hour bus ride to the tiny village of Maxhimiha on Lake Baikal's eastern shore, a location suggested by the women's group. Under pouring rain, we staggered into the village, wheeling our suitcases. We had no idea where to start looking for a place to stay, but as we came down the road, two middle-aged women wearing babushkas maneuvered through the mud puddles and approached us.

"You will stay with me in my log cabin," Babanina said. Her face was as sweet, alive, and soft as she was hearty and generous. She took us home, built a fire for us, and heated borscht soup. We slept well in her warm rooms, Laura and I in one room, Babanina and Olga in the other.

Since there was no stone in Maxhimiha, we hitchhiked the next day around the lake to the village of Turka, which supposedly had some outcroppings. Along the lakeshore we found a magnificent natural stone altar jutting out over the water. The view from this rock took my breath away—a luminous lake surrounded by forest. As I explored the outcropping, a big wave broke over it and drenched me. On one side, some stones formed a baptismal pool. I thought this might be the ideal site, although I had some misgivings about working so close to the water when it turned stormy. I had seen Lake Baikal in a storm, raging and dark like pewter, with exploding silver tips on the waves.

But Turka itself depressed us. It was an industrial town with trucks that pulled in and out all day. So we thought we might go on to Gurrunekinko, a prettier spot from which we could commute to the stone site. The next day, we dragged our luggage onto the bus from Maxhimiha to Gurrunekinko, and called at the home of a family I had met during my first visit to Lake Baikal. They had a cottage for rent. When they eventually responded to our persistent knocking, the smell of vodka nearly overpowered us. They were completely drunk. Their log cabin on the lakeshore was adorable, quiet and secluded, and perfectly suited to our needs, but before we had decided to rent it, they asked for money to buy more vodka. We knew we would have to find somewhere else.

We scoured the village for another place to stay. One old woman we spoke to said that she expected her grandchildren to arrive any day to help with the potato harvest. At last, a seventy-year-old man said we could live in his house. Desperate, I paid him half the month's rent in advance, and he rushed off to buy vodka even before he had shown us around or had given us a key. Inside, the place was filthy, with old scraps of food lying everywhere. While we deliberated about what to do, I went to the outhouse and found the seat unusable, covered in excrement. When I got back, Laura and Olga had simultaneously decided that we couldn't live there.

We set off once again, dragging our luggage to the hotel in Turka, the most practical solution to our dilemma. But on the way, I admitted that I just wanted to be back with Babanina in Maxhimiha. Torn between the perfect stone site and Babanina, Babanina won. We flagged down a car to take us "home," and Babanina, ecstatic at our return, made us eggs and sausages as Olga translated our story.

That evening, Laura and I walked along the shore of Lake Baikal at sunset when the water and the mountains turned purple. This was the Lake Baikal we had heard about—clear, calm water surrounded by snow-tipped mountains, silent except for the gentle lapping of the waves.

The day Olga left to go back to school in Ulan Ude, Laura and I went hiking. We took the path into the forest, and then I left the trail, wandering mesmerized as its virgin darkness drew me in. The forest was dangerous, villagers had warned me. "Three people were mauled by bears," they had said, and I did feel the presence of bears. As I wandered, I marveled again at the myriad plants covering the ground like a carpet, and at the mushrooms and fungi growing out of leaf mold and tree bark. I imagined myself standing two feet from a great grizzly, looking into its eyes. I thought, if for the privilege of being here I paid with my life, I would feel gratified that at least my flesh had given nourishment to one living creature. After some time I joined Laura on the path again. When we returned to the village, we saw huge bear tracks in the sand where we had entered the forest.

Soon I found a site for the stone circle I had envisioned when we were in the museum. It was located on the bank of Lake Baikal, where the darkness of the forest met the bright light of the lake.

Laura and I wanted to talk with Babanina, and we put together some sentences in Russian Cyrillic. *Who can give us approval for the sculpture in Maxhimiha? Who can help us carry stone from the river to the forest?* These were all the words we could find in our tourist books. Babanina took me out and asked the men who were building a house down the lane if they could help.

Yes, they said they could, but they had no truck. More men gathered around, and I showed them photos and the single page of writing about the World Wheel that Olga had translated into Russian.

Babanina and I returned to the cottage with the understanding that when the men found a truck, they would come and get us. We assumed that this would take some time, if it happened at all.

Laura and I went down to the river, and I began to choose stones for the earth wheel. Just as I had located the ninth stone, the large one for the center, I heard the voices of the men behind me. They had returned with an enormous eight-wheeled truck, which drove easily across the stream. It took three men to unearth the large upright stone that would form the center of the earth wheel. One man ran for a plank and called for more men, until, in all, about a dozen of them arrived. They slowly wedged the stone up the plank onto the truck. They loaded the other eight stones with no difficulty, and we drove off together to the site. The truck could barely get through the trees, but it did, and they unloaded the large stone into its place. The men dug it into the ground and stood it upright. We placed the other stones in a circle around it. The circle immediately held power, and my heart warmed to see how much these men enjoyed helping us.

I tried to pay the driver of the truck, a young Russian boy, by sticking money in his pocket, but he refused it twice. Working with these men couldn't have been more different from the drunken encounters we had experienced up until then.

When Laura and I got back to the cottage, Babanina had prepared us a delicious fish dinner of *omal,* which she and her Buryat woman friend had caught the day before out on Lake Baikal in their little green rowboat. For dessert we had Russian pancakes with homemade strawberry jam. We ate until we were ready to burst.

The next day's work on the sculpture was pure fun. I took a string, one end of which Laura held on top of the center stone, and, with a chisel tied to the other end, I walked in a circle cutting into the ground. Then with my compass, I marked north, east, south,

Curious wolf and Vijali meet in the Siberian forest

and west with stones. The men had unknowingly placed the four large stones right on the marks.

I transplanted all the living plants that were inside the circle out into the forest. First a little pine sapling, next different kinds of mosses, then grass and other small Siberian forest plants whose names I didn't know. Some roots prevented us from leveling the ground, so I pulled them out with a shovel and my hands.

While I worked at the forest site, carving the stones that formed the wheel and placing pebbles demarcating a Russian cross on the inside, wolves came, gentle and curious. One even came up and sniffed my hand. In the villages, people kept these wonderful creatures chained up, and they turned into the most ferocious animals I had ever seen. When we walked by, they bared their teeth and foamed at the mouth, pulling and rearing against their heavy chains.

Babanina's family came to stay at the house, and they drove us to a place where colored stones had washed up from the lake. I envisioned defining the cardinal directions using these stones, so we gathered golden, red, black and white stones, which had been smoothed and rounded by tumbling in the lapping tide of the lake. We each chose a color to gather in buckets, which we then dumped into the rear of the car, trying to keep the colors separate.

The next day, I went to the site and sat in the morning sunlight facing the center boulder. I didn't close my eyes in meditation, as was my usual habit, but gazed at the stone with unfocused eyes until I saw it radiate light outward, just as I had experienced with the stones so many years ago in the Santa Monica Mountains. Then the light became a web of spirit running through the stone connecting everything in the universe.

The thought of Laura arriving at the site broke my concentration, but, instead of feeling irritated by this distracting thought, as I might have at another time, I saw the thought rise up out of the web and dissolve back into it, returning to its source, its base of spirit. The thought became a part of the breathing process as it rose with my chest and then fell again. The thought did not take away from the web—it was contained within it. Space within form. And form within space. I saw that my earlier efforts to cling to the thought, not the thought itself, had kept me stuck. Grasping the thought was like trying to hold onto a piece of the web, as if it were a solid and separate "thing," rather than a moment in an ongoing dance of energy.

I pulled myself out of this reverie when I heard Laura on the path. I knew then what form the sculp-

Vijali carving in the Siberian forest on the banks of Lake Baikal

ture needed to take, and in my work meditation each tap, tap, tap was a song of praise. Earth, why do I love you so? Why do I feel a heavy mantle of restriction lift when I enter you? A doorway opens through you into space, into freedom, into my borderless self.

By the end of the day, I had carved a doorway recess into the heart of the stone. The next day I picked up an even harder stone in the forest. It fit nicely into the palm of my hand, and I rubbed and rubbed the surface of the sculpture. It acted like a natural sandpaper as I smoothed the surface to make it ready to paint. Then I painted the center shape with blue shaded into white at the bottom so that it appeared luminous: an opening into the stone, into the understanding of ourselves. I called the boulder *The Within of Matter*.

Because I had already set a date for the ceremony when I was in Ulan Ude, and also because I had a ticket leaving Beijing shortly for Japan (and Laura had her ticket to return to the United States on the same day), I continued working through rain and high winds so the site would be ready on time. To keep warm I borrowed Babanina's fishing boots and wore all my clothes in layers.

The lake was wild by my side, and the mountains on the other side of the bay were painted white with snow as I worked in the fierce Baikal winds. I finished placing the stones in the cross ditches, adjusting the outer circle and leveling uneven ground where neces-

Buryat children sing and help with earth wheel in Siberia

Buryat children gather stones for the earth wheel

sary. As I worked, I realized my own fulfillment. The myth of a separate God was broken. The myth of a mate was broken. The myth of a perfect teacher was broken. My soul stood naked in the *void*. I knew fulfillment because people *really are* God, nothing less. And to love that radiant source in everything is to go deeper than the surface manifestation of forms to the Reality within nature, the Spirit within matter. Such a love is too vast for our ordinary minds to grasp, and yet it is simply an infinite deepening and expansion of the little, limited love we experience in loving someone. My own search to find love had led me to the underlying ocean of all love.

Shortly before I completed the site, a class of Buryat children turned up from Ulan Ude with their teacher. They loved the earth wheel and helped me place stones and shovel earth, chattering away in Buryatian. The government had only allowed them to have their own schools since 1990. They demonstrated their pride in their language and music by singing a Buryat song for me before they left.

Because of a storm, we had no phone or electricity for ten days, so I had no way of knowing who would show up for the actual ceremony. I was going on the assumption that only people from the village would attend. In the kitchen with Babanina and Laura, I prepared a talking stick. I took a stick that I picked on my first walk in the forest, and around it I wound colored yarn. With the yarn complete, I carved and painted sections of the wood. Laura contributed to the piece, as did Babanina, along with her daughter and her daughter's husband, both of whom had arrived early on the morning of the ceremony. Lastly, I tied on a feather I had found at the site and a heart-shaped stone.

Minutes before the scheduled ceremony a convoy of cars arrived. Lena had brought the television crew again and carloads of people eager to participate in the ceremony. The circle consisted of people from widely varied backgrounds—simple hunters and fishermen, sophisticated scientists from the capital, artists from the theater group, and writers—all a mixture of Buryats and Russians. We passed the talking stick around, and each person answered the three questions.

The presence of the television crew was tremendously important. These Siberians felt that they were cut off from the rest of the world, that no one recognized their plight. At last their voices would be heard. In the circle, their strong faces shone with passion. At the beginning of the ceremony, I gave each person a stone to commemorate the day. At the end, with prayers for world peace, we tied pieces of cloth to the trees as prayer flags, envisioning that the breeze from Lake Baikal would blow these prayers for peace into the world. The earth wheel, called *Light Within Darkness*, was created like a planted seed where the dark of the forest, the depression of the people, was dispelled by the light of the luminous lake—a seed of hope for their future.

My presence in Buryatia influenced the lives of others. In Ulan Ude, I spent an evening with an artist whose aristocratic family had been banished to Siberia from St. Petersburg. He had been born in one of the *gulags*, the Siberian concentration work camps where many aristocrats were worked and starved to death during the Soviet era. When I suggested he do

Light Within Darkness, where the dark Siberian forest meets the luminous light of Lake Baikal

something to improve his situation, he said, "You're a rich American. You can do something, but we can't." He had been unable to take action on his own behalf for so long under Communism that, even with that control lifted, he no longer knew how to express himself or to initiate action.

But when I showed my slides and talked about the World Wheel, people saw that someone with virtually no money could take action in a simple way, with whatever talents they had. By the time of the ceremony, many of those who attended had already made significant changes in their lives. Svetlana, manager of the Childrens Theater in Ulan Ude, felt so inspired by the World Wheel, and by me as a woman making a statement in the world, that she started a women's group where the women not only supported each other, but also helped the elderly and the flood victims. I understand that the group has grown and remains active.

While I traveled in Siberia, I carried a book in which people could write their answers to my questions. Ojunbulig, a young Mongolian girl, wrote: "I'm Mongolian. And I'm very proud that I was born here. One of our Mongolian poets said, 'One of our problems is to understand each other. If we will love all things in the world, we can return to the harmony.'" And Oxana, my Russian friend in Ulan Ude, wrote: "When we have the opportunity to connect with nature, we become better than we are. I think that one problem is misunderstanding between us. Sometimes we can hear our own voice, but not the voice of the people who surround us." These young women gave me hope for the future of Buryatia and Russia—and hope for our planet.

Lake Baikal, Siberia

CHAPTER TWENTY TWO

My Sacred Mountain

Santa Monica Mountains
1982-1987

Boney Mountain, Santa Monica Mountains, California

EVEN THOUGH I WAS married to Oscar and our house often swarmed with guests, I often felt alone, apart. A distance grew between Oscar and me that I didn't know how to bridge. Oscar often fell asleep at the television, exhausted from his psychiatric work. I noticed he rarely looked into my eyes. Our social events, in which I was primarily the cook, dishwasher, and onlooker, left me feeling empty and frustrated.

One evening, when Oscar came home from a long day of psychiatric work, I noticed that the lines on his forehead and at the corners of his eyes had deepened in his rugged Mediterranean face, even since the morning. That night his friend, Ivan Tores, arrived. I brought the steaming roast beef, potatoes, and onions to the table on a platter, followed by a salad. As we ate, the two of them talked of Hollywood, of friends, and of old times. I poured wine and water, offered seconds, removed the dishes, brought in coffee and cheesecake, and removed more dishes. Two hours passed with Oscar and Ivan deep in conversation and, when I went to the kitchen, I felt as if I were far away, looking at a play on a stage. With the dishes finished and my presence not missed, I went to my room and wept.

The next morning, I asked Oscar to accompany me on a pilgrimage to the Hopi Reservation. It was a holiday weekend and I knew he didn't have clients until the middle of the week.

"*Bubbala,*" he said, using the Yiddish term of endearment. "I have guests coming over. I need to stay, but you go ahead."

The Hopis keep cornmeal in their cars. When they pick herbs in the hills, they first offer prayers and then sacred cornmeal. On the reservation most of them live in the old Hopi traditional ways.

Old Oraibi is the oldest village in the United States, continuously inhabited since it was first built over two thousand years ago. Homes in Old Oraibi, and also in the old section of Hotevilla, are either built upon the original ruins or are the ancient ruins themselves. These villages have no electricity, no heating, no bathrooms, and no running water. How cold the winters must be on those six-thousand-foot high mesas! Yes, but the Hopis remain rich in a social, cultural, and spiritual heritage that has never been broken.

I drove into Old Oraibi with Biphisi, a Hopi medicine woman who had helped me the last time I was on the reservation. I had been ill during that visit, and had been directed to her for a healing. Normally white people may not enter Old Oraibi, but because I was with Biphisi, no one spoke against my presence.

As Biphisi worked with an elderly woman who had fallen and broken her hip, she talked about the villagers. "They have chosen to live without facilities. They feel that if they accept plumbing and electricity, they will also take on the evils of the white man. So they would rather live in this way."[26]

That night, Biphisi and I hiked to a mesa on the reservation with our sleeping bags. We climbed into our bags to protect ourselves from the mosquitoes, and we looked up at the brilliant stars moving across the sky. "You are an alien, but in a good sense," she said. "You're here to bring people back to their relationship with nature so they can also know who they are."

Quietly we fell asleep under the pulsating stars.

The next morning, we sat in silence looking out over the Hopi mesas and listening to the scurry of an animal, to the wind blowing leaves. Suddenly I got a strong feeling that Hopiland was the heart of this half of the globe. I saw the western hemisphere as a giant body with its seven chakras. In the north, Alaska, Canada and the upper part of the United States form the crown, brow, and throat chakras. Hopiland is the heart chakra, and southern California the solar plexus. To the south, Mexico and South America are the navel and base chakras. On the other side of the globe are similar geographic chakras.

I imagined sculptures I could develop in different areas of the world to reactivate these power places, these acupuncture points of the earth. The sculptures, I thought, would be similar to the Chinese acupuncture needles used on the body. They would create a flow of energy through a blocked location, allowing people to feel the power of place through the art.

Biphisi nudged me out of my reverie, "I can feel your thoughts. You are being led into your right destiny. This rock, this power place is helping you see."

After a few weeks of living with Biphisi, her husband, Michael, and their four children, I phoned Oscar to tell him about the *Kachina* dances for which we were preparing. "Please come share this with me," I said. "I know you'll find it interesting."

"*Bubbala,* I have my patients to see. I can't go."

"But we have a long weekend coming up. Can't you come?" I hung the phone up, carrying his "no" in my heavy heart.

The next morning, we started cooking for the *Kachinas*, spirits that live in the San Francisco Peaks. Hopis consider this mountain range in northern Arizona to be sacred. I was told that the *Kachinas* would arrive on Saturday and Sunday to dance, sing, and give out colorful food presents in a ritual similar to a western Christmas. Evanette, Biphisi's eleven-year-old daughter, showed me how to make Hopi cookies. With Biphisi, we also baked bread, made pies, and soaked the corn to make the traditional hominy and pigs feet soup. The older children, cousins, and neighbors joined in the preparations, and deftly kept the younger ones away, so they would believe that the *Kachinas* would really come bringing gifts like Santa Claus.

As I found out later, the *Kachinas* really *do* come.

Michael, too, prepared intensively to dance as one of the *Kachinas.* Only men can do this, and they spend hours at night in the *kiva*, an underground ceremonial chamber, where they pray and prepare themselves. The warm evening breeze carried the sound of drumming and chanting into the kitchen, overlaying the sound of the television.

While we worked, one of the village women came to the door to see Biphisi. Although Biphisi was not supposed to treat patients during these holidays, she never turned away anyone who arrived at her door. The cooking stopped, and she sat on the living room couch talking with the distraught woman until she became calm. When Biphisi returned, she said quietly, "At times my thirty-eight years feel very old."

At eight-thirty the next morning, Biphisi and I walked down to a cleared area in the center of New Oraibi and found our seats. The *Chakwainas,* or long-haired *Kachinas* were already in the Plaza dancing in a long curved line, chanting to the beat of the drums. A *Chakwaina* is a *wuya,* one who has achieved a state of wisdom and power comparable to that of a religious elder, but who is also a great warrior. The long black hair on their masks reached to their waists in the back and half covered their faces in front. The black mask had crescent moons for eyes and a decorative band for the mouth. A leather tongue hung down from its center. As the dancers moved to the drum beat, their bodies looked like dancing earth and stone, painted as they were in colored clays.

The drummer was dressed as a buffoon with a mud headdress, a big belly, and black skirt and scarf. Occasionally, he walked along the line of dancers, dropping sacred cornmeal at their sides and at the shrine in the center. He represented the "ordinary human." Earlier, he had asked the *Kachina* spirits to come from the San Francisco Peaks. He thanked them now for gracing us with their presence and their wisdom given through song and dance and gifts.

Another day of dances, cooking, dishes—and Michael and Biphisi's relatives and friends poured into the house between dances. All were welcome; all were fed.

At the dancers' noon break, a couple from Walpi (another Hopi village), who were makers of fine Hopi pottery, came to the house. The woman had been in a severe depression. She told me she had known Biphisi and Michael for many years, but hadn't realized their healing skills. She had come to see them the week before, and Biphisi's prayers and Michael's herbs had lifted her depression.

We returned to the *Kachina* dances and found our seats. Biphisi translated the singing. "There will come a day when there will be disorder on this earth, when there will be no hunting and crops will fail. But one of you young men could change that; just one of you could change the course of these tides."

The *Kachinas* gave baskets of beautifully colored food to the crowd. Then they threw Hopi bread (called *piki*), oranges, and Crackerjacks to the people standing and sitting on the rooftops. They passed and threw food to my left, to my right, in front, and in back of me. I was obviously being skipped. This is how it feels to be a member of a minority. The child inside me, with her need for love and acceptance, cried quietly. Then a *Kachina* moved forward and gave me a basket of food.

"Aswali," I said. "Thank you." From his armband I recognized it was Michael.

Late that night, I heard a knock on the door. A Hopi man brought in his wife. She had had a stroke at the dance and was unable to talk. Despite Biphisi's exhaustion, she massaged and manipulated the woman's tongue and face for about an hour and brought back the feeling and movement. Michael told me how to boil the appropriate herbs and gave her the tea. Later Biphisi said, "If she hadn't come right away, she could have been permanently paralyzed on one side of her face."

The *Kachina* dances continued. On the first day I had wondered why they couldn't add an extra little syncopated beat or give an extra kick to vary the rhythm and movement. But by the third day, I understood. The continual repetition of the heartbeat rhythm of the drum, the bells on one foot, the clap of the tortoise shells on the other, punctuated every few beats by the rattle and the low guttural sound of the songs, set up a vibration in the atmosphere that gradually changed the chemistry of the body. The sound felt as if it were coming from the bowels of the earth, and the thump of the feet on the earth was a summoning of the Earth's spirit. As the hours passed, the Earth's voice slowly, deeply penetrated my flesh, the muscles and marrow of my bones. She entered my body and circulated in my blood. I became Earth.

Michael and each of the other dancers, with their masks and movements, were transformed into the spirit of the *Kachina.* They became living deities, a funnel through which the energy of the All Pervading, the *Void,* speaks to us, interacts with us, plays with us. The rhymic pounding of their feet and the weaving movements of their arms made the spruce boughs tucked in at their waists sway, until the trees themselves danced before us. The black sky of the *Kachina* masks looked down, and the stars laughed. The Earth swelled up out of the *Void* and heaved her breath, giving birth to form.

One dancer drew my attention. I felt that Spirit moved through him more strongly than through the others. I kept my eyes on him and, although I sat still, the inside of my body moved and my spirit was released to dance with the *Kachinas.* I sat by Biphisi's side, thankful for privacy behind the sunglasses I wore, when I uncontrollably broke into tears. A wave of energy flushed through me, touching every cell until I felt as if I would climax. Instead, the energy moved up through my body in waves and lifted me into the world of the *Kachinas*—another consciousness, my borderless world. As if I had been touched by a magic wand, everything became bright and radiant. Once again, I experienced Spirit in everything. My beloved boulders spoke through those dancing forms, the trees came to me singing. The power of the *Kachinas* poured through my body as if they spoke to me. "See as we see! Know as we know!" For four days I stayed in this altered state, moving and seeing through the eyes of the *Kachinas.*

Though I longed to stay, I previously had scheduled a talk at Santa Monica City College. When the *Kachina* dances ended and everyone went back to their normal routines, I sadly gathered my belongings and packed my car for the drive back. The whole family came out to say good-bye and I hugged each one.

As I drove down Highway 89, a red earth cliff rose from the desert floor on my left. Ahead of me were the snow-capped San Francisco Peaks, home of the *Kachinas*, drawing me toward them. A lone shack in the desert enchanted me, and I fantasized about living there with the view of those mountains before me, perhaps forever, as each morning I awoke to the glory of the sun on red earth.

Still in an altered state, I drove straight through to Santa Monica, a thirteen-hour drive that normally would have exhausted me. This time, I practically flew across the Mojave Desert, and the thirteen hours seemed like three. As I drove, I remembered the *Chakwaina,* the long-haired dancing *Kachinas*. I saw their movements—the movement of the head toward the earth as the arms moved upward, one slightly higher than the other as the right foot hit the ground and the left rose slightly. Mesmerized again by the memory of their movements, I felt the energy pulsing through me.

As I neared Los Angeles, once again I could feel and see the air thicken and congeal around me. My shoulders tightened. Breathing became an effort. As I drove toward the city, I saw smog streaked across the horizon. Cars swarmed onto the freeway as if herded toward their destiny by some unknown slaughterer. People appeared sandwiched between smog and pavement. *What am I doing here?* I asked my self silently. I've found my sacred earth art, my real work, but where is my spirit-based home and community within my own culture? Where is *my* sacred mountain?

One morning before sunrise, I sat up in bed with a start. I had been waking up every morning with the words running through my mind like a mantra, Where is *our* sacred mountain? Where is *our* sacred mountain? On this particular morning, however, I woke up remembering the first time I had laid eyes on Boney Mountain, the highest ridge of the Santa Monica Mountains. In my mind, I saw its backbone of stone pillars rising like a row of deities. We *do* have a sacred mountain, I thought. Only no one is honoring its spirit.

I jumped out of bed and hurriedly fixed breakfast. When Oscar sat down to eat, I said, "I need to go into the mountains to explore."

Oscar looked worried. "I was going to bring friends over for dinner and—"

I interrupted him. "I'll have dinner on the table by six o'clock."

"No. No. I know you'd like to stay overnight. You go. We'll go out to dinner."

We hugged awkwardly, silently, knowing that our separate interests pulled us apart. When he went upstairs with his first patient, I threw my backpack and sleeping bag into my car and drove toward the mountains.

On the last curvy stretch of dirt road, I found a place to park and hiked up an overgrown switchback toward the top ridge. "This range runs east and west, a sacred alignment for us Chumash people," Kote, a medicine man and friend had told me on my first trek to this area. His voice rang out in my memory. "We used this area for special rituals and vision quests in ancient times. Even now there are pictographs in some of the caves and shelters."

Rose-streaked sandstone boulders ascended ten stories above my head and formed the top ridge. The day sparkled after a rain. I had an awe-inspiring view of the ocean and surrounding hills. When I reached the top of the plateau, the landscape opened up into gently rolling valleys with massive rock formations jutting out, rising boldly from their centers, no human defacement visible. I sat on a cool, craggy stone and thought about the Santa Monica Mountains. They compose the largest wilderness area close to a major U.S. metropolis. I looked out over the ocean. I saw the Channel Islands off Santa Barbara, at the western tip of this range. Then I turned eastward and saw the Santa Monica Mountains running through Malibu. In my mind's eye I could see the range continuing, sloping down to its other end through the Hollywood Hills to end in Griffith Park.

In the distance I spotted a cave, and curiosity pulled me out of my reverie. When I approached it, I saw it was so large that twelve people could comfortably sleep in it. I also saw an enormous cat print and stooped down to measure it with my hand. Six inches across—a mountain lion.

By this time, pink light streaked across the turquoise sky. I needed a place to sleep, but the mountain lion print made this cave seem dangerous. I made my way back to a ravine I had spotted earlier and hiked up a dry streambed, through a narrow channel created by boulders that had once touched. Water erosion had created a long, upward birth passage. I crawled through it, finding my footing on the rugged, pitted surface of the stone. Finally, the sky illuminated a small opening at the other end, and I emerged onto a large flat rock with a sandy place just big enough for my sleeping bag. As stars popped out one by one, I listened to the coyotes and an owl and felt the cool breeze blowing like silk spun from the rays of the full moon overhead.

Golden morning light awakened me. The air was gold, the rocks were gold, and I was gold. I wanted to live here. I felt the spirit of the mountain and remembered my time with the *Kachinas* and the spirit of *their* sacred mountain on the Hopi Reservation. There were people—at this very moment—who were living with the spirit of the Earth at the very center of their lives. I took a deep breath. I could live that way as well!

I stuffed my sleeping bag into my backpack and hiked back down the trail. Not far from the bottom of the switchback I had hiked up, I found an abandoned trailer with its windows broken and its door banging in the breeze. The roof leaked and rats' nests occupied the corners. Birds nested in the ceiling light fixtures. It stood at the end of a mile of eroded dirt road bordering the National Forest Service Land. As I left, a rattlesnake slithered from underneath.

From the closest neighbor I got the phone number of the owner.

Oscar sat in the living room watching television when I entered the house. I gave him a hug and went into the kitchen to start supper. As it cooked, I called the number and reached the owner at home.

"I found your trailer on the slopes of Boney Mountain. Can I repair it and use it as my home?"

"It's falling apart," he said. "I'd be delighted to have someone fix it up and live in it."

During supper I broke the news to Oscar. "This feels urgent. I want to live with the rhythms of nature and with my own unfolding nature. I want to move to the mountains and live in a trailer that I found today."

Oscar said, "I knew this was coming."

"But if we could buy the land, we could build you a place there also."

The twinkle went out of Oscar's eyes. After some time, he said, "I can't leave my life here, my patients."

"But what about having both places?"

"I don't think so, *Bubbala.*" He seemed resigned when he left the table. He went into the living room and turned on the television.

A jumble of dishes sat in the sink, laundry was in the washer, and Oscar's jacket lay on the floor where he had left it, but I did not rush to straighten up as I had always done before. I went over to Oscar, put my hand on his shoulder, and sat on the arm of the chair, tears streaming down my face.

He clicked off the television. His eyes closed as if the pressure of this truth was too much. Then his head drooped and the chair seemed to grow in size as it held him in his sleep.

A month later, I moved into the trailer on Boney Mountain where I intended to live without the compromise of a double life. I was forty-three. Oscar and I had been together for seven years, we had been married for three. I had believed that, through perseverance, I could integrate our two worlds, but I had failed. I left a husband I loved because he could not join me in my life, any more than either of us could find a way to incorporate our two lives into one.

Oscar and his friends felt that I was pulling away from the world, but I felt I was entering the world *more.* I urgently wanted to enter into the *heart* of the world. I could not live an integrated life when television and advertisements bombarded me with the message that we are separate and must acquire

Vijali meditating in her trailer on Boney Mountain

possessions, sometimes at the cost of the earth and others, to build up our egos and survive in this life.

I arrived at the trailer in February with tools for cleaning and repair, and with all of my belongings. As I surveyed the trailer, I saw that rats had eaten holes through it everywhere. I spent the first day cleaning, throwing out nests, beer cans, and debris. I found rats' nests in the drawers, in the broken heater, and under the cracked sink—eight nests in all. They were quite beautiful and filled with matches, as if matches were their favorite possessions.

Each garbage bag filled, each scrape of the putty knife through composite layers of rat excretion and filth, brought me closer to a new space for myself on the earth spot that felt the most sacred to me.

I lived without electricity or water, with only the stars illuminating the beautiful black nights. In such a simple state, every act became a ritual—carrying water, bathing from a bucket with a ladle, gathering herbs and wild food from the hillside. My toilet was a trowel behind a bush. Everything became sacred. I couldn't get enough of silence, and even the sound of music despoiled its sweetness.

Yet life was not without challenges. I could live only in the back of the trailer because I couldn't keep the rats out of the front. They were enormous and noisy, with bodies eight inches long. They pulled themselves out of large rat traps, apparently unharmed, to scramble around the defunct heater as if it were a personal gym.

A heavy storm arrived on the night of the full moon, the first Sunday after I moved in. Rain driven by strong winds beat like arrows against the trailer until it shook. I had covered the cold, uninsulated floors with rattan mats and had kept the space simple, without furniture. On the floor, I had placed a mattress and some wildflowers in a ceramic vase that a potter friend had given to me. Two rooms leaked, so I put out buckets and laid plastic covering over the mats.

The next day, when the storm broke for a few moments, I walked down the gutted muddy road in my high rubber boots. I saw yellow daisies, orange monkey flowers, blue nightshade, and musk mustard with small purple flowers underfoot. Because of the changing angle of the lowering sun, the rows of stone forms at the top of the range looked like gods dancing in a line with the coming of the rose-colored evening light. From the shadows of their deep-set eyes, they looked down upon me from an ancient past.

Soon afterwards, in the middle of the night, an electrical storm broke over my little trailer as if the tall stone formations at the highest point of the mountain had created a conduit attracting an electrical charge. I had never been so close to lightning so blindingly brilliant, nor thunder so loud. It rolled through my body. I was sure the lightning struck right outside the trailer, and I realized that the metal trailer wasn't grounded.

Vijali in Hindi means "a flash of lightning," so I worried for an hour and then decided that if it was "my time," I was okay with that. All night the wind pounded the trailer and the plastic over the windows broke so that rain flooded the front room.

First thing the next morning, a new sound drew me out of the trailer an hour before the next storm—waterfalls! The side of Boney Mountain had been transformed into white waterfalls, two of them just behind and to the left of the trailer. A few yards away, in the ravine, two more waterfalls poured into a rushing river. The sound of flowing water surrounded me.

Each morning I rose early to greet the sun from an outlook on my plateau and, at the end of each day, I returned to wish the sun farewell. Because I paid no rent and went nowhere except to the market for food every other week, I had few expenses. I had decided that *time* was my most important treasure. Time to create and meditate meant more to me than having new clothes, a house, or expensive things. So, during this time I wrote, sang and composed music, danced on full moon nights, sculpted, meditated, read, and took hikes into the mountains for ceremony. Every other week, I drove down to the market about an hour away to buy food and other necessities. I supplemented the provisions I bought with food I gathered from the hillsides and canyons. Oscar had bought several pieces of art from me when we parted, which gave me enough money to survive. Occasionally, I carved a small sculpture, and then a friend would find their way to my retreat and purchase it just in time for me to buy food.

I could not get enough of being alone. I steeped in the silence. When evening came, I ate a dinner of wild greens gathered from the hillside, potatoes, and tea brewed from the fragrant sweet sage I often picked in the afternoons. I rested on cushions inside the trailer and lit candles that threw shadows against the walls. The mantra Swami gave me at thirteen had become ingrained in my cells. Sometimes it died away, but when I needed it, it was there, pounding like my heartbeat. And the same happened with other practices as well. The Vipassana meditation of following the breath while noticing thoughts and emotions, something I had once practiced for several years, now came to me spontaneously, so that I fell into it naturally.

One night, as I boiled water on the propane stove for tea, I watched the flickering kerosene lamps throw my shadow against the trailer walls. I pulled a few leaves off the white sage I had gathered from the hillside the week before, dropped them in my cup, and poured in the hot water. Sage aroma filled the air. Without the pressures of society and marriage, I was able to integrate my borderless experience into every moment of my day.

In May that first spring on Boney Mountain, when the days became warm, I took my typewriter outside, spread a blanket on the ground, and removed my clothes to drink in the sun before I started to write. Just as I stretched out on my back, I heard a rattlesnake by my arm. I jerked my head in the direction of the sound and saw a black-tailed rattler coiled four inches from my face. Eye to eye on the same level, I watched her forked tongue dart in and out. Before I had time to remember that one should be perfectly still when confronted by a snake, I leapt into the air. The snake writhed away, her head raised, her rattles vibrating.

For the rest of the day, I could not get the image of that broad black head and darting tongue out of my mind. With each step, I anticipated another encounter and, as I went to sleep that night, I examined my covers. Each fold, each shadow contained the possibility of a snake. In bed, images of snakes consumed me—snakes hanging from the ceiling, crawling into the trailer from the crack under the door, working their way into my bed sheets, and crawling into my vagina. Finally, I fell asleep and they entered my dreams.

The next day I created a ceremony for the snakes. I took water, food, and flowers to the spot where I had seen the rattler. I placed them in a circle on the ground and I talked with the rattlesnakes. "I respect you and know that the trailer was your home long before I came to live here. I will never hurt you, but please give me permission to live here also. May we live in harmony."

I think the ritual was more for me than for them, but it worked. My fear left. During the next week I saw five rattlesnakes near the trailer, but from the day of the ceremony onward they never coiled, but just lay there looking at me. My fear never returned. They became my teachers and companions, in that they taught me to be still and wait for the right moment, to live close to earth, and to be conscious of each step.

I thought about my marriage, about Oscar, and I recalled the words of Thomas Merton, the Trappist monk whose writings so beautifully expressed my own feeling:

> *"Withdrawal from other men can be a special form of love for them . . . it may well be a quiet and humble refusal to accept the myths and fictions with which the social life cannot help but be full—especially today. To despair of the illusions and facades which man builds around himself is certainly not to despair of man. On the contrary, it may be a sign of love and of hope."* [27]

I believe that all spiritual practices have come from people who have had time alone to play with experience and then to repeat it and observe what happens. At Boney Mountain, I liked to be playful like that. After sunset, I often put myself in a state of gentle flow in which I felt the interconnectedness of my body. Then I followed the energy moving through me. I practiced a kind of spontaneous, undisciplined Tai Chi. In the past, I had been very rigid about practices, but now felt that this could be a trap. Rigidity smothers subtle internal messages. Goal orientation takes over, and we say to ourselves, "I'm going to do this practice and it's going to give me this and that." And that is the death of innate wisdom.[28]

Sometimes I sat in the dark for hours and hours. I lay back on the cushions and looked out the window at the moon moving across the sky. I heard the crickets or an owl calling. Something gentle came around me then, as if I had been touched by an unknown hand, and I felt in total harmony with myself and everything around me. I felt loved for the first time. Sometimes it seemed as if a current from my heart would pulse out into the universe, pause, and come back into me; then out of me, again and again. I saw streams, matrices, and lattices of light that must have some universal pattern. Sometimes the patterns were visible and sometimes they were not, but I saw them as a great web that connects everything—a great web of light that had always been there.

Vijali carving beneath Boney Mountain ridge, Santa Monica Mountains, California

One evening I returned to the trailer feeling such a release of new energy that I could almost believe the dormant, wild dark roots of human origin had come to life, that I was about to grow new branches and leaves. I needed to trust this, not knowing what the shape of those new branches would be.

I finished my supper of rice and vegetables and opened the door of the trailer. The hot summer wind tore it from my hand and banged it against the metal side. I braced my body against the step and managed to get it closed behind me. Then, stepping onto the earth road that wound through my beloved boulder friends, I started running, held by the hot wind . . .

From the Earth, Boney Mountain, Santa Monica Mountains

CHAPTER TWENTY THREE

World Wheel-Spoke Twelve

Tenkawa, Nara, Japan
1993

Sunset

UNLIKE MY VISITS TO OTHER countries of the World Wheel, where I had arrived with one contact—if I was lucky—and found my way into the homes and hearts of ordinary people, friends had pre-scheduled my time in Japan. Dominique Mazeaud, an artist and curator from Santa Fe, and Ishi Nikeda, an artist friend of hers in Japan, had set up a collaborative network of talented artists, activists, and spiritual leaders interested in working with me. The result was a fast-paced pilgrimage, during which I created three environmental sculptures and three performances, and presented four slide lectures—all in the space of six weeks.

Dominique arrived in Japan from the United States just before I arrived from Siberia. A young Japanese woman, Taiko Doi, met us both at Narita Airport. Dominique had befriended Taiko on one of her previous trips to Japan. She and her husband drove us across Tokyo to their home. Tokyo was extremely orderly and organized, and a surprise to me after my time in the Siberian forest. Taxi doors opened automatically as one approached, and vending machines existed for every need. Large crowds waited silently at street corners for the lights to turn green. A bow and a show of politeness accompanied every exchange, although none of this eased the palpable tension that pervaded the air. I had the sense of being on a tight wire that could snap at any moment.

The pace of life was numbing. Everyone had a day job and a night job. They raced from place to place even faster than we do in the United States. I glimpsed what it must be like for someone from a third world country to arrive in North America.

When we reached Taiko's home, Dominique and I were still exhausted from our respective journeys. However, within a few minutes of our arrival, Taiko invited us to join the class she was teaching at her Globalist Institute nearby. Dominique gave us both a dose of bee pollen to perk us up. I had never taken bee pollen before. Suddenly I felt a terrible thirst, then nausea, followed by difficulty breathing. I didn't know what was wrong with me. Dominique called a doctor friend for guidance as I went slowly, but inexorably, into anaphylactic shock.

Through jammed Tokyo traffic, Taiko and two of her students rushed me to the hospital. My entire body had taken on a purple hue and was glazed with welts as I gasped for breath, emitting a gruesome rattle with every attempt. Each moment I found it more difficult to breathe. At the hospital, nurses rushed me into the emergency ward where they kept me on an intravenous drip until two o'clock in the morning, my hostess and her students by my side. The kind generosity of our new friends deeply touched me. In the midst of their busy lives they insisted on staying with me all night, and when the sun rose they each went to work without sleep.

Although I was still exhausted from my ordeal the night before, I attended a party the following evening given by Taiko for Dominique and me, and gave a slide show talk about the other countries of the World Wheel. I ended the evening by asking each person my three questions. The women were excruciatingly shy. No matter how bright or how beautiful, they quivered with shyness, barely making eye contact, and giggling behind their hands in a way that was both playful and painful to watch.

Later that week, I had the opportunity to share my slides and stories with the Web of Life Deep Ecology Group founded by Tamio Nakana, a graduate of the California Institute for Integral Studies in San Francisco. During my slide show presentation, I had the impression that my audience was falling asleep. Everyone looked blank or, more probably, bored. For the final circle I passed a talking stick. As the stick went around, I discovered to my great surprise that people were very enthusiastic about the World Wheel project and that what they had seen had moved them. I had completely misread their facial expressions and body language, or lack of it—an instructive cultural misunderstanding.

Dominique had arranged for me to create a sculpture and a ceremony at the Kuimaru Cultural Re-Education Center with the artist Ishi Nikeda. The Center had been founded for the express purpose of creating lively cultural exchanges between Japanese villages and the cities. To get to the Center, we took a train to Chowa Mura, a remote village in the mountains, three and a half hours north of Tokyo. Hiroshi Fujimori, the Center's director, met us at the station and drove us into the mountains.

For this first piece in Japan I was to collaborate with Ishi, and the ceremony was scheduled for the full moon. But I soon discovered that people didn't understand the process of the World Wheel. They were under the impression that I had a "gig," a set performance that I presented around the planet. I had to teach them about my approach to art, but also, because of the prearranged schedule, I had to approach my work differently. In this case, it was necessary for me to do solo pieces and to speak with my own voice rather than facilitating the community to speak. This challenge pushed me to extend the boundaries of my art and my work.

On the grounds of the Cultural Center, Ishi created a water wheel by digging a large circular ditch, lining it with plastic, and filling it with water and blue dye. In the center of his wheel I built an earth wheel, lined it with stones, and in the center of that, I created a fire sculpture to be lit during the ceremony. The day before the event, we worked in the rain and the earth turned to mud. There is nothing I love more than working and playing in the mud, so I worked with great fun and joy, especially because Ishi and his assistants were working alongside me on their own project in the same conditions.

Dominique and I were living in a rice-growing village, which delighted us both. But that year Japan suffered one of its coldest and wettest summers since the war. Every day the local newspaper carried a picture of a worried farmer in a rice paddy investigating his crop. As we worked in the woods to gather materials for the performance, we looked out toward the rice fields and often saw an inspector examining the rice. Later, we learned that Japan had lost almost its entire rice crop, an event that devastated the economy.

The night of the performance, clouds moved across the sky. Throughout the evening, their movement created dramatic changes in light and tone, hiding and then revealing the moon. Despite continuing rain, a crowd of about thirty people gathered, both villagers and people from the cities. Dominique had prepared garlands of dry leaves and branches, which she offered as a way of honoring and welcoming the audience. Ishi set the water flowing in the water wheel. He had dyed the stream blue and it flowed in a spiral around the water wheel to the accompaniment of his own music—the sound of breath through water. He and I began the performance by speaking about the meaning of the two wheels, the water wheel and the earth wheel.

Just as I began my part of the ceremony—a slow moving dance around the earth wheel holding two sticks of fire—the rain stopped miraculously and the moon rose. I honored the four directions with burning sage and singing, and then I addressed the problems surrounding us. Holding rice stalks, I offered a prayer for a successful rice crop.

After the ceremony, volunteers brought out sushi, rice balls, mushrooms, and shrimp dishes, and the city and village people mingled together. Dominique and I spoke with the older women of the village, who were fascinated with my light-colored hair. Convinced it was not real, they said, "Real hair is black!" I felt deeply satisfied—youth and old age connecting, water wheel and earth wheel resonating, Japanese and North American artists working together—weaving the world into one family.

Vijali in performance ceremony in Japan

By the end of the evening only a light rain fell, luminous, almost like snow, more like drops of silver light than rain, a blessing from the moon. We quickly disassembled the tables and video equipment and said *sayonara*, satisfied with a magical end to our first ceremony in Japan and the beginning of our one-month pilgrimage.

The next day, Dominque and I left for the Myogonji Temple in Chiba Prefecture. There we did an "Iki-Iki Seminar," which means "Exploring the Positive You." For some years, Dominique had been traveling the world documenting examples of art rooted in spirituality. When we gave presentations together in Japan, she introduced me by placing my work in this context, and I presented slides and drew people into a dialogue. Fifteen friends of the temple attended the seminar. We were touched by the manner in which they overcame their shyness and opened their hearts. We left with the hope that this sharing had provided some opening and support in people's lives.

Back in Tokyo, at the International Christian University, I showed my slides to about two hundred students in the Intercultural Communications Department. Afterward, Dominique and I spent several hours with a smaller group that had expressed interest in a more in-depth exchange. Many of those who stayed for this gathering wanted to challenge the social status quo and were eager to meet two women who had chosen unconventional lifestyles. Some of them had lived abroad for long periods of time and felt unwelcome in Japan. We encouraged them to see themselves as "bridge people" who could facilitate cross-cultural understanding.

The second World Wheel sculpture and performance event in Japan was planned to take place at the home of Rui Sekido, a successful Japanese performance artist who lived in Yuguchizawa, two hours west of Tokyo. Every summer Sekido organized the Yuguchizawa-eza, a forum on his family's land, to coincide with the village festival at the end of July. This year he accommodated my schedule by holding it in October instead, and the event was like a tribal gathering of artists.

Sekido was a leader amongst his peers, a respected artist known for his acrobatic performances. We arrived a few days early to help our host prepare for the gathering. He treated us in the most generous way, preparing delicious Japanese meals and giving us his quarters while he moved into his parents' home for the duration. We assisted in the construction of several grass-covered huts that would house the guests during the two-day event. I delighted in the hard work and the fluid spirit of cooperation.

Everything was ready by Sunday, including the weather, which miraculously had cleared once more.

We set up a schedule sheet, and visiting performers wrote down when and where they wanted to perform. There was a diverse representation of artists, young and old, but the acknowledged elders of the group were Yutaka Matsuzawa and Shoji Kaneko, both highly respected in Japan. As the artists prepared their pieces, I felt a great sense of community, although we each worked on our individual projects. In an ironic juxtaposition of contrasting efforts—a microcosm of global dissonance—while we honored the earth through art and community, only a few feet from us a road crew was busy tearing into the mountain to widen the road.

Sekido made a wonderful spiral down into the earth, something I dreamed of doing when I owned land. At the bottom of the spiral was a large flat stone for meditation. With Sekido's kind permission, I carved the stone with three concentric circles and painted the center "emptiness blue." This was my physical representation of spirit within matter.

In the evening the performances began. The artists and about thirty people in the audience held candles as they walked down the spiral into the earth, making a wonderful visual effect. I slowly walked down the candlelit path to the bottom of the pit and stood on the meditation stone I had carved and painted earlier. Here I answered my first two questions using voice and movement—*What is our essence? What is our problem?* It came to me as I stood and spoke that there had been an evolution in my own performances. I had started in Malibu as the cooling lava, crusting earth, as Gaia, the Earth herself. Then on the Seneca Reservation I covered myself in leaves, the plant life of the planet, honoring the elements of fire, wind, and water. In Italy, I emerged from stone as the wolf. In ceremony after ceremony, Earth evolved into the ordinary person I played in this performance, speaking to my fellow humans, equal to equal.

For the answer to my third question—*What is the solution?*—I passed a talking stick among the audience. As they gave their responses, they enacted my own answer: connecting with community. The group received the performance enthusiastically and understood what I had done, despite the language barrier. I felt honored to be a part of this community of artists.

Of the many wonderful performances presented that night, some were quite profound. Sekido, wearing his trademark red costume, walked a tightrope suspended from up on the mountain to the center of the pond. As he emerged out of the darkness in slow motion, he looked like a dancing flame. His collaborator, Mifune, dressed in white, set hundreds of lighted candles in bamboo containers afloat on the water. When Sekido reached the end of the tightrope, he slid down the pole head first into the water and stayed there for some time, head submerged, feet and legs pointing to the sky. He looked like a heavenly flame merging into the lake of spirit, the meeting of heaven and earth.

From Yuguchizawa, we set out to join the poet and activist Nanao Sakaki on his fourth twelve-day walk to save the Nagara River from developers who wanted to dam it. To reach Nanao and his group, we changed trains five times and negotiated six train stations. Then we walked twelve miles to their campsite, where we joined them in a day of rest before we resumed the protest pilgrimage.

According to local environmental activists, more than two hundred rivers in Japan had been dammed already. Preventing the damming of the Nagara was considered to be a crucial step in the struggle to save the natural waterways of the country. At the camp Nanao and his group welcomed us to the campfire circle, and though we were different ethnically, we felt related—part of a new tribe, brothers and sisters of the River and of the Earth. We washed our clothes in the river, helped cook and collect mushrooms, listened to poetry read by Nanao, and joined in the music of the group. Sometimes in the course of conversation we talked about the World Wheel project, but primarily we were there to listen, honor, and support. When we left, Nanao's last words rang out, "Tell the people that the fight for the Nagara River is a fight of the world for the world."

Dominique had arranged for us to stay at the home of Suil Moon in Kyoto. Born in Scotland, Suil's path had taken her to Korea, where she was a Buddhist nun for three years. She lived now in Kyoto and made her living as a psychotherapist, meditation teacher, and hypnotherapy trainer. Part of a community of Westerners who loved Japan, known in Kyoto as "bridge people," Suil had the energy of a great river, flowing effortlessly. She attracted more than forty people to our presentation. The evening closed with a women's circle, an intimate gathering at which we prayed and wrote a joint poem in answer to my first question, *What is our essence?* We shared from our hearts, one by one, our answer to the third question, *What will help us return to harmony?* The evening felt like the beginning of what could become a strong women's support system.

In our women's circle, one woman asked the question, "Do you think it is easier for women to feel connected with the whole of life than it is for men?" I answered that I feel it is. Because we're closer to the cycles of our own bodies and thus closer to the cycles of nature, we have to let go and accept the next cycle. Men can also achieve this connection, but have to work harder at it.

Before I left Japan, I carved and painted a stone, naming it *Spirit Within Matter.* It showed an opening into the essence of ourselves, that spaciousness that is our birthright. I left it with Suil as a focal point for the women's group, which continued to meet long after my visit.

The third World Wheel piece in Japan was scheduled to take place at Tenkawa, an ancient Shinto site in the mountains of Nara Prefecture. The shrine honors Benzaiten, the Japanese version of the Hindu goddess Saraswati, who embodies the arts, wisdom, and water. In the old temple, the Noh stage was part of the main shrine. Artist performances were viewed as offerings not just entertainment. This deeper, more sacred purpose for art excited me, so different from contemporary usage, but similar to my own performance work, which I have called, "Theater of the Earth."

On the full harvest moon in October, we arrived at the bus station in Tenkawa and were met by Ishi and his wife, Mihoko. They took us to the site where Ishi was creating another water wheel, which we planned to use as the stage for our performance. From the banks of the nearby Tenkawa River, I picked twelve of the largest stones I could carry. Dominique helped me lug them back to the site and place them in a circle.

I carved the stones with patterns from nature—the spiral, the wave, the double helix. Each stone and pattern represented one of the countries on the World Wheel. On the stone representing Japan, I carved concentric circles symbolizing closure and the synthesis of all the countries. While I worked, Dominique collected branches and logs from the forest and placed them in a circle within the circle of stones.

I carved ecstatically, tuning into the stone. Once a part of the stone cracked and broke off, so that the shape of the pattern changed. I saw myself working in co-creation with the stone. Each stone represented the love I felt for my family in all countries, not only in those of the World Wheel, but in the entire world.

Often what people call "love" is actually attachment or desire. Even service to others often stems from the *need* of a person to feel good about themselves. I realized, as I listened to the sound of my chisel against the stone, that we truly love when we come to a place free of desire, a place of inner and outer connection, where we live in a *state* of love. This universal love is bestowed on all life equally. Usually when I worked, my mantra flowed with each breath. Now I noticed that it had stopped, and a silence and stillness permeated my being.

The priest of the Shinto temple, Reverend Mikinosuke Kakisaka, came by to see what we were creating. He expressed his unhappiness with the way Dominique had piled the firewood. He said, "Not Shinto," as he stood by the pile of wood. Clearly uncertain about us, he nevertheless agreed to close our performance with a Shinto fire ceremony.

That night it poured rain, and the next morning the sound of rain on the roof drew me from my dreams. Penetrating my half-sleep, the beat of the rain formed into words. I listened as they bounced off my tongue: "Our essence is the connecting force of life." Tip, tip, tip, tip. "We are part of God's body." Tip, tip. "God is simply the matrix of wisdom innate in the whole. We are not God's children. Our very nature is divine, and the purpose of life is to *re*member, *re*connect to our divine nature." Tip, tip, tip, tip.

I dressed for the rain and started carving the stones, wondering how we would manage the outdoor ceremony in this weather. I pulled the hood of my raincoat over my head. Soon the tip, tap sound of my work resonated with an inner stillness, and another shift occurred in my consciousness. I realized we perceive this material world at a certain frequency, but another world exists at another frequency. I could turn to that other frequency and be there if I wished. I experimented as I worked—going back and forth, changing the frequency of perception. Is this what Jesus meant when he said, "The kingdom of God is at hand"?

I turned the stone as I worked to get a better angle to carve, and continued to chisel. As I worked I felt such love for the stone, for the tree growing on my left, for the river flowing on my right. I gave thanks for the periods in my life isolated in nature. They had given me the time and silence to experience these subtle frequencies and shifts of consciousness, and to begin to see and understand how we are put together, how we function within the whole.

I carved the sunburst pattern of the big bang on the stone that represented Malibu, the first site of the World Wheel. I remembered how my childhood feelings of abandonment had surfaced in my relationships with the performers when tensions arose during our work together. At the time I wondered if those old voices would ever die. I had shifted back and forth from an expanded consciousness to the contraction of that small child crying out in fear or longing. Finally, I experienced a place beyond or beneath the tides of emotion, where all experience exists and never leaves. There I am always stable like a mountain, regardless of the storms that may pass over me or the circumstances that may develop in my life. I still express the whole range of emotions, but a deep, peaceful knowing accompanies them, as if the waters have become so deep, the view so wide, that the hurt child's voice is but a bubble in the foam. The shift of identity from the small self to the limitless infinite leads to the awakening of the spirit of peace.

I finished carving the last stone and noticed that the branches and wood that Dominique had collected were soaking wet. Concerned about the ceremony, I quickly put my tools away and looked for the priest in the shrine. He seemed to be waiting for me and immediately asked a novice attendant to bring us tea. When I expressed my concern about rain, Reverend Mikinosuke Kakisaka was all smiles.

He said, "This rain is the will of the Goddess Benzaiten. Her grace has brought us together in this way because she wants you to join us inside her Shrine."

I remembered that Her domain was water, wisdom, and the arts.

The priest asked me to describe the ceremony.

"It is a prayer that we will remember that our true nature is without boundaries," I said, "because this is what will lead us to world peace."

He looked delighted and kept asking me questions about the sculptures and the performance. I explained the symbols I had carved on the stones and drew them on a paper with the meaning written next to them:

1. This pattern is where I started in Malibu, California. The place of my beginning is like the big bang, the starting point.

2. Then the thrust of that explosion creates the moving line. This is the second site, at the Seneca Indian Reservation. The indigenous peoples hold that original thrust of our human race.

3. Then, as the universe expands and evolves, in Spain that line begins to curve, to take a more complicated shape.

4. In Italy, with the continuing development of culture, it becomes even more complicated, the wave.

5. Then, in Greece, we see the patterns of chaos and the great god Cronos from which new life, ideas, gods, and goddesses emerge.

6. In Egypt, the DNA pattern shows the growing complexity of our life structures.

7. In Palestine and Israel, the branch pattern of our capillary system reflects our ceremony at the Dead Sea, where the Palestinian and Israeli children planted a tree of peace.

8. In India, the butterfly effect represents the reproduction of the mirror image in physics. I see our times, through science, mirroring the ancient wisdom of the Indian Vedas.

9. The spiral on the two-dimensional plane and the funnel in three dimensions show Tibet as the direct connection with other dimensions and vortices of energy.

10. China's pattern is the oval shape, the beginning of a closure, or "noosphere" as Pierre Teihard De Chardin has termed it—when Earth has developed to the point where it can observe itself through us, and this awareness has circled the globe, lifting us to a new level of consciousness. I see this in China because the ancient Tao is now re-surfacing and, instead of being just the property of China, is spreading throughout the world.

11. In Siberia, the circle showed the struggle to rebuild the social circle of equality—the need for people to find their place around the round table.

12. Japan, the last country of the World Wheel, represents closure with the image of concentric circles. Each ring is a country, unique in itself, but sharing the center point of the circle—unity through the heart.

The priest and his helpers brought the stones into the Shinto shrine and placed them in a large circle in the center. They then created another concentric circle with cedar branches and candles within my circle of stones. I became aware that, without conscious intent, I had used the pattern of concentric circles at each of the three Japanese sites. I realized that this was the symbol for me of the essence and culmination of the World Wheel, which had began as a Native American medicine wheel, and which had taken new form in each country. These concentric wheels were unique in themselves, but all shared one point as the center, the heart. I realized that the most common answer in all the countries to my third question, *What is the solution?*, was to develop more love for one another.

Shinto priest in the Tenkawa Temple for the World Wheel ceremony

On the morning of the ceremony, in the pouring rain, Ishi presented his water piece, assisted by Dominique. In the evening we gathered in the shrine. The priest, dressed in flowing white robes, drummed on a giant Shinto drum. I stood in the dark at the center of the circle, dressed in black with my face painted as an open blue sky—emptiness. As I stood, I contacted my deepest longing: to dance and sing the divine spirit and awaken people to their own divinity, bringing peace into the world. Half an hour passed; I slipped into the stillness and borderlessness of my own essence.

When the drumming came to an end, the priest and I walked to the altar and gave offerings and prayers. He lit the twelve candles in the stone circle as I returned to the center. I moved slowly in each of the four directions, accompanied by the sound of a didgeridoo played by a local musician. At each direction, I stopped and the didgeridoo stopped with me. I offered a prayer with voice and movement, then returned to the center, where I waited for the music to draw me out again.

As some inner force pulled me to the South, the wail of Earth's sadness and the sorrow of her children rose from my belly and poured through my lips. In the West, I felt the darkness of hibernation and dream, and our awakening visions on this earth. In the North, I sang an ancient Sanskrit hymn honoring the Divine Mother of the Universe. My movement stopped in the East and, as emptiness, I stood at the point of new beginnings, the rise of a new sun. Spontaneously, I expressed the answers to my three questions through my body. As I performed the ceremony, I lost my sense of individual identity and opened to universal energy.

The priest entered the circle and sat in the South, where he performed a Shinto fire ceremony. He asked Dominique and me to sit in the West and East. The altar of the Goddess Benzaiten was in the North, and the fire burned in the center.

At the completion of the ceremony, the priest turned to me and said, "The Earth and Cosmos have heard your sincere prayer dance and it will be answered."

I felt that his words came from a larger part of the universe rather than from his personality alone. He asked me to come to the main altar and kneel. Then he said a prayer in Japanese and initiated me into the Shinto priesthood by placing a mantle around my shoulders, similar to the one he wore. This so surprised me that at first I didn't realize what had happened.

Within the shrine a small plot of ground was roped off. In Shinto temples no icons or images of the Goddess are visible, but a mountain, a stone, or lake will often represent her. In this temple, this plot of earth represented the sacred body of the Goddess, and no one had permission to enter there, not even the priests. But the priest asked me to reach into this holy place and bury my offerings—the earth I had brought from the twelve World Wheel countries and a stone blessed by the Dalai Lama. I parted the earth, Her body, and placed my objects in the folds of Her flesh. Then I raked with my fingers to close the earth again. There the objects remain, buried within the sacred body of the Goddess—as if the Universe had accepted the closure of my pilgrimage, and the seeds of harmony and peace.

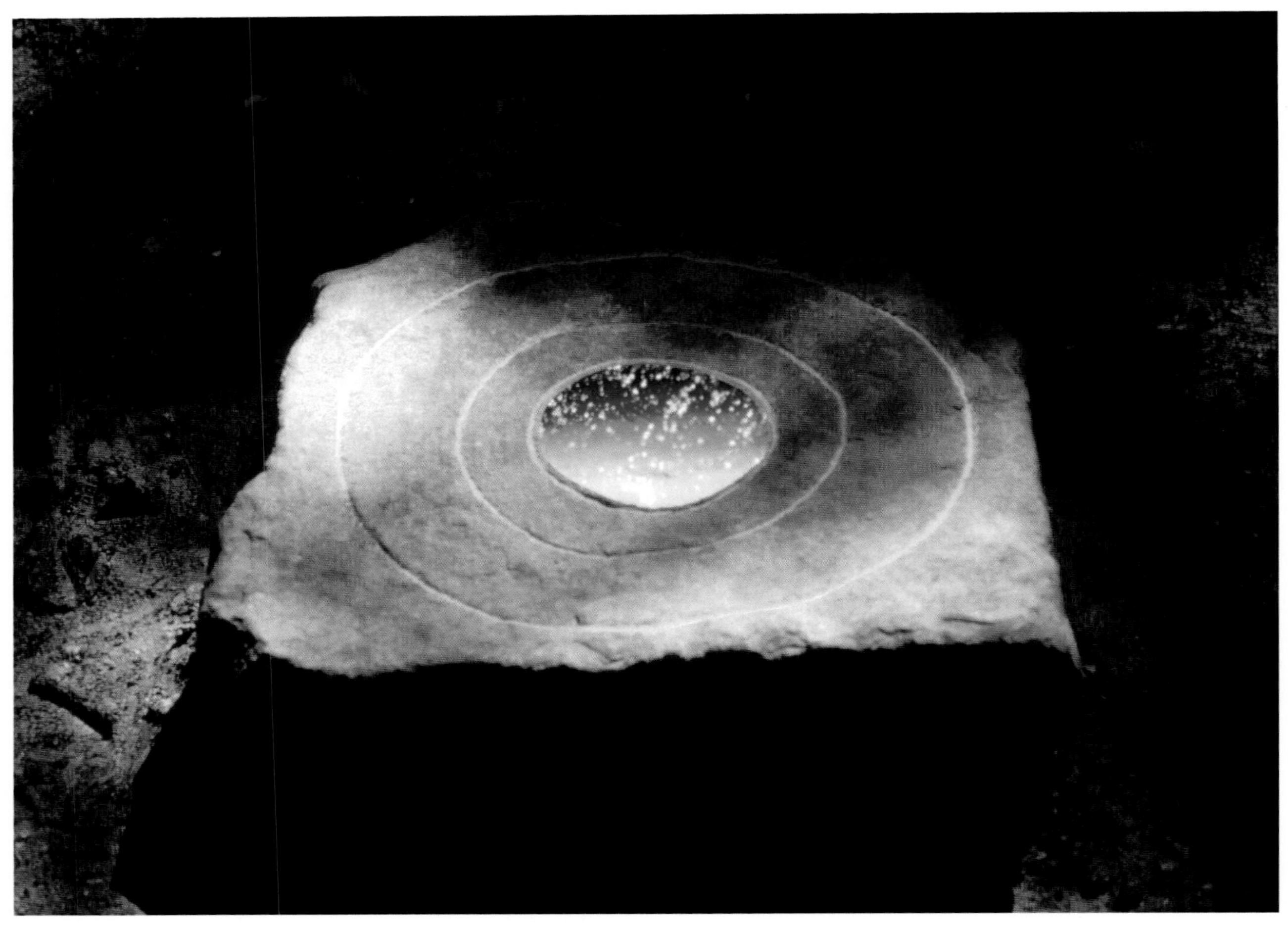

Concentric Circles: One Heart

CHAPTER TWENTY FOUR

Return

Canyonlands of Utah, USA
1994-1998

Rainbow at World Wheel Retreat Center, Canyonlands of Utah

AFTER THE FINAL CEREMONY in Japan I returned to the United States, to the now unfamiliar haunts of Los Angeles. One day, feeling the flatness of life in southern California after my seven-year World Wheel pilgrimage, seeing people flock to workshops for wisdom but return to lives unchanged, I got in my truck and drove east. I left the overcrowded freeways and the polluted air behind as I moved through Arizona into Utah. I had a prayer on my lips—please guide me to the place where I can live in harmony with my own spirit, the environment, and the community.

The desert skies opened as I drove, and I realized that there were no words that could describe my view of the world, having been free from the influence of our censored newspapers, television, and magazines for seven years, having been nourished by community kindness in villages and by the hospitality of the poor.

As I entered the red-earth country of Moab in southeast Utah with its striking plateaus rising on all sides, an eagle flew across my windshield and I looked into its eyes. A chill ran up my spine, and I knew that something important for me was imminent. A few minutes later, I stopped at a local bakery in Moab. A pleasant looking girl dressed in jeans and hiking boots, tanned and rosy-cheeked from the sun, served me.

"Where would I find land for sale in this red rock heaven?" I asked.

She gave me a thoughtful look, pointed north, and gave me directions to a location forty minutes outside of Moab.

I drove along the Colorado River with its spectacular walls of red sandstone. I turned off the river road, drove up over a rise and down into a green valley with the snow-capped La Sal Mountains in the distance and Round Mountain rising like a woman's breast in the center. Towering red plateaus and pinnacles defined her body and, as my breath deepened and my shoulders relaxed, I realized I was home.

I knew no one in Utah, so I stayed a week sleeping in the back of my Toyota truck. I asked realtors and everyone I met about land. By the end of the week I had exhausted the possibilities and, because of a lecture already scheduled in Arizona, I had to leave. At the very last moment I stopped in at the realtor's office to say goodbye.

"We've been trying to find you all day," he said. "We were afraid you had already left. Five acres have become available which we think you would like. The property has two enormous boulders, trees and views, and it's very wild."

I drove out to the property alone, insisting that the realtor should go home to his supper because it was so late. I arrived at the land just as the sun was setting on two thirty-foot boulders. The La Sal Mountains were blushing with pink snow, and the plateaus were bursting into red flames. My prayer had been answered.

Behind me, I heard a truck drive up the road. I signed an offer for the land on the hood of the realtor's truck as his wife, holding their new baby, looked on from the passenger's seat.

After they drove off, I walked the red earth, down a path among stones. My eye caught a darkened shadow and I crawled into a cave laced with cobwebs, the earth pawed to a fine dust, soft and silky for a bed.

The offer was accepted and I moved onto the land. I lived in a small camper set among the juniper trees, the piñon pines, and the giant boulders which created a powerful site for ceremony. As the first year passed, local friends gathered weekly in the cave for meditation, and in the spring and fall people brought tents for retreats I held on the land.

With the help of friends, I built a straw-bale home that I call a *hogan* because it resembles the traditional house of the Navajo American Indians. It is sixteen feet in diameter. We gathered aspen trees from the La Sal Mountains, stripped their bark, and inserted twenty-nine poles (*vigas*) around a steel circular band holding up the sky-well. The ceiling was constructed with willows gathered from the banks of the Colorado River and nailed in place on top of these *vigas*. A silo roof, used by the local farmers to store their grain, became my roof. I gather the rainwater that falls on the roof, running it into a tank located under the house, where it is protected from freezing during the winter. Drinking water I bring to the land by truck from a spring nearby, and solar panels provide electrical power. We poured a stabilized adobe floor for the hogan. When it was almost dry, I carved a mandala wheel in the center and, within that, I painted a circular sky with flower petals reaching out to the four cardinal directions. When it was thoroughly dry, my sacred space was complete and I moved in.

As I write the last chapter of this book, it is snowing in the La Sal Mountains. The wind is pounding against the *hogan* and I am warm inside, sitting close to the fireplace. How grateful I am to have the companionship of the piñon pines and the deer that make this land their home. Sitting here, looking out the window, I see Castle Rock rising into the clouds and the snowflakes sailing past.

I get up and put another log on the fire. The winter draws my mind inward and, as I settle down again, my thoughts run across the many threads that have made up the tapestry of my life. Memory carries me back to my childhood. I think about my retreat into shyness, resulting perhaps from my parents' abandonment when I was two—the curse of shyness that barred me from spontaneity and exiled me from a full expression of life. But art and my love of nature, which connected me with my own spirit, became my road out of that exile. When I had grabbed the brown crayon and vigorously scrolled a twisting trunk across the paper and pressed my green crayon into the surface for leaves, I felt at one with the gnarly tree growing in the front yard of my grandparents' home.

I think of my father, now known as Swami Amohananda in the Vedanta Monastery, where he continued to live even after I had left the convent. For a year, my father had been thinking of leaving the monastery, and in May, 2007, he drove his truck with his few possessions from California and moved into an apartment for elders in Moab. Both of us are grateful for the opportunity to get to know each other better and to share this last part of his life. He is ninety-six years old, healthy and at peace.

Vijali dancing in front of cave

During this month I asked him, "Where is the body of my mother?"

"It is owned by the state," he answered.

Was it used for experiments called research? Were her organs taken to save someone's life? Was she then buried in a communal grave similar to that at Auschwitz. These are the questions I have long lived with.

"Honey," he said, "from the University of Southern California in Los Angeles, I learned where your mother's body is buried. A body, found in the street or at a hospital that is not claimed, is cremated. The

Ceiling of the *hogan,* a straw bail cottage built by Vijali

ashes are held for four years and then are buried at the cemetery in Boyle Heights at East First and Lorena Street in Los Angeles."

"Is there a marker?" I asked.

"I have never gone to see," he answered. "We can go together and see."

A glowing log gives way and rolls onto the hearth with a pop. I push it back into the fire with iron tongs and put another log on the embers. I remember a few years ago driving for two days across the desert floor. "Is it too late? Is it too late?" I chanted. When I arrived at the hospital in Los Angeles, Oscar was on heavy doses of morphine to ease the contractions of his frail body as his kidneys failed to siphon off the poisons in his system. As I entered his room, he was lying on his side, propped up by pillows. He was breathing through a respirator, and a tube had been placed down his throat into his stomach for forced feeding. The nurse had just removed the antibiotic drip, telling his sons, Rob and David, "We can do no more for your father." A clothespin attached to Oscar's ear held wires to the monitor that showed his blood oxygen level. Two adhesive pads on his chest were wired to the monitor measuring his heart rate. Periodically we looked at the readings, then back to Oscar's half-conscious face.

Rob told me as I stood by the hospital bed holding Oscar's hand, "He is calmer now that they have increased the morphine. The nurses have just released Dad from the restraints on his legs and arms. He was continually yanking the wires and tubes from his body saying, 'Take me home! Take me home! Take me home!'" Rob looked pensive and said, "I thought perhaps he would turn around, perhaps his life would be saved for a few more months, or weeks, or days."

Oscar's chant rang in my ears, "Take me home! Take me home!" I remembered him telling me, just a month before, that he hated hospitals, that he wanted to die at home. Oscar, my husband of many years ago, twenty-two years older than myself—how deep was this bond that would not break even as other ties were formed.

I held Oscar's unresponsive hand even tighter and I gave thanks for the two weeks we had recently spent together. What a surprise from the universe! After our divorce, Oscar had married a young woman, Cathy, much younger than me—partly for the security of having a mate who would not be leaving to do her own projects, someone who would outlive him and take care of him in his old age. A few months ago, however, Oscar woke up to find Cathy lying dead beside him in their bed; she had died without obvious cause. Cathy had been very jealous of me and would not let me call or see Oscar for the ten years they had been married. In my wildest imagination I did not dream of this scenario.

Hearing of Cathy's death from Rob, I drove to Oscar's house in Manhattan Beach, and we spent two weeks together. During our walks he spoke openly of his feelings about our marriage with an honesty that he had never ventured to reveal during our seven years together. "Vijali," he said, "I was insecure about you having your own career and leaving on your projects. I realize that now." Oscar seemed to get stronger

Interior of the *hogan*

during my visit and lifted out of the depression that had haunted him most of his adult life.

"I need to turn Dr. Janiger," the young nurse said, shaking me out of my reverie, "while I change the sheets." I let go of Oscar's hand and it dropped limp by his side.

Because of the change of position, Oscar's lungs filled with phlegm and he sputtered and gasped for breath. His mouth and throat were sucked clear by a tube that the nurse held in his mouth. His eyes closed, but the rattle continued deep in the cavern of his body. Hour after hour after hour, I held his hand and cooled his burning forehead, chest, and neck with wet cloths to lower his fever.

Just before two a.m., Oscar opened his eyes in full consciousness. We looked into each other's eyes for more than ten minutes without letting our gaze break. So much was said through that gaze. I poured my heart out into the silence between us. The last time we had seen each other, he had asked me to be with him at his death, and I had promised him I would. For years I had had a repeated dream that Oscar was dying and that I was with him. I had carried a deep desire that I could share these last precious moments of his life with him, even though our lives had taken different directions, even though he had been married to someone else.

He seemed not to be breathing, but his eyes were clear and fastened to mine. Then he took one deep breath and there was stillness, peace—a peace that he did not experience during his lifetime. His eyes glazed over. His always-ruddy cheeks paled, then ashened.

I pull the wicker chair closer to the fireplace and balance my laptop on my knees. I remember the last time I went to the Hopi Reservation in Arizona. I had taken the same route that I had always driven to see Biphisi and Michael. I had stopped at the Hopi Cultural Center in New Oraibi and called their telephone number. A recording said, "This number is no longer in use."

"Where are they now?" I asked the Hopi woman behind the counter.

"They have withdrawn from the functions of the pueblo and are living most of the time in Flagstaff," she answered.

The telephone rings and it is Dale. As we talk I muse how we have become friends again after so many years of silence—remembering our time with Anandamayi Ma in India, and feeling the threads of connection that had brought us to her feet thirty-five years ago.

When I hang up the phone I see that the storm has passed. Stepping out from under the archway of the door of the *hogan* into the crisp air, the evening sky, ablaze with the setting sun, encircles me in its flaming arms. I walk the land, touching the stones and feeling their welcome. The sky fades into darkness, into the void. This spaciousness is my real home—and the sky reminds me of who I am. As my feet walk in peace on the red earth sprinkled with crystals of snow, I look up to the stars, clear and beckoning, to the universe that gave birth to this earth, to our bodies. It speaks through all our cells—"Remember, remember, remember."

Om,
Filled full with Brahman (God) are the things we see,
Filled full with Brahman are the things we see not,
From out of Brahman floweth all that is:
From Brahman all—yet is he still the same.
Om . . . Peace, peace, peace.

Brihadaranyaka Upanishads, 2000 BCE [29]

Hogan with view of mesas

POSTSCRIPT

Second World Wheel

Andes and Amazon, Ecuador
1999–2007

Vijali in her cave

IN MAY OF 1999, I learned that the child of a friend had died. I wept when I got the news, not just for my friend, but for all the children of the planet—babies deformed because of the nuclear disaster in Chernobyl, children living with cancer because of our nuclear testing on Bikini Island in the South Pacific, teenagers with no hope for any future committing suicide in the United States, children starving because of our sanctions and war in Iraq. And the question arose, as it always does, *What can I do?*

I walked on my land to the two giant boulders that touch at the base with just enough space between them to see a strip of sky. I had named them ShivaShakti because one was male and the other female. Entering the cave that had been formed in the female stone, I sat in meditation. Her craggy walls held me in her earth womb, and in the silence of her sanctuary, I began to feel something growing in me, an answer to my question. At first it was just a feeling—that something was calling me, pulling me. Then, in meditation, I saw another circle around the planet, this time close to the equator. Twelve new countries formed a wheel, a second World Wheel. As the hours passed, the conviction rose in me that my question prayer had been answered, and that it was the children of our world who were calling.

I left the cave and went to the *hogan* where I kept a world globe. My eyes fell on the equator as I turned the globe. I knew then, as I had known thirteen years earlier when I began the first World Wheel pilgrimage, that this would be my way of walking peace for the next period of my life—perhaps until my death. The countries of a new World Wheel passed under my eyes as the globe revolved. I fell into sleep and dreamed of the first country—Ecuador.

Now, in January of 2007, I am sitting on the banks of the Yukias River in the Ecuadorian Amazon with Shuar children splashing by my side in the pristine waters flowing from the wild Cutucú range. In the Amazon rainforest east of Macas, generous donations to my Second World Wheel Project have made it possible to purchase three hundred acres of virgin rainforest for a nature reserve, complete with a lagoon, an island, waterfalls, and two rivers.

I have returned this land to the indigenous Shuar families of the area (it had been taken from them by Silesian missionaries) to be caretakers of our precious rainforest, the lungs of our planet. I am in the process

Yukias River, Ecuador with Shuar children playing, Second World Wheel Project: *Refugio Amazonico*

of sculpting *Anaconda Woman* near the sacred waterfall with my new Shuar friends and their children. Along the river, we have established a Wisdom Center, *Refugio Amazonico,* with traditional buildings of thatch and bamboo siding, tree houses for guests, and a school for the Shuar children taught by the elders. This is a way to preserve the Shuar culture, the knowledge of the rainforest medicinal plants, and how to live in a sustainable way within the environment—all knowledge necessary for the survival and health of our life on this planet.

Tuntuam Camilo Tsamaraint with Amazon butterfly

Solania and Nantar, Shuar mother and child

Ceremony with indigenous Shuar musicians, *Refugio Amazonico,* Second World Wheel Project, Ecuador

Traditional Shuar dance and music

Nantar

Nantar drawing

Federico Tsamaraint teaching in the Shuar Refugio School
started by the Second World Wheel Project

Vijali giving out drawings from children from New Mexico, USA

Peacemaker Ceremony, Vijali as Spirit of the Rainforest with Shuar children as the animals of the Amazon bringing the fire of peace to the world

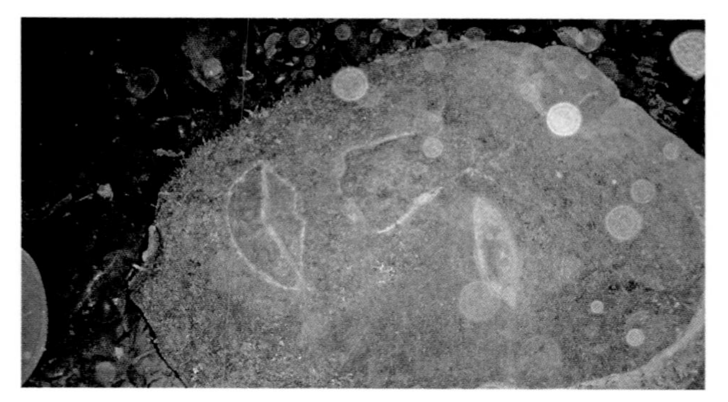

Anaconda Woman, sculpture in progress

Vijali and Tuntuam Camilo carving by the sacred waterfall

Shuar children learning from Vijali how to carve

Achili Pachacamac, lava boulder carved by Vijali with the help of the Peguche community, Second World Wheel Project, Andes of Ecuador

In 1999, as work on the Second World Wheel Project began, another Wisdom Center was started in the Andes of Ecuador. Visitors to the tiny Otavaleñan village of Peguche, high in the Andes, will find a two-story stone sculpture of *Achili Pachacamac*, their pre-Incan deity, that I carved with the help of the village. Three new projects flourish: an indigenous women's group called *Hwari Maki* that helps single women develop crafts to sell so that they can be independent, a charming bed and breakfast inn, and a school for the Otavaleñan children to preserve their culture.

Achili Pachacamac (detail of corn)

Matico Lema (right), founder of *Hwari Maki,* women's group for Otavaleñan women

Vijali carving *Achili Pachacamac* with Chino from the village Peguche

Inti Raimi, harvest ceremony with the *Achili Pachacamac* sculpture in Peguche. Left to right: their local shamans, Vijali, Edie Hartshorne (Outreach Coordinator for the World Wheel), Matico, and friend

Vijali with Otavaleñan children

Shairy, Otavaleñan healer from Peguche

The vision of the World Wheel Project has evolved. It now focuses on the creation of Wisdom Centers in a second World Wheel. These Centers will be established in twelve countries circling the planet to preserve, as well as develop, knowledge critical for the healing and survival of our planet. They will serve as crucibles for the birth of wisdom necessary for our future.

The two Wisdom Centers in Ecuador are the results of my last seven years of work on the Second World Wheel. The Wheel continues– I am planning to start Wisdom Centers in the additional ten sites, each dedicated to the well-being of our children. This spring, in the Caribbean waters of Costa Rica, I created the *Ocean Spiral,* a painting performance prayer for the waters of our planet with organic colors. In the Galapagos Islands, I would like to create a ceremony with the animals as a prayer that our relationship be healed. Each Wisdom Center preserves a disappearing culture, and each ceremony event is an attempt to protect the health of our earth–the people, the flora and fauna–the biosphere of our planet.

Andean children

Woman Made of the Cosmos (detail)

May we each find our own footsteps with the clarity of who we are—different as each snowflake pattern is different, but all equally beautiful. We are luminous beings—only for a moment clothed in the trappings of darkness with which society and our ego-centered minds have burdened our souls.

Today, I shake off this darkness that eats into our lives. I shake off this view of separation and isolation, to know that each person is our own, that our true nature is one with every child, every creature, every plant, every stone, and every atom of the universe.

Vijali

Chronology

Vijali as Gaia in the *Western Gateway* performance

1939 Born in Los Angeles, California, May Day.

1941 My parents divorce, and my father places me in a series of foster homes over the next two years.

1943 My father sends me to his parents in Dallas, Texas.

1944 My mother takes me and leaves me on a farm in Little Rock, Arkansas.

1946 My mother is institutionalized in a mental hospital as a schizophrenic. She remains hospitalized for the rest of her life.

1948 Move to Hollywood, California with my grandparents, and am introduced to the Vedanta Society by my father.

1949 Start boarding school at the Temescal School for Girls in Pomona County, California.

1950 Transfer to the Parnell Preparatory School for Girls in Whittier, California.

1953 Enter the Vedanta Society convent in Santa Barbara, California as a nun.

1964 Leave the Vedanta Society convent and go to Ottawa, Canada. I go to work as an illustrator for the National Research Council, and take graduate courses at night.

1965 Move to Montreal and attend Sir George Williams College, majoring in art.

1966 My mother passes away in a mental hospital.

1967 Return to Santa Barbara, California and marry Dale Clark. We live in Santa Barbara.

1972 Dale and I travel to India and meet Anandamayi Ma.

1973 Begin my friendship with Anaïs Nin.

1974 Dale and I get divorced.

1976 Experience a powerful "uncoiling" of Kundalini energy, which changes my life. I come to see the underlying unity of all life. I close my studio in Santa Barbara and begin to create stone sculptures in nature and ritual performances with communities in the Los Angeles area. I sculpt *Winged Woman* and *Continuum* in Southern California. I visit Don Hildé in the Amazon and sculpt *Homage to Andean Women* in the Andes of Peru. Swami Prabbavananda, my guru at the Vedanta Society, dies.

1977 Pepperdine University in Malibu, California gives me permission to create environmental sculptures in Winter Canyon. I sculpt the *Shelter Sculpture* and the *Sculptural Amphitheater, The Within of Matter*. I receive a Masters of Fine Arts in Environmental Sculpture from Goddard College, Plainfield, Vermont.

1978 Become engaged to Dr. Oscar Janiger, and carve two environmental sculptures in Southern California: *Spirit Within Matter* and *The Seed of Space*.

1979 Marry Oscar Janiger.

1980 Live with Biphisi, a Hopi medicine woman on the Hopi Reservation in New Oraibi, Arizona.

1981 Carve *She Who Opens the Doors of the Earth* with the help of the community in Yelapa, Mexico.

1982 Get divorced from Oscar. Move alone into an abandoned trailer on Boney Mountain in the Santa Monica Mountains of Southern California for a five-year retreat. I develop a life style that includes meditation, dancing, writing poetry, composing music, and creating environmental sculptures. I begin to write my autobiography.

1984 Dream I see myself circling the globe as I create environmental stone sculptures and ceremonies in many countries. Community is developed as we work together. This dream came to fruition in the first World Wheel Project.

1986 Begin work on the first World Wheel site in the Santa Monica Mountains of Malibu, California on Frank Lloyd Wright's family land.

1987 Complete the World Wheel site 1. The sculpture is named the *Earth Wheel,* and the ceremony called *Western Gateway* is performed on August 16th, the date of the Harmonic Convergence.

1988 Leave my mountain retreat to live with Yehwehnode, a Seneca medicine woman, on the Cattaraugus Seneca Reservation in upstate New York. I carve the sculpture *Unity* for World Wheel site 2 on the Reservation. The ceremony, called *The Peacemaker,* is performed in June.

Journey to Alicante, Spain to create World Wheel site 3. Both the sculpture and the ceremony, performed the first day of January, 1989, are named *Woman of Sky with the Sun in Her Belly*.

1989 Travel in June to the Umbrian Forest in Italy to create World Wheel site 4. The ceremony performed August 15th is called *Voices of the Umbrian Forest*.

Journey to the Greek island of Tinos in the Aegean Sea to create World Wheel site 5. The site included a number of environmental art works: the sculpture *Serpent*, the painting *Woman Made of the Cosmos*, *Gaia's Laboratory* (a cave with seven paintings), and the *Tower of Fire*, a structure of driftwood twelve feet high set on fire during the performance. The ceremony performance, called *Phidusa Woman*, is performed in November.

1990 Journey to Egypt to create World Wheel site 6, *Woman with the Wings of an Eagle, Sun at Her Forehead, Moon at Her Feet,* at Saint Paul's Monastery on the South Gallala Plateau. In April, I created a private ceremony with myself, the sculpture, and the vast sky and sands of Egypt.

Travel to Palestine and Israel to create World Wheel site 7 overlooking the Dead Sea. During the ceremony held on October 27th, the *Tree of Peace* is planted by a Palestinian boy and an Israeli girl in the center of a circle of stone carvings named *Earth Wheel.*

1991 Journey to India; first, to Rewalsar for a retreat with Lama Wangdor; then to Dharamsala to see the Dalai Lama; then to Calcutta to visit the Kali Temple (the home of Ramakrishna) and to meet with Mother Teresa. Finally I travel to Shantiniketan in West Bengal to create World Wheel site 8 in a village of Baul minstrels. Rather than a sculpture, I build a community house, *Baul Kutir,* to serve as a school room, a community meeting place, and a place where the Baul minstrels can practice, perform, and sleep. We hold the inauguration ceremony on May 7th feeding 700 people.

1992 Make a pilgrimage to Tibet to create World Wheel site 10 in Shoto Terdrum, home of Padmasambhava, one of the most revered figures in Tibetan Buddhism, and Yeshe Tsogyal, one of Tibet's most prominent holy women. I receive a Chöd Empowerment initiation from Lama Pema Samdup, a lama living for eighteen years in a cave in the area. For this site I create the incised cave painting, *Rainbow Bodhisattva*, and hold the ceremony in May.

Travel to Kunming in southwest China to create World Wheel site 10. This site was located in the Shisan Forest Park, and included a number of environmental sculptures: *Kuan Yin of the People I, II, III, Woman of the Sky Holding a Lotus*, *Emptiness,* and *Endagered Panda*. The ceremony called *Return to Harmony* is performed in October.

1993 Journey to Russia to create World Wheel site 11 in Buryat, Siberia. Both the sculpture, built on the shores of Lake Baikal, and the ceremony, performed in August, are called *Light Within Darkness.*

Travel to Japan to create World Wheel site 12 and complete the first World Wheel. I create three environmental sculptures and three ceremonial performances collectively called *Concentric Circles; One Heart*. The last ceremony was held in October.

1994 Buy five acres of land in Moab area of Utah, and start the World Wheel Retreat Center.

1999 Start the Second World Wheel Project. The purpose of this project is to develop Wisdom Centers to preserve indigenous cultures by developing schools for children, establishing nature preserves, and creating community through environmental art projects.

Travel to Ecuador to start work on the first site of the Second World Wheel Project in the Andean village of Peguche. With extensive community involvement, I create the statue *Achili Pachacamac*. The ceremony for the completion of the sculpture is held at the time of Inti Raimi, a traditional harvest ceremony on June 21st.

This site now includes three projects: an indigenous women's group, *Hwari Maki,* that helps single women develop crafts to sell so that they can become or remain independent, a bed and breakfast inn, and a school for the Otavaleñan children to preserve their culture.

2000 Start work on the second site of the Second World Wheel Project in the rainforest with indigenous Shuar of the Ecuadorian Amazon.

2001 to 2005 Raise funds in the United States to purchase 300 acres of virgin rainforest to create the *Refugio Amazonico,* a nature reserve to protect the Amazonian rainforest environment, and a Wisdom Center to preserve the indigenous culture of the Shuar.

2006 The Shuar Refuge School is started with Edie Hartshorne as co-director.

Publish *Liberty, Enlightening the World*, an illustrated poem celebrating the Statue of Liberty as our symbol of freedom, and *Of Earth & Fire*, a book of personal poetry and works of art expressing the integration of body, nature, and spirit.

2007 Continue work on the *Refugio Amazonico.*

Create a water sculpture/painting and ceremonial performance called the *Ocean Spiral* in the Caribbean of Costa Rica as a prayer for the waters of our planet.

Publish *World Wheel: One Woman's Quest for Peace*, an account of the first World Wheel journey interwoven with an autobiographical account of my early life.

Future Plans

1. Continue to develop the first two sites of the Second World Wheel Project in Ecuador.
2. Continue to hold workshops and retreats at the World Wheel Retreat Center in Utah.
3. Continue the creation of *Ocean Spiral* paintings and ceremonial performances around the world as prayers for the waters of our planet.
4. Create a ceremony performance in the Galapagos Islands honoring and calling for the preservation of all animal life on our planet.
5. Continue the development of the remaining ten sites of the Second World Wheel Project circling the planet.

Acknowledgments

World Wheel site 1: Audience in Malibu, California for the *Western Gateway* performance

I wish to thank the spirit within all life that has guided me throughout this journey, as well as the many friends and organizations that made it possible to complete the World Wheel Pilgrimage: Andrew Beath of EarthWays Foundation, Marion Rockefeller Weber of the Flow Fund, Elizabeth Robinson of the Morgan Trust Co., the Skages Foundation, the Anton Haardt Foundation, Markell Brooks, Louisa of the Putnam Foundation, Pia Gallegos, Marion Hunt, Elizabeth Beath, Dr. Oscar Janiger, and many other friends and friends of friends.

Thank you, Joaquin Gil, for your assistance in many countries; Nyland Nido, for your help in China; and Patricia and Lee Sanders, for your endless enthusiasm and help. Thank you, Wata Arieli, for your collaboration in Israel and Palestine, and Dominique Mezeaud and Ichi Ikeda for your collaboration in Japan. Thank you, Mary and Eric Lloyd Wright, for the use of your land, and Georgianne Cowan and Anne Mavor for your collaboration at the first site and all the great help in getting started. My gratitude to you, Twylah Nitsch (Yehwehnode), for your wisdom of the medicine wheel and your wise grandmother support. Thank you to all who participated in the World Wheel events.

And for the emergence of this book, I want to thank Rochelle Freeman for your hours of pouring over my journals and notes for the first draft of the book, Sherry Ruth Anderson for your guidance, and to Patricia Hopkins, Martin Lee, Kathryn Wilder, Cris Coffee, Laura Kamala, Stephanie Gayer-Stevens, Michael Ellsberg, Henry Swan III, Robin Hartshorne, Pearl Luke, Vivien Feyer, Cathleen McGuire, Coralyn Dailey, and Jan Sells for your editing at different stages of the manuscript. Thank you, Shelley Firth, for your many hours of work with InDesign, and thank you, Henry Swan III, for your many hours of work on the graphics. Thank you, Gloria Feman Orenstein, for your inspiring introduction. Thank you, Terry Tempest Williams, for your continual encouragement and belief in the book and me. Thank you, Henry Swan III, Markell Brooks, and Edie Hartshorne, for your financial support that made the completion of this book possible. Thank you also to all the people I have not mentioned by name. Thank you all!

Woman with the Wings of an Eagle, Sun at Her Forehead, Moon at Her Feet, Egypt

Photo Illustrations

Georgianne Cowan in the *Western Gateway* performance

Cover

Kuan Yin of the People, limestone, 18′ high; sculpture and photo Vijali Hamilton

Frontmatter

1. *Winged Woman* (detail); photo Vijali Hamilton
2. *Achili Pachacamac* (detail moon); photo Vijali Hamilton
3. *Achili Pachacamac* (detail sun); photo Vijali Hamilton
4. *Woman of Sky* (detail hand holding lotus); photo Vijali Hamilton
5. *Spirit within Matter*, sandstone, 4′x 2′x 1′; photo Vijali Hamilton
6. World map; watercolor and photo Vijali Hamilton
7. *Sculptural Amphitheater* (detail), sandstone, Pepperdine University, Malibu, California; photo ©Eric Lawton
8. *The Other Self* (detail face); photo Steven Smith
9. *She Who Opens the Doors of the Earth,* granite, 15′x 8′x 10′, Yelapa, Mexico; photo Vijali Hamilton
10. *Dark Roots Luminous*, roots, cloth and plaster life mask, 5′x 3′x 1′, Canyonlands of Utah; photo Chick Heburt

Chapter 1: WORLD WHEEL—SPOKE ONE
Malibu, California, USA, 1984 -1987

11. *Western Gateway* performance; photo ©Eric Lawton
12. Vijali sitting outside of her trailer at Boney Mountain, Santa Monica Mts., California; photo James Woolsey
13. Santa Monica Mountains, California; photo Vijali Hamilton
14. Setting the center stone for *Earth Wheel* with help from the Wright family; photo Mary Wright
15. Peter Levitt, Mary Wright, and Vijali working together to create *Earth Wheel;* photo Andrew Beath
16. *Earth Wheel* at the first World Wheel site, Malibu, California, lava and gathered stones, 30′ diameter, photo ©Eric Lawton
17. Vijali working on *Shelter Sculpture* in Winter Canyon, Pepperdine University, Malibu, California, 10′x 12′x 10′; photographer unknown
18. Vijali carving in cave for *Sculptural Amphitheater* in Winter Canyon, Pepperdine University, Malibu, California; photographer unknown
19 The grass tunnel in Winter Canyon; photo Vijali Hamilton
20. *Sculptural Amphitheater* (detail) with Vijali, 200′ x 500′; photo ©Eric Lawton
21. *Sculptural Amphitheater* (detail); photo Vijali Hamilton
22. Spectators gathering for the *Western Gateway* performance; photo ©Eric Lawton
23. Georgianne Cowan as androgenous being in the *Western Gateway* performance; photo ©Eric Lawton
24. Georgianne Cowan and partner in the *Western Gateway* performance; photo ©Eric Lawton
25. Georgianne Cowan birthing as Woman in the the *Western Gateway* performance; photo Vijali Hamilton
26. Vijali as Gaia in the the *Western Gateway* performance, Malibu, California; photo ©Eric Lawton
27. Vijali as Gaia sitting on precipice after the *Western Gateway* performance; photo ©Eric Lawton

Chapter 2: INVISIBLE SOURCES

28. *Invisible Sources,* pencil drawing on paper, 8″x 10″, 1974; photo Vijali Hamilton
29. *Alone,* ink drawing on paper, 8″x 10″, 1972; photo Vijali Hamilton
30. *Introvert*, ink drawing on paper, 5″x 7″, 1972; photo Vijali Hamilton

Chapter 3: WORLD WHEEL—SPOKE TWO
Seneca Cattauragus Reservation, New York, USA, 1988

31. *Unity* (detail), Seneca Cattauragus Reservation, New York; photo Vijali Hamilton
32. Seneca lodge at Yewehnode's home; photo Vijali Hamilton
33. *Unity,* sculpture in granite and crystal with four directional faces, 5′x 4½′ x 3′; photo Robert Holland
34. *Forest Wheels* hanging, 6′ diameter; photo Morna Watson
35. Vijali in her lace leaf veil and ceremonial dress for *The Peacemaker* performance; photo Jonathan Glasier
36. Yehwehnode (Twylah Nitsch) telling the Seneca creation story; photo Andrew Beath
37. Seneca drummer leading us into *The Peacemaker* ceremony; photo Morna Watson
38. Gathering in forest for *The Peacemaker* performance; photo Andrew Beath

39. The Peacemaker and Hiawatha with the *Forest Wheels;* photo Morna Watson
40. *Seed of Space* (detail), sculpture in Santa Monica Mountains; Photo Sasha Burger

Chapter 4: THE VEDANTA CONVENT

41. *One* (Ramakrishna and Sarada Devi), sculptured marble painting, 4'x 4½'x 2", 1970; photo Dale Clark
42. *The Other Self,* sculptured marble painting, 4'x 4'x 3", 1972; photo Steven Smith
43. *Swami Prabhavananda,* oil painting on canvas, 18"x 24", 1956; photographer unknown
44. *Kali*, sculpture in clay for Kali Puja, 3' high, 1957; photographer unknown
45. *Mary and Jesus,* oil painting on wood door, 6'x 3½', 1956; photographer unknown
46. *Mary and Jesus* (detail); photographer unknown
47. *The Kiss*, ink drawing on paper, 8"x 10", 1970; photo Vijali Hamilton
48. *Sri Kali Yantra* (detail), sandstone, 7'x 5'x 6', ancient East Indian symbol for the divine feminine, womb of the cosmos, carved by Vijali, 1997; photo Vijali Hamilton

Chapter 5: WORLD WHEEL—SPOKE THREE
Alicante, Spain, 1988

49. *River of Light,* painting and incising on river stone, 2½' x 2'x 2'; photo Vijali Hamilton
50. Vijali drawing Christina's shadow for sculpture image *Woman of Space Pregnant with Sun*; photo Joaquin Gil
51. *Woman of Space Pregnant with Sun,* conglomerate, Alicante, Spain, 5'x 3'; photo Vijali Hamilton
52. *Woman of Space Pregnant with Sun* (detail); photo Vijali Hamilton

Chapter 6: INTO THE WORLD

53. *90% Bliss* (detail), 1967; photo Dale Clark
54. *Ghosts from the Past,* sculptured marble painting, 1967; photo Steven Smith
55. Vijali in her and Dale's home with the sculptured marble painting, *Sailing Free;* photo Dale Clark
56. *The Great Mother,* sculptured marble painting, 5'x 4'x 3'; photo Steven Smith

Chapter 7: WORLD WHEEL—SPOKE FOUR
Umbrian Forest, Italy, 1989

57. *Rainbow Seeing,* marble, 8" x 12" x 10"; photo Out Take: Alison & Richard
58. Script and diagram from the Eugubbine Tablets; tourist brochure
59. *Ancient Roots,* Umbrian Forest, Italy, local limestone (pietra viva), 3'x 2'x 2'; photo Out Take: Alison & Richard
60. *Trinity,* Umbrian Forest, Italy, Carrara marble, 3'x 2'x 2'; photo Vijali Hamilton
61. Gate Guardian, *Voices of the Umbrian Forest* performance; photo Out Take: Alison & Richard
62. Vijali as Stone next to sculpture *Goddess of the Underworld;* photo Out Take: Alison & Richard
63. Vijali as Wolf speaking to the community in the *Voices of the Umbrian Forest* performance; photo Out Take: Alison & Richard
64. Drinking milk and honey on the ascent in the *Voices of the Umbrian Forest* performance; photo Out Take: Alison & Richard

Chapter 8: A ROOM OF MY OWN

65. *The Room Inside,* sculptured marble painting, 2'6"x 2'x 3", 1973; photo Dale Cark
66. *Anandamayi Ma,* sculpted marble painting, 5'x 4'x 2", 1973; photo Dale Clark
67. *Anaïs Nin,* sculpted marble painting, 5'x 6'x 3", 1973; photo Steven Smith
68. *25% Bliss,* cast aluminum and stretched canvas over wood, 8'x 5'x 1', 1968; photo Vijali Hamilton
69. *95% Bliss,* marble composition with wood inserts, 4'x 4'x 8", in gratitude to Markell Brooks, 1969; photo Steven Smith

Chapter 9: WORLD WHEEL—SPOKE FIVE
Tinos, Greece, 1989

70. *Serpent* (detail) with actress in *Phidusa Woman* performance; photographer unknown
71. *Serpent,* granite and enamal, 12'x 2'x 6'; photo Vijali Hamilton
72. Vijali with *Serpent* (detail) sculpture; photo Joaquin Gil
73. *Woman Made of the Cosmos*, 12'x 8'; photo Vijali Hamilton
74. *Woman Made of the Cosmos* (detail); photo Vijali Hamilton
75. Vijali as Seaweed Gaia in the *Phidusa Woman* performance; photographer unknown
76. Greek musicians playing in the *Phidusa Woman* performance; photographer unknown
77. Sea the Unconscious, dancer Shirley Graham, in the *Phidusa Woman* performance; photographer unknown
78. Vijali as Seaweed Gaia at the Aegean Sea; photo Jan Semmal

Chapter 10: KUNDALINI

79. *Within* (detail); photo Steven Smith
80. *Roots of Consciousness,* cover *Roots of Consciousness* by Jeff Mishlove, 4'x 4'x 3,"1972, photo Steven Smith
81. *Within,* sculptured marble painting, 4'x 4'x 3", 1973; photo Steven Smith
82. *Borderless,* drawing from journal, pen on paper, 6"x 3", 1976; photo Vijali Hamilton

Chapter 11: WORLD WHEEL—SPOKE SIX
South Gallala Plateau, Egypt, 1989

83. *Woman with the Wings of an Eagle, Sun at Her Forehead, Moon at her Feet* (detail of feet); photo Vijali Hamilton

Chapter 12: WINGED WOMAN

Chapter 13: WORLD WHEEL—SPOKE SEVEN
Palestine and Israel, 1990

Chapter 14: THE AMAZON JUNGLE

Chapter 15: WORLD WHEEL—SPOKE EIGHT
West Bengal, India, 1991

Chapter 16: FREEDOM

Chapter 17: WORLD WHEEL—SPOKE NINE
Shoto Terdrom, Tibet, 1992

Chapter 18: MARRIAGE

Chapter 19: WORLD WHEEL—SPOKE TEN
Kunming, China, 1992

Chapter 20: SPIRIT WITHIN MATTER

Chapter 21: WORLD WHEEL—SPOKE ELEVEN
Lake Baikal, Siberia, Russia 1993

Chapter 22: MY SACRED MOUNTAIN

Chapter 23: WORLD WHEEL—SPOKE TWELVE
Tenkawa, Nara, Japan, 1993

Chapter 24: RETURN

Postscript: Second World Wheel, Amazon and Andes
Ecuador, 1999 - 2007

173. Ceremony with the indigenous Shuar musicians, Refugio Amazonico, Second World Wheel Project, Ecuador; photo Edie Hartshorne
174. Traditional Shuar dance and music; photo Edie Hartshorne
175. Nantar; photo Edie Hartshorne
176. Nantar drawing; photo Edie Hartshorne
177. Federico Tsamaraint teaching in the Shuar Refugio School, started by the Second World Wheel Project; photo Edie Hartshorne
178. Vijali giving out drawings from children from New Mexico, USA; photo Edie Hartshorne
179. *Peacecemaker Ceremony*, Vijali as Spirit of the Rainforest with Shuar children as the animals of the Amazon bringing the fire of peace to the world; photo Catherine Allport.
180. *Anaconda Woman,* (sculpture in progress), basalt, 6′x 6′x 4′; photo Vijali Hamilton
181. Vijali and Tuntuam Camilo carving by the sacred waterfall; photo Edie Hartshorne
182. Shuar children learning from Vijali how to carve; photo Sherry R. Anderson
183. *Achili Pachacamac,* lava boulder carved by Vijali with the help of the Peguche community, 30′x 20′x 15′; Second World Wheel Project, Andes of Ecuador; photo Vijali Hamilton
184. *Achili Pachacamac* (detail of corn); photo Vijali Hamilton
185. Matico Lema (right), founder of *Hwari Maki,* women's group for Otavaleñan women; photo Edie Hartshorne
186. Vijali carving *Achili Pachacamac* with Chino from the village Peguche; photo Edie Hartshorne
187. Inti Raimi, harvest ceremony with the *Achili Pachacamac* sculpture in Peguche. Left to right: their local shamans, Vijali, Edie Hartshorne (Outreach Coordinator for the World Wheel), Matico, and friend; photo Cherese Udell
188. Vijali with Otavaleñan children; photo Edie Hartshorne
189. Shairy, Otavaleñan healer from Peguche; photo Edie Hartshorne
190. Andean children; photo Vijali Hamilton
191. *Woman Made of the Cosmos* (detail); photo Vijali Hamilton

Chronology

192. Vijali as Gaia in the *Western Gateway* performance; photo ©Eric Lawton

Acknowledgements

193. World Wheel site 1: Audience in Malibu, California for the *Western Gateway* performance; photo ©Eric Lawton
194. *Woman with the Wings of an Eagle, Sun at Her Forehead, Moon at Her Feet*, Egypt; photo Vijali Hamilton

List of Photo Illustrations

195. Georgianne Cowan in the *Western Gateway* performance; photo Vijali Hamilton

Endnotes

196. *Shelter Sculpture,* Pepperdine University, Malibu, California; photo Vijali Hamilton
197. Vijali as Space in the *Return to Harmony* performance, China; Photo Patricia Sanders

Bibliography

198. Scroll for treasure container buried in Tinos, Greece; photo Vijali Hamilton
199. *Woman of Sky* (detail); photo Vijali Hamilton

Books Featuring Vijali Hamilton

200. Vijali as Gaia in the *Western Gateway* performance, Malibu, California; photo Georgianne Cowen

Other Works By Vijali Hamilton

201. Vijali preparing to be Gaia in the *Western Gateway* performance, Malibu, California; photographer unknown

Biography

202. Vijali carving in the Andes of Ecuador; photo Edie Hartshorne
203. Vijali in ceremony; photographer unknown
204. Vijali as Gaia in the *Western Gateway* performance, World Wheel, site 1, Malibu, California;

Back Cover

205. Vijali carving in the Andes of Ecuador: photo Edie Hartshorne

Endnotes

Shelter Sculpture, Pepperdine University, Malibu, California

Introduction

1. *From a Broken Web*, Catherine Keller, Boston: Beacon Press, 1986

Chapter 1: WORLD WHEEL, SPOKE ONE

2. See *lingam* and *yoni* in *A Concise Dictionary of Indian Philosophy, Sanskrit Terms Defined in English,* John Grimes, Albany, New York: State University of New York Press, 1996, page 175 and 361
3. In talking about the ancient peoples who worshipped monolithic stones, it seems to me that these stones were more than just symbols of fertility—they conducted a force, the knowledge of which vanished as civilization developed. Ancient Hindu scripture considered upright stones to be emblems of the supreme godhead and ascribed to them the sound "Om." They believed that upright stones having a particular shape and position in the ground were conduits of low-frequency vibrations which entered the body hitting the spinal cord directly and traveling straight to the hypothalamus gland. Located in the most protected cavity of the brain, this gland controls the autonomic nervous system, including our response to stress.
4. *The Time Tables of History*, Bernard Grun, based upon Werner Stein's Kulturfahrplan, The New Third Revised Edition, New York: A Touchstone Book, Simon & Schuster, 1991, pages 620 and 621

Chapter 3: WORLD WHEEL, SPOKE TWO

5. *The White Roots of Peace: The Iroquois Book of Life,* Paul Wallace, Santa Fe, New Mexico: Clear Light Publishers, (originally the University of Pennsylvania Press), 1994
6. After many weeks of debate in the Constitutional Convention, a committee was formed to combine the main agreements into a formal document. John Ruthledge, Chairman of the Committee of Detail, proposed a model similar to that of the Iroquois Confederacy, which had been functioning as a successful democratic government for hundreds of years. He had observed its functions firsthand. As a result, our U.S. Constitution now parallels the Iroquois Confederacy in the structure of our Executive, Legislative, and Judicial branches of government. *The Constitution of the Iroquois Confederation,* Modern History Source Book, Gerald Murphy, August 1997, http:/www.fordham.edu/halsall/mod/iroquois.html

Chapter 4: THE VEDANTA CONVENT

7. *Ramakrishna and His Disciples,* Christopher Isherwood, Hollywood, California: Vedanta Press, 1980
8. *Vedanta for the Western World,* Christopher Isherwood, Hollywood, California: Vedanta Press, 1985.
9. *The Gospel of Sri Ramakrishna*, Mahindranath Gupta, translated into English by Swami Nikhilananda, New York: Ramakrishna-Vivekananda Center, 1942

Chapter 7: WORLD WHEEL, SPOKE FOUR

10. *The Descent of Inanna-Ishtar,* Jalaja Bonheim, in *Goddess: A Celebration of Art and Literature,* Jalaja Bonheim (Editor), New York: Stewart, Tabori & Chang, 1997, pages 131 and 133

Chapter 8: A ROOM OF MY OWN

11. *Anandamayi, Her Life and Wisdom,* Richard Lannoy, Shaftesbury, Dorset: Element Books Limited, 1996

Chapter 9: WORLD WHEEL, SPOKE FIVE

12. *The Greek Myths*, Robert Graves, Vol. I, Manchester, United Kingdom: Carcanet Press Ltd., 2001, page 54.
13. *Mythology*, Edith Hamilton, Boston: Little, Brown, 1942, page 72

Chapter 10: KUNDALINI

14. *Kundalini: The Arousal of the Inner Energy*, Ajit Mooerjee, One Park Street, Rochester, VT: Destiny Books, 1986

Chapter 11: WORLD WHEEL, SPOKE SIX

15. *Articles: House of Hermits*, Hermitary, *The Desert Mothers: A Survey of the Feminine Anchoretic Tradition in Western Europe* by Margot H. King (reprinted with permission from Peregrina Publishing Co.), www.hermitary.com/articles/mothers.html

Chapter 14: THE AMAZON JUNGLE

16. *LSD, Spirituality, and the Creative Process: Based on the Ground-breaking Research of Oscar Janiger, M.D.*, Marlene Dobkin de Rios, Oscar Janiger, Forward by Rick Strassman, South Paris, Maine: Park Street Press, 2003

    A Different Kind of Healing, Oscar Janiger and Philip Goldberg, Los Angeles: J.P. Tarcher, 1993
17. *Amazon Healer, The Life and Times of an Urban Shaman,* Marlene Dobkin de Rios, Dorset, Great Britain: Prism Press, 1992

Chapter 15: WORLD WHEEL, SPOKE EIGHT

18. *Teachings of Love,* Thich Nhat Hanh, Berkeley, California: Parallax Press, 1997
19. *Kali: The Black Goddess of Dakshineswar,* Elizabeth Harding, Berwick, Maine: Nicolas-Hays, 1993
20. *The Path of the Mystic Lover: Baul Songs of Passion and Ecstasy,* Bhaskar Bhattacharyya with Nik Douglas and Penny Slinger, Rochester, Vermont: Destiny Books, 1993
21. A Baul song written by Lalon Kakir from Bangladesh, India. He was born in a Hindu family and his parents floated him in a basket on a river. He was found and brought up in a Muslim family. He believed in humankind, not Vaishnava (Hindu) or Islam (Muslim). This song and the story of Lalon Kakir's life were taught to me by Purna Das Baul.

Chapter 18: MARRIAGE

22. *The Prophet,* Kahlil Gibran, New York: Borzoi Books, Published by Alfred A. Knopf, Inc., 1997, pages 15, 16

Chapter 20: SPIRIT WITHIN MATTER

23. To protect the owner of the site, I have placed *Spirit Within Matter* in Winter Canyon and condensed many trips and projects into one story.
24. *Biologic and Clinical Effects of Low Frequency Magnetic and Electric Field,* James Beal, Springfield, Illinois: Chas. C. Thomas Publishing Co., 1974

Chapter 21: WORLD WHEEL, SPOKE 11

25 *The Jewel of Siberia: A Report on Penny Newman's Trip and the Environmental Challenges Facing their Country. With Specific Information on Lake Baikal,* www.ccaej.org/projects/lakebaikal.htm

Chapter 22: MY SACRED MOUNTAIN

26. *The Hopi Survival Kit,* Thomas E. Mails, New York: Welcome Rain, 1997
27. *Disputed Questions (Notes For a Philosophy of Solitude),* Thomas Merton, San Diego, New York: A Harvest Book, Harcourt Brace & Co., 1985, page 192
28. *Hermits: The Insights of Solitude,* Peter France, New York: St. Martin's Press, 1996, page 177

Chapter 24: Return

29. *The Upanishads: Breath of the Eternal,* translated by Swami Prabhavananda and Frederick Manchester, Hollywood, California: Vedanta Press, paperback edition, 1983, page 131

Vijali as Space in the *Return to Harmony* performance, China

Bibliography

Scroll for treasure container buried in Tinos, Greece. A treasure scroll was buried in each World Wheel country.

Introduction

The Theatre of the Marvelous: Surrealism and the Contemporary Stage, Gloria Feman Orenstein, New York: New York University Press, 1975

The Reflowering of the Goddess, Gloria Feman Orenstein, New York: Pergamon Press, Athene Series and Columbia University Teachers' College Press, 1990

Multicultural Celebrations: The Paintings of Betty LaDuke, 1972–1992, Gloria Feman Orenstein, Petaluma, California: Pomegranate Art Press, 1993

Reweaving the World: The Emergence of Ecofeminism, co-edited Gloria Feman Orenstein and Irene Diamond, San Francisco: Sierra Club Books, California, 1990

Chapter 1: WORLD WHEEL–SPOKE ONE

Six Easy Pieces: Essentials of Physics as Explained by Its Most Brilliant Teacher, Richard Feynman, New York: Perseus Books Group, 1996

The Dream of the Earth, Thomas Berry, San Francisco: Sierra Club Books, 1988

Chapter 2: INVISIBLE SOURCES

Man's Search for Meaning, Viktor E. Frankl, New York: Washington Square Press, Inc., 1968.

The Spiritual Life of Children, Robert Coles, Boston: A Peta Division Book, Houghton Mifflin Company, 1990

Chapter 3: WORLD WHEEL–SPOKE TWO

Profiles in Wisdom, Steven McFadden, Chapter 6, "She Whose Voice Rides on the Wind: Grandmother Twylah Nitsch," Santa Fe, New Mexico: Bear & Company, 1991

Chapter 4: THE VEDANTA CONVENT

Upanishads, Breath of the Eternal (the ancient vedic scriptures of India), anonymous, translated by Swami Prabhavananda and Frederick Manchester, Vedanta Press, Hollywood, California, 1975

Chapter 5: WORLD WHEEL–SPOKE THREE

Don Quixote, Cervantes, New York: New American Library, A Mentor Book, 1957

Chapter 6: INTO THE WORLD

Taoist Secrets of Love: Cultivating Male Sexual Energy, Aurora Press, New York, 1984

Healing Love through the Tao: Cultivating Female Sexual Energy, Mantak Chia and Maneewan Chia, Healing Tao Books, Huntington, New York, 1986

Chapter 7: WORLD WHEEL–SPOKE FOUR

Inferno, The Divine Comedy of Dante Alighieri, translated by Allen Mandelbaum, New York, A Bantam Book, 1982

Chapter 8: A ROOM OF MY OWN

Women of Power and Grace: Nine Astonishing, Inspiring Luminaries of Our Time, Timothy Conway, Ph.D., Santa Barbara, California: The Wake Up Press, 1994

Matri Vani, Anandamayi, Varanasi: Shree Shree Anandamayee Charitable Society, 1977

Chapter 9: WORLD WHEEL–SPOKE FIVE

The Heroine's Journey, Maureen Murdock, Boston & Shaftesbury: Shambhala Publications, 1990.

Chapter 10: KUNDALINI

The Shambalah Guide to Yoga, George Feuerstein, "The Serpent Power," Boston, Shambhala Publications, Inc., 1996

A Chakra & Kundalini Workbook, Dr. Jonn Mumford, St. Paul, MN: Llewellyn Publications, 2003

The Madness of the Saints: Ecstatic Religion in Bengal, June McDaniel, Chicago and London: University of Chicago Press, 1989

Talks with Sri Ramana Maharshi, Sri Munagala Venkataramiah, Tiruvannamalai, India: Sri Ramanasramam, 2000

Emptiness Dancing, Selected Dharma Talks of Adyashanti, Los Gatos, California: Open Gate Publishing, 2004

Chapter 11: WORLD WHEEL–SPOKE SIX

The Lives of the Desert Fathers, translated by Norman Russell, introduction by Benedicta Ward SLG, London and Oxford: A. R. Mowbray & Co. Ltd. and Kalamazoo, Michigan: Cistercian Publications, 1981

The Way of a Pilgrim and *The Pilgrim Continues His Way,* translated by Helen Bacovcin, New York: Image Books Doubleday, 1992

Chapter 19: WORLD WHEEL–SPOKE EIGHT

The Bauls of Bengal, Krishnendu Das, Calcutta: Das International Publication. 1980

Chapter 20: SPIRIT WITHIN MATTER

The Heart of Matter, Pierre Teilhard de Chardin, New York: a Harvest Book / Harcourt, Inc., 1976

Chapter 21: WORLD WHEEL–SPOKE NINE

Sky Dancer: The Secret Life and Songs of the Lady Yeshe Tsogyel, Keith Dowman, Ithaca, New York: Snow Lion Publications, 1996

Tibet, Lonely Planet Guide, Robert Strauss, Hawthorn, Australia & Berkeley, California: Lonely Planet Publications, 1992

The Power Places of Central Tibet: The Pilgrim's Guide, Keith Dowman, London & New York: Routledge & Kegan Paul, 1988

The Anguish of Tibet, edited by Petra K. Kelly, Gert Bastian, and Pat Aiello, Berkeley, California: Parallax Press, 1991

Magic and Mystery in Tibet, Alexandra David-Neel, New York: Dover Publications, Inc., 1971

Forbidden Journey, The Life of Alexandra David-Neel, Barbara and Michael Foster, New York: Harper & Row, Publishers, Inc., 1987

Chapter 24: RETURN TO THE STATES

The Green Belt Movement, Wangari Maathai, New York: Lantern Books, a division of Booklight Inc., 2004

Consciousness in Action: The Power of Beauty, Love, and Courage in a Violent Time, Andrew Beath, New York: Lantern Books, a division of Booklight Inc., 2005

Peace Pilgrim: Her Life and Work in Her Own Words, Peace Pilgrim, Santa Fe, New Mexico: Ocean Tree Books, 1992

Freedom in Exile, Autobiography of the Dalai Lama, Tenzin Gyatso, New York: Harper Perennial, a division of Harper Collins Publishers, 1990

Reason for Hope, A Spiritual Journey, Jane Goodall with Phillip Berman, New York: Warner Books, a Time Warner Company, 1999

Woman of Sky (detail)

Books Featuring Vijali Hamilton

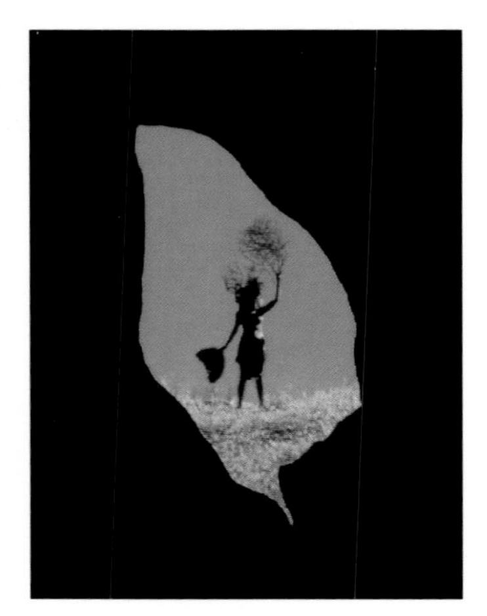

Vijali as Gaia in the *Western Gateway* performance, Malibu, California

Roots of Consciousness, by Jeff Mishlove, New York: Random House, 1975: cover art by Vijali Hamilton

Women Saints of East and West, Swami Ghanananda and John Stewart-Wallace, Hollywood, California: Vedanta Press, 1979: cover art by Vijali Hamilton

Once and Future Goddess, by Elinor Gadon, San Francisco: Harper and Row, 1989: art and life of Vijali Hamilton

The Reflowering of the Goddess, Gloria Feman Orenstein, New York: Pergamon Press, Athene Series and Columbia University Teachers' College Press, 1990: art and life of Vijali Hamilton

Reweaving the World: The Emergence of Ecofeminism, co-edited Gloria Feman Orenstein and Irene Diamond, San Francisco, California: Sierra Club Books,1990: art and life of Vijali Hamilton

Dharma Gaia: A Harvest of Essays in Buddhism and Ecology, edited by Allan Hunt-Badiner, Berkeley: Parallax Press, 1990: art by Vijali Hamilton

The Feminine Face of God, Sherry Anderson and Patricia Hopkins, New York: Bantam, 1991: life of Vijali Hamilton

The Box, the Terma Foundation, Santa Fe, New Mexico: Terma Press, 1993: art and life of Vijali Hamilton

Sculpting with the Environment: A Natural Dialogue, Baile Oakes, New York: Van Nostrand Reinhold, 1995: art and writing by Vijali Hamilton

Proceedings of the Twelfth International Conference on the Study of Shaminism and Alternate Modes of Healing, edited by Ruth Inge Heinze, Berkeley: Independent Scholars of Asia, 1995: writing by Vijali Hamilton

Skydancing Earthwalker, Women's Pilgrimages to Sacred Places, edited by Laila Castle, Berkeley, California: Frog Limited, 1996: cover art and writing by Vijali Hamilton

From the Realm of the Ancestors; An Anthology in Honor of Marija Gimbutas, edited by Joan Morler, Manchester, Cincinnati: KIT, 1997: art and writing about Vijali Hamilton

On Turning 60, Cathleen Roundtree, New York: Harmony Books, 1997: photos and life of Vijali Hamilton

The Flow Fund Circle, Marion Rockefeller Weber, 1997: writing about Vijali Hamilton

Goddess: A Celibration in Art and Literature, Jalaja Bonheim, New York: Stewart Tabori & Chang, 1997:

Creative Healing, Michael Samuals, M.D. and Mary Rockwood Lane, R.N., M.S.N., San Francisco: Harper, 1998: art and life of Vijali Hamilton

The Ways of Spirit: 50 Visionaries Share Philosophies, Paths, and Practices, edited by Susan Averrete: Tempe, Arizona: Galileo Publishing, 2003: writing by Vijali Hamilton

Cultural Creatives, Paul Ray and Sherry Ruth Anderson, New York: Harmony Books, 2000: life of Vijali Hamilton

Sophia: Goddess of Wisdom, Bride of God, Caitlin Mathews, Wheaton, Illinois: Quest Books, 2001: Cover art (front and back) by Vijali Hamilton

Mandala: Journey to the Center, Bailey Cunningham, New York: DK Publishers, 2002: art and writing by Vijali Hamilton

Spiritual Awakenings: Glimpses into the Higher Realms, Maggie Erotokritou, Baltimore: Publish America, 2005: writing by Vijali Hamilton

Consciousness in Action, Andrew Beath, New York: Lantern Books, 2005: reference to life of Vijali Hamilton

Other Works By Vijali Hamilton

Books

In the Fields of Life, poems and artwork, Canyonlands Utah: Earth Mandala Press, 1998. (out of print)

Liberty, Enlightening the World, poem and artwork, Canyonlands, Utah: Earth Mandala Press, 2001, second edition, Canyonlands, Utah: World Wheel Press, 2006

Of Earth & Fire, poems and artwork, Canyonlands, Utah: World Wheel Press, 2006

Audio Cassettes and CDs

Refuge, Gabrielle Roth & The Mirrors, Red Bank, New Jersey: Raven Recording, 1998: cover art by Vijali Hamilton

Awaken Your Heart from Its Ancient Sleep, original music by Vijali Hamilton and Edie Hartshorne, cover art by Vijali Hamilton, Earth Mandala Records, 2000

Atahualpa Manta, Traditional Andian Music from Ecuador, Earth Mandala Records, 2000: cover art

Sacred Chants, Vijali Hamilton with Edie Hartshorne, World Wheel Studio, 2007

Calendar and Cards

Healing Our Earth, calendar, published by Brush Dance, 2003

Healing Our Earth, greeting card series, (three images) published by Brush Dance, 2002

Mother of Tears, card for Women in Black (NGO), 2002

Rainbow Bodhisattva, greeting card, Rivers Press, 2004, reprint 2005, 2006, 2007

Periodicals

Los Angeles Weekly, 1985: cover art by Vijali Hamilton.

Connections, Institute of Noetic Sciences, 1998: cover art by Vijali Hamilton

EarthLight, Reawakening to Communion, 2000: front cover and back cover art, and feature article by Vijali Hamilton

Buddhist Review, Finding the Spirit in Stone, 2002: cover art and feature article by Vijali Hamilton

Films

World Wheel I, One Woman's Pilgrimage for Global Peace, 60 min., World Wheel Productions, 2003

World Wheel II, One Woman's Pilgrimage for Global Peace, 30 min., World Wheel Productions, 2003

Heart of the Jaguar, The Amazon, 6 min., World Wheel Productions, 2004

The World Wheel Journeys, 6 min., Lightningwood Productions, 2007

Vijali preparing to be Gaia in the *Western Gateway* performance, Malibu, California

Biography

Vijali carving in the Andes of Ecuador

Vijali Hamilton is a visionary multimedia artist, sculptor, poet, musician, author, and teacher. Over one thousand of her artworks are in museums, public places, and private collections. She gives seminars and retreats on meditation and the creative process, internationally and at her retreat center home in the Canyonlands of Utah. Early in her life, Vijali spent ten years as a monastic member of the Vedanta Society convent in Santa Barbara. Later she received her Masters in Fine Arts from Goddard College. She is a fellow of the World Academy of Art and Science.

In 1986, she founded her first World Wheel Project, a seven-year spiritual and artistic pilgrimage during which she circled the globe creating monumental stone sculptures and community-based performances in twelve countries. In 1999, she began the Second World Wheel Project. This project again circles the planet, now creating Wisdom Centers in twelve countries to preserve as well as develop knowledge for the healing and survival of our planet. These Centers create a crucible for the cross-cultural emergence of wisdom needed for our future. The Second World Wheel Project is dedicated to the children of our world.

The account of Vijali Hamilton's journeys and her poetry and artwork are available in her books: *World Wheel: One Woman's Quest for Peace*; *Liberty: Enlightening the World;* and *Of Earth & Fire*. She has also produced two music albums (with Edie Hartshorne) and a video documentary, *World Wheel: One Woman's Pilgrimage for Global Peace*. Vijali's art, writing and life have been described in numerous books, articles, radio interviews, and television documentaries. More information about her work as well as her books and CD/DVDs are available through her web site: www.vijali.net.

Vijali in ceremony

Vijali as Gaia in the *Western Gateway* performance, World Wheel site 1, Malibu, California

May Peace Prevail on Earth

If you would like to be a part of the Second World Wheel,
there are many ways to participate.

Please visit our website:
www.vijali.net

To read current and past World Wheel
newsletters, visit:
www.vijali.net/newsletter.html

Order books, cards, CDs, DVDs, VHDs,
sculptures, and prints of sculptures:
www.worldwheelpress.org